CL 7/12
1 5 AUG 2012

C000215250

7/4
1·20

Leeds Library and Information Service
24 hour renewals
http://librarycatalogue.leedslearning.net
or phone 0845 1207271
Overdue charges may apply

LD 4410617 3

The Dracula Secrets

JACK THE RIPPER
AND THE DARKEST SOURCES OF
BRAM STOKER

NEIL R. STOREY

The
History
Press

For Molly – My angel of the darkness

First published 2012

The History Press
The Mill, Brimscombe Port
Stroud, Gloucestershire, GL5 2QG
www.thehistorypress.co.uk

© Neil R. Storey, 2012

The right of Neil R. Storey, to be identified as the Author
of this work has been asserted in accordance with the
Copyrights, Designs and Patents Act 1988.

British Library Cataloguing in Publication Data.
A catalogue record for this book is available from the British Library.

ISBN 978 0 7524 8048 0

Typesetting and origination by The History Press
Printed in Great Britain

CONTENTS

FOREWORD

(With a digression on Ripper research)
By Stewart P. Evans

In any list of literary and film subjects that have acquired cult status the names of Jack the Ripper and Dracula must figure prominently. The former, although his identity remains unknown, was a real-life murderer, but he is one who has attracted great mythology and fictional trappings; the latter character is fictional but he has attracted much research in an effort to establish a real historical basis. Both rank highly as nightmare figures that continue to haunt the imagination. To seek actual links between the two is an intriguing quest, which has never before been fully explored. The author of the present work, however, has sought out some very real associations and presents his findings here, adding new facts to our knowledge. In this computer age of digital online searching, when many researchers and writers seldom stray from their keyboards, Neil Storey has travelled widely researching his subject.

In presenting his work, the author grounds his findings on much solid biographical and genealogical information and gives us an excellent insight into those dark Victorian days of the *fin de siècle*, when London was subjected to a reign of terror the like of which had not been seen before. He seeks out all the players; Bram Stoker, Henry Irving, Hall Caine, Francis Tumblety and others, and adds to our knowledge. In the pages of the contemporary press the London exploits of the unknown Jack the Ripper were broadcast to a horrified nation and, indeed, to the world. In the pages of an 1897 novel the London exploits of the fictional Count Dracula were likewise broadcast to the nation and the world. Both were the subjects of stage plays and, later, films. The infamy of both grew and spread over the years in equal measure. Both attracted a cult following, which has now migrated to the Internet. In an age when codes, esoteric associations and mysterious links are very popular, is it really possible to establish anything of a tangible nature to link Jack the Ripper with Count Dracula? Well, I believe that Neil Storey has shown us that it really is and that cannot be gainsaid. We know that Bram Stoker was in London during the relevant period and that the murders attracted his attention. The problem is, however, to try and establish firm connections between the Ripper (described at the time as a 'vampire' and 'drunk with blood') and Stoker's fictional blood-feasting Count. It must be no mere coincidence that Stoker had Dracula venturing into the East End of London.

Both subjects have been of great interest to me almost as far back as I care to remember. I recall first reading about Jack the Ripper in 1961 and around the same time I read Bram Stoker's novel about the sanguinary Count. Although I have never published anything on *Dracula* I have followed the associated literature and movies over the years. My interest in Jack the Ripper has, however, been the object of much reading and research for me for just as long and I have published several works on the subject; I may be entitled to at least claim to be an authority in the field. Back in 1993 sheer serendipity led to my discovery of a fresh and genuine contemporary Ripper suspect, one 'Dr' Francis Tumblety, an Irish-American, and this led to my first Ripper book, co-authored with Paul Gainey, some two years later.

This is not a book seeking to establish the identity of 'Jack the Ripper', although it does cast some interesting sidelights on that vexed question. It also provides new and relevant information on the decidedly odd Francis Tumblety 'M.D.', a genuine Ripper suspect of the time. It enhances our understanding of those fraught times and the characters playing out the drama. Of its nature no book that makes out the best case for any particular individual being Jack the Ripper can hope to be totally objective. It is, naturally, subjective. It is therefore necessary to be selective with contemporary press material as well as to indulge in speculation. Even so, honesty and accuracy should be maintained and all relevant material, where known, should be included. I endeavoured to follow these requirements but it did not prevent me from being labelled 'the Tumblety man'. This is a tag that I have found very difficult to shake off, despite the totally objective reference works I have since written. I have stated my position over this question in order to explain my own lack of research into Tumblety since the publication of the updated edition of my book in 1996. I felt that the best research on Tumblety would be carried out by those better placed than myself to do so and to maintain objectivity it was better for me to not indulge one suspect. The USA was where the best material was to be found. Many researchers took up the torch and some excellent research was carried out by such dedicated souls as Joe Chetcuti, Mike Hawley, Roger Palmer, Tim Riordan and Wolf Vanderlinden. They have all added greatly to our knowledge. *Dracula* and Stoker, too, have their champions of research and much relevant material and opinion has been added by such dedicated followers as Barbara Belford, Richard Dalby, Carol Margaret Davison, Robert Eighteen-Bisang, the late Dan Farson (who also contributed greatly on Jack the Ripper), Radu Florescu and Raymond McNally, Clive Leatherdale, Harry Ludlam, Elizabeth Miller, Paul Murray, my old and valued friend the late Leslie Shepard, Leonard Wolf and others too numerous to mention.

Neil Storey has bravely taken up the diverse threads and has looked at Tumblety's connection, and possible links, with the relevant cast of Victorian characters. To forge a real link between the factual Jack the Ripper and the fictional Dracula adds, in my opinion, great interest to both, but it is a daunting task and I can only admire his dedication to the cause. All that said, I feel that this book is a valuable addition to both areas of interest and I recommend it to the relevant readers as a necessary addition to their (probably creaking) bookshelves.

ACKNOWLEDGEMENTS

This book has been made possible and enriched by many who have generously opened their archives and shared their knowledge with me. I am particularly indebted to a man I am proud to call my friend, crime historian – Stewart P. Evans. I would also like to express my gratitude to Manx National Heritage *Eiraght Ashoonagh Vannin* and particularly their archivist Wendy Thirkettle. It is thanks to the generosity of Manx National Heritage that many of the letters sent by Francis Tumblety to Thomas Henry Hall Caine are published for the first time in this book.

I would also like to record my appreciation and thanks to the following: Heather Wolfe and Rebecca Oviedo at Folger Shakespeare Library, Washington; Nicole Contaxis, The New-York Historical Society; Karen Schoenewaldt, Registrar at Rosenbach Museum & Library, Philadelphia; Shakespeare Centre Library and Archive, Stratford-upon-Avon; Claire-Hélène Lengellé, Marie-Chantal Anctil and Suzanne Grégoire at Bibliothèque et Archives Nationales du Québec; Paul Hambleton, National Library of Scotland; The Victorian and Albert Museum; The British Library; The National Archives; The Library of Congress; United States National Archives, War Department Records, Judge Advocate General Office; Legislative Library of New Brunswick; The Library and Archives of Trinity College Dublin, Trinity College Dublin Historical Society ('The Hist'); Whitby Museum & Library; Whitby Public Library; St Mary's Parish church, Whitby; Whitby Abbey; Michael Shaw, The Sutcliffe Gallery, Whitby; Golders Green Crematorium; Norfolk Library and Information Service; Sotheby's London; Liverpool Record Office, Carol Collins; Ruth Myers; Helen Tovey at *Family Tree Magazine*; Joe Chetcuti; Robert Eighteen-Bisang; Clive Leatherdale; James Nice; Roger Palmer; Robert Smith; Jo de Vries, Mark Beynon and Cate Ludlow at The History Press; Colin Wilkinson, Bluecoat Press, Liverpool; Rusty Clark; David Drummond; Donald Rumbelow; Andrew Selwyn-Crome; Martin and Pip Faulks; the late Leslie Shephard and The Walt Whitman Archive, edited by Ed Folsom and Kenneth M. Price, published by the University of Nebraska–Lincoln http://www.whitmanarchive.org/.

INTRODUCTION

When I asked him if he knew Count Dracula, and could tell me anything of his castle, both he and his wife crossed themselves, and, saying that they knew nothing at all, simply refused to speak further. It was so near the time of starting that I had no time to ask anyone else, for it was all very mysterious and not by any means comforting.

> Jonathan Harker's journal
> Bram Stoker, *Dracula* (1897)

It was one of those clear, bright December mornings – when the sun hurts your eyes and the cold breezes nipping around your neck cause you to turn up your coat collar – when I stepped out from the sepulchral gloom of the Underground station. Setting out along Finchley Road as the cars and buses flew past, after a short walk I turned off up the quieter suburban Hoop Lane where I arrived at a large Italianate edifice of smart red brick walls and buildings and found my way to the office. Upon entering I was greeted by a receptionist and I told her the reason for my visit. She was a smart young lady with kind eyes, who politely asked me if I would like to take a seat while she made the necessary call. As she picked up the phone I heard her say, 'There is a gentleman to see Bram Stoker.' Just for a golden, wish-fuelled moment, it felt as if the tall, well-built figure of the great man with the paw of Hercules and the smile of Machiavelli would walk through the door, but it was not to be, for this was Golders Green Crematorium and through the window I found myself gazing at the chapel where Bram's funeral service had been conducted almost a hundred years previously.

My guide arrived and we set out through an archway and walked up the arcade where the walls were decked with memorial plaques. Some to those who were special only to their family and friends, while others marked those who had touched all of our lives and remain in immortal memory as household names: beloved entertainers, actors and musicians whose carved tablets record the names of Vesta Victoria, Sid James, Marc Bolan, Ray Ellington, Bud Flanagan,

Jack Hawkins, Joyce Grenfell, Robert Harbin the magician, Ivor Novello, Anna Pavlova, Kathleen Ferrier, Matt Munro and Peter Sellers – the list just goes on and on to create one of the greatest and most diverse playbills of all time.

We arrived at the door of the East Columbarium and while it was being unlocked my gaze lingered over the long, green swards that stretched out beyond. I took a last breath of fresh air as we stepped inside. The air within, however, was not fetid and the atmosphere of the building was filled with a serene sense of the past. We climbed up solid old stairs to the top floor and entered a room filled from floor to ceiling with stone shelves and divides, each one containing an ornamental urn or a carved stone box in a cornucopia of classic designs. Some of the alcoves were decorated, some had tiny well-fashioned iron or bronze gates in front of them, some had ornaments but I was directed to one alcove, that was, like the majority, quite plain, and there, in a tastefully formed stone casket little larger than a shoebox, was all that was left of Bram and his son, Noel, whose ashes were blended with those of his father after his death in September 1961. Bram had suf-fered the same ultimate fate as his most infamous creation, for they both had been turned to dust, but the legacy of Bram's book will ensure that neither he nor the vampire Count will ever really die. For me it was the moving end of one journey and the beginning of another. The books and research I had collected for years had given me a mass of information, the archives I had waited for were available to me and I had begun the first of many research trips for this book with a visit to Bram Stoker.

I have known, like many of us, the character of Dracula for as long as I can recall. Coming from an old Norfolk family I grew up surrounded by folktales, history and memories of the past in a county blessed with wide open skies – a gentle landscape punctuated with medieval churches, castles, the ruins of once mighty religious houses and views far enough to transport a young man's imagi-nation anywhere it wanted to go. I was always drawn to the darker aspects of history and was more fascinated by the old ghost stories recorded as fact by wit-nesses and tradition than any fiction. I suppose I must have been in my early teens when I bought my first Jack the Ripper book; to me it seemed like a natural progression from ghosts and legends to a true story of five horrific murders that seemed to be committed by some entity, half-beast, half-man with a vicious thirst for blood, who was never caught – he just seemed to disappear into the darkness.

I do not consider myself unique nor the first to see the tall gent dressed in his top hat, evening dress and long cape, the iconic 'Gentleman Jack the Ripper', easily transposed with the vampire Count; the synergy has always been there and I think for good reason: *Dracula* was born out of the Jack the Ripper crimes of 1888. I am not suggesting Bram used his book solely as a vehicle to retell the story of the Whitechapel murders, nor were they his only inspiration, however, as we shall see, they are surely entwined within it. *Dracula* is a fantastic mixture, skilfully drawn from so many of Bram's experiences and the characteristics of people he had encountered over the years; it includes some of the cutting-edge technology of its day, such as typewriters and phonographs, as well as elements of new science and pseudo-sciences, such as psychology, mesmerism and phrenology.

Bram had been fascinated by the stories of ghosts and legends he heard as he grew up in Ireland and maintained his fascination into manhood, where he read more about the occult, the strange and the uncanny. He pondered and discussed such matters with friends like Thomas Henry Hall Caine and Henry Irving in their all-night conversations, which lasted until the edges of the blinds became etched with rays of the dawn. *Dracula* is a story set in what was, for Bram and his readers, the modern world. Yet despite all the advances of technology, medicine and knowledge in the Victorian age, the characters are rendered impotent when confronted by the malevolent powers of ancient evil and it is to the past, to the knowledge of long-held traditions and lore that had been dismissed and disregarded by modern society, that our brave adventurers turn to confound and slay the forces of darkness. *Dracula* not only explores the esoteric but provides a justification for its learned study.

There were once those who railed against the idea of there being any connection between *Dracula* and the Whitechapel murders. That is, until 1986 when Richard Dalby uncovered and had translated the author's preface of the first foreign language (Icelandic) edition of *Dracula* (1903): it specifically mentioned Jack the Ripper.[1] It was to be another chance discovery of a single document that would reveal Francis Tumblety as the Special Branch prime suspect for Jack the Ripper. Stewart P. Evans recognised the significance of what has become known as the 'Littlechild Letter', one of four letters he purchased from antiquarian book dealer Eric Barton in 1993. With co-author Paul Gainey, Evans carried out the first research into Tumblety as a Jack the Ripper suspect; they published their findings in *The Lodger: The Arrest and Escape of Jack the Ripper* (1995). A Channel 4 television documentary presented by David Jessel followed a year later. In the documentary a short interview with Vivien Allen, the biographer of Thomas Hall Caine (one of the most popular authors of the late nineteenth century, but almost forgotten today), revealed a connection between him and Francis Tumblety. Suddenly a startling connection was made in my mind. I recalled the enigmatic dedication in *Dracula*, 'To my dear friend Hommy Beg'; *Hommy Beg* being Manx for 'Little Tommy' – the affectionate name given to Caine by his Manx grandmother.

I began to research these links but was only able to focus on the Whitechapel murders in my first book about those crimes and times, *A Grim Almanac of Jack the Ripper's London* (2004). However, I took the opportunity to mention this fascinating connection between Stoker, Caine and Tumblety in it.[2] In the course of researching Jack the Ripper's London it was my good fortune to be introduced by my editor to crime historian Stewart P. Evans, and an enduring friendship has resulted. Over the ensuing years I have enjoyed the hospitality of Stewart and his wife Rosie on many occasions. Stewart and I have discussed and debated the

Ripper case as well as many others at length, but it was the Hall Caine, Tumblety and Stoker connection that continued to fascinate me. As time went on more and more resources became available on the internet, notably newspapers in America and Canada, which allowed me to trace far more about Tumblety than had been previously possible in the UK.

The problem of further research into Hall Caine was that his papers were not easily accessible: they were hundreds of miles and a ferry journey away from me on the Isle of Man. Furthermore, the cataloguing of the papers had only begun after their closure period expired on 1 January 2000 and remains, to some extent, ongoing. In 2011 my work as a historian brought me to the Isle of Man for a short project and I took the opportunity of enquiring about the availability of the Hall Caine papers at Manx National Heritage. I met their archivist, Wendy Thirkettle; the welcome was warm and the reply was that the papers were now available. My wait was over and I soon made a return journey to the archive where there were over fifty letters and telegrams from Tumblety to Hall Caine, and even more from Bram. This year, 2012, marks the centenary of the death of Bram Stoker and the 125th anniversary of the publication of *Dracula*. There really was no better time to draw together my research, follow up leads that have taken my enquiries all over the world and, having had access to some of the best public and private collections of relevant material in the world, combined with advice, contributions and encouragement from fellow crime historians and *Dracula* experts, shed new light on the darkest sources of the book that changed gothic horror forever.

Neil R. Storey
The Eve of St George's Day, 2012

YOUNG BRAM

Abraham Stoker was born on 8 November 1847 at 15 Marino Crescent, in the Dublin suburb of Clontarf, the third child of Abraham and Charlotte Matilda Stoker. His older siblings were a brother, William Thornley, born on 6 March 1845, and Charlotte Matilda, born just over a year later on 9 June 1846. Stoker was named after his father, but rather than being called Abraham Junior or any other nom de plume he was always known as Bram.

At the time of Bram's birth the Stoker family had lived in Ireland for a number of generations. The Stokers had originally come over to Ireland from Morpeth, Northumberland, in 1690, when Peter Stoker was serving as part of William of

Orange's army. He had settled there, married, and his son, also named Peter, was born at Portlaoise, Queen's County, Leinster, in 1710. When the boy grew up he married Mary Senior and they had three children: Richard, born at Maryborough, Queen's County (in 1731); Bartholomew (1732); and William (1740), born in Ossory, Leinster. The eldest child, Richard (Bram's great-grandfather), was recalled by the Stoker family as having served as a quartermaster in the Second Irish Horse (later the

Abraham 'Bram' Stoker in 1893.

5th Dragoon) Guards, known as the 'Green Horse' after the green facings of their tunics; he died in Dublin in 1780. Richard's children were William (1755), Peter (1769) and John (1770). William married Frances Smyth, a Leinster girl, in 1780 and they were blessed with six children, among them, a son, Abraham (Bram's father), born in 1799.

Young Abraham was brought up in a Protestant household where prayers and religious observation were features of daily life; he embraced this and was an active member of the Sunday School Society for Ireland for many years. His faith never left him and he would regulate his own and his future family's life in the same way. Shortly after his sixteenth birthday, Abraham was fortunate to obtain a position in the civil service as a junior clerk in the Chief Secretary of Ireland's office, Dublin Castle, in June 1815. He remained in that grade for almost forty years; his work ethic reflected his outlook on life and would, on occasion, be repeated to his family: 'Honesty is the same in every relation of life and anything obtained by a different course cannot be right.' When he applied for the post of senior clerk in 1853 his application stated 'I have now been upwards of thirty-seven years in the Chief Secretary's office … For the last twenty years I have had charge of Parliamentary business, a branch which I believe I am justified in stating as not the least responsible or laborious portion of the duties of the office …'[3] His candidature was supported by a letter from Alex McDonell, former chief clerk at the castle, in which he proclaimed he had 'never known a better public servant' and expounded his praise for Stoker by saying 'I consider him a model man in all the great points required in one who is to fill such an office as that which he is for – thorough integrity – good temper – judgement – close appreciation and devotion to his duty and thorough knowledge of the business of the department'. McDonell also claimed he would not be acting justly by the government or 'by this most meritorious & modest man'[4] if he had not written such a testimony in his favour. Abraham was awarded the job.

In 1844, while still an assistant clerk, Abraham had married Charlotte Matilda Blake Thornley of Sligo; they made a home in Clontarf and started a family. The birth of Abraham 'Bram' Stoker was followed by the birth of another sister, Marion, the following year. When Charlotte rapidly fell pregnant again Abraham was only too aware space would be at a premium at Marino Crescent, and so moved his family to a larger house – Artane Lodge in the village of Artane (a few miles from the centre of Dublin). Here Thomas was born on 20 August 1849, followed by Richard Nugent (31 October 1851), Margaret Dalrymple (20 March 1853) and George on 20 July 1854.

Bram had been baptised at the Church of Ireland church of St John the Baptist at Clontarf on 30 December 1847. The service was not carried out by the usual incumbent but, by an interesting turn of fate, the officiating minister was the Reverend Edward, a visiting clergyman from the diocese of Ossary – land of Bram's Stoker ancestors in the eighteenth century. All of Abraham Stoker's children were baptised at St John the Baptist but sadly nothing remains today of the old church that served the parish for 250 years; it was demolished in favour of a new, larger edifice, which was built in 1866.

Much has been said about the Stokers and Clontarf in previous books and undoubtedly there would have been family outings to the seaside there, but Clontarf was a home for the Stokers for only a handful of years and they moved away when Bram was about eighteen months old. The majority of Bram's young life was actually spent in Artane where the Stoker family lived in a fine villa. When the Stokers knew Artane in the 1850s it was a quiet and rural village with a population of about 450, on the Dublin to Malahide road (about 2½ miles from Dublin post office). Described as 'one of the most cheerful highways near Dublin', it was surrounded by green fields and richly cultivated farms with views of the islands of Lambay and Ireland's Eye, the wooded lands of Clonshagh were nearby, with the hill of Howth and the Dublin and Wicklow Mountains as a magnificent backdrop. Abraham could continue to catch his train to get to work at Dublin Castle from Clontarf station on the Dublin and Drogheda railway, leaving Charlotte and the loyal family nurse, Ellen Crone, to look after the children. Charlotte Stoker was an impressive and strong-minded woman, held in some awe by her family; she was determined her sons should do well and progress in life and made no attempt to conceal her dissatisfaction if they failed to excel in their studies. Family members would recall she always put the boys first and was known to declare she 'did not care tuppence'[5] for her daughters.

Artane Lodge was to be Bram's home for most of his early years but, unlike his brothers and sisters, Bram did not play in the garden, run across the surrounding fields or play in the woods; young Bram suffered what still remains a mystery illness. Stoker recalled in this in an unpublished section of his manuscript of *Personal Reminiscences*:[6]

When the nursery bell rang at night my mother would run to the room expecting to find me dying. Certainly till I was about seven years old I never knew what it was to stand upright. All my early recollection is of being carried in people's arms and of being laid down somewhere or other. On a bed or a sofa if within the house, on a rug or amid cushions or on the grass if the weather were fine. To this day if I lie on the grass those days come back to me with never-ending freshness. I look among the stalks or blades of the grass and wonder where the sound come from – that gentle hum of nature which never ceases for ears that can hear. I wonder anew what is below the red brown uneven earth which seems as level at a little distance but is in reality so rugged. Then came back the wisdoms of those half-formed thoughts which use the rudiments of philosophy. Naturally I was thoughtful and the leisure of long illness gave opportunity for many thoughts which were fruitful according to their kind in later years.[7]

During those years of illness young Bram was told many stories, undoubtedly a heady brew of recollections, local traditions, tales and folklore, by both his mother and the beloved family nurse, Ellen Crone. William Thornley, known just as Thornley, kept a photograph of the latter and a lock of her hair for the rest of his life, adding a photograph of her gravestone at Rathfarnham to the collection after her death. A plaque in the cemetery records she was 'for many years the devoted nurse and friend in the family of Abraham and Charlotte Stoker and in whose services she died on 29 March 1869, aged 68 years'.

Bram's mother, Charlotte, was a wonderful teller of stories, some drawn from or influenced by the difficult events of her childhood. Charlotte was the daughter of Thomas and Matilda Thornley. Thomas was from Ballyshannon, Co. Donegal, and was a serving lieutenant of the 43rd (Monmouthshire) Regiment of Foot who had served in the American War of 1812; he had married Matilda in 1817. She had been one of the Blakes of Galway, who had settled in Sligo. Charlotte was their first child and she grew up in the family home on Correction Street (now known as High Street), which was named after the House of Correction that once stood there. The new county prison was begun in 1818, the year Charlotte was born, and opened in 1823. It was a considerable building of polygon shape designed to hold 200 prisoners, with a governor's residence in the centre. The new prison had wings for both male and female inmates, and had its own hospital wing, surgery, dispensary, cookhouse, clothing store and school within its walls. Hard labour was served on its treadmill, along with picking oakum, breaking stones and chopping wood to fuel the prison's furnaces; the men were sentenced to industrial labour served in workshops making shoes, tailoring, tinsmithing, glazing, painting or gardening, and the female prisoners sewed, knitted or worked in the laundry. No indolence was allowed.

After Derry, Sligo was the second biggest town in the north-west of Ireland, but the prison and stories of what occurred behind those high walls were familiar to all. Executions were still carried out in public view and during her years there Charlotte may well have witnessed the hanging of murderers Owen Healy and Thomas Tuffy in July 1835. She also lived through famine when the potato and oat crops failed in 1822, but the events that were to become engraved upon her memory occurred during the Sligo cholera epidemic of 1832. Charlotte was aged 14 at the time and at that impressionable age she was living in a society that was gripped by mortal fear and witnessed desperate and inhuman acts, some of which exposed the very worst of human nature. In a memoir of these events, which she wrote in later life, Charlotte recalled:

> Rumours of the great plague broke on us from time to time, as men talk of far-off things which can never come near themselves, but gradually the terror grew on us as we heard of it coming nearer and nearer … Then with wild afright, we began to hear the whisper passed, 'It is in Ireland!' Men's senses began failing

An echo of the Sligo cholera epidemic, William's Fitzgerald's eerie depiction of the 'invisible giant', the bringer of pestilence, in *Under the Sunset* (1882 edition).

them for fear, and deeds were done, in selfish dread, enough to call down God's direct vengeance upon us.

One action I vividly remember. A poor traveller was taken ill on the roadside some miles from the town, and how did those Samaritans tend him? They dug a pit and with long poles pushed him living into it, and covered him up quick, alive. Severely, like Sodom, did our city pay for such crimes …

In a very few days the town became a place of the dead. No vehicles moved except the cholera carts or doctors' carriages. Many people fled, and many of these were overtaken by the plague and died by the way. Some of the doctors 'made good of it' as they said themselves, at first, but one by one they too became victims and others came and filled the gaps, then others once again filled their places. Most of the clergy of all denominations fled, and few indeed were the instances in which the funeral service was read over the dead.

The great County Infirmary and Fever Hospital was turned into a cholera hospital, but was quite insufficient to meet the requirements of the situation. The nurses died one after another, and none could be found to fill their places but women of the worst description, who were always more than half drunk, and such scenes were perpetrated there as would make the flesh creep to hear of.

One Roman Catholic priest remained (there may have been others, but I knew of this one). His name was Gilern, and he told us himself that he was obliged to sit day after day, and night after night, on top of the great stone stairs with a horse whip, to prevent those wretches dragging the patients down the stairs by the legs with their heads dashing on the stone steps, before they were dead.[8]

There is little doubt such stories, related in such a personal and powerful manner, stayed with Bram all his life and were drawn upon by him in a number of his books and stories, notably in his early tale *The Spectre of Doom*, later reprinted in Stoker's strange collection of fairy tales, *Under the Sunset* (1881), and in *Dracula*.

Further tales in Charlotte's memoir speak of the dead becoming undead: those believed to have succumbed to the cholera and who were being prepared for burial or piled up among the bodies who were then discovered to be alive. Such a one was an old soldier known as 'long Sergeant Callen':

He took the cholera and was thought dead, and a coffin was brought. As the coffin maker had always a stack of coffins ready on hand, with burials following immediately on the deaths, they were much of a uniform size and, of course, too short for long Sergeant Callen. The men who were putting him in, when they found he would not fit, took a big hammer to break his legs to make him fit. The first blow raised the sergeant from his stupor, and he started up and recovered.[9]

Charlotte records a red scarf being wound around a body as a folkloric talisman to banish sickness, while her recollections of the naive but determined attempts to cleanse houses and prevent the spread of infection on the streets based on old beliefs and lore have clear resonance in *Dracula*. Charlotte explains how they believed they could ward off the cholera:

> There was a constant fumigation kept up. Plates of salt on which vitriolic acid was poured from time to time were placed outside all the windows and doors. Every morning as soon as we awoke, a dose of whiskey thickened with ginger was given us all, in quantities according to our ages. Gradually the street in which we lived thinned out, as by twos and threes our dead neighbours were carried away. Our neighbours on both sides died. On one side a little girl called Mary Sheridan was left alone and sick, and we could hear her cries. I begged my mother's leave to help her, and she let me go, with many fears. Poor Mary died in my arms an hour after. I returned home and, being well fumigated, was not affected … At night many tar barrels and other combustible matters used to be burned along the street to try to purify the air, and they had a weird, unearthly look, gleaming out in the darkness.[10]

In *Dracula*, Professor Van Helsing and Dr Seward grimly set about a similar task in the bedroom of Lucy Westenra to repel the contagion of the vampire:

> We went into the room, taking the flowers with us. The Professor's actions were certainly odd and not to be found in any pharmacopeia that I ever heard of. First he fastened up the windows and latched them securely. Next, taking a handful of the flowers, he rubbed them all over the sashes, as though to ensure that every whiff of air that might get in would be laden with the garlic smell. Then with the wisp he rubbed all over the jamb of the door, above, below, and at each side, and round the fireplace in the same way.

When Charlotte's family saw a number of their own poultry dead in their back-yard they decided it was time to leave and father, mother, Charlotte, her two brothers and a servant left on the mail coach for Ballyshannon:

> It was a damp, drizzling morning, and we felt very miserable, as if we had a forewarning of what lay before us. All went well until we got within a mile of a village about four miles from Ballyshannon, when the coach was met and stopped by a mob of men armed with sticks, scythes and pitchforks. They were headed by a Dr. John Shields, who was half mad. He was the son of one of the first physicians and most respected men in the county but did not take after his father. The coach was stopped and were ordered out, our luggage taken off, and no entreaties could prevail on those men to allow us to pass. Fear had maddened them. After a long parley and many threats of the vengeance of the law, the coach was allowed to proceed and we were left on the roadside sitting on our trunks, cold, wet and hungry, and well-nigh hopeless.[11]

What happened to them has resonance in Jonathan Harker's arrival in Transylvania where, on seeing the caleche (carriage) from Castle Dracula, the crowd made the sign of the cross and pointed two fingers at Harker to ward off the evil eye in a 'chorus of screams from the peasants and a universal crossing of themselves'; one of Harker's fellow travellers even whispered a line from Burger's *Lenore*: '*Denn die Todten reiten Schnell*' (For the dead travel fast). This was perhaps another echo of the old Irish tales of phantom coaches that would clatter along at ungodly hours as harbingers of death. The folklore attached to the manifestation insists that at the sight or sound of the coach all gates should be thrown open, then the coach will not call for a family member but will foretell the death of a relative some distance away. One such tale from Co. Clare dates from December 1876:

> a servant of the Macnamaras was going his rounds at Ennistymon, a beautiful spot in a wooded glen, with a broad stream falling in a series of cascades. In the dark he heard the rumbling of wheels on the back avenue, and, knowing from the hour and place that no mortal vehicle could be coming, concluded that it was the death coach, and ran on, opening the gates before it. He had just time to open the third gate, and throw himself on his face beside it, when he heard a coach go clanking past. On the following day Admiral Sir Burton Macnamara died in London.[12]

Charlotte and Nurse Ellen were steeped in Celtic folklore; Charlotte swore she had heard a banshee wail before her own mother died. Although it is not known exactly which folk tales were told to young Bram, there are many touchstones from Celtic folklore that resonate in *Dracula*, for the ancient tales and lore of Ireland is permeated with stories of encounters, challenges and fights won and lost between humans and the supernatural. Many of them are tales of witches, devils, demons, spirits, entities, the undead and shape-shifters, where a creature would be seen as an animal or a bird such as a raven by day, but by night would turn into a man. Each tale would demonstrate cunning on both sides and would often explain the parameters of power endowed upon the supernatural being and how they would be deterred by certain objects, symbols or natural features such as the sign of the cross, a Bible and holy water, running water or the crowing of a cock.[13]

Blood also features in a number of Celtic folk tales as a life force drained and used to empower diabolical creatures, such as the blood-sucking demon the *deamhan-fhola* and witches. In one tale recorded in popular Irish oral tradition, a servant girl observes three men warming themselves by a fire at a remote inn. After the men drowse off into a stupor, brought about more by magic than drink, three hags enter, bleed the men and use the blood in the mix for a cake. The men awake in a very weak state and can only be revived when the servant girl gives them some of the cake to eat. This was a story made only too real when food was

scarce during the Irish famines of the nineteenth century, as living animals were
bled and their blood mixed with a handful of oatmeal or yellow meal and vegetable residue to make 'relish cakes' for human consumption.[14]

Akin to many other folk traditions and legends, vampires feature in Irish folklore and one may easily be seduced by the idea that the roots of Bram's inspiration
for *Dracula* may be found amongst them.

Although published after his boyhood, in *The Origin and History of Irish Names
of Places* by Patrick Weston Joyce (1875), a story that may have been told to young
Bram from the oral tradition in Co. Derry was as follows:

> There is a place in the parish of Errigal in Derry, called Slaghtaverty, but it
> ought to have been called Laghtaverty, the laght or sepulchral monument
> of the abhartach or dwarf. This dwarf was a magician, and a dreadful tyrant,
> and after having perpetrated great cruelties on the people he was at last van-
> quished and slain by a neighbouring chieftain; some say by Fionn MacCumhail
> [Finn McCool]. He was buried in a standing posture, but the very next day he
> appeared in his old haunts, more cruel and vigorous than ever. And the chief
> slew him a second time and buried him as before, but again he escaped from the
> grave, and spread terror through the whole country. The chief then consulted a
> druid, and according to his directions, he slew the dwarf a third time, and buried
> him in the same place, with his head downwards; which subdued his magical
> power, so that he never again appeared on earth. The laght raised over the dwarf
> is still there, and you may hear the legend with much detail from the natives of
> the place, one of whom told it to me.[15]

The oral tradition of the story has a variation to the written tale, whereby the
abhartach was slain by another chieftain named Cathrain and rose from his
grave to wreak a terrible revenge on Cathrain's subjects by drinking their blood.
Cathrain consults a Christian saint who advises him that the risen abhartach is
neamh-mairbh, or walking dead, and that he can only be returned to his grave if
he is killed by a sword of yew wood. After that, a great stone should be placed
atop the grave and the area around planted with thorns to hold him fast.[16] This
achieved, the abhartach, it is said, rests to this day in a grave now known as
Slaghtaverty Dolmen – covered by a large stone and two others with a hawthorn
growing beside it.

Montague Summers also records ancient tales of the walking dead who were
feared across the land, notably the '*Dearg-dul*', or red blood sucker.[17] The name
takes a variety of forms, such as *dearg-dur* or *dearg-dililat*, while many tales talk of
the *dearg-diúlai*, the drinker of human blood, which features in stories from across
the rural counties of Ireland. The stories have echoes of the old Irish tale of the
demon bride, where a beautiful but evil spirit steals the souls of men with a kiss.
The *dearg-diúlai* can be male or female; the latter – often noted for appearing pale

but beautiful and sensuous – linger in graveyards at night ready to seduce unwary travellers with their irresistible charm, but when they kiss they suck the life blood from their victims' bodies. In another tale, from Antrim, a beautiful vampire was said to walk as undead until she could turn another beauty into a vampire to take her place.

It was Cathal Ó Sándair who observed that Bram may have been guided to use the name Dracula for its resonance with the Irish *droch-fola* (pronounced drok'ola), meaning bad blood, or even the Kerry folk tale of *Dún Dreach-fhola* (pronounced drak'ola), the castle of blood visage; a story claimed to have been enlarged upon in the lectures of Seán Ó Súilleabháin, the archivist of the Irish Folklore Commission and author of *A Handbook of Irish Folklore*, as a fortress inhabited by *neamh-mhairbh*, the undead, who sustained themselves by the blood of wayfarers.[18]

Whichever stories were heard by young Bram, they pervaded his young imagination and endowed him with a legacy of remarkable material that he would draw upon again and again for the rest of his life. Meanwhile, as Bram recovered from his childhood illness he grew strong and with time became the largest member of his family.

In 1858 the Stoker family moved yet again, this time to 17 Upper Buckingham Street in the Mountjoy district of Dublin City. Dublin was quite a change from the rural village of Artane, and began a time of broadening horizons for Charlotte. She had developed a keen interest in matters of social concern before she was married and the move to Dublin had seen her active participation in the new feminine movement for education. The late 1850s and early 1860s were a remarkable time for women in general, although there were still many who would disparage and mock them for attempting to enter the political arena.

Women were still decades away from obtaining the right to vote, but the first women's groups to apply pressure for the right of equal franchise and raise awareness of issues of social concern were being created – notably with the foundation of The Queen's Institute in London in 1841, which offered a course of general education to governesses in an attempt to improve their status. This was followed, in 1859, by the Society for Promoting the Employment of Women, which was founded by Barbara Bodichon, the author of *Women and Work* (1858), with the English poet and philanthropist Adelaide Anne Procter, and Jessie Boucherett. These ideas spread to Ireland through the meeting of the Social Science Congress in Dublin in 1861,[19] and with the formation of The Queen's Institute for the Training and Employment of Women in Dublin – Charlotte (and sometimes her husband) regularly attended their meetings. Charlotte also began to give speeches and proved herself a well-informed and powerful orator who judiciously illustrated her lectures with examples from her own research.

Charlotte's first significant paper was delivered at a meeting of the Statistical and Social Enquiry for Ireland on 13 May 1863, and was entitled 'On the

Sackville (now O'Connell) Street, Dublin's main thoroughfare as Bram would have known it in the 1860s.

Necessity of a State Provision for the Education of the Deaf and Dumb in Ireland'.[20] The speech was well received and enjoyed support from census commissioner Dr William Wilde, a man who would form a friendship with the Stoker family. Meanwhile, Charlotte's social work saw her become a workhouse visitor. Dublin had two workhouses known as the North Union and the South Union and it is testimony to her strength of character that she chose to become a visitor at the latter, for its reputation was far the worst of the two. The events of 1862 may well have had a bearing on her decision.

Westmoreland Street, Dublin, viewed from College Green, with the statue of the poet
Thomas Moore (1779–1852) on the right, photographed in the 1860s.

In November 1862 there was a violent uprising by a number of the pauper
inmates, who routed the wardmasters of the Union to fly before them as they
threatened vengeance. Fires were started in three separate parts of the building
and when the fire engines arrived they were hindered in their work by the paupers, who had armed themselves with broom handles, hammers and pieces of
iron bedsteads and were determined to see the building burn to the ground. It

took about 200 soldiers and police to restrain the rioters and maintain order, and about twenty arrests were made.[21]

The trial of those involved in the insurrection was brought before the Crown Court in December 1862, and, perhaps significantly for Charlotte, the first to face judgement were two women, Anne Duffy and Ellen Carey, who both pleaded guilty to setting fire to the workhouse. They made it clear that they had no regrets and were firmly of the opinion that convicts were much better treated than paupers. When sentenced to four years' penal servitude, they said, 'Thank your Lordship; we have got out of hell at all events.' Seventeen male paupers followed them facing the same charges: all received the same punishment as Anne and Ellen and all also thanked the judge and jury for being 'got out of a house of persecution'. Four more were brought up on charges of rioting and found guilty: they received twelve months with hard labour.[22]

Charlotte became a workhouse visitor soon after and from her observations within those walls she wrote a paper entitled 'On Female Emigration from Workhouses', which was read before the Statistical Society in January 1864. The object of her paper was to show that the only suitable way to provide for workhouse girls was to help them emigrate. In her paper Charlotte argued that, under the present system, it was impossible for girls in workhouses to gain a proper education and, as a result, they failed in their placements as servants and in other employment and became 'outcasts from public sympathy and protection. No wonder they should gradually sink into the lowest phases of vice and misery.' She directly referred to the insubordination at the south Dublin workhouse in 1862 'as evidence of the bad effects of workhouse education', and explained she had seen as many as three generations of one family within it. She continued, 'When the young girls passed into the adult ward their demoralisation was completed. They became utterly depraved, and after passing through every stage of vice outside the house, they ended their wretched lives in the hospital, leaving to another generation the inheritance of their sin and misery.'[23]

The paper was also produced as a pamphlet and, while Charlotte would go on researching and presenting papers, none would attract such media interest as 'On Female Emigration'. It is interesting here to consider what impressions and views of those who had fallen into 'vice and misery' Charlotte instilled in her shy and impressionable son, Bram.

At about the age of 11, Bram commenced his first formal education as a day boy at Bective House College, a school run by Dr John Lardner Burke. Stoker was taught by the Reverend William Woods (who later bought the school from Burke in 1869). Bective House, situated at No. 15 Rutland Square East, (now the eastern side Parnell Square), was founded by Dr Burke in 1834 as 'a seminary for young gentlemen' with facilities for both boarding and day scholars; it was named in honour of the Earl of Bective, the proprietor of houses on the square.

The school was ideally situated for recreational activities, as a green field within the Rotunda Gardens was across from the college (now occupied by the Garden of Remembrance). Reverend Woods, affectionately remembered as far as Stoker was concerned, as 'a man of broad scholarship, fearless eloquence … a kindly disposition and almost limitless patience', was keen to promote the new sport of rugby among the boys and the big, sturdily built young man that Stoker had grown to be was first blooded to the game of rugby here and proved himself a promising forward.

Still quite a shy and introspective lad, Bram only made a few friends at school: one of those we know of with any certainty was Valentine Dillon, who in his maturity became a notable Dublin solicitor, acted as a lawyer for the Land League and defended Charles Stewart Parnell, the leader of the Irish Party and the Land League, after his arrest in 1880. Dillon remained a staunch supporter of Parnell and went on to be Lord Mayor of Dublin in 1894 and again in 1895. Bram was always proud to say Val Dillon was an old friend and spoke highly of him as 'a man with broad views of life and of the dignity of the position which he held'. [24]

Dillon and Stoker seemed, however, a strange match: Dillon was a Roman Catholic with a strong nationalist background, while Stoker was a Protestant with parents who were sympathetic towards the Free State, and who became active in Home Rule politics and remained friends with Val's uncle John Dillon, one of the original committee members of the Irish National Land League.

Perhaps not too much can be read into Bram and Dillon's unlikely relationship, however. After all, they were just young lads and school friends. Although they were to meet again on occasion they went their separate ways in higher education: Dillon to a Catholic university while Bram, like many of Reverend Woods' boys, to Trinity College.

2

TRINITY

Trinity College did not have the intimate relationship with its city, Dublin, that was synonymous with Oxford or Cambridge; as in all university centres there were 'town and gown' disagreements, but in Dublin there were also far deeper divides on religious grounds. The college was founded by letters patent from Elizabeth I in 1592 and from the day it admitted its first students in January 1593 remained a Protestant seat of learning, exclusive of all other religious denominations, until 1845, when the college founded scholarships for students of any creed (although rarely Catholic). It was only in 1873, when cordial support was given by the university to the act that abolished religious tests, that Catholics were accepted as students (with the exception of the School of Divinity).

Bram Stoker matriculated at Trinity in 1864, a few weeks short of his seventeenth birthday. The buildings he studied in and came to know well were described by Samuel Ossory Fitzpatrick in 1907:

> The main characteristic of the College is the sense of roominess, the absence of cramping confinement in her spacious enclosures. In all some twenty-eight acres, now in the very heart of a busy city, are included within her boundary walls. The west front facing College Green is a Palladian facade 300ft in length and 65 feet in height. The great gateway is flanked on each side by two Corinthian columns resting on bases of rustic ashlar, and supporting a bold pediment surmounted by an entablature ... Passing through the gateway we enter Parliament Square through an octagon vestibule 72 feet in length, with a groined and vaulted roof, piercing the main building, and having on the left the porter's lodge. Above the gateway, extending the full depth from east to west, is the Regent House, 63 feet by 46 feet, now used as an examination hall. It is approached from the gateway by a handsome staircase on the right of the vestibule, the supports of which are singularly massive and rich in their design. The interior facade is simpler, and the pavilions are replaced by the residentiary buildings of Parliament Square, running at right angles to the main front. At the

extremities of these are, on the left or north side, the Chapel, and on the right or south, the Theatre, while in the centre rises the campanile, beyond which is Library Square.[25]

Of the past alumni Fitzpatrick wrote: '… the bonds uniting the Irish metropolis to the centre of Irish learning are strong and permanent; and Trinity College has struck its impress deeply on the lives of many of Ireland's greatest sons, has moulded and shaped their destinies, and through them has profoundly influenced the history of the Irish nation.' His words were indeed true, for the cornerstones of modern Irish civilisation were taught at Trinity, as symbolised in the figures sculpted by Thomas Kirk at the base of the campanile that represent divinity, science, medicine and law.

The Trinity alumni has a remarkable dichotomy, whereby a number of those who became leaders of Ireland's national movements and uprisings can be found alongside those who came to prominence for upholding the laws and statutes against which the rebels had riled. Among the rebels was no lesser man than Wolfe Tone (1763–98), the 'Father of Irish Republicanism' and leader of the 1798 Rebellion; Robert Emmet, Irish nationalist and Republican who led the abortive rebellion against British rule in 1803, and after capture and trial was executed for high treason; Thomas Osborne Davis (1814–45), the revolutionary writer and composer of rousing ballads, who became the leader and poet of the Young Ireland movement and who dedicated his life to Irish nationalism; Chartist and reformer James Bronterre O'Brien (1805–64); and the militant Chartist leader, Irish patriot and former Repeal of the Union Member of Parliament Feargus O'Connor (1794–1855).

The men of law included barristers and judges such as John George (1804–71) and Christopher Palles (1831–1920); distinguished Irish QC brothers John George Gibson (1846–1923) and Edward Gibson (1837–1913), the man largely responsible for drafting the Purchase of Land (Ireland) Act 1885 who was made Lord Chancellor of Ireland in 1885; Edward Carson (1854–1935) QC and Privy Counsellor, who was engaged by the Marquess of Queensberry to lead his defence against Oscar Wilde's action for criminal libel in 1895, and who went on to become leader of the Irish Unionist Alliance and Ulster Unionist Party between 1910 and 1921 and the founding father of the Northern Irish State; and barrister Sir Robert Anderson (1841–1918), a man who would hold the position of Assistant Commissioner (Crime) in the Metropolitan Police from 1888 until his retirement in 1901 – and a man we shall encounter again.

Although other members of the extended Stoker family had preceded Bram at Trinity, his father had not attended university. Elder brother Thornley had studied medicine at Queen's College, Galway, so Bram would be the first of Abraham and Charlotte Stoker's children to go up to Trinity. Class distinction was still applied and Bram was admitted as a 'pensioner', which meant his parents were in receipt

The Trinity College campanile (bell tower) built in 1853 by Sir Charles Lanyon, pictured *c.* 1870. The four figures at the base of the belfry, sculpted by Thomas Kirk, represent the learned arts – divinity, science, medicine and law – which were taught there.

of only a modest income. He was thus of a middling sort; with fellow common-ers with wealthy parents above him and sizars, the children of poorer parents, below. Bram did not take up residence in halls but continued to live at home with his parents, and the introspective young man could easily have remained so but for the fact that his entry to Trinity became a glorious voyage of discovery, which Bram later compared to his life before in an autobiographical passage in *The Mystery of the Sea*: 'Hitherto my life was an uneventful one. At school I was, though secretly ambitious, dull as to results. At College I was better off, for my big body and athletic powers gave me a certain position in which I had to overcome my natural shyness.'[26]

Bram employed no false modesty to his academic prowess here; he came fortieth out of fifty-one in his entrance exams. While he did not lack intelligence, it always seemed that he would only excel in the things that really captured his imagination or interest. Perhaps John Butler Yeats, who entered Trinity in 1857, summed up the situation when commenting, 'the Trinity College intellects, noisy and monotonous, without ideas or curiosity about ideas and without sense of mystery, everything was sacrificed to mental efficiency ... Trinity college is intellectually a sort of little Prussia.' This was a view shared by H.A. Hinckson in *Student Life in Trinity College, Dublin* (1892):

> The Fellows exercise but little influence on the college life of the students except in their capacity as examiners. In the Exam Hall they meet 'as victim and executioner', and consequently the relations between them are often somewhat strained. There is little or no social intercourse between them and the students, to whose intellectual level they rarely deign to descend. They give no entertainments to the students like their confreres at Oxford and Cambridge. The professional gown seems always to cling to them, and the majesty of their high position is ever before their eyes. No wonder the undergrads regard them with fear and trembling. As might be expected, they are very conservative, especially the senior fellows, and view with grave suspicion any suggestion of reform.[27]

The good people of Dublin did not appreciate students loafing about the streets, especially indulging in occasional pranks such as 'blowing off doors with gunpowder, wrenching off city knockers and drawing obnoxious individuals on the walls and doors of their chambers', thus the students were policed by the college janitors resplendent in their liveries of dark blue with brass buttons bearing the college arms, and velvet hunting caps. An old chronicler describing the college recorded:

> On the left side as you enter the vestibule is the porter's lodge, as it is called, and although it is but an humble apartment, and its occupants sober and discreet men, yet its influence is, by a certain class of students, technically known as 'Town Haunters', considered more depressing and pestiferous than the vapours of Trophonious's cave or those of the celebrated Grotto del Cani. When Great Tom has ceased to toll the hour of nine, this portal is closed and then vigilance puts into activity her sharpest features, that none may enter without being 'noted down'.[28]

Yet, even within the confines of Trinity, students were not encouraged to enjoy their surroundings when not attending lectures:

> it is not given to dream too long in the green Wilderness or beneath the trees of the park. One may not pace the walks over long with a chosen friend, dear in that fresh confidence of a college friendship ... The authorities have so ordained it, that neither Wilderness nor park is allowable at a time when one would enjoy them most. After 6pm in the summer evenings, all day long on a summer Sunday, the gates are locked, and the student may swelter in his dark rooms, and swear at officialism in general and in particular. Even the grass plots of the Front Square are sacred, and one may not lie thereon, or swing on the chains which guard them without incurring a severe reprimand.[29]

Charles Barrington, a contemporary of Stoker, recalled how student sons of the more wealthy families would retreat to halls and enjoy afternoons of billiards, cards and whiskey, while some would take a sojourn down Grafton Street dressed in attire so smart such men became known as the 'Grafton Street Hussars'. However, there was so much more to student life, and the boys like Bram who did not excel within the prescribed curriculum could flourish at sports and within the university societies. This Bram did and he was beginning to make his name when, after less than a year at university, his personal situation changed. Bram's father was suffering from increasing bouts of illness that forced his retirement from the civil service in October 1865. Granted a 'retired allowance' of £650 a year, he moved his family to 5 Orwell Park in the expanding southern Dublin suburb of Rathgar, next Rathmines. Bram moved yet again in 1870 to live with Thornley in his smart four-storey Georgian terraced house at 43 Harcourt Street, Dublin. Wanting to contribute to the family finances, Bram applied to the civil service in 1866, was employed as an unestablished member of staff and, having been examined for a clerkship, was entered as a clerk, second class, in the Fines and Penalties Department in 1867.

Bram wanted to carry on at university but initially found it difficult to balance his new job and his college commitments: his attendance at the latter suffered and he was 'degraded' by his tutor's order in 1867, but he did not give up. His Bachelor degree should have taken four years, it was six years before Bram was listed among the pensionarii who had graduated in pure mathematics in March 1870. Entitled to purchase his Masters, he did so and was conferred with his Magistri in Artibus in the examination hall of Trinity on 9 February 1875.[30]

Despite the problems early on, Bram appears to have made a work and university balance acceptable to all sides and even had time to make his mark in the Civil Service Athletic Sports, in university societies and sporting clubs. It was said that Trinity was 'a good foster mother of vigorous sons' and athletics flourished there. A small collection of newspapers cuttings amongst the vast number he would later amass for Henry Irving bear mute testimony to the outstanding sporting achievements of Bram Stoker.

At the 1867 Civil Service Athletic Sports event held on the Leinster Cricket Ground in Rathmines, Bram was booked in for the 'stranger's race' which he won 'in admirable style'. At the same event the 'throwing the cricket ball' had but one entrant on the day, a Mr L. Fyers Banks, who threw the ball 60 yards and carried off the prize of a flask; Bram, who had not formally entered the contest, picked up the ball and sent it flying – 105 yards! Bram also played for the Trinity first XV and was awarded caps for the 1868/70 and 1870/71 seasons 'for superior play'. His athletic abilities were truly outstanding and included prizes for gymnasium weights, and 2-, 5- and 7-mile walking races.

The annual Trinity Sports, held over two days on the College Park, would attract in excess of 30,000 spectators and the athletic prowess of Stoker consistently stood out and drew interest from both the crowd and the press. His versatility was very impressive: during the Trinity Sports of June 1870 Stoker not only came first in putting the 42lb weight, the 16lb shot, and slinging the 56lb and 42lb weights, he also took joint first in vaulting, high jump, the long jump and trapeze.

Bram's sporting achievements would become known far beyond the prism of Trinity and the cups he was awarded were treasured for the rest of his life.

Bram also found time to perform with the University Boat Club Dramatic Society, but his most significant achievement was to become both Auditor of the Trinity Historical Society (known as the Hist) and President of the Philosophical Society (known as the Phil). This was no mean feat, for both these offices are the highest that can be achieved in both these esteemed university debating and literary societies, and it is a clear mark of what an active and popular figure Bram was at Trinity.

The Phil can trace its lineage back to The Dublin Philosophical Society founded in 1683 by William Molyneux. The society known to Bram had been created in 1860 after the Dublin University Philosophical Society dissolved, and the Undergraduate Philosophical Society changed its name to the University Philosophical Society, incorporating both societies. The Phil was an active forum for reading and discussing papers and had counted among its members such luminaries as the classicist and polymath John Pentland Mahaffy (president 1858–59), popular Trinity master Professor Edward Dowden, poet and literary critic John Todhunter and artist John Butler Yeats.

Bram presented his inaugural paper, 'Sensationalism in Fiction and Society', to the Phil on 7 May 1868 and from that time onwards regularly attended the meetings, where papers exploring a variety of aspects of the supernatural in literature, such as the demonology of Milton, the legend of *Faust* and Byron's work, were discussed. Bram was elected President of the Phil in May 1870: during his tenure he read an essay on Dante Gabriel Rossetti's poems. He stood down at the closing meeting for the session 1869/70, held in the New Buildings at Trinity in June 1870, after delivering an address on 'The Means of Improvement in Composition'. Bram continued to attend and participate in the meetings of the Phil until 1877.

While at Trinity, Bram got to know the two sons of his parents' friends Sir William and Jane Wilde: William, known to his friends as Willie, and, of course, Oscar. All three boys attended Trinity College: Willie and Bram were in the same year and were good friends while the younger Oscar was below them. Although Bram would have encouraged and supported the motion for Oscar to join the Phil in 1871, he was actually proposed by its president, Charles Arundell, and secretary, Kendal Franks. Oscar's application to the Hist was proposed by his brother Willie, and seconded by Charles Arundell, the correspondence secretary.[31]

Bram loved the cut and thrust of debate in the Hist. This university society was established within the college in 1770, but able to trace its origins to the society founded by the philosopher Edmund Burke in Dublin in 1747. Its notable members included two future revolutionaries, Theobald Wolfe Tone and Robert Emmet, while the Extern Historical Society (as it was named from 1815–43) counted Thomas Davis, John Blake Dillon and a number of other key figures from the nationalist cause among its membership, along with Joseph Sheridan Le Fanu, the author of numerous gothic tales and mystery novels, notably *Uncle Silas* (1864) and *In a Glass Darkly* (1872).

Bram was of the firm belief that the Hist '… is no ornamental appanage to the College, but is its supplementary school, and it must always keep its relative position within its progress if it is to live and flourish'.[32]

He was among the principle speakers of the 1868 season and was elected to the general committee in May 1869. Stoker recalled, 'In my university days I had been something of a law-maker in a small way, as I had revised and carried out the revision of the laws of order of the college historical society.'[33]

At the opening meeting of the thirtieth session of the Hist, as auditor, Bram was required to give an address. He chose to be topical in addressing the subject of 'The Necessity for Political Honesty'. The backdrop for his speech was a troubled Ireland in the aftermath of the abortive Fenian Rising of 1867, when inflamed political and sectarian divides threatened the future of the nation. Just over a year had passed since a serious riot had occurred after police used truncheons to disperse a crowd of men, women and children attending a Fenian amnesty meeting in Dublin's Phoenix Park in August 1871.[34] Bram would have been only too aware that the emotions and beliefs of his audience could and would be touched by his words; he chose them well. His powerful speech presents a significant and rare insight of the opinions, beliefs and incisive vision of Bram Stoker as a young man.

It was the evening of Wednesday 13 November 1872, the setting was the lofty eighteenth-century dining hall of Trinity College. Half panelled in dark wood, the room was illuminated by lamps that gave a rich golden glow to the heavy gilded frames that held the portraits of the luminaries of the past, which gazed down from the upper walls. Filled by a larger than usual attendance, the room was 'thronged in every part by both visitors and students', there had been some good-humoured noise but the audience rigidly obeyed the injunction implied in the statement on the invitation cards that 'any party demonstration would be out of place'. Shortly after eight, the chair was taken by the president of the society, the Right Hon. Sir Joseph Napier, Bart. He was joined on the dais by an august group of dignitaries and senior academics, men of the clergy and the law, among them the Lord Mayor of Dublin, Judge Warren, the Right Hon. John Thomas Ball QC MP, Professor Edward Dowden and Sir William Wilde.

One of the secretaries, Mr H. Tydd Lane, rose first to read the minutes of the last meeting. Then Bram rose purposefully. His presence was immense; he was a tall, athletic and impressive man, a million miles away from the sickly and intro-spective boy of a decade before. He began his oration:

> Mr President and Gentlemen, I have chosen as the theme of my address, the necessity for political honesty, because such seems to me to be the grandest subject that the whole world of thought affords to young men. Whatever we may think or say, gentlemen, we are beginning our public life in taking part in the working of this old society and at the threshold of our lives there is surely no subject which touches us so deeply as that which contains the germs of our future. Success or failure awaits us according to how we work and it is vitally important that we should begin properly, that we may not be doomed to failure at the very start. I hold that the same rules of right and wrong, which are our springs of personal action should be through our life guides in state matters and that the only policy whose effects will for ever influence the world for good is that which is but the enlargement and perfection of our personal truth and justice. In this age in which cynicism is too often considered ability and in which the worker and his critics are creatures of different worlds, the advocacy of an ideal honesty may seem as wild as the dreams of Don Quixote; and this one idea only will I therefore venture to put forward, and urge with what force I can – that we should have a theory in which we have perfect belief and which we may carelessly endeavour to carry into practice. We are here now not as practical politicians but as theorists; and we are learning the principles which will guide and mould our future deeds. Our time of action will come soon enough, and in trial and temptation when the lessons which we have learned have borne us in safety through the flame, we will be grateful for the theoretic teaching which brought us forth unscathed. I appeal to the men behind me – men with the experience, the personal experience of half a century in the world of facts, to tell you that unless theory is sound practice is at best a chance.

> It may be that affairs are regulated for a time by it and that the issue seems good till tested; but in the end, when the time of trial comes, he who trusts in practice without theory finds out too late that in scorning the belief of a

possible perfection he has fallen into the error of a blind credulity of what is weak. On three grounds – moral, utilitarianism, and patriotic – we should have as our object of ambition political honesty – the testing as just or unjust in itself, as well as taken in consideration with this great scheme of which it is a part, every proposed measure which is to affect the community.

Just consider for a moment the position in which we stand and you will see the great necessity for political purity, both for our protection and our progress. There is war without and war within. The force of nationalities is manifesting itself, and in the settling down of races are such mighty upheavals that our little country is in danger of being crushed. States which we used to consider as collectively not our equals in force are becoming so great that unless our growth keeps pace with theirs, we must evidently be stifled. We cannot increase in territory, we cannot increase much more in numbers but in liberality and honesty there are no bounds to progress and when we have ceased to be mart of the world, we may become the arbiter of its destinies and its temple of justice.

All around no ancient forms are being renewed, and new ones cropping up. The spirits of Caesar and Brutus rise from the slumber of eighteen centuries, and United Germany marches on the one hand, and Republican France on the other. The Slavonic nations awake from their long lethargy, and Russia with her millions threatens the future peace of Europe, and stretches already a greedy arm towards British India. Another Reformation, not by theologians, but by politicians, is at hand, and the bells are being founded that are to ring the death-knell of the union of Church and State throughout the world. Across the Atlantic, not now an illimitable waste, but a strait crossed by a bridge of boats, the great Republic, a century old, is growing so vast that the merits and de-merits of ideal democracy may ere long be tested. And even here, this vast nation, splitting up into factions, whose collision would effect materially the progress of our affairs. At home the strife of arbour and capital, so ruinous to a commercial country, is carried on with increasing bitterness, and actual want stares many of our people in the face. The influence of individuals for good or ill is struggling for supremacy, with the force of many, united to gain one temporary advantage; and the educated one contends against the ignorant, en masse. Add to these difficulties the hollowness and artificialness of society within and its wastefulness and extravagance without, and you will see in what a plight we really are.

Who is to see the end of all these things; what statesman, were he even gifted with tenfold force of intellect, can see even the probable solution of the difficulty? So interwoven are the myriad warps and wefts in the giant web of the world that on attempting investigation we have to fall back amazed and abashed. Try to follow even one thread and after a moment your intellect will fail, and your eyes grow dim from the intensity of your fruitless gaze; but to consider the whole fabric were indeed a task. Everything is so gigantic nowadays that no man should hope to match his puny intellect against the vast combination of forces which surround him. And yet we see Statesmen trying to subordinate every circumstance to their own schemes, and form a maze of political combinations of which they alone may hold the clue. And further, we see men who are blind enough and credulous enough to support them in all their schemes – who fulfil their behests by weight of numbers, and make laws and carry reforms, knowing often that the things which they do or sanction are wrong in themselves. They put the faith that should only be given to God in the intellects of men, and support false measures under the flimsy pretext that, although they are wrong in themselves, the scheme of which they are a necessary part is, in the main, right. There is still another reason why we should regard the purity and honesty of our political views of paramount importance.

The voice of patriotism should be heard in our councils; as well as that of utility; and there is a cogent reason why we here in the Historical Society in especial should hearken to it – one which involves our love for our country and belief in the future of our race. We are at the heart of the university which is the intellectual centre of Ireland. The college teaches, and we in our time of maturity, shall teach, not the people directly, but the teachers of the people. Be our professions the church, the senate, the bar, the platform or the press; we may each of us become leaders of opinion.

In what ratio then will our honesty or dishonesty – our good lesson or bad, be multiplied when it reaches the masses in another generation? And what may even now be multiplied a thousand fold will be increased a million fold when the people – the great mass of the hewers of wood and drawers of water – have learned the lesson, and have become in turn the fountain of political truth. The Celtic race is waking up from its long lethargy and another half century will see a wondrous change in the position which it occupies amongst the races of the world. Just conceive what the teaching of a principle may be by the Irish in America alone. There the development of the race is a patent fact. To a vital energy which is unequalled, the Irishman unites an intellect which only requires to be directed by experience to make its influence felt, and an instinct for right and wrong almost poetical in its intensity. These powers will have an ample field for exercise in that great country, where the native Anglo-Saxon race is dwindling and can never be restored to equal vigour by the new immigration from the East; and they will serve to counterbalance effeteness in the American, and want of principle in the Mongolian.

And as it is a law, so far as we can judge from history, that the qualities of a race manifest themselves despite all difficulty, this race – this leavening race of future America – this race which we young men may each of us directly and indirectly influence for good or ill, may become in time the leading element of Western civilization. But not in America alone will Ireland manifest herself – abroad and at home alike will she make her influence felt. I have merely taken this example, because here the change is already in progress. Ireland in all her suffering of centuries has gained this one advantage – her people have remained the same whilst other people have slowly changed for the worse. The very same individuality and self-ascertain and passionate feeling which prompt to rebellion, and keep alive the smouldering fire of disaffection, become shrewdness and enterprise and purpose in commercial prosperity and high spirit continues the same power in wealth as in poverty. Surely through all their sad career the courage and devotion of our countryman have never been found wanting.

In the midst of all her sorrow Ireland's hope has remained unshaken: and the valour of her sons has been proved in every great battle of Europe from Fontenoy to the Redan. Aye, truly at home or abroad, with the wisdom of education to guide her force, and the certainty of safety to secure her commerce and to develop her resources, the Ireland of the future is a subject for ambitious dreams. But the new order must be based on no sectarian feuds. The old animosities must be forgotten and all the dead past left to rest in peace. There have been wrongs, but they have been atoned for – there have been errors, but they are corrected – there have been insults, but they are wiped away. It is wise to remember what to have suffered is our shame? Is it good for the cause of freedom that free men should treasure up the chains that bound their sires? If we are ever to be great we must forget that we have been little: if we are ever to be noble we must begin by generosity and forgive what had long been acknowledged a wrong. It may be for us to be the foremost men of the advancing race. We can choose whether we shall live for the future or follow the past; and it needs little effort to see the nobler choice.

In our society we begin our lives as men thinking for ourselves, and every step is not indirect, but direct to the final end. We here, a few young men with traditions of the past to direct us, and the responsibility of guiding the future to make us prudent, may do much. We are young enough to hope and action lies the future of ourselves, our country and our race.[35]

Bram's speech was received with hearty and sustained applause and he was awarded a certificate for oratory. As usual for the auditor's speech, Bram's address was printed at the expense of the society and was widely reported, with much of its content reproduced in the press. The tenor in which it was received is summed up by the reporter from *Saunders Newsletter* who described the address as 'conceived in an excellent spirit, manly, honest and well phrased'.[36] Bram was to reflect in later life, 'In fact I feel justified in saying I represented in my own person something of that aim of university education *mens sana in corpora sano* [a sound mind in a sound body]'.[37]

Bram may not have excelled in the written aspect of academia but no one could deny his eloquence and he was, moreover, a very amiable young man who gained the affection and admiration of his peers and was well liked by his tutors. Bram formed particular a bond with two of them.

First, there was Dr George Ferdinand Shaw (1821–99), the tutor assigned to
Bram. Shaw had been a newspaper man and had served a short tenure as the first
editor of the *Irish Times* when it was re-established in 1859; he proceeded to work
as an editor on *Saunders Newsletter* and wrote for *The Nation* and *Evening Mail*.
However, Shaw spent the majority of his adult life in academia. He had entered
Trinity as a sizar in 1841 then returned, becoming a fellow, senior fellow, senior
dean and registrar. Above all, he was a well-known man about town in Dublin and
never at a loss for banter, wit or anecdote. His entry in *Who's Who* simply states
his interests as 'Novels, plays and operas', but he was also regularly found keeping
company with the leading actors and actresses of the day. Considered something
of a maverick among the fellows, a history of Trinity concluded, 'Overflowing
with tireless, if not clearly focussed energy … He contributed little, perhaps, to
the education of Dublin but a good deal to its entertainment.'[38]

Shaw inspired Bram in many ways and the conversations they had were avidly
recorded in Bram's notebook, revealing an 'easy intimacy'[39] between the two
men. It was Shaw who moved that Stoker's auditor address to the Hist should
be printed and open the debate orations, although it must be said he began by
stating he 'knew nothing more revolutionary or contrary to his experience than
a politician should turn honest' and left it to Mr Gerald Fitzgibbon QC to say a
few words in praise of honesty.[40] However, during his speech Shaw, no doubt to
the delight of Bram, referenced James Albery's comedy *The Two Roses*, and the
character of Digby Grant. Both Shaw and Stoker had seen the play at Dublin's
Theatre Royal in May 1871 with a young, up-and-coming actor, Henry Irving,
in the role of Grant. Both men had been impressed with Irving's performance;
Bram was particularly entranced, believing Irving had 'stood out star-like' from
the company, and was so interested he went to see the play three times.[41] Shaw
and Stoker stayed in contact for years after university and Shaw visited Bram at
London's Lyceum Theatre on a number of occasions.

The greatest influence upon Bram at Trinity was, however, Edward Dowden
(1843–1913), the charismatic Professor of English Literature. He was on the dignitaries' dais during Bram's auditor speech to the Hist and must have glowed
with pride when he heard many of the views he held so dear being so eloquently
understood and expressed by his student. A Trinity man himself, Dowden was a
past president of the Phil, he was the winner of the vice-chancellor's prize for
English verse and prose, and had been awarded the first senior moderatorship in
ethics and logic. Filling the newly created Chair of English Literature at Trinity
in 1867 (a position he would hold until his death), at the time Dowden knew
Bram he would have been working on his first book *Shakespeare, His Mind and Art*
(1875); a book that would be well received and first bring Dowden's name to a
wider audience as a critic. Hinkson evokes the man in *Student Life*:

Dr Dowden, Professor of English Literature, in appearance recalls the features which Vandyke so loved to paint. He has a handsome, dreamy face, with pointed beard, and a soft, somewhat melancholy voice. He is surrounded by a little coterie of literary and would be literary people, from the youth who has just discovered that some difference exists between the style of Matthew Arnold and that of Robert Browning, to the enthusiast who sought inspiration by spending the night on the tomb of Wordsworth. Yet to each and all he is affable and sympathetic, and can easily come down to the intelligence of his company. By his admirers he is regarded with an almost idolatrous affection. He can speak well, too, though his speeches are somewhat redolent of the lamp.[42]

Dowden made his name with his *Life of Shelley* (1886) and would publish schol-arly works on Shakespeare, Southey, Browning, Goethe and Wordsworth in which he demonstrated a profound knowledge of the currents and tendencies of thought in various ages. Dowden also took a proactive interest in living authors and dramatists, and maintained a regular correspondence with a number of them, including Robert Browning, George Eliot and the dramatist Henry Taylor whose play *Philip van Artevelde* (1834) elicited comparisons with Shakespeare among con-temporary critics. However, it was Dowden's connection with and appreciation of the American poet Walt Whitman that would forge the friendship between Stoker and himself, as Bram was to recount:

> In 1868 when William Michael Rossetti brought out his 'Selected Poems of Walt Whitman' it raised a regular storm in British literary circles. The bitter-minded critics of the time absolutely flew at the Poet and his work as watch-dogs do at a ragged beggar. Unfortunately there were passages in the Leaves of Grass which allowed of attacks, and those who did not or could not understand the broad spirit of the group of poems took samples of detail which were at least deter-rent. Doubtless they thought that it was a case for ferocious attack; as from these excerpts it would seem that the book was as offensive to morals as to taste. They did not scruple to give the ipsissima verba of the most repugnant passages.
>
> In my own University the book was received with homeric laughter, and more than a few of the students sent over to Trübner's for copies of the com-plete Leaves of Grass that being the only place where they could then be had. Needless to say that amongst young men the objectionable passages were searched for and more noxious ones expected. For days we all talked of Walt Whitman and the new poetry with scorn especially those of us who had not seen the book. One day I met a man in the Quad who had a copy, and I asked him to let me look at it. He acquiesced readily:
>
> 'Take the damned thing,' he said; 'I've had enough of it!'
>
> I took the book with me into the Park and in the shade of an elm tree began to read it. Very shortly my own opinion began to form; it was diametrically

opposed to that which I had been hearing. From that hour I became a lover of Walt Whitman. There were a few of us who, quite independently of each other, took the same view. We had quite a fight over it with our companions who used to assail us with shafts of their humour on all occasions. Somehow, we learned, I think, a good deal in having perpetually to argue without being able to deny in so far as quotation went at all events the premises of our opponents.

However, we were ourselves satisfied, and that was much. Young men are, as a rule, very tenacious of such established ideas as they have – perhaps it is a fortunate thing for them and others; and we did not expect to convince our friends all at once. Fortunately also the feeling of intellectual superiority which comes with the honest acceptance of an idea which others have refused is an anodyne to the pain of ridicule. We Walt-Whitmanites had in the main more satisfaction than our opponents. Edward Dowden was one of the few who in those days took the large and liberal view of the *Leaves of Grass*, and as he was Professor of English Literature at the University his opinion carried great weight in such a matter.[43]

In an attempt to stimulate a more considered academic discussion, Dowden brought the subject of the poems before the Philosophical Society on 4 May 1871, with a paper on 'Walt Whitman and the Poetry of Democracy'. Bram was given the honour of opening the debate on the paper; but the criticism of Whitman, for or against, would not be won or lost in one night.

In July 1871 Dowden published *The Poetry of Democracy: Walt Whitman* in the *Westminster Review*, and contacted William Rossetti, the complier of *Selected Poems of Walt Whitman*, in Cork for Whitman's address. Although he was informed that a copy of the article had already been forwarded to Whitman, Dowden was not to be denied the pleasure of sending a second copy and accompanied it with a letter that leaves us in no doubt of his sincere interest and appreciation of Whitman's work:

I ought to say that the article expresses very partially the impression which your writings have made on me. It keeps, as is obvious, at a single point of view and regards only what becomes visible from that point. But also I wrote more coolly than I feel because I wanted those, who being ignorant of your writings are perhaps prejudiced against them, to say: 'Here is a cool judicious impartial critic who finds a great deal in Whitman – perhaps after all we are mistaken.' Perhaps this will be unsatisfactory to you, and you would prefer that your critic should let the full force of your writings appear in his criticisms and attract those who are to be attracted and repel those who are to be repelled, and you may value the power of repulsion as well as that of attraction. But so many persons capable of loving your work, by some mischance or miscarriage or by some ignorance or removable error fail in their approach to you, or do not approach at all, that I think I am justified in my attempt.

You have many readers in Ireland, and those who do not feel a qualified delight in your poems – do not love them by degree, but with an absolute, a personal love.

We none of us question that yours is the clearest, and sweetest, and fullest American voice. We grant as true all that you claim for yourself. And you gain steadily among us new readers and lovers. If you care at all for what I have written it would certainly be a pleasure to hear this from yourself. If you do not care for it you will know that I wished to do better than I did.[44]

Whitman did appreciate what Dowden had to say and they exchanged a number of letters of mutual appreciation and interest. Bram also drafted a letter to Whitman in 1872: it was an impassioned one but he did not send it and allowed it to lie dormant. Meanwhile, he continued to publicly defend and praise Whitman's poetry, and was to recall:

Little by little we got recruits amongst the abler young men till at last a little cult was established. But the attack still went on. I well remember a militant evening at the 'Fortnightly Club' a club of Dublin men, meeting occasionally for free discussions. Occasionally there were meetings for both sexes. This particular evening February 14, 1876 was, perhaps fortunately, not a 'Ladies' Night'. The paper was on 'Walt Whitman' and was by a man of some standing socially; a man who had had a fair University record and was then a county gentleman of position in his own county. He was exceedingly able; a good scholar, well versed in both classic and English literature, and a brilliant humorist. His paper at the 'Fortnightly' was a violent, incisive attack on Walt Whitman; had we not been accustomed to such for years it would have seemed outrageous. I am bound to say it was very clever; by confining himself almost entirely to the group of poems, 'Children of Adam', he made out, in one way, a strong case. But he went too far. In challenging the existence in the whole collection of poems for mention of one decent woman which is in itself ridiculous, for Walt Whitman honoured women he drew an impassioned speech from Edward Dowden, who finished by reading a few verses from the poem 'Faces'. It was the last section of the poem, that which describes a noble figure of an old Quaker mother. It ends:

'The melodious character of the earth,
The finish beyond which philosophy cannot go,
and does not wish to go,
The justified mother of men.'

I followed Dowden in the speaking and we carried the question. I find a note in my diary, which if egotistical has at least that merit of sincerity which is to be found now and again in a man's diary when he is young: 'Spoke I think well.'[45]

It seems there was doubt in young Bram's mind as to whether they really won the debate. He was certainly impassioned enough to work into the night writing another letter, which he did send to Whitman:

Dublin, Feb. 14, 1876.
My dear Mr. Whitman,

I hope you will not consider this letter from an utter stranger a liberty. Indeed, I hardly feel a stranger to you, nor is this the first letter that I have written to you. My friend Edward Dowden has told me often that you like new acquaintances or I should rather say friends. And as an old friend I send you an enclosure which may interest you. Four years ago I wrote the enclosed draft of a letter which I intended to copy out and send to you – it has lain in my desk since then – when I heard that you were addressed as Mr. Whitman. It speaks for itself and needs no comment. It is as truly what I wanted to say as that light is light. The four years which have elapsed have made me love your work fourfold, and I can truly say that I have ever spoken as your friend. You know what hostile criticism your work sometimes evokes here, and I wage a perpetual war with many friends on your behalf. But I am glad to say that I have been the means of making your work known to many who were scoffers at first. The years which have passed have not been uneventful to me, and I have felt and thought and suffered much in them, and I can truly say that from you I have had much pleasure and much consolation – and I do believe that your open earnest speech has not been thrown away on me or that my life and thought fail to be marked with its impress. I write this openly because I feel that with you one must be open. We have just had tonight a hot debate on your genius at the Fortnightly Club in which I had the privilege of putting forward my views – I think with success. Do not think me cheeky for writing this. I only hope we may sometime meet and I shall be able perhaps to say what I cannot write. Dowden promised to get me a copy of your new edition and I hope that for any other work which you may have you will let me always be an early subscriber. I am sorry that you're not strong. Many of us are hoping to see you in Ireland. We had arranged to have a meeting for you. I do not know if you like getting letters. If you do I shall only be too happy to send you news of how thought goes among the men I know.

With truest wishes for your health and happiness believe me
Your friend

Bram Stoker[46]

The 1872 draft that Bram enclosed to Whitman is revelatory and commits to paper some of the deepest personal feelings of young Bram Stoker; it remains the most personal letter to survive from all of his correspondence:

Dublin, Ireland, Feb. 18, 1872.

If you are the man I take you to be you will like to get this letter. If you are
not I don't care whether you like it or not and only ask you to put it into the
fire without reading any farther. But I believe you will like it. I don't think there
is a man living, even you who are above the prejudices of the class of small-
minded men, who wouldn't like to get a letter from a younger man, a stranger,
across the world – a man living in an atmosphere prejudiced to the truths you
sing and your manner of singing them. The idea that arises in my mind is
whether there is a man living who would have the pluck to burn a letter in
which he felt the smallest atom of interest without reading it. I believe you
would and that you believe you would yourself. You can burn this now and test
yourself, and all I will ask for my trouble of writing this letter, which for all
I can tell you may light your pipe with or apply to some more ignoble purpose
– is that you will in some manner let me know that my words have tested your
impatience. Put it in the fire if you like – but if you do you will miss the pleasure of this next sentence, which ought to be that you have conquered an
unworthy impulse. A man who is uncertain of his own strength might try to
encourage himself by a piece of bravo, but a man who can write, as you have
written, the most candid words that ever fell from the lips of mortal man – a
man to whose candour Rousseau's Confessions is reticence – can have no fear
for his own strength. If you have gone this far you may read the letter and I feel
in writing now that I am talking to you. If I were before your face I would like
to shake hands with you, for I feel that I would like you. I would like to call you
Comrade and to talk to you as men who are not poets do not often talk. I think
that at first a man would be ashamed, for a man cannot in a moment break the
habit of comparative reticence that has become a second nature to him; but
I know I would not long be ashamed to be natural before you. You are a true
man, and I would like to be one myself, and so I would be towards you as a
brother and as a pupil to his master. In this age no man becomes worthy of the
name without an effort. You have shaken off the shackles and your wings are
free. I have the shackles on my shoulders still – but I have no wings. If you are
going to read this letter any further I should tell you that I am not prepared to
'give up all else' so far as words go. The only thing I am prepared to give up is
prejudice, and before I knew you I had begun to throw overboard my cargo, but
it is not all gone yet. I do not know how you will take this letter. I have not
addressed you in any form as I hear that you dislike to a certain degree the conventional forms in letters. I am writing to you because you are different from
other men. If you were the same as the mass I would not write at all. As it is
I must either call you Walt Whitman or not call you at all – and I have chosen
the latter course. I don't know whether it is usual for you to get letters from
utter strangers who have not even the claim of literary brotherhood to write
you. If it is you must be frightfully tormented with letters and I am sorry to

have written this. I have, however, the claim of liking you – for your words are your own soul and even if you do not read my letter it is no less a pleasure to me to write it. Shelley wrote to William Godwin and they became friends. I am not Shelley and you are not Godwin and so I will only hope that sometime I may meet you face to face and perhaps shake hands with you. If I ever do it will be one of the greatest pleasures of my life. If you care to know who it is that writes this, my name is Abraham Stoker (Junior). My friends call me Bram. I live at 43 Harcourt St., Dublin. I am a clerk in the service of the Crown on a small salary. I am twenty-four years old. Have been champion at our athletic sports (Trinity College, Dublin) and have won about a dozen cups. I have also been President of the College Philosophical Society and an art and theatrical critic of a daily paper. I am six feet two inches high and twelve stone weight naked and used to be forty-one or forty-two inches round the chest. I am ugly but strong and determined and have a large bump over my eyebrows. I have a heavy jaw and a big mouth and thick lips – sensitive nostrils – a snubnose and straight hair. I am equal in temper and cool in disposition and have a large amount of self control and am naturally secretive to the world. I take a delight in letting people I don't like – people of mean or cruel or sneaking or cowardly disposition – see the worst side of me. I have a large number of acquaintances and some five or six friends – all of which latter body care much for me. Now I have told you all I know about myself. I know you from your works and your photograph, and if I know anything about you I think you would like to know of the personal appearance of your correspondents. You are I know a keen physiognomist. I am a believer of the science myself and am in an humble way a practicer of it. I was not disappointed when I saw your photograph – your late one especially. The way I came to like you was this: A notice of your poems appeared some two years ago or more in the Temple Bar magazine. I glanced at it and took its dictum as final, and laughed at you among my friends. I say it to my own shame but not to my regret for it has taught me a lesson to last my life out – without ever having seen your poems. More than a year after I heard two men in College talking of you. One of them had your book (Rossetti's edition) and was reading aloud some passages at which both laughed. They chose only those passages which are most foreign to British ears and made fun of them. Something struck me that I had judged you hastily. I took home the volume and read it far into the night. Since then I have to thank you for many happy hours, for I have read your poems with my door locked late at night, and I have read them on the seashore where I could look all round me and see no more sign of human life than the ships out at sea: and here I often found myself waking up from a reverie with the book lying open before me. I love all poetry, and high generous thoughts make the tears rush to my eyes, but sometimes a word or a phrase of yours takes me away from the world around me and places me in an ideal land surrounded by realities more than any poem I ever read. Last year I was sitting on the beach on a summer's day reading your preface to the Leaves of Grass as printed in Rossetti's edition (for Rossetti is all I have got till I get the complete set of your works which I have ordered from America). One thought struck me and I pondered over it for several hours – 'the weather-beaten vessels entering new ports', you who wrote the words know them better than I do: and to you who sing of your own land of progress the words have a meaning that I can only imagine. But be assured of this, Walt Whitman – that a man of less than half your own age, reared a conservative in a conservative country, and who has always heard your name cried down by the great mass of people who mention it, here felt his heart leap towards you across the Atlantic and his soul swelling at the words or rather the thoughts. It is vain for me to try to quote any instances of what thoughts of yours I like best – for I like them all and you must feel that you are reading the true words of one who feels with you. You see, I have called you by your name. I have been more candid with you – have said more about myself to you than I have ever said to any one before. You will not be angry with me if you have read so far. You will not laugh at me for writing this to you. It was with no small effort that I began to write and I feel reluctant to stop, but I must not tire you any more. If you ever would care to have more you can imagine, for you have a great heart, how much pleasure it would be to me to write more to you. How sweet a thing it is for a strong healthy man with a woman's eyes and a child's wishes to feel that he can speak so to a man who can be if he wishes father, and brother and wife to his soul. I don't think you will laugh, Walt Whitman, nor despise me, but at all events I thank you for all the love and sympathy you have given me in common with my kind.

Bram Stoker.[47]

Whitman *was* pleased to reply to young Bram:

March 6, '76.
My dear young man,

Your letters have been most welcome to me – welcome to me as Person and as Author – I don't know which most – You did well to write me so unconventionally, so fresh, so manly, and so affectionately, too. I too hope (though it is not probable) that we shall one day meet each other. Meantime I send you my friendship and thanks.

Edward Dowden's letter containing among others your subscription for a copy of my new edition has just been received. I shall send the books very soon by express in a package to his address. I have just written E. D.

My physique is entirely shattered – doubtless permanently, from paralysis and other ailments. But I am up and dressed, and get out every day a little. Live here quite lonesome, but hearty, and good spirits. Write to me again.

Walt Whitman

Stoker and Whitman carried on their correspondence and met many years later when Bram was in America while on tour with the Lyceum Company.

Whitman's *Leaves of Grass* has many poems that can easily be seen as sexually ambiguous, certainly erotic and even homosexual, but perhaps it was their ambiguity that particularly touched Bram and in writing so frankly and intimately to Whitman perhaps Bram was seeking a male role model for the man he wished to become, that he desired or wished to understand in himself. It must also be remembered that at this time homosexuality was seen as abhorrent and unnatural, and was against the law. As a result, the culture of and the communication between homosexuals was driven underground, cloaked in secrets and even developed its own parlance. It has been argued, from a number of perspectives, that *Dracula* has a homosexual or homoerotic subtext, but it is in *The Man* (1905) where it seems that Stoker expresses himself most overtly. *The Man* has been criticised for its lack of understanding or empathy with the female characters within it but, consider, perhaps it is more an attempt for Bram to express his own latent homosexual awakening masked in the character and expressed through the voice of a woman he ambiguously named Stephen:

> In the train she began to review, for the first time, her visit to the university. All had been so strange and new and delightful to her that she had never stopped for retrospect. Life in the new and enchanting place had been in the moving present. The mind had been receptive only, gathering data for later thought. During her visit she had had no one to direct her thought, and so it had been all personal, with the freedom of individuality at large. Of course her mother's friend, skilled in the mind-workings of average girls, and able to pick her way through intellectual and moral quagmires, had taken good care to point out to her certain intellectual movements and certain moral lessons; just as she had in their various walks and drives pointed out matters of interest – architectural beauties and spots of historic import. And she had taken in, loyally accepted, and thoroughly assimilated all that she had been told. But there were other lessons which were for her young eyes; facts which the older eyes had ceased to notice, if they had ever noticed them at all. The self-content, the sex-content in the endless tide of young men that thronged the streets and quads and parks; the all-sufficing nature of sport or study, to whichever their inclinations tended. The small part which womankind seemed to have in their lives. Stephen had had, as we know, a peculiar training; whatever her instincts were, her habits were largely boy habits. Here she was amongst boys, a glorious tide of them; it made now and again her heart beat to look at them. And yet amongst them all she was only an outsider. She could not do anything better than any of them. Of course, each time she went out, she became conscious of admiring glances; she could not be woman without such consciousness. But it was as a girl that men looked at her, not as an equal. As well as personal experience and the lessons

of eyes and ears and intelligence, there were other things to classify and adjust; things which were entirely from the outside of her own life. The fragments of common-room gossip, which it had been her fortune to hear accidentally now and again. The half confidences of scandals, borne on whispered breaths. The whole confidences of dormitory and study which she had been privileged to share. All were parts of the new and strange world, the great world which had swum into her ken.

As she sat now in the train, with some formulation of memory already accomplished in the two hours of solitude, her first comment, spoken half audibly, would have surprised her teachers as much as it would have surprised herself, if she had been conscious of it; for as yet her thinking was not self-conscious:

'Surely, I am not like that!'

It was of the women she had been thinking, not of the men. The glimpse which she had had of her own sex had been an awakening to her; and the awakening had not been to a pleasant world. All at once she seemed to realise that her sex had defects – littlenesses, meannesses, cowardices, falsenesses. That their occupations were apt to be trivial or narrow or selfish; that their desires were earthly, and their tastes coarse; that what she held to be goodness was apt to be realised only as fear. That innocence was but ignorance, or at least baffled curiosity. That ...

A flood of shame swept over her, and instinctively she put her hands before her burning face. As usual, she was running all at once into extremes.

And above all these was borne upon her, and for the first time in her life, that she was herself a woman![48]

3

LOVE OF NO
COMMON ORDER

Abraham Stoker had been a keen theatregoer all his life and took in many shows with Bram, who looked back affectionately on those times:

> In those days, as now, the home Civil Service was not a very money-making business, and it was just as well that he preferred the pit. I believed then that I preferred it also, for I too was then in the Civil Service![49]

A love of theatre, actors and actresses grew to become a consuming passion for young Bram. Father and son would talk of performances they had seen, both good and bad, and recall those of the greats of their day such as Charles Kean, G.V. Brook, T.C. King, Charles Dillon and Vandenhoff who had all graced the Dublin stages over the years. However, as Bram reminisced:

> provincial playgoers did not have much opportunity of seeing great acting, except in the star parts. It was the day of the stock companies, when the chief theatres everywhere had good actors who played for the whole season, each in his or her established class; but notable excellence was not to be expected at the salaries then possible to even the most enterprising management. The 'business', the term still applied to the minor incidents of acting, as well as to the disposition of the various characters and the entrances and exits was, of necessity, of a formal and traditional kind. There was no time for the exhaustive rehearsal of minor details to which actors are in these days accustomed. When the bill was changed five or six times a week it was only possible, even at the longest rehearsal, to get through the standard outline of action, and secure perfection in the cues in fact, those conditions of the interdependence of the actors and mechanics on which the structural excellence of the play depends … This adherence to standard 'business' was so strict, though unwritten, a rule that no one actor could venture to break it. To do so without preparation would have been to at least endanger the success of the play.[50]

The greats of the stage up to the nineteenth century had maintained a performance tradition that revolved around larger-than-life characters – the 'greats' were defined by dramatic movements and flamboyant gestures. The theatre-going audiences would also anticipate, nay, expect, each performance, each year to be consistent and would look forward to the set piece highlights of the play.

Thus, when Bram first saw Henry Irving at the Theatre Royal, Dublin, on the evening of Wednesday 28 August 1867, he saw an actor whose performance was so different it left an indelible impression upon him for the rest of his life. Miss Herbert, the manger of the St James's Company, had brought them on tour with com-

Illustration of Bram Stoker published in some of his early books.

edies old and new. On that particular night it was Sheridan's *The Rivals*, in which a young up-and-coming actor named Henry Irving played Captain Absolute:

> To this day I can remember the playing of Henry Irving as Captain Absolute, which was different from any performance of the same part which I had seen. What I saw, to my amazement and delight, was a patrician figure as real as the persons of one's dreams, and endowed with the same poetic grace. A young soldier, handsome, distinguished, self-dependent, compact of grace and slumbrous energy. A man of quality who stood out from his surroundings on the stage as a being of another social world. A figure full of dash and fine irony, and whose ridicule seemed to bite; buoyant with the joy of life; self-conscious; an inoffensive egoist even in his love-making; of supreme and unsurpassable insolence, veiled and shrouded in his fine quality of manner. Such a figure as could only be possible in an age when the answer to offence was a swordthrust, when only those dare be insolent who could depend to the last on the heart and brain and arm behind the blade.[51]

Bram did not see Irving again until May 1871, when he saw the comedy *Two Roses*. The magic of Irving's performance had not diminished in any way for Bram but he was exercised by the failure of any Dublin newspaper to mention the standard of acting or even the names of the players. He approached Dr Henry Maunsell of the Dublin *Evening Mail* to ask if he would allow him to perform the function of theatre critic for the paper. Maunsell was interested in the proposal but was frank enough to admit he could not afford to pay him. Bram confidently replied he would 'gladly do it without fee or reward'. He was given the job. It was the first step towards the life that Bram had dreamt of and an escape from the drudgery of life in the civil service; Bram was overjoyed:

> From my beginning the work in November 1871 I had an absolutely free hand. I was thus able to direct public attention, so far as my paper could effect it, where in my mind such was required. In those five years I think I learned a good deal. 'Writing maketh an exact man'; and as I have always held that in matters critical the critic's personal honour is involved in every word he writes, the duty I had undertaken was to me a grave one. I did not shirk work in any way.[52]

The position of theatre critic provided Bram with the magical entrée that transported him from theatregoer to a person and personality in the theatrical world; known to theatre staff, his preferred seat would be saved for him. Bram was welcomed backstage to mix with actors and actresses, often their meeting would move beyond a brief encounter for he befriended and corresponded with a number of them for years, providing encouragement and advice, and even becoming their confidant. It was a hallmark of Bram's that if he became a friend it was a real friendship that would endure and he could be trusted with your darkest secrets. Actress Helen Barry not only asked his opinions on her play but unburdened herself to him, hinting darkly at an unsuitable 'past'; Bram answered with a fourteen-page letter of advice.[53] But as a theatre critic it was Bram's first sight of the performance of and his meeting with Genevieve Ward that was to leave a particular impression upon him:

> On the evening of Thursday, 20th November 1873, I strolled into the Theatre Royal, Dublin, to see what was on. I had been then for two years a dramatic critic, and was fairly well used to the routine of things. There was a very poor house indeed; in that huge theatre the few hundreds scattered about were like the plums in a fo'c's'le duff. I sat down in my usual seat, which the attendants, knowing my choice, always kept for me if possible: the end seat 'O.P.' or left-hand side looking towards the stage. The play was Legouvé's Adrienne Lecouvreur, a somewhat machine-made play of the old school. The lady who played Adrienne interested me at once; she was like a triton amongst minnows. She was very handsome; of a rich dark beauty, with clear cut classical features, black hair, and great eyes that now and again flashed fire. I sat in growing admiration of her powers ... she was so masterful, so dominating in other ways that I could not understand it. At the end of the second act I went into the lobby to ask the attendants if they could tell me anything about her as the name on the bill was entirely new to me.[54]

Bram was entranced, and when he returned again on 24 November he had a chance meeting with an old friend, Wilson King the American consul. King had known Genevieve since childhood and arranged an introduction, 'And there and then began a close friendship which has never faltered, which has been one of the delights of my life and which will I trust remain as warm as it is now till the death of either of us shall cut it short.'[55]

As Bram established himself as a critic he also began to establish himself as an independent young man. For reasons that were probably both financial and influenced by his ailing health, Abraham Stoker decided to move to France where the air was good and a reasonable standard of living could be had in retirement. He obtained a loan of £300 and with Charlotte and daughters Matilda and Margaret bade farewell to Dublin in the summer of 1872, settling, at least for the time being, in Caen, Normandy. Bram also moved out of his brother's house, describing his new situation as 'living in the top rooms of a house, which I had furnished myself',[56] where he enjoyed the life of a bachelor. These rooms may well have been in the house he shared with Herbert Wilson and artist William Delany at 11 Lower Leeson Street. Although his family may have feared such a bohemian household could lead Bram astray from the upright path of his career in the civil service, the environment in which Bram was living appeared to be highly conducive to his literary output. Bram's first major work of fiction, *The Crystal Cup*, was accepted and published in the popular monthly magazine, *London Society*, in September 1872. He then seized the opportunity to become editor of the *Irish Echo* when it was offered to him in November 1873, but the money was not good and he could not afford to give up his job with the civil service. In his letters, Bram's father, despite initial pleasure for his son achieving the editor's job, supported him when he stepped down early in the following year, counselling that he felt the pay he received could not reflect the effort Bram put into the job, and adding that 'the government did not approve of its officers being connected with a newspaper – even if it was not a political one'.[57]

Bram was residing at 47 Kildare Street in 1874 and was back with Thornley at his new home at 16 Harcourt Street by the end of the year. Thornley's splendid new home had been part of Clonmell House, Dublin's original Mansion House, the residence of Attorney General John Scott, later Lord Clonmell, in 1778. Scott served as Lord Chief Justice of the King's Bench for Ireland from 1784 to 1789 and was described by Sir Jonah Barrington in *A Compendium of Irish* Biography (1878), as:

> Courageous, vulgar, humorous, artificial; he knew the world well, and he profited by that knowledge. He cultivated the powerful; he bullied the timid; he fought the brave; he flattered the vain; he duped the credulous; and he amused the convivial. Half liked, half reprobated, he was too high to be despised, and too low to be respected. His language was coarse, and his principles arbitrary; but his passions were his slaves, and his cunning was his instrument.

A hard man in court and one who acquired a formidable reputation as a duellist, he was the original 'Copper-Faced Jack'.

The residence on Harcourt Street provided Bram with the inspiration for *The Judge's House*, a superb short story first published in the *Illustrated Sporting and Dramatic News* in December 1891, and rediscovered after his death and published in *Dracula's Guest and Other Weird Stories* (1914). The story, with some interesting biographical touches, relates how student Malcolm Malcolmson sought a quiet place to stay as he read for his exams, 'He feared the attractions of the seaside, and also he feared completely rural isolation, for of old he knew its harms, and so he determined to find some unpretentious little town where there would be nothing to distract him.' Finding what he believed to be the ideal residence, Malcolmson was warned against staying there for it had been 'the abode of a judge who was held in great terror on account of his harsh sentences and his hostility to prisoners at Assizes' and was still haunted by his malevolent spirit. Brushing aside such tales for, 'A man who is reading for the Mathematical Tripos has too much to think of to be disturbed by any of these mysterious "somethings"', he dismissed the warnings to his peril.

Whether *The Judge's House* was written around the time it was published or, like many other stories by Bram, was recalled later is unclear. Regardless, Bram's literary output for 1875 was, yet again, a remarkable one: he published three serials in the *The Shamrock*, a Dublin weekly illustrated journal that ran a regular array of part-work stories. Bram's first work accepted by them appeared as a ten-chapter serial, *The Primrose Path*, which ran between 6 February and 6 March. It was a Hogarthian tale of Jerry O'Sullivan, an honest theatrical carpenter who, against the advice of those around him, removes himself and his faithful wife Katey from Dublin to London, seeking a better job. He ends up working in a squalid theatre where a series of misfortunes befall him, he takes to drink and it becomes his ruin.[58] *The Primrose Path* was followed by a four-chapter serial entitled *Buried Treasures*, published over two issues of *The Shamrock* from 13 March to 20 March 1875. It embraced a number of themes that fascinated Bram and which can be found in many of Bram's later works. Various elements in this story clearly resonate in *Dracula*, for example, for there is unstinting love of the kind that would be between Mina and Jonathan, there is shipwreck, storm and a mysterious iron chest, a dogged pursuit to discover the contents in defiance of forces both natural and supernatural and, not least, Bram evokes death as a winged creature as Robert Hamilton makes a final attempt to recover the iron chest from the shipwreck:

> The wind was rapidly rising to a storm, and swept by him, laden with the deadly mist in fierce gusts. The roaring of the tide grew nearer and nearer, and louder and louder. Overhead was a pall of darkness, save when in the leaden winter sky some white pillar of mist swept onward like an embodied spirit of the storm. All the past began to crowd Robert's memory, and more especially the recent

past. He thought of his friend's words – 'Nothing short of death shall keep me away', and so full of dismal shadows, and forms of horror was all the air, that he could well fancy that Tom was dead, and that his spirit was circling round him, wailing through the night. Then again, arose the memory of his dream, and his very heart stood still, as he thought of how awfully it had been fulfilled. There he now lay; not in a dream, but in reality, beside a ship on a waste of desert sand. Beside him lay a chest such as he had seen in his dreams, and, as before, death seemed flapping his giant wings over his head. Strange horrors seemed to gather round him, borne on the wings of the blast. His father, whom he had never seen, he felt to be now beside him. All the dead that he had ever known circled round him in a weird dance. As the stormy gusts swept by, he heard amid their screams the lugubrious tolling of bells; bells seemed to be all around him; whichever way he turned he heard his knell. All forms were gathered there, as in his dreams – all save Ellen. But hark! even as the thought flashed across his brain; his ears seemed to hear her voice as one hears in a dream. He tried to cry out, but was so overcome by cold, that he could barely hear his own voice. He tried to rise, but in vain, and then, overcome by pain and excitement, and disappointed hope, he became insensible.[59]

Bram's serialised novels were clearly popular and he was able to develop the supernatural elements of his stories into his first full-blown published gothic horror story, *The Chain of Destiny*, which appeared over four issues of *The Shamrock* between 1 May and 22 May 1875. Rather than the reader being left with the ambiguity of ghosts being tricks of the mind suffered by the character in the grip of tempest, as in *Buried Treasures*, Bram created them as vivid manifestations of the paranormal who cause the hero, Frank Stanford, to struggle with his own mind and understanding of what he sees and experiences. *The Chain of Destiny* contains several literary prototypes revived by Bram for *Dracula*. The scene is set in a large old mansion house known as Scarp, perhaps Bram's first germ of his later vision of the forbidding Castle Dracula:

It was so late in the evening when I arrived at Scarp that I had but little opportunity of observing the external appearance of the house; but, as far as I could judge in the dim twilight, it was a very stately edifice of seemingly great age, built of white stone. When I passed the porch, however, I could observe its internal beauties much more closely, for a large wood fire burned in the hall and all the rooms and passages were lighted. The hall was almost baronial in its size, and opened on to a staircase of dark oak so wide and so generous in its slope that a carriage might almost have been driven up it. The rooms were large and lofty, with their walls, like those of the staircase, panelled with oak black from age. This sombre material would have made the house intensely gloomy but for the enormous width and height of both rooms and passages.[60]

The story of the damnation of the house of Scarp was revealed during a casual perusal of the library:

> We proceeded to look for some of those old books of family history which are occasionally to be found in old county houses. The library of Scarp, I saw, was very valuable, and as we prosecuted our search I came across many splendid and rare volumes which I determined to examine at my leisure, for I had come to Scarp for a long visit … From the text we learned that one of the daughters of Kirk had, in the year 1573, married the brother of Fothering against the united wills of her father and brother, and that after a bitter feud of some ten or twelve years, the latter, then master of Scarp, had met the brother of Fothering in a duel and had killed him. Upon receiving the news Fothering had sworn a great oath to revenge his brother, invoking the most fearful curses upon himself and his race if he should fail to cut off the hand that had slain his brother, and to nail it over the gate of Fothering. The feud then became so bitter that Kirk seems to have gone quite mad on the subject. When he heard of Fothering's oath he knew that he had but little chance of escape, since his enemy was his master at every weapon; so he determined upon a mode of revenge which, although costing him his own life, he fondly hoped would accomplish the eternal destruction of his brother-in-law through his violated oath. He sent Fothering a letter cursing him and his race, and praying for the consummation of his own curse invoked in case of failure.[61]

In much the same way, Jonathan Harker would casually research the background of the unknown country where he would be going:

> Having had some time at my disposal when in London, I had visited the British Museum, and made search among the books and maps in the library regarding Transylvania it had struck me that some foreknowledge of the country could hardly fail to have some importance in dealing with a nobleman of that country … I read that every known superstition in the world is gathered into the horse-shoe of the Carpathians, as if it were the centre of some sort of imaginative whirlpool; if so my stay may be very interesting.
> (Mem., I must ask the Count all about them.)[62]

Significantly, early on in *The Chain of Destiny* there is an encounter that Bram would revisit upon Jonathan Harker in *Dracula*, but while Jonathan became drowsy in the ladies' apartments of the castle, in *The Chain of Destiny* Frank Stanford retires to a bedroom where sleep eventually comes upon him:

> I thought that I awoke suddenly to that peculiar feeling which we sometimes have on starting from sleep, as if someone had been speaking in the room, and

the voice is still echoing through it. All was quite silent, and the fire had gone out. I looked out of the window that lay straight opposite the foot of the bed, and observed a light outside, which gradually grew brighter till the room was almost as light as by day. The window looked like a picture in the framework formed by the cornice over the foot of the bed, and the massive pillars shrouded in curtains which supported it.

With the new accession of light I looked round the room, but nothing was changed. All was as before, except that some of the objects of furniture and ornament were shown in stronger relief than hitherto. Amongst these, those most in relief were the other bed, which was placed across the room ... The light in the room continued to grow even brighter, so I looked again out of the window to seek its source, and saw there a lovely sight. It seemed as if there were grouped without the window three lovely children, who seemed to float in mid-air. The light seemed to spring from a point far behind them, and by their side was something dark and shadowy, which served to set off their radiance.

The children seemed to be smiling in upon something in the room, and, following their glances, I saw that their eyes rested upon the other bed. There, strange to say, the head which I had lately seen in the picture rested upon the pillow. I looked at the wall, but the frame was empty, the picture was gone. Then I looked at the bed again, and saw the young girl asleep, with the expression of her face constantly changing, as though she were dreaming.

As I was observing her, a sudden look of terror spread over her face, and she sat up like a sleep-walker, with her eyes wide open, staring out of the window. Again turning to the window, my gaze became fixed, for a great and weird change had taken place. The figures were still there, but their features and expressions had become woefully different. Instead of the happy innocent look of childhood was one of malignity. With the change the children had grown old, and now three hags, decrepit and deformed, like typical witches, were before me.

But a thousand times worse than this transformation was the change in the dark mass that was near them. From a cloud, misty and undefined, it became a sort of shadow with a form. This gradually, as I looked, grew darker and fuller, till at length it made me shudder. There stood before me the phantom of the Fiend. There was a long period of dead silence, in which I could hear the beating of my heart; but at length the phantom spoke to the others. His words seemed to issue from his lips mechanically, and without expression – 'To-morrow, and to-morrow, and to-morrow. The fairest and the best.'[63]

While, in *Dracula*, Jonathan Harker records:

I was not alone. The room was the same, unchanged in any way since I came into it. I could see along the floor, in the brilliant moonlight, my own footsteps marked where I had disturbed the long accumulation of dust. In the moon-light opposite me were three young women, ladies by their dress and manner. I thought at the time that I must be dreaming when I saw them, they threw no shadow on the floor. They came close to me, and looked at me for some time, and then whispered together.[64]

The women in Dracula's chamber did not metamorphose into hags, but they came towards Jonathan, and the Fiend that appeared in the later incarnation of the scene was Dracula, who threw off the vampiric sirens, exclaiming, 'How dare you touch him, any of you? How dare you cast eyes on him when I had forbidden it? Back, I tell you all! This man belongs to me! Beware how you meddle with him, or you'll have to deal with me.' Indeed, the coquettish riposte of one of the women to Dracula and the ensuing laughter caused Harker to comment, 'It seemed like the pleasure of fiends.' Dracula retorts with his own promise of 'tomorrow': 'Well, now I promise you that when I am done with him you shall kiss him at your will. Now go! Go! I must awaken him, for there is work to be done.'[65]

The year 1875 had been both productive and a successful one for Bram and he was able to move onto new lodgings shortly before Thornley's marriage to Emily Stewart on 23 August. Directories show Bram retained 16 Harcourt Street as a reliable permanent address for correspondence while he was living in rooms at 116 Lower Baggot Street, a short distance from John Todhunter, a former medical graduate of Trinity who had tired of medicine and turned to literature. Todhunter remained a close friend of Thornley and was a literary confidant of Bram at the time; they both shared a great interest in the paranormal and folklore, themes that were reflected in some of the books Todhunter published in the 1880s and 1890s such as *The Banshee and Other Poems* (1888) and *The Irish Bardic Tales* (1896).

In October 1876 word was sent to Bram that his father was gravely ill. To reach the bedside was not easy; his parents and two sisters had moved to Naples and his father lay in the Pensione Suisse in the Cava di Terrini district of Naples. Bram set off as swiftly as he could but tragically did not arrive in time. He paid his final respects in the vault of the church at La Cava, where he pressed his lips to his dead father's forehead. After the funeral, Bram returned to Dublin with his sister Margaret while his mother and sister Matilda chose to stay in Naples; they only decided to return to Dublin in the 1880s, when they moved into 72 Rathgar Road, Rathfarnham, where Bram's mother died in 1901.

At the time Bram returned from Italy, the Dublin newspapers were advertising Bateman's Lyceum Company, which was on tour and coming to Dublin Theatre Royal for eight nights. The Theatre Royal had suffered a chequered past. Built on land acquired by Henry Harris in 1820 as the Albany New Theatre for £50,000 it could seat 2,000 but, despite being visited by King George IV and becoming a patent theatre, proudly changing its name to the Theatre Royal, audience

ROYAL

LYCEUM THEATRE,

LICENSED BY THE LORD CHAMBERLAIN TO

MR. H. L. BATEMAN,

Sole Lessee and Manager.

MONDAY, DEC. 18, AND EVERY EVENING, AT 8.

Will be performed

THE NEW DRAMA,

IN THREE ACTS,

BY

LEOPOLD LEWIS,

ENTITLED

THE BELLS,

Adapted from " THE POLISH JEW,"

A DRAMATIC STUDY BY

MM. ERCKMANN-CHATRIAN.

Mathias	Mr. HENRY IRVING.
Walter	Mr. FRANK HALL.
Hans	Mr. F. W. IRISH.
Christian	Mr. HERBERT CRELLIN.
Doctor Zimmer	Mr. DYAS.
Notary	Mr. COLLETT.
Tony	Mr. FREDERICKS.
Fritz	Mr. FOTHERINGHAM.
Karl	Mr. EVERARD.
Catherine	Miss G. PAUNCEFORT.
Annette	Miss FANNY HEYWOOD.
Sozel	Miss ELLEN MAYNE.

With New and appropriate Scenery by

HAWES CRAVEN, H. CUTHBERT, and Assistants.

OVERTURE AND ORIGINAL MUSIC

COMPOSED AND ARRANGED BY M. E. SINGLA.

Musical Director, Mr. MALLANDAINE.

The Mechanical Effects by Mr. H. JONES.

The Properties by Mr. A. ARNOTT and Assistants.

Costumes by Mr. SAM. MAY and Mrs. RIDLER.

The whole produced under the immediate direction of

MR. H. L. BATEMAN.

Cover of the programme for Bateman's production of *The Bells* in which Irving made his name in the role of Mathias during the London Lyceum season 1871/72.

figures were low and several boxes were soon boarded up. Great performers of the day such as Paganini, Jenny Lind and the enormously popular Irish actor Barry Sullivan performed at the Theatre Royal and drew large audiences, but these were the exception and by 1851 financial difficulties caused the theatre to close. Reopened under John Harris, the theatre enjoyed something of a renaissance and saw Dion Boucicault and his wife make their first Dublin appearances there in 1861, in Boucicault's own play, *The Colleen Bawn*. In 1874 Brothers John and Michael Gunn became the new owners of the theatre. The boys had lost their father in an infamous Dublin accident – he and five others were drowned when an omnibus plunged into the canal at Portobello Bridge – but the tragedy did not leave its mark upon them. Both became ebullient impresarios with Michael Gunn, the builder of Dublin's Gaiety Theatre in 1871, taking over as manager of the Theatre Royal. The Royal was a theatre in new ascendancy and eagerly anticipated the arrival of Bateman's Company, especially the star that would be taking the lead in their performances – Henry Irving.

The run began with three evening performances of *Hamlet*, with Irving in the lead. The second night, Wednesday 28 November, drew an enormous audience and was attended by His Grace the Lord Lieutenant, accompanied by a party including Lady Georgina Hamilton and the Marchioness of Blandford. The Dublin *Evening Mail* reported 'Every part of the house, from floor to ceiling was overflowing.' Many were refused admission and it was noted that during the ghost scene the hurrahs of the crowd on the street were heard but 'although the audience knew of the approach of the party, they remained perfectly quiet till the close of the scene, when a storm of welcome burst forth that did one good to hear'.

On Saturday 2 and Monday 4 December Irving performed his great creation, Mathias in *The Bells*, which had already been heralded as creating 'the most profound impression' for many successive months during the London Lyceum season 1871/72. The Dublin run concluded on Tuesday 5 and Wednesday 6 December with a performance of *Charles I*.

Bram attended two of the three performances of *Hamlet* and wrote two reviews of Irving's performance. Perhaps it was the exchanges between Hamlet and the ghost of his dead father, and the contemplation of life and death in the play that touched Bram; or perhaps something of Bram's own memories of his father were evoked by Irving's performance; it may even have been the effusion of passion for an actor Bram had come to love that stimulated him to produce the most important review he would ever write. Bram was soon to discover his comments on Irving's characterisation and instinctive understanding of the role particularly impressed the actor, especially his view of Irving's portrayal of Hamlet as a mystic:

> Mr. Irving works out with a rare and beautiful completeness with that soupçon
> of doubt which the spectator should and must have regarding the facts of the

lives of others whose secrets are known only to themselves and heaven. The actor who throws on such touches of character and facts of life the fierce light of absolute certainty is as great a barbarian as he who, as Oliver Holmes[66] says, 'insists on the brutality of an actual checkmate'. To give strong grounds for belief, where the instinct can judge more truly than the intellect, is the perfection of suggestive acting; and certainly with regard to this view of Hamlet, Mr. Irving deserves not only the highest praise that can be accorded, but the loving gratitude of all to whom this art is dear.

There is another view of Hamlet, too, which Mr. Irving seems to realise by a kind of instinct, but which we recommend to his notice as one requiring to be more fully and intentionally worked out ... It is the great, deep, underlying idea of Hamlet is a mystic. In several passages Mr. Irving seems to have a tendency towards this rendering; when with far introspective gaze he appears on the scene; when he delivers the words, 'In my mind's eye, Horatio', whenever his thoughts turn toward suicide and the mystic's psychic sensibility recognises a danger and a purpose far away; and noticeably in the rendering of the debated passage 'Look upon this picture and upon this.' To the latter he leaves aside the idea of corporeal pictures either hanging on walls or in lockets and sees the stern reality in the peopled air above and around him. It seems to us that in the high strung nerves of the man there is a natural impulse to the spiritual susceptibility – that in his concentrated action. Spasmodic though it sometimes be, and in the divine delirium of his perfected passion, there is the instinct of the mystic which has but to render a little plainer that the less susceptible senses of his audience may see and understand. Of the haunting thought of suicide, Mr. Irving makes a strong point, ever showing the struggle between the desire and the obedience to Divine authority.[67]

The review was published in the Dublin *Evening Mail* on 1 December 1876; in fact Bram was to record Irving was 'so pleased he asked on reading my criticism on Tuesday morning that we should be introduced. This was effected by my friend Mr. John Harris, Manager of the Theatre Royal', although the chances are Bram's memory did not serve him well in this instance and it was in fact Michael Gunn, the then current manager, that arranged the meeting. Such an error of memory is hardly surprising when the focus of the meeting was with a man Bram already admired and came to idolise:

Irving and I met as friends, and it was a great gratification to me when he praised my work. He asked me to come round to his room again when the play was over. I went back with him to his hotel, and with three of his friends supped with him.[68]

Bram was invited to join Irving again at the magnificent Shelbourne Hotel, St Stephen's Green, Dublin, on Sunday 3 December 1876 when Irving had invited a few friends to dinner, 'It was a pleasant evening and a memorable one for me, for then began the close friendship between us which only terminated with his life if indeed friendship, like any other form of love, can ever terminate.'[69]

The group discussed theatre criticism and portrayal of characters: Irving had received fine reviews from notable critics but a special bond emerged between him and Stoker:

> my host's heart was from the beginning something toward me, as mine had been toward him. He had learned that I could appreciate high effort; and with the instinct of his craft liked, I suppose, to prove himself again to his new, sympathetic and understanding friend. And so after dinner he said he would like to recite for me Thomas Hood's poem 'The Dream of Eugene Aram'.[70]

Hood's poem was a standard text in schools of the nineteenth century, boys would be instructed to learn and present the piece to their class or even in front of their school and it was certainly familiar to all those present at their gathering, but 'such was Irving's commanding force, so great was the magnetism of his genius, so profound was the sense of his dominance that I sat spellbound'.[71]

In his *Personal Reminiscences of Henry Irving*, published the year after Irving's death, Bram vividly recalled Irving's performance and in doing so left a eulogy to the theatrical skills, presence and sheer power of his friend's performances. It also gives some indication of why Irving came to be regarded as the greatest actor of his age:

> That experience I shall never can never forget. The recitation was different, both in kind and degree, from anything I had ever heard … Outwardly I was as of stone; nought quick in me but receptivity and imagination. That I knew the story and was even familiar with its unalterable words was nothing. The whole thing was new, re-created by a force of passion which was like a new power. Across the footlights amid picturesque scenery and suitable dress, with one's fellows beside and all around one, though the effect of passion can convince and sway it cannot move one personally beyond a certain point. But here was incarnate power, incarnate passion, so close that one could meet it eye to eye, within touch of the outstretched hand. The surroundings became non-existent; the dress ceased to be noticeable; recurring thoughts of self-existence were not at all. Here was indeed Eugene Aram as he was face to face with his Lord; his very soul aflame in the light of his abiding horror. Looking back now, I can realise the perfection of art with which the mind was led and swept and swayed hither and thither as the actor wished. How a change of tone or time denoted the personality of the 'Blood-avenging Sprite' and how the nervous, eloquent hands slowly moving, outspread fanlike, round the fixed face set as doom, with eyes as inflexible as Fate emphasised it till one instinctively quivered with pity.

Then came the awful horror on the murderer's face as the ghost in his brain seemed to take external shape before his eyes, and enforced on him that from his sin there was no refuge. After this climax of horror the Actor was able by art and habit to control himself to the narrative mood whilst he spoke the few concluding lines of the poem.

Then he collapsed half fainting … That night for a brief time, in which the rest of the world seemed to sit still, Irving's genius floated in blazing triumph above the summit of art. There is something in the soul which lifts it above all that has its base in material things. If once only in a lifetime the soul of a man can take wings and sweep for an instant into mortal gaze, then that 'once' for Irving was on that, to me, ever memorable night. [72]

In the moments after Irving's performance the room remained silent, in awe of what they had seen, before erupting into applause; Bram was overwhelmed and in his own words, 'I burst out into something like a violent fit of hysterics.'[73] However, let us not forget that his extraordinary reaction may also have been intensified by grief. Bram had had little time to mourn the loss of his father, a father who introduced young Bram to the theatre, shared his love for it and bonded with the son to whom he would become closest: he was not there to share this sublime moment, and at that very moment Bram realised he never would be again.

Irving was moved by Bram's reaction to his performance and realised he had found a kindred spirit; that Bram's 'capacity for receptive emotion was something akin in forcefulness to his power of creating it'. Irving went to his room and returned with a photograph with an inscription on it, the ink still wet as he held it out towards Bram; the inscription read, 'My dear friend Stoker. God bless you! God bless you!! Henry Irving. Dublin, December 3, 1876.' The significance of the gesture was not lost; Bram recorded, 'In those moments of our mutual emotion he too had found a friend and knew it. Soul had looked into soul! From that hour began a friendship as profound, as close, as lasting as can be between two men.'[74]

Irving moved on with the tour but both men were keen to keep in contact. In the aftermath of that fateful meeting, Bram's theatrical critiques began to tail off. Bram had worked his way up the civil service to become head of the junior clerks and had been promoted to Inspector of Petty Sessions in March 1876. Perhaps his managers in the civil service had taken a dim view of a man in his position being associated with a newspaper; undoubtedly something had to give in Bram's life and a release from meeting the regular deadlines of the paper week after week may well have been welcome to him. Although he continued to frequent the Dublin theatres it may have been that, having seen the genius of Irving and been accepted into the intimate circle of his friends, Bram was content to gradually stand down as critic, almost as if he had found what he sought.

In 1877 Bram moved to what proved to be his last Dublin address, above Smyth's grocer and wine merchants at 7 St Stephen's Green, a short distance from the Shelbourne Hotel. Irving continued to correspond with Bram and returned to Ireland on a number of occasions, each time meeting up with his friend who would have made certain preparations for dinners and social occasions at his behest. The pair seemed very comfortable in each other's company and Bram seemed to know instinctively what would please Irving.

In understanding why their bond emerged it is worthwhile considering the background of Henry Irving. At the time they met in 1876 Irving was 38 years old and Bram had recently had his twenty-ninth birthday. Irving had been born into a working-class family at Keinton Mandeville in Somerset on 6 February 1838. Christened John Henry Brodribb, his lineage was a simple one: on his father's side 'a long line of sturdy but unimaginative Somerset farmers, on his mother's an obscure line of Cornishmen who never appear to have set the Fal on fire'.[75] Young John received limited schooling at Miss Penberthy's dame school while his family were living at Halsetown, near St Ives, Cornwall. His family then moved to London and occupied rooms on the top floor of a house at 68 Old Broad Street, near Whitechapel, and young Brodribb was sent to the City Commercial School that stood between Lombard Street and Cornhill. He was an average student and enjoyed his classes as much as any other boy, but his greatest achievement was a very personal one, for he used Dr Pinches' elocution class to conquer his stammer, something he did with aplomb. In much the same way that Bram rose from his bed of childhood illness and went on to develop his remarkable athletic prowess, when young Brodribb had conquered his stammer he approached set readings with maturing confidence and gusto.

His first taste of performance before a more public audience came at successive annual school speech days held at Sussex Hall on Leadenhall Street. When the time came for him to leave school, Mr and Mrs Brodribb sent their son to work as a junior clerk at Messrs. Paterson & Longman, solicitors of Milk Street, Cheapside. He knew what drudgery office work could be to an artistic soul and after a number of amateur theatrical performances and nights haunting the theatre at Sadler's Wells, he made the acquaintance of William Hoskins. Hoskins, an actor-manager, saw something in the young John Brodribb and secured him his first engagement with a new professional theatrical company in Sunderland. His parents attempted to dissuade him from forsaking the stability of a clerking job to take up the more precarious life of an actor, but the boy felt it was his destiny to act.

To gain a place in a theatrical company was Brodribb's dream come true. In many ways he felt reborn, and rechristened himself with a name he hoped would 'look good on playbills'. He admired the American author Washington Irving; he adopted his own middle name as his first, and thus when he made his debut with Mr Davis's company as Gaston, Duke of Orleans, in Bulwer-Lytton's *Richelieu* on 29 September 1856 at Sunderland, it was Henry Irving that strode out. He liked the name, it sat well with the young actors, and he eventually assumed it by royal licence.

Irving spent the following ten years in various stock companies, performing mostly in Scotland and in the north of England in more than 500 minor character roles. He even worked for a short while as stage director at the St James's Theatre, where he found himself well placed to join a better-known touring company and subsequently enjoyed his first conspicuous success as Digby Grant in *Two Roses*, when it opened on 4 June 1870 at London's Vaudeville Theatre. It ran for 300 nights. Irving began his long association with the Lyceum in 1871 when he joined Bateman's Company and rejuvenated the fortunes of the house with his portrayal of Mathias in *The Bells*, a version of Erckmann-Chatrian's *Le Juif Polonais* (*The Polish Jew*) by Leopold Davis Lewis, a property which Irving had discovered himself.

The story was a simple one but its success or failure hinged on the power of the performance of the character Mathias, a man who murders a Polish Jewish merchant with an axe in order to rob him of his money. Mathias becomes insane with guilt, his mind haunted by his heinous deed; only Mathias and the audience can see the ghostly manifestation of his victim or hear the bells of his sledge. The denouement of the play was an ideal set piece for Irving, as the character Mathias suffers a vivid nightmare that he is facing trial for the murder and is condemned to death by hanging. He awakes and attempts to pull the noose from his neck but the terror is such his heart gives out in the process and he slumps to the ground, dead. It would be commented:

> The play left the first-nighters a little dazed. Old fashioned playgoers did not know what to make of it as a form of entertainment. But when the final curtain fell the audience, after a gasp or two, realised that they had witnessed the most masterly form of tragic acting that the British stage had seen for many a long day, and there was a storm of cheers.[76]

The Bells ran for 151 performances; it established Irving at the forefront of the British drama and would prove a popular vehicle for him for the rest of his professional life. Bram had undoubtedly followed Irving's progress and it may well have been published accounts of *The Bells* that inspired Stoker to include the booming sound of bells among the spirits of the dead that Richard Hamilton had known and which swirled around him in the teeth of the storm at the climax of *Buried Treasures* (1875).

While with Bateman's company, Irving toured the provinces in the lead roles in *Eugene Aram*, in *Richelieu*, *Macbeth*, *Othello* and *Hamlet*; the latter performance the one that would first bring Bram to his notice and friendship in 1876.

The notion of Irving and Stoker having a homosexual relationship has been debated; the root of the discussion originated from Stoker's great-nephew and biographer Dan Farson in *The Man Who Wrote Dracula* (1975).[77] Stoker may have struggled with his sexual identity, but if there was homosexual love from Bram for Irving, there is no evidence of it being requited in a sexual way by Irving. Both men had, however, known the love and loss of women. Irving's losses had been particularly cruel. His first love was a charming young actress named Eleanora 'Nelly' Moore, who had made her London debut in the comedietta of *Cupid's Ladder* at St James's Theatre on 9 October 1859. Nelly, described as 'fair, with bright yellow hair, well-proportioned, a pleasant and sympathetic actress and a woman of unblemished reputation',[78] made her name in comedies and melodrama; in life and on stage she was the epitome of the heroine so acceptable to the Victorian stage.

Irving had first met Nelly while she was still playing the provinces during summer season at Cambridge Theatre Royal in 1862. Their love blossomed during a run of *Blanche of Nevers* at Manchester in 1866. After meeting the glamorous socialite Florence O'Callaghan on his way to a party thrown by Clement Scott at Linden Gardens, Kensington, in 1867, however, Irving abandoned Nelly. Or, at least, that is how it appeared. The rout of their romance had come about after green-room gossip about her dalliance with another actor, and 'supposed friend', who, Irving was told confidentially, had caused Nelly to suffer 'a grave injury at his hands'.[79] The dramatic phraseology was typical Victorian parlance for a woman being seduced and losing her virginity, some went so far as to suggest she had been made pregnant as a result.[80]

In his biography of his grandfather, Laurence Irving recounts the following story, presumably related to the family at the time by Irving's old friend and confidant, the character actor John Lawrence Toole:

> Later in cold anger, he [Irving] confronted this man and made it clear to him that although evidence of his guilt had been buried with his victim, suspicion would rest upon him as long as his accuser lived. Toole, fearful for Irving's self-control, was near at hand and never forgot the faces of the two men when they came from the room in which they had faced one another alone.[81]

Whether Nelly actually confessed any infidelity to Irving is unclear, nor is it certain that she had been seduced or made pregnant at all, but Irving's reaction was one of theatrical proportions. Feeling he no longer had any obligation to Nelly, Irving not only signified the termination of the romance by rebounding into a high-profile relationship with Miss O'Callaghan, he asked her to marry him, and their engagement was formally announced in April 1869.

If there were any pain or acrimony caused by the separation, it did not manifest in the professional lives of Nelly and Irving; they would soon work together again. Indeed, it was when they were together in the cast of *The Lancashire Lass*, with Nelly in the lead role of Ruth Kirby, at the Queen's Theatre in December 1869, that she was taken ill and had to leave the cast. Irving's grandson would recount how Irving 'was deeply anxious for the girl he still loved'[82] and went to visit her at her house at 31 Soho Square only to encounter Ann Shepherd, the woman who came to nurse her. According to Laurence Irving, Ann informed Irving that Nelly had scarlet fever.[83] Nelly's close family were touring in America and Irving was concerned she was quite alone, so he asked their mutual friend Laura Friswell if she would be kind enough to call upon her and this she did. Poor Nelly hovered between life and death for three weeks and Irving continued to visit until the morning of 22 January. Bringing a fine bunch of violets to her door, he was given the news that Nelly was dead. She was just 24 years old.

By the time of her death, Nelly had become a new star of the stage and her passing was reported in the theatre pages of London newspapers and across Britain and Ireland. The *Pall Mall Gazette* reported the cause of her demise as 'typhoid fever',[84] the cause of death recorded on her death certificate. Nelly's death was described in the *Morning Post* as from 'a lingering malady which, unhappily for her friends and profession, has brought a young life and a bright career to an unexpected termination. But "whom the gods love die young".'[85] Newspapers were deluged with poems and eulogies for the dead actress, *The Era* even had cause to announce 'We have not space for your poetry upon the death of Miss Nelly Moore. We have received sufficient to fill more than one page of our paper.'[86] Nelly's funeral was arranged for 1 February; she received full theatrical 'honours' with attendance by many of the well-known theatrical personalities of the day whose presence was as avidly reported in the press as any premiere. Among them were well-known actor managers W.H. Chippendale and Charles Wyndham, leading comic actor Lionel Brough, character actor, J.L. Toole, John Billington, Sidney Bancroft and Arthur Sketchley the author. Actresses Miss Maria Simpson, Maria and Nelly Harris and many more also attended to mourn the passing of one of their number.

Crowds gathered at Nelly's house and for her funeral service at St Anne's Church, Soho. The cortège was led by a hearse drawn by four magnificent black horses with black plumes relieved in silver. The glass sides of the hearse revealed a black coffin surmounted by a great wreath of white camellias. Three mourning coaches and three private carriages followed the hearse to Nelly's committal at Brompton Cemetery, while Miss Fanny Josephs, Miss Larkin, Mrs Billington and Miss Lydia Maitland were 'assiduous in their almost hopeless exertions to soothe the deep afflictions' of Nelly's mother.

As the last prayers were repeated and the mourners bent over the grave the winter wind sighed through the fir trees and sang the requiem for Nelly Moore. While Irving was not among the published list of mourners – it would have been considered bad form for her former suitor to have appeared amongst them, nor would have Miss O'Callaghan approved – it was noted that a small bouquet of azaleas and violets was tied to the foot handle of her coffin with white ribbon.[87] The symbolism of flowers would not have been lost on the feminine Victorian audience who, as part of their social upbringing, would have been taught the nuances of the language of flowers.[88] It was a gesture that would have been all the more poignant for those close enough to know the truth about the split between Irving and Nelly: azaleas, the symbol of fragile passion; and violets, the symbol of modesty, virtue, faithfulness and love, were the very same flowers Irving had brought to Nelly's door on the morning of her death. There was no card or attribution for the flowers – there didn't need to be.

Irving married Florence O'Callaghan at the parish church of St Marylebone almost seven months after the death of Nelly on 15 July. Very soon married life exposed Florence's capricious temper, which could not be ignored or humoured as it had been during their courtship. Florence did not like the traffic of theatre types who frequently cluttered their home, moreover she soon made no effort to disguise her dislike of Irving's professional friends or the fact she despised his profession. The atmosphere of nagging disapproval in the house drove Irving to hire a cheap lodging in Drury Lane where he could rehearse in peace.

It was during the carriage ride home in the glory and exhaustion of his triumphant opening night of *The Bells* of 25 November 1871 when, after a pregnant silence, Florence's smouldering and jealous temper loosed her tongue to bring him down to earth as she scowled: 'Are you going to go on making a fool of yourself like this all your life?' Irving told the driver to stop as they were crossing Hyde Park Corner and, with irony that would not have been out of place in a Thomas Hardy novel, they came to a halt near the spot Irving had proposed to Florence: the place his impetuous love had reached its peak was also where it was extinguished once and for all. Irving got out of the carriage and walked off into the cold night air, never to return home and never to speak to his wife again.

Bram had also known love; while the big 'perhaps …' is that Bram was bisexual, he certainly showed an interest in women. Often this love was from afar; his private notebook from his young manhood shows he certainly admired and discussed young women with his friends.[89]

Bram had an exchange of letters with Genevieve Ward in which both spoke in affectionate terms to one another, they also socialised together when she came on theatrical tours to Dublin. Bram even stayed with Genevieve and her mother in Paris as he passed through on a visit to his parents at their new home in Clarens, Switzerland, in 1875.[90] It appears he did not actually make it to see his parents but, equally, there is no direct evidence that Bram and Genevieve had become intimate. What is intriguing is that Bram wrote to his parents that he had met a mysterious lady he described as 'Miss Henry' in Paris, and, clearly enamoured with the girl, was going to write a play for her. The surviving correspondence between Bram and Genevieve in the mid-1870s confirms he was writing a play based on the story of Madame Roland, a supporter of the French Revolution who later disagreed with the policies of the new regime and had her life terminated upon the guillotine during the Terror. Genevieve took an interest in its research and progress, going so far as to suggest Bram should come and stay with her in Paris again so they could research the story together at the Bibliothèque Nationale.

In 1876, however, Bram received a disuasive letter from his father, shortly before his death. In it, his father reminded Bram that he had known actors and actresses and their society, and that while they were agreeable, their kind were not desirable. Bram did not complete his play, nor did he write for a long while, blaming illness, and he and Genevieve remained merely friends.

Love can, however, spring eternal and by 1878 Irving and Stoker may both have spoken of new love in their lives. For Bram it was Florence Balcombe. At the time they met she was living with her parents at 1 Marino Crescent, the street where Bram was born and had spent the first eighteen months of his life. Florence Ann Lemon Balcombe had been born at Falmouth in Cornwall on 17 July 1858. She was the third of five daughters of Crimean War veteran Captain James Balcombe of the 57th Regiment and his wife Phillippa. James retired as a lieutenant colonel from the South Down Militia in 1876 and they had only been at Marino Crescent a short while when Florence began walking out with Oscar Wilde. A little over two years later, Bram caught her attention and she forsook Oscar for him. Florence was 19, bright, witty and, above all, beautiful; she was regarded as one of, if not *the*, most beautiful woman in all Dublin. The pair quickly became swept up in a whirlwind romance and very soon plans were being made for their marriage.

Irving, meanwhile, may have had Zaré Thalberg on his mind at that time. A pretty, young opera singer, Zaré was believed to have been the illegitimate daughter of Sigismund Thalberg, composer and distinguished virtuoso pianist, following a liaison with the composer and singer Elena Angri. Zaré was born in New York during Thalberg's American tour in April 1857. She made her own London debut with the Royal Italian Opera at Covent Garden as Zerline in Mozart's *Don Giovanni* to great acclaim in April 1875. She was thus certainly performing in London at the same time as Irving. The exact nature of their relationship is still unknown, but a single photograph found pasted back to back with one of Irving was found in Irving's pocketbook after his death in 1905. Believed for many years to be an image of Nelly Moore it is, in fact, a photograph of Zaré Thalberg.

Regardless, or perhaps in spite of these romances, Bram had shown that he understood Irving and was dedicated to him. After a flying visit to Dublin in June 1877, Irving invited Bram over to London to see him in *The Lyons Mail*. Bram was honoured to sit with Irving in his dressing room between acts and they saw much of each other over the next few days as Irving gave him a taste of the life there. To demonstrate doors could be opened for Bram in 'the City', Irving arranged an introduction to James Knowles, editor of the magazine he had recently founded, the *Nineteenth Century*. The pair hit it off; Bram came to write for *Nineteenth Century* and they remained friends for many years after.

Irving was in no doubt that Bram understood the business of acting and thought, like poacher-turned-gamekeeper, what better man than a theatre critic to manage a theatre? During a return visit to Dublin in the autumn of 1877, Irving, Bram and a small coterie of friends suppered in the restaurants that were once a famous feature of men's social life in Dublin: Jude's, Burton Bindon's, and Corless's, so famous for their 'hot lobster'. Irving was clearly near to achieving his goal of taking over a theatre of his own and broached the idea of Bram giving up his job in the civil service and sharing his fortunes. The idea had been certainly mooted since their first meeting and now Bram could see his dreams could just become a reality:

> The hope grew in me that a time might yet come when he and I might work together to one end that we both believed in and held precious in the secret chamber of our hearts. In my diary that night, November 22, 1877, I wrote: 'London in view'.[91]

Bram was invited back to London by Irving again on 8 June 1878 to see the opening night of William Gorman Wills' *Vanderdecken*, a new version of the eerie tale of the *Flying Dutchman*: the ship and crew damned after its captain, Henrick Vanderdecken, swore at the wind and defied the Devil while trying to weather a storm around the Cape of Good Hope. As a result, the ship was doomed to sail the oceans forever as a ghostly portent of violent storm and foul weather to all who saw her. Irving was out to impress, he wanted to show what *he* could do as a producer as well as an actor. The effect was not lost on Bram, who was to recall the scene and Irving's appearance years later with crystal clarity:

> Irving … gave one a wonderful impression of a dead man fictitiously alive. I think his first appearance was the most striking and startling thing I ever saw on the stage. The scene was of the landing-place on the edge of the fiord. Sea and sky were blue with the cold steely blue of the North. The sun was bright, and across the water the rugged mountain-line stood out boldly. Deep under the shelving beach, which led down to the water, was a Norwegian fishing-boat whose small brown foresail swung in the wind. There was no appearance anywhere of a man or anything else alive. But suddenly there stood a mariner in old-time dress of picturesque cut and faded colour of brown and peacock blue with a touch of red. On his head was a sable cap. He stood there, silent, still and fixed, more like a vision made solid than a living man.[92]

Bram was particularly drawn to Irving's eyes: 'It was marvellous that any living man should show such eyes. They really seemed to shine like cinders of glowing red from out the marble face.'[93] These features seared into Bram's mind and he was to resurrect them in his description of the vampires in *Dracula*, notably, the Count himself: 'His eyes were positively blazing. The red light in them was lurid, as if the flames of hell fire blazed behind them. His face was deathly pale, and the lines of it were hard like drawn wires.'[94]

Despite Irving's impressive characterisation, Bram, the critics and audiences felt there was something lacking. The following day, Bram met Irving at his rooms on Grafton Street and the pair worked hard to cut and tighten up the performance; they later took the revised work to the rehearsal. Bram attended that evening's performance and went to supper with Irving at the Devonshire Club, where they talked over the play and continued the conversation in Irving's own rooms, as both men loved to do, through the night, only concluding their discourse after 5 a.m. The following day Bram went to Paris and on his return saw the play again. He felt it was tighter and the cast more at ease, but sadly *Vanderdecken* was not destined to be a success. Irving, however, was convinced, more than ever, that Bram was the man who shared his vision and understanding and that he really should have been involved in the project from its conception.

Irving returned again to Dublin as an actor on 23 September 1878 to commence two weeks of performances. During that time Bram was with him a great deal through rehearsals and performances. Even outside the theatre, the two continued to keep company and could be seen driving almost every day, dining out with friends and Bram's family. As Bram recalled, it was not only the best of times, it was the beginning of a new life for him:

It was a sort of gala time to us all, and through every phase of it and through the working time as well our friendship grew and grew. We had now been close friends for over two years.

We understood each other's nature, needs and ambitions, and had a mutual confidence, each towards the other in his own way, rare amongst men. It did not, I think, surprise any of us when six weeks after his departure I received a telegram from him from Glasgow, where he was then playing, asking me if I could go to see him at once on important business.

I was with him the next evening. He told me that he had arranged to take the management of the Lyceum into his own hands. He asked me if I would give up the Civil Service and join him; I to take charge of his business as Acting Manager. I accepted at once … I was content to throw in my lot with his. In the morning I sent in my resignation and made by telegram certain domestic and other arrangements of supreme importance to me at that time and ever since. We had decided that I was to join him on December 14 as I should require a few weeks to arrange matters at home. I knew that as he was to open the Lyceum on December so time was precious, and accordingly did all required with what expedition I could. [95]

Among the first preparations for his departure Bram tendered his resignation to the civil service, but he did not just walk away from his job at Dublin Castle. He ensured all the arrangements had been made for the completion of the book he had been working on since his appointment as Inspector of the Petty Sessions.

It had been no mean feat to compile the material for his legal administration manual, *The Duties of Clerks of Petty Sessions in Ireland*, in which Bram aimed to present the model for an effective system of procedure, not only for Ireland, but for adoption across the empire. When the book was published in 1879 it included the endorsement of the registrar, Richard Wingfield, who recommended it to all clerks of petty sessions. It became the standard text on the subject for years afterwards. Bram would freely admit the book was 'dry as dust'[96] but it was to be his first published book.

'And last, not least', as Bram would say, he married Florence. In a situation that would be echoed in *Dracula* when Jonathan Harker's wedding to Mina was postponed when he was summoned by the Count in Transylvania, then under-taken in haste in Budapest as he recovered from the trauma of his time at Castle Dracula, Bram's plans were hastily brought forward when he was summoned by his new master. The wedding of 31-year-old Bram and Florence, aged just 19, was conducted by the Reverend Charles W. Benson at the then fashionable St Ann's Anglican Church, on Dawson Street, Dublin, on 4 December 1878. There was no time for a honeymoon and five days later Bram Stoker, the new acting manager of the Lyceum, joined Irving at the Plough and Harrow at Edgbaston; as Bram was to recall 'he was mightily surprised I had a wife – the wife – with me'.[97]

4

ARRIVAL

When Irving took control of the Lyceum in August 1878 he had done so as the prosperity of Victorian England was fast approaching its apogee, in the knowledge that a new discerning clientele had emerged. This clientele shunned the coarse entertainments and had come to stigmatise music halls, seeking, instead, an evening of sophisticated theatre. But Irving would not be satisfied with a just a good play, he wanted, and knew his audiences wanted, to see performances in a comfortable and attractive theatre where the sense of spectacle and occasion began on the street outside and swept on majestically through the entrance to the auditorium; this was a place where one could see and be seen among the better

Irving exits stage left on the opening night of *Hamlet*, on the opening night of the Lyceum, under Irving's management on 30 December 1878. The artist, Alfred Bryan, captures the faces of the many dignitaries in the audience and in the boxes, including Edward, Prince of Wales, and Benjamin Disraeli.

classes of society. It was Irving's intention to make the Royal Lyceum, as he liked to call it, the beating heart of this, and in so doing elevate the acting profession to one of respectability.

The first incarnation of the Lyceum was built by the architect James Payne, who, having been elected President of the Society of Artists, agitated for funds and grandly opened the new building as an edifice for the exhibitions of the Society of Artists on 11 May 1772. The society only lasted for some three years then the building passed through a number of hands. The lessees were happy to rent it out to any who could afford to pay the rent, hence all manner of events were seen at the Lyceum, from meetings of a public debating society to exhibitions of sports such as fencing or boxing, from Count Zambeccari's air balloon to a number of performances of the 'Optical and Mechanical Exhibition' *Phantasmagoria*, which saw images of skeletons, shrouded phantoms, devils and other gruesome objects projected upon the walls, then appear to move and fly about by means of a specially designed magic lantern. It seems the walls of the Lyceum were enchanted by the strange and the macabre from these early years. Even Madame Tussaud, invited by magic lantern and *Phantasmagoria* pioneer Paul Philidor, first exhibited her work, including her display of the heads of the nobility she modelled after their visit to the guillotine, alongside his show at the Lyceum in 1802.

The fire at the Drury Lane Theatre in February 1809 caused the removal of The Drury Lane Company to the Lyceum and the theatre was granted its first license from the Lord Chamberlain to present plays; among them was James Robinson Planché's adaptation of John Polidori's *The Vampyre*, entitled *The Vampire, or the Bride of the Isles*. Brought out on 9 August 1820, it proved very popular and was performed a further thirty-seven times during the season and frequently afterwards. The 'Vampire Trap' stage effect was designed especially for this play and enabled the prince of darkness to make his final disappearance. The effect and the device created an enormous sensation in its day and the device was installed in a number of other London theatres.[98]

The Lyceum suffered a major fire of its own in February 1830 and could only be rebuilt after alteration had been carried out on the Strand, but rebuilt it was, to the classical designs of architect Samuel Beazley, as a bigger theatre with a magnificent and highly conspicuous portico facing the newly created Wellington Street. The portico, consisting of six lofty, fluted columns of the Corinthian order supporting a well-proportioned entablature and pediment, was a structure that was both impressive and gave a new gravitas to the building, making the Lyceum a landmark in its own right. While inside, well, it is best to leave the description to one who saw it first hand, and what a sight it must have been:

Passing through a hall with an arched roof, we enter a vestibule, opening into a circle of boxes, with a tasteful double staircase on each side, leading to the upper boxes and saloon. The auditory is in front semi-circular and at the sides of the horse-shoe form or that which is best adapted for hearing. The architectural design consists of an elegant entablature surmounted with a light balustrade, forming the front of the gallery and slips, surmounted on slender columns rising from the dress circle. The enrichments are raised in burnished gold on a white ground.

The ceiling, which is circular, and slightly concave, is ornamented with coloured arabesques in compartments of chaste effect. There are two tiers of boxes. In front of the lower or dress circle is a projection called 'the balcony' answering to the 'première galerie' of the French Theatres, the front consisting of an ornamental trellis work of gilt metal.

The front of the dress circle is ornamented with classic subjects in the fresco style, and the first or upper tier is embellished with an intimation of rich tapestry, which is novel in an English theatre. The balustrades of the gallery and slips are lined with rose colour. There is only one gallery but it is extensive.[99]

The auditory was lit by a spectacular glass chandelier, 'suspended by ten massive glass cords, surmounted by a brilliant feather, divided into eight festoons of prismatic icicles, which produce a dazzling effect with the gas lights darting through 400 prismatic spheres, so that the whole appears to be ablaze of sunshine upon a coruscation of icicles.'[100]

When Irving took over the Lyceum its reputation had become rather like the fabric of the building – tired and worn. Now he had control, Irving was determined to restore this theatre of his very own to its former glory and more. He began with its refurbishment, the only major change being the colour scheme of trad..onal rich crimson with gilded highlights, but all this had to be effected in time for the opening night. When Bram arrived there were only two weeks left until the opening night, and:

the theatre which was to be opened was in a state of chaos. The builders who were making certain structural alterations had not got through their work; plasterers, paper-hangers, painters, upholsterers were tumbling over each other. The outside of the building was covered with scaffolding. The whole of the auditorium was a mass of poles and platforms. On the stage and in the paint-room and the property-rooms, the gas-rooms and carpenter's shop and wardrobe-room, the new production of Hamlet was being hurried on under high pressure.[101]

Bram stepped into the breach as Irving's acting manager, but he had not anticipated the sheer scale of the job:

The week at Birmingham had been a heavy time. I had taken over all the correspondence and the letters were endless. It was the beginning of a vast experience of correspondence, for from that day on till the day of his death

I seldom wrote, in working times, less than fifty letters a day. Fortunately for both myself and the readers, for I write an extremely bad hand the bulk of them were short. Anyhow I think I shall be very well within the mark when I say that during my time of working with Henry Irving I have written in his name nearly half a million letters! [102]

Then there were the finances to consider; while the theatre was 'dark' during renovations there was no revenue coming through the doors and Irving was left with his savings and money from his tours to sustain the situation. As Bram would point out, 'before the curtain went up on the first night of his management he had already paid away nearly ten thousand pounds, and had incurred liability for at least half as much more by outlay on the structure and what the lawyers call "beautifyings" of the Lyceum'.[103]

Bram was keen to roll up his sleeves and get on with the job in hand, and while it certainly proved to be a steep learning curve, it was one he handled with aplomb:

Nearly all the work was new to me, and I was not sorry when on the 19th my colleague, the stage manager, arrived and took in hand the whole of the stage matters. When Irving and the company arrived, four days after, things both on the stage and throughout the house were beginning to look more presentable.

When the heads of departments came back to work, preparations began to hum ... The production with which the season of 1878–9 opened was almost entirely new. When Irving took over the Lyceum the agreement between him and Mrs. Bateman [the previous lessee] entitled him to the use of certain plays and material necessary for their representation. But he never contented himself with the scenery, properties or dresses originally used. The taste of the public had so improved and their education so progressed, chiefly under his own influence, that the perfection of the seventies would not do for later days. For *Hamlet* new scenery had been painted by Hawes Craven, and of all the dresses and proper-ties used few if any had been seen before. What we had seen in the provinces was the old production. I remember being much struck by the care in doing things, especially with reference to the action. It was the first time that I had had the privilege of seeing a play 'produced'. I had already seen rehearsals, but these except of pantomime had generally been to keep the actors, supers and working staff up to the mark of excellence already arrived at. But now I began to understand why everything was as it was.

Within a handful of days after the announcement of the opening night of the Lyceum under its new management, every seat in the house for *Hamlet* on 30 December 1878 was sold. Among the invitations sent out at the behest of Irving was one in letter form written, unusually, by Henry Loveday, his trusted stage manager, on the morning before the opening night (no wonder it was 'in haste'). The letter was addressed to T.H.H. Caine Esq., Anderton's Hotel, Fleet Street, London, on paper headed 'Royal Lyceum Theatre, Strand'. The message was a brief one:

> Monday
> My dear Mr Caine
>   No rehearsal today – delighted to see you tonight – see Mr. Bram Stoker – he has a seat in Box for you – come round after – in haste
>
>   Sincerely Yours
>   H.J. Loveday[104]

The friendship between Hall Caine and Irving dated back to October 1874 when Caine was a freelance reporter in Liverpool and wrote to Irving to ask if he would allow him to insert his portrait in a new monthly magazine he was trying to get off the ground, entitled the *Rambler*.[105] Irving was clearly flattered and replied in the affirmative with a very kindly letter. Sadly the magazine did not survive long, but the friendship between Caine and Irving endured for the rest of Irving's life. A fortnight after they first met, on 31 October 1874, Caine attended the first night of *Hamlet* at the Lyceum in his capacity as critic of the *Liverpool Town Crier*, quite an honour indeed for a provincial and little-known critic. Perhaps Irving saw a something in him similar to that which he saw in Bram; like Bram, Caine was spellbound by Irving's performance and his eloquent criticism published in the newspaper was so well appreciated that he was asked to reprint it in pamphlet form, as Bram would recollect:

> though I knew nothing of them at that time, two criticisms of his Hamlet had been published in Liverpool. One admirable pamphlet was by Sir (then Mr.) Edward Russell, then, as now, the finest critic in England; the other by Hall Caine a remarkable review to have been written by a young man under twenty.[106]

Irving was clearly delighted with Caine's reviews and two years later, during a visit to Liverpool whilst on tour, they met at Irving's request. It is intriguing to note that in describing how the relationship between these two men matured in his *Personal Reminiscences of Henry Irving*, Stoker mirrors and analyses his own relationship with and understanding of the great actor:

> There began a close friendship which lasted till Irving's death. Caine seemed to intuitively understand not only Irving's work but his aim and method. Irving felt this and had a high opinion of Caine's powers. I do not know any one whose opinions interested him more. There was to both men a natural expression of intellectual frankness, as if they held the purpose as well as the facts of ideas in common. The two men were very much alike in certain intellectual ways. To

both was given an almost abnormal faculty of self-abstraction and of concentrating all their powers on a given subject for any length of time. To both was
illimitable patience in the doing of their work. And in yet one other way their
powers were similar: a faculty of getting up and ultimately applying to the work
in hand an amazing amount of information. When Irving undertook a character
he set himself to work to inform himself of the facts appertaining to it; when the
time for acting it came, it was found that he knew pretty well all that could be
known about. Hall Caine was also a 'glutton' in the same way. He absorbed facts
and ideas almost by an instinct and assimilated them with natural ease.[107]

The first meeting between Caine and Stoker was an auspicious one that could
have had two outcomes, both of them extremes. One could have been that they
found each other a threat, rivals for the love and attention of Irving, each believing they had the greater understanding and appreciation of the man, while the
other outcome was the polar reverse. Fortunately, the latter triumphed. Bram
and Caine became intimate friends, personal and literary confidants only to be
parted by Bram's death in 1912. Brought together because of their adoration for
Irving, they shared many seminal interests in the world of the occult, the strange
and the supernatural: both men adored the poetry of the English Romantics and
Walt Whitman; Caine had corresponded with Edward Dowden, the tutor Bram
respected above all at others at Trinity; both were blessed with the gift of story-
telling and both were authors in what little time their paying jobs would allow,
dreaming of success but not knowing if it would come to them.

Thomas Henry Hall Caine was born in Runcorn, Cheshire, on 14 May 1853. He
disliked his name, preferring to be known simply as Hall Caine; only those closest
to him would call him Tom. His father, John Caine, had been born a Manxman,
the younger son of a farmer in Ballaugh on the Isle of Man while his mother,
Sarah Hall, had come from a Cumbrian family born in the air of the Solway Firth.

Tom's father had served an apprenticeship with a blacksmith at Ramsey but
when he had learned his trade he found that work on the Isle of Man was simply
not available and he emigrated to Liverpool. Here, he re-trained as a ship's smith,
married and made his first home together with his wife. Tom would have been
born in Liverpool had his father not taken his pregnant wife with him when he
was on a temporary job at Runcorn Docks.

On their return to Liverpool, John Caine found a home for his family in Toxteth
where many of the shipyard and dock workers lived in long rows of back-to-back
terraced houses. It was a place where the sanitation was poor and times were hard,
but the common bonds were strong among the many Manx who had made their
homes there, having come to Liverpool to find work. Nevertheless, Tom, with his
family, often visited the Isle of Man to see his Manx grandmother, Isabella Caine. A
widow since 1844, she had lived in the Isle of Man all her life and, in her old age, she
lived with one of her sons, William, in a typical rural Manx cottage at Ballavolley:

One side of the porch was the parlour, which also served as a dairy, redolent of milk and bright with rare old Derby china. On the other side was the living room, with its undulating floor of stamped earth and grateless hearthstone in the ingle, to the right and left of which were seats. Here in the ingle-nook the little boy would sit watching his aunts cooking the oaten cake on the griddle, over a fire of turf from the curragh, and gorse from the hills, or the bubbling cooking-pot slung on the slowrie ... The walls of this room were covered with blue crockery-ware and through the open rafters of the unplastered ceiling could be seen the flooring of the bedrooms above. These were the bedrooms, with the bed in the angle where the roof was lowest. One had to crawl into bed and lie just under the whitewashed 'scraa' or 'turf roofing'.[108]

Caine recalled:

She believed in every kind of supernatural influence, the earth and the air were full of spiritual things ... she knew when the storms were coming by a look at the sky and she could tell the time within a few minutes by sight of the stars. She knew a bad man as she knew the clouds and she could see a good heart through a clear countenance as she saw the stones at the bottom of the well. I think of her now feeding the fire with the crackling gorse while she told me wondrous tales of the 'little men' and I tell myself now that, bewildered as she would have been to hear it, my old Manx grandmother was a poet.[109]

The story Caine liked best to listen to, although it frightened him so much he would run and hide his face in the folds of his grandmother's blue Spanish cloak, was how his grandmother, as a girl in the first blossom of womanhood, had seen the fairies with her own eyes when she had been out one night to meet her sweet-heart. As she was returning in the moonlight she was 'overtaken by a multitude of little men, tiny little fellows in velvet coats and cocked hats and pointed shoes, who ran after her, swarmed over her and clambered up her streaming hair'.[110]

Caine would recall that his grandmother spoke in the native Manx tongue and had an affectionate boyhood name for him, 'She called me Hommy Beg, which was Manx for Little Tommy' but he would reflect that although he could speak some Manx, he freely admitted his pronunciation sounded akin to 'hard swearing'.[111]

Some criticism was levelled at Hall Caine by his detractors for his emphasis on his Manx memories of childhood but, in comparison with the grimy streets and industrial brickwork of Liverpool, this was an escape to a beautiful rural idyll of clean air, wide open spaces, green fields, hills and mountains. The streets of Liverpool were unsanitary and sicknesses such as typhoid, influenza or whooping cough could spread rapidly and claim many lives, especially the old and the very young. When he was just 9 years old, Tom lost two of his little sisters in less than a year: 5-year-old Sarah to hydrocephaly and 14-month-old Emma, who died in convulsions brought on by whooping cough. Tom was devastated and, as he was suffering from whooping cough too, his parents, fearing for his health and emotional wellbeing if he stayed in Liverpool, sent him to convalesce with family on the Isle of Man. Despite being tinged with some sadness, Caine would recall his visits to the Isle of Man as the happiest memories of his young life and, as an aspiring romancer, it is hardly surprising he would evoke this imagery again and again in both his literary work and the interviews he gave. Hall Caine's 'run for cover' would become a recurrent feature of his adult life as Caine's biographer, Vivien Allen, pointed out: 'Whenever he felt ill or worried or under strain he would opt for that panacea, "a change of air". Unfortunately he himself did not change so that he frequently returned home or moved on still feeling exhausted and unwell.'[112]

Tom received his formal education at the British Schools on Hope Street in Liverpool and spent many hours on his own reading books, notably at the Liverpool Free Library where his mind would 'run wild in a wilderness of books'. Caine was a bookish boy, spurning games in preference for reading, but the books he enjoyed were not typical for boys, for he delved into theological works, histories, metaphysics, poetry and even parliamentary speeches of great orators, which he keenly concentrated into his young mind. Caine also experienced what he described as the 'scribbling itch' for writing; he could not recall a time when it wasn't there, but his outpourings were an eclectic range of essays, poems, novels and overview histories produced in 'unguided ardour' with little thought of them being published: 'as soon as a thing was done it was done with and it found its way to the bottom of a trunk'.[113] When Caine left school at 14 he was apprenticed to John Murray, an architect and land surveyor. Murray was a distant relative of Prime Minister William Ewart Gladstone and it was through this connection Caine first encountered the great man in 1868. The meeting occured on the day of the general election, when Caine was charged with running telegrams announcing the results as they came in from across the country to Murray's brother's office in Union Court. This day was etched into Caine's memory, as he described his vision of Gladstone almost forty years later:

> I see him as he was then, sitting behind an office table, a tall man in a stiff-looking frock-coat of the fashion of an earlier day, with a pale face and side whiskers and very straight black hair, thin on the crown and brushed close across the forehead. He was my hero, my idol, my demi-god, in those days, but that did not prevent my blurting out the big news of great majorities before he had time to open his telegrams, and then his pale, serious shadowed face, almost sad and apparently preoccupied, would lighten into a smile that was like sunshine.[114]

A short while later Caine was to come to Gladstone's notice again when he was sent by Murray to supervise the survey of his estate at Seaforth. The chief surveyor had failed to turn up and Caine was acting as his deputy. The great man was surprised such a small 'lad' in charge of the chain men; he went over to talk to him, asked about his maps, and Caine gave an overview of suggested improvements. Gladstone listened intently then, as he look his leave, patted Tom on the head and told him he 'would do something some day'.[115]

In 1870 Caine suffered what he would describe as 'the first hint of one of the nervous attacks which even then beset me'.[116] The exact cause is unclear, but it may have been due to a culmination of the death of Caine's Grandfather Hall a few months earlier, pressure from his work in the architect's office or, as Caine would suggest, frustration and disappointment after the failure of a magazine he had written for

William Ewart Gladstone c. 1868.

and in which he had invested the high hopes of youth collapsed, more or less before it got off the ground, due to lack of public interest. As a result, Caine threw up his job at the architect's office and went to live with his schoolmaster uncle and his aunt, James and Catherine Teare, at Maughold on the Isle of Man. Caine was made more welcome than he had expected: his uncle was suffering from tuberculosis and if Caine was willing to step into the breach at the school he would be welcome to stay as long as he wished. It was to prove to be another bittersweet time for Caine; he evocatively recalled the school and his time as teacher there:

> The schoolhouse was a quaint-looking structure that stood alone like a light-house on the bleakest of the Manx headlands, Kirk Maughold Head and the wind in the winter swirled round it and lashed it as with a knout … Sometime we had to tie a rope from the door of the dwelling house to the door of the school that I might shoulder my way round by the walls without being swept off my feet and sometimes we saw the children who came from the farms in the valleys on either side, with laughter and shrill cries, creeping up to our aerie on hands and knees. It was a stern sort of schooling for all of us, but I think we came through it to our mutual content, though the children taught me more than I was able to teach them.[117]

In his spare time Caine restored a tumbledown cottage, made it a home and used his skills as a stonemason, taught to him by his dear departed Grandad Hall, to carve 'Phoenix Cottage' and the date of 8 January 1871 on the lintel over the door. When his uncle was finally claimed by TB in December 1871 he lovingly carved the headstone for him, too. As a respected, educated and literate man of the village where many were illiterate, Caine also took his uncle's place as the person many would turn to for help in personal and business matters; he recalled the diversity of this extraneous unpaid work that could involve the, 'Making of wills for farmers round about, the drafting of agreements and leases, the writing of messages to banks protesting against crushing interest and occasionally the inditing of love letters for young farm hands to their girls in service on farms that were far away.'[118] This gave Caine plenty of material that he would later use to good effect in many of his books – much to the chagrin of the Manx people.

Caine had been offered the position of schoolmaster and could have spent the foreseeable future in Maughold, but in many ways that dear little village was no longer a challenge to him. He had come with nothing, risen to a physical and mental challenge and achieved much; in many ways he had grown up and his work was done, so when a letter came from John Murray in March 1872, advising Caine that his job was still open to him and that he should come back to Liverpool, Caine returned home and settled back into his work in the surveyor's office.

While on the Isle of Man Caine had written a number of articles for local newspaper *Mona's Herald*, vehemently arguing the case for political independence. However, these articles attracted little notice beyond that of Uncle James, who much admired them and encouraged Caine to write, informing his sceptical relations that if Hall Caine failed as an architect, he would certainly be able to make a living with his pen. When he returned to Liverpool, Caine set about taking his literary work further and assimilating his knowledge from the drawing office into some articles on building, land surveying and architecture; thus Caine's first works to be published for a national audience appeared in *The Builder* and *Building News*. The life in Murray's surveyor's offices pleased Caine's parents but it was not for Caine, as Ramsey Muir would incisively point out in *A History of Liverpool* (1907):

> The conditions of the clerk's life usually render him conventional, respectable, timid and unadventurous. His work does not encourage, but rather represses, individuality and openness of mind. For that reason it is ill-paid, yet convention requires him to live in a way that perpetually strains his income. This class, though it includes many capable and clear-headed men, is also largely recruited from among the half-hearted, the listless, the unimaginative and the dull; and so in any period of stress or depression many of them will drift helplessly, especially if one their moorings of respectability are cut.[119]

It was not many editions of Liverpool newspapers that would separate the latest account from the police court of a clerk gone bad, turned to drink and theft, from an account of a clerk or one of similar class appearing under the 'Coroner's Inquests' as suicide or *felo de se*.

Caine sought to be published on the arts and to have his own compositions of prose and poetry appear in print, even if it be more for love than money. Just like Bram, Caine began by offering his services to a number of Liverpool newspapers as theatre critic for free and was accepted, although, unlike Bram, letters in the Hall Caine papers reveal he regularly frustrated his editors by delivering copy late. In 1873 the Caine family moved to a larger house at 59 South Chester Street, Toxteth, where Tom shared a cramped room with his younger brother John who had got himself a position as a shipping clerk.

It was a time of change for Hall Caine: he was in his early 20s and, describing it as 'Partly from the failure of faith in myself as a draughtsman and partly from a desire to be moving on', he left Murray's and obtained employment in the offices of builders, Bromley & Son. Caine recalled it as:

> the best move I have yet made, though I remember with a certain shame that it must have been considerably less advantageous for my employer, for my new employment fostered my literary activity after a fashion that could hardly have been contemplated by my indulgent chief. Making no particular demand on my intellect, it left me free to read more and more books of many sorts and to write stories and dramas and essay and articles. I remember that I had a snug little office to myself in which I did these things for several years, while all the time my face bore an expression of intense absorption in the affairs of the building trade. The literary conscience in its early manifestation is an elastic one.[120]

Caine sought solace in matters aesthetic and needed to challenge his brain and find focus to explore the subjects that interested him in discourse with others of like mind. If Caine had been able to gain a place at university he would have undoubtedly found the forum he needed so desperately and would have flourished as Bram Stoker did. Tragically, like so many bright young men and women of his day, constraints of finance and social strata precluded entry into the hallowed walls of higher education.

Ignorance was, however, identified as a 'social evil' and efforts had been made among the philanthropic, both within and separate from the council, to stimulate and improve the minds of the Liverpool populace. The middle years of the nineteenth century saw the foundation of the free library that Caine loved so well, along with a museum and art gallery housed in impressive buildings that filled the whole north side of William Brown Street across the way from the noble St George's Hall. Built in the neo-Grecian style with long porticos of Corinthian columns, St George's Hall was opened in 1854 as a senatus, combining both law courts and one of the most impressive concert halls of the Victorian age. High above the Minton tiled floor, in the tunnel vault roof supported on columns of polished red granite, the panelled plasterwork depicts the allegorical figures of Virtues, Science and Arts. These buildings represented the new cultural aorta of

Liverpool and the young Hall Caine sensed that it was within this world that he belonged.

The latter half of the nineteenth century saw the burgeoning new middle classes of Britain clamour to create clubs and societies for the improvement of the mind through study of the arts and sciences. In Liverpool, their Literary and Philosophical Society dated back to 1812 and was joined by a coterie of smaller societies for the study of specific sciences and new inventions, such as photography in the 1860s and 1870s. Liverpool was well enough regarded to host the annual meeting of the British Association for the Advancement of Science in 1870. Many of these societies held their meetings at the Free Public Library and Museum and the posters or newspaper adverts and accounts of the proceedings would not have escaped the attention of Caine, nor could he have failed to observe the distinguished and well-dressed membership attending them.

Caine resolved a new society should be started and with old school friend, William Tirebuck, and a number of other aspirational young men they formed a society of their own. Caine was to recall:

> I was making various grandiose efforts in Liverpool and one of these was an effort to establish a branch of the Shakespeare Society, the Ruskin Society and the Society for the Protection of Ancient buildings, all rolled into one. We called our own organisation 'Notes and Queries Society', held our meetings at the local Royal Institution and invited public men to discourse to us in person or by proxy. The 'Notes' were often provided by persons of no less distinction than Ruskin and William Morris, but the only 'Queries' I can remember came from our landlords and concerned the subject of rent.[121]

Although Caine may have been dismissive of the success of the Notes and Queries Society in his biography, it was no more or less successful than many other such societies of its day; in fact, it was far from hard done by. The Liverpool newspapers soon picked up on their meetings and they were reported along with accounts of the meetings of the other acknowledged learned societies of Liverpool such as the Art Club, the Chemist's Association, the Engineering Society, the Geological Society,

Hall Caine aged 25.

the Microscopical, Mineralogical Naturalists' Field Club and the Numismatic, Philomathic and Polytechnic Societies as well as the Literary and Philosophical Society.[122] Caine was Notes and Queries' president and their meetings were held at the Liverpool Royal Institution buildings on Colquitt Street. This was no side street venue; before the opening of such Liverpool Borough Council facilities as the William Brown Library (1860) and the Walker Art Gallery (1877) the Royal Institution was the place for the promotion of literature, science and the arts in Liverpool. Science courses held here met the needs of medical students and practitioners, the literature and arts programme covered topics such as English and foreign literature, philosophy, history, fine art and music, while its galleries housed a fine art collection, a small library and a museum of natural history and antiquities.

The Notes and Queries Society was also graced by a number of notable speakers: Edward Russell read a masterly essay on Shakespeare; Philip Rathbone, chairman of the Liverpool City Council committee responsible for the Walker Art Gallery, spoke on 'Nudes in Art'; and there was a recital by the composer and organist W.H. Jude. Even Henry Irving made an appearance, as Caine recalled:

> then a young man in the first flush of his success, came to us on one occasion to defend what he called the 'craven' view of 'Macbeth' and I remember that much to his amusement a rugged Unitarian minister, who had been, I think, a postman, dressed him down as if he had been a naughty boy who required the cane of a schoolmaster.[123]

Caine edited a booklet of the papers presented to the society by William Morris, Samuel Huggins and John J. Stevenson on the progress of public and professional thought on the treatment of ancient buildings – it was described as 'well worth reading'.[124] Caine's own lectures presented at both the Free Library and for the Notes and Queries Society at their meetings at the Royal Institution were reported in the local newspapers, and some were printed and circulated in pamphlet form. He received particular praise for his lecture on Shakespeare from Lord Houghton, the biographer of Keats, and notable praise for his lecture on the theme of 'The Supernatural in Poetry' in July 1878 for which he had persuaded Professor Edward Dowden to chair the meeting, even receiving a long letter of eulogy from Matthew Arnold in response to the published paper. But it was Caine's correspondence and relationship with Dante Gabriel Rossetti that is of particular note. His lectures on the works of Rossetti moved the great man so deeply that Caine became his close confidant and even moved in with him, for what was to prove to be the final twelve months of Rossetti's life, until his death in April 1882.

When Bram Stoker and Hall Caine had met in 1878 their backgrounds may have been different, but they shared many touchstones in their lives. They looked forward to the brave new decade of the 1880s as two kindred souls brought together at the start of their literary careers, blessed with a friendship that would see them become further entwined in literature and love over the years to come.

5

WHO IS THE GREAT AMERICAN DOCTOR?

Tumblety had a killing air,
Though curing was his professional trade,
Rosy of cheek and glossy of hair,
Dangerous to man to widow or maid.

The Poem of Dr Tumblety, 1866[125]

When Hall Caine was working freelance and often unpaid for the newspapers in Liverpool during the mid-1870s, the pressure of his frantic trips to deliver copy to newspaper offices, visiting plays and writing his own novels and plays, and suffering the indignity of rejection took its toll. He had suffered with his nerves since an early age: as his biographer would point out, 'hectic periods of research and creative work were often succeeded by gloomy depths of exhaustion, frequently prostrating him in a state of "nervous collapse".' It could be argued he was suffering from long-term depression, perhaps a bipolar condition, that led to him becoming a hypochondriac.

Caine had consulted a number of doctors to no avail and, unfortunately, he was now moving in new social circles of newspapers, theatre and literature, where the unwary young man could fall prey to the pretentious, the hangers on, con artists, sycophants and sociopaths who were also drawn to this world – enter Dr Francis Tumblety.

Tumblety was a quack doctor and a charlatan whose life story is obfuscated by the lies he told in his publications and in his personal claims to reporters or those who encountered him over the years. It can be said, without equivocation, that he was a controversial and remarkable character.

According to his family, Francis Tumblety was born in or near Dublin in the early months of 1830, the youngest of eleven children born to James and Margaret Tumblety. His siblings were Margaret (1826–93), Patrick (1823–58), Lawrence (1819–98), Elizabeth (born 1814), Jane (born 1815), Mary (1810–76), Alice (1809–1903), and twins Julia and Bridget (born 1821).

The dramatic illustration of the arrest of Tumblety in St Louis, Missouri, used on the cover of his first biography *A Few Passages in the Life of Dr. Francis Tumblety* (1866).

Little is known of his early life in Ireland: Tumblety would claim he was educated at the 'University of Dublin', where he graduated and then studied medicine. It was claimed he displayed diplomas reflecting these qualifications,[126] but this is extremely unlikely as he would not have had enough time there to qualify, even if he had achieved a place, as his parents emigrated, taking both Francis, then aged 17, and his sister Anne, to New York in 1847.

Their actions were far from unique, they joined thousands in an exodus to escape the horrors of the potato famine but, in their instance, they would not be arriving in a land filled with strangers. James and Margaret's son Lawrence had emigrated a few years earlier and had settled in to his new life in Rochester, New York.

After travelling from Ireland to Liverpool, the family left Liverpool aboard the packet boat *Ashburton* and, after a journey of about four weeks, arrived in New York on 21 June 1847 and settled with Lawrence on Sophia Street in Rochester. They were later joined by another son, Patrick, who lodged nearby. James Tumblety may well have fallen ill and been hospitalised in 1850 (he died in 1851), as the Federal census for that year shows his wife Margaret Tumblety as head of household, with son Lawrence working as a gardener and Francis as a labourer – hardly the work of a man qualified in medicine.

An old resident of Rochester, Captain W.C. Streeter, had memories of 'Frank Tumblety' from 1848:

> He was selling books and papers on the packets and was in the habit of board-ing my boat a short distance from the town. The books he sold were largely of the kind Anthony Comstock suppresses [sic] now. His father was an Irishman and lived on the common south of the city on what was then known as Sophia Street, but is now Plymouth Avenue and is about a mile from the center of the city. There were but few houses there then and the Tumblety's had no near neighbors. I don't remember what the father did. There were two boys older than Frank and one of them worked as a steward for Dr. Fitzhugh, then a prom-inent physician.[127]

With regard to the books referred to as 'of the kind Anthony Comstock sup-presses': Comstock was a moral crusader who had created the New York Society for the Suppression of Vice in 1874. His ideas of what constituted something being 'obscene, lewd or lascivious' had a wide scope, from overt pornography to certain types of anatomy textbooks to anything written or practical pertaining to birth control. The material referred to by Streeter could have been pornographic books for sailors or more likely books on birth control. That Tumblety was a peddler is confirmed in *Rochester City Directory* of 1851/52, but no employer is indicated.

Edward Haywood, of the Bureau of Accounts in the State Department at Washington, also recalled Tumblety as a young man in Rochester:

I remember him very well when he used to run about the canal in Rochester, N.Y., a dirty, awkward, ignorant, uncared-for, good-for-nothing boy. He was utterly devoid of education. He lived with his brother, who was my uncle's gardener ... The only training he ever had for the medical profession was in a little drug store at the back of the Arcade, which was kept by a 'Doctor' Lispenard, who carried on a medical business of a disreputable kind.[128]

Dr Lispenard was a pseudonym used by Dr Ezra J. Reynolds who operated from rooms at 14 Exchange Place, Rochester. Reynolds placed separate adverts in the *Rochester City Directory* (1857) for both his incarnations. Dr Reynolds could be consulted 'on all diseases of a private or delicate nature', claiming he could be 'successfully consulted' on diseases of the liver, kidney and bladder as well as a wide range of ailments, among them: jaundice, dropsy, all forms of scrofula, neuralgia heart conditions, bronchitis, swelling on the bones, ulcers of legs, mouth, tongue, nose, throat and lips, mercurial and syphilitic affections – he even offered a cure for the 'secret habits of young men'. However, the chances are that if Tumblety was selling books for Lispenard, they would have been literature on sexual diseases.

Reynolds' alter ego was more explicit; the advert under his name offers Dr Lispenard's *Practical Private Medical Guide* as 'The most popular work ever published on the disease of the genital organs'. In it he offered cures for a variety of venereal diseases as well as 'Midwifery, Miscarriages, Impotence and Barrenness'. The advert was keen to point out, 'Dr Lispenard continues to dispense his invaluable remedies to those afflicted with Secret Diseases ... None leave his treatment half cured. He always gives the best of satisfaction. Gonorrhea, Gleet, Syphillis, Stricture, Suppression of the Menses in females &c. Successfully treated.'

Tumblety appears to have progressed rapidly from pedlar to protégé of Reynolds', but the man who was to become the role model for Tumblety was undoubtedly Dr Rudolph Lyons, who extolled the secret medical knowledge of the Native Americans in 'the reformed Indian vegetable practice'.[129] Unlike Reynolds, who would place occasional adverts in almanacs and the city guide, Lyons knew the value of impact publicity: he would also publish an impressive list of conditions he had successfully treated where other doctors had failed, took out large adverts in newspapers and cultivated respectability by emphasising a specialisation in the treatment of women and children rather than the diseases of vice. Lyons was savvy: he based himself in fashionable addresses, dressed well and sought his clientele from among the better social classes and elite – those best placed to pay him well for his services. He did not remain in one area, but maintained consulting rooms at number of locations in upstate New York where he would herald his arrival at certain times every month in his newspaper advertisements.

New York had always been a great draw for all manner of medical practitioners; those both certified and legitimate, and those less orthodox and charlatan. A marked decline of 'botanical practitioners' from the mid-1840s was contrasted by a rise in sexual disease 'specialists' advertising contraceptives and abortifacients. Increasing numbers of alternative medical practitioners were also having to become geographically mobile.[130] By the time Tumblety decided to practice in his own right, he knew he would be entering a community where there was

BE WISE BEFORE IT IS TOO LATE

CALL, WITHOUT DELAY, AND SEE

THE INDIAN HERB DOCTOR!

AT

No. 18, Great St. James's Street,
(OPPOSITE THE ST. LAWRENCE HALL,)

MONTREAL, C.E.,

Where he will remain from 1st Sept. to 1st March, 1858, when he will return to his Office in Toronto, C.W.

By so doing you will escape the iron grasp of Mercury, and other baneful poisons. Nay, more, you will become, once more, in possession of that greatest of all earthly blessings—HEALTH.

I desire your prostrate hearts to lift,
Your bleeding wounds to cure,
And with the treasures of Nature's gift,
Relieve the rich and poor.

The people of MONTREAL and Surrounding Country are respectfully informed that the well-known and justly-celebrated INDIAN HERB DOCTOR,

FRANCIS TUMBLETY, FORMERLY OF ROCHESTER, N.Y.,

Can be consulted, and his safe and efficacious Medicines from Nature's Garden obtained at No 18, Great St. James's Street, opposite the St. Lawrence Hall, Montreal, C.E. The following is a list of Chronic Complaints which are treated by him with unparalleled success.

Diseases of the Lungs, Heart, Liver, and Throat; Dropsy, Dyspepsia, Fits, St. Vitus' Dance, Rheumatism, Diseases of the Kidneys and Bladder, and all Diseases arising from Impurity of the Blood, such as Scrofula or King's Evil, Erysipelas, St. Anthony's Fire, Cancers, Fever Sores of however long standing, &c., &c., &c.

Also, all other complicated Chronic complaints, which have baffled the science and skill of Calomel Doctors. "A good tree is known by its good fruits," and a good Physician by his successful works.

TESTIMONIAL.

DESPAIRING, read the following, and be convinced! Recommendation of Doctor TUMBLETY by a number of well-known and prominent men of the City of Rochester, N.Y.

"TO ALL WHOM THIS MAY COME.—We, the undersigned citizens of Rochester, N.Y., do hereby certify that we are acquainted with Dr. FRANCIS TUMBLETY, an esteemed fellow-townsman, and learning that he is about leaving for the West, feel desirous of recomending him as a gentleman entitled to public confidence."

CHARLES J. HAYDEN, Mayor of Rochester.	S. W. D. MOORE, Esq., Justice of Rochester.	J. W. TOMPKINS, Esq.	E. DARROW, Esq.
CHARLES J. HILL, Ex-Mayor. "	Ald. G. W. PARSONS, Supt. Gas Works.	J. ROBINSON, Esq.	D. M. DEWEY, Esq.
ASHLEY SAMPSON, late 1st Judge Monroe Co.	H. B. WHITE, Attorney-at-law.	A. K. AMSDEN, Esq.	J. M. FRENCH, Esq.
Rev. J. B. SHAW, Pastor 2nd Pres. Church.	D. ANTHONY, Esq., Insurance Agent.	JAS. McMAHON, Esq.	E. W. ARMSTRONG, M.D.
B. F. BACON, M. D., Western House of Refuge.	JOSEPH CURTIS, Publisher " Daily Union."	DAVID ELY, Esq.	H. BRADLEY, M. D.
WM. H. CHENEY, President of Eagle Bank.	JAMES E. CHENEY, Esq.		

MOST IMPORTANT TO YOUNG MEN!

Whose hollow cheeks, pallid countenances, and attenuated forms, tell the story of their sufferings. They should lose no time in consulting the INDIAN HERB DOCTOR, at No. 18, Great St. James's Street, opposite the St. Lawrence Hall, Montreal, C.E.

TO FEMALES, YOUNG AND OLD, MARRIED OR SINGLE!

If you are suffering with any Disease peculiar to your sex, you will do well to consult, without delay the Indian Herb Doctor, F. TUMBLETY. The experience and success of several years' practice justifies him in saying, without the least boast, that he has not his superior America in the treatment of Female Complaints.

The cover of Tumblety's pamphlet of testimonials he published in Montreal, Canada, in 1857. (*Stewart P. Evans Archive*)

already a surfeit of practitioners and, to have the impact he wanted, he would have to go somewhere he was unknown and where there was far less competition. Emulating the methods of Lyons and shamelessly copying much of the content of his literature, Tumblety travelled to Canada and heralded his arrival in the press as 'the Great Indian Herb Doctor' in 1856.

Tumblety travelled across southern Ontario offering his services as the Herb Doctor to the communities he passed through. During this time a strange encounter occurred between Tumblety and a patient named as Mrs Carden. While on a professional call to her house in London, Ontario, it was claimed, Tumblety had asked her to brush some dust from his coat. Considering this an insult she had Tumblety arraigned before the mayor in May 1856, who agreed with her and meted out a fine of £5 to Tumblety.[131] It seems there was more to the case than was reported; perhaps a matter of decency that would have besmirched the married lady concerned if it had been reported in the press.

Tumblety moved on to Toronto in late 1856. Initially working out of the International Hotel, he then opened offices at 111 King Street where he displayed, as a sign, a large pair of buck horns, which he claimed were presented to him by an Indian chief named 'Sundown', a savage of the plains with whom he was 'intimately acquainted'.[132] His adverts also upped their game, featuring testimonials from 'cured' clients, and he even branched out into a mail order service. But his past was catching up with him. Before the days of mass media, news would travel by word of mouth, newspapers and broadsides. News of mountebanks and charlatans would often follow them in the form of rumours, but if they were exposed in newspapers they would have little defence and would usually move on. In December 1856 Tumblety was consulted by Adolphus Binkert about his facial eruptions, only to be informed by Tumblety that he was suffering from advanced consumption and did not have very much longer to live, but that Tumblety could cure him for $50. Binkert could not afford to pay that amount of money but persuaded Tumblety to treat him in exchange for his gold watch and a promissory note for the excess. Magnanimously, Tumblety acquiesced, and gave him the medicine, advising Binkert to see a priest and get absolution lest the medicine not work!

It was not long afterwards that Binkert happened upon a newspaper that ran an exposé on Tumblety, describing him as an 'unprincipled and wicked imposter' – the incensed Binkert took Tumblety to court. The hearing was postponed until March 1857 and it appears there was an out-of-court settlement.[133] Tumblety did continue to practice in Toronto but soon began planning his next move, and in September Montreal beckoned.

Some 543 kilometres away from Toronto, Tumblety took rooms at 18 Great St. James Street, Montreal, and, as ever, he invested heavily in regular advertising. Typical of these adverts was this one published in the *Montreal Pilot* on 14 September 1857:

Listen to the voice of Truth and Reason and be Profited by it

The time has come that all who will, can escape the iron grasp of Mercury and other mineral poisons, by calling without delay to see the well-known and justly celebrated Indian Herb Doctor F. Tumblety, who will remain at No. 18 Great St. James Street, nearly opposite the St. Lawrence Hall, a few doors below the post office, from 1st September to 1st May next, to administer those only true and safe medicines from Nature's garden which has for its author the great and All-wise Physician above!

The following diseases can be cured by Dr. T. in the most obstinate stage of their existence, viz; Diseases of the Lungs, Heart, Liver and Throat. Also Dyspepsia, Dropsy and all Diseases of the Blood, such as Scrofula, Erysipelas, Salt-rheum, Fever-Sores and all other Chronic complaints of years standing.

P.S. – The Doctor will also give particular attention to all diseases peculiar to females and children.

The poor will be liberally considered.

OFFICE, No. 18 GREAT ST. JAMES STREET, A FEW DOORS BELOW THE POST OFFICE.

(Nearly opposite St. Lawrence Hall.)

N.B. – Persons residing at a distance wishing to consult the doctor can do so by letter, postpaid, enclosing One Dollar, if they wish for an answer.

All letters of this nature will receive immediate attention.

Letter should be directed in a plain, bold hand to the Indian Herb Doctor, F. Tumblety, Montreal, C.E.

The problem for Tumblety was that such a high-profile arrival of a new doctor drew flack from the extant medical practitioners in the community, or perhaps something of his reputation had preceded him. In any case, a letter was published in the local press:

Sir, – When a new 'Doctor' takes up his residence amongst us, apparently without or perhaps Colonial Diploma, should not the medical men of the city call the attention of the Chief Magistrate to the fact?

Failing redress in that quarter, let them find out a case where some poor unfortunate being has perhaps been made miserable for life by swallowing some horrible mixture destructive to both stomach and bowels, and thereon take legal proceedings.

I am, Sir, our obedient servant, CIVIS[134]

Shortly after his arrival complaints were lodged with the police that Tumblety had been distributing pamphlets and medicines associated with female conditions, named in the press as 'Dr. Tumblety's Private Medical Treatise'. It was said he circulated among these 'young girls and lads especially' and contained such information and language 'such as no parent would wish his young children to peruse'.[135] There had also been rumours in both Toronto and now in Montreal that Tumblety was an abortionist[136] and it had become currency on the streets of Montreal that he had administered remedies to women in the city for that purpose – a felony that carried a prison sentence in Canada. The police investigated and laid a trap on 22 September; the *Montreal Pilot* recounted what happened:

> Detective Simard of the Government Police paid a visit to Dr. Tumblety at his office in Great St. James Street, and enquired from him whether he could give any remedies to procure a miscarriage, as there was a young girl of his acquaintance in the family way.
>
> Doctor Tumblety replied that he could, but inquired whether the intended patient was a Protestant or a Catholic, to which he received an answer that she was a Protestant, whereupon the doctor said he would assist her. Simard then inquired his terms, which he stated would be $20 cash. The detective then left, promising to come back the next day, and in the meantime stated that he would inform the young girl of what had taken place. On Tuesday morning Simard returned and informed Dr. Tumblety that the young girl was afraid to take his medicines unless she was assured by the Dr. in person that there was no danger to her own life. He then left. A little after twelve the same day he returned to the doctor's office accompanied by a young girl, about seventeen years of age, named Philomene Dumas, who stated she was in an interesting condition. After being questioned by the Doctor regarding her symptoms, she got from him a bottle of medicine and a box of pills, and was assured they would make her all right and relieve her from her present condition. Before leaving the doctor's office she drank some of the medicine. Simard then paid the Doctor his fee of $20, and left in company with the young girl.
>
> Almost four hours after this he was arrested by the High Constable, on the warrant of C.J. Coursol, Esq. Inspector and Superintendent of Police.[137]

Tumblety took no chances and hired Bernard Devlin and Lewis Drummond, two of the foremost lawyers in Montreal, for his defence. The case opened before magistrate Charles Coursol at the police court on 25 September. Significant testimony came from the chemist, Mr John Birk, who had been given a bottle of the medicine in question to analyse and 'found that it contained some black helebore [sic] or heleboreen and a small quantity of syrup. The black helebore is a medicine which druggists never sell without a prescription from a medical man; for it is known to be a strong medicine, used to cause miscarriage. He had also examined a box of pills carefully which were sent to him, and found that they contained Cayenne pepper, aloes, oil of savine, and cantharadies.'[138] Birk stated that in his experience, 'aloes, oil of savine and cathardies, have the effect of procuring abortion'.[139] A Dr Picault and a Dr Sutherland then gave evidence on the effects of hellebore, confirming that its violent action on the stomach and bowels was capable of producing abortion. Sutherland pointed out, 'and moreover, that the effect of a combination of medicines, such as are said to be contained in the pills, tend to render the action of the former less uncertain'.[140]

Matters looked black for Tumblety as the court was adjourned for the day. During the second day of the hearing evidence given by Kenneth Campbell, an assistant chemist who made pills for Tumblety, testified that:

> a young man representing himself to be in the employ of Dr. Tumblety, came to the shop of Johnston Beers and Co., known as the Medical Hall, and handed me a paper containing a prescription for making about eleven and a half ounces of pill mass. This mass was to contain five ounces of socotrine aloes, one half ounce cast steel soap, one ounce gamboge, One ounce colicinth, one ounce extract of gentian, one ounce mandrake, two ounces capsicum, one half drachm oil of peppermint. This was made and taken by our porter to Dr. Tumblety's office. We made no liquid for the doctor. He has seen in the Police Office two pills, said to have been analised [sic] by Mr. Birk, and he believed they were made from the above prescription, which he made. In the preparation which he made for Dr. Tumblety, there was neither oil of savine nor cantharadies.[141]

Campbell also examined some fluid analysed by Mr Birk. But could not, by the taste or smell at least, detect any black hellebore in the medicine.

The case was sent to be heard before the grand jury on Friday 23 October; Tumblety was only granted bail on the third application. During the interregnum between the hearing and Tumblety's appearance before the grand jury, samples of the medicine and pills were sent by order of the Honourable Procurator for Lower Canada for examination by François Alexandre Hubert LaRue, Licentiate of Medicine and Professor of Legal Medicine, Toxicology and Hygiene at the Laval University of Quebec, who made a thorough toxicological examination of them. In summary, his findings were that there were no significant quantities of any toxic elements found in the pills or medicine supplied to him and, as a result, the trial was thrown out as 'no bill'.

Tumblety's adverts continued to appear through the period of his trial and in the aftermath he attempted to restore his damaged reputation in Montreal, flooding the newspapers with adverts where he spoke of the 'foul and criminal conspiracy by which it was sought to ruin my character and degrade me in your esteem'.[142] A pamphlet of testimonials presenting the names of dignitaries of Rochester in New York who 'were desirous of recommending him as a gentleman entitled to public confidence' on the cover, with testimonials from residents of the Canadian cities of London, Brantford, Hamilton and Toronto inside appeared,[143] and a new broadside published in December 1857 named almost forty people of Montreal who were prepared to sign certificates of attestation saying that he had 'cured' them using his medicines, and from such diverse ailments as rheumatism, consumption, scurvy, blindness, jaundice, 'female complaint' and palpitation of the heart.[144]

Although a number of the testimonials to him were not quite as he would have his public believe, and some were outright fabrications, it seems that no matter what mud was flung at Tumblety there were still those who believed in him and held him in some esteem. The damage was, nevertheless, done and Tumblety continued his odyssey in Canada, crossing to the United States and Boston in September 1859 and then back to Saint John, New Brunswick, Canada, in late June 1860, where his newspaper adverts announced:

> The Indian Herb Doctor from Canada has arrived and may be consulted free of charge at his Rooms in the American House, King Street. The Doctor will describe disease and tell his patients the Nature of their Complaints of Illness without receiving any information from them.[145]

Tumblety, the man, also left a lasting impression and would be recalled years later as 'a tall, handsome man and a beautiful rider' who would 'canter along like a circus man' on a beautiful white horse with a couple of greyhounds following him.[146] Tumblety's problem was, yet again, those who saw his high-profile adverts and behaviour and decided to look a little closer at him and, in particular, his qualifications. Tumblety always signed his name with the letters MD boldly written after, and he used the appellation 'Dr'. But he had no qualifications to back this up and in 1860 he was taken to court in Saint John on Friday 10 August for misrepresenting himself to the public. He was fined $20 and 30s 6d costs and ordered to desist from using the letters MD in association with his name or practice.[147]

A few other newspapers, particularly those who had experiences of Tumblety in the past, picked up on the story and saw it as an opportunity to get a sideswipe in about the lack or regulation of medical practitioners in the city:

> Tumblety Fined!
> Read this: Tumblety, a resident of Boston, who has written M. D. after his name in that city with impunity, did the same thing in St. Johns, N.B. on Friday last, and got fined $20 for his impudence. The Medical Act in that Province does not tolerate any but regular practitioners.
>
> What outside barbarism. How ignorant people are 'away down East?' We know better here. Let Tumblety come here. Does anyone suppose he will get fined? By no means. If he knows no more about medicines, than some of the convicts of our police court, and has a full share of impudence, he can here acquire a most glorious patronage until one more ignorant arrives.[148]

Back in Saint John, Tumblety continued to advertise his services, showing his name without the MD. He would not go down without a fight, however, and immediately set about getting the judgement overturned. Incredibly, he achieved this when Judge Robert Parker formally reversed the decision on 10 September.[149] Tumblety may have won that courtroom battle but a more serious incident was just around the corner. Fifty-nine-year-old James Potmore had been suffering with an increasingly painful disease of the kidneys and from gravel in his urine for over ten years, and had recently been unable to carry out his work as a carpenter. Seduced by Tumblety's adverts and their promises of cures for longstanding ailments, Potmore applied to him and purchased two bottles, each containing about a gill of medicine 'that looked like water'. Potmore took them back to his Sheffield Street home; what happened next was reported from his wife's testimony at the inquest:

> He [Potmore] took a teaspoonfull [sic] of this in water three times a day. When first he took it he cried out that 'that would burn the heart out of a man'. He continued, however, to take it for nine or ten days regularly. He always complained of the same burning sensation in the stomach after taking it, and he lost his appetite, which previously was good. On the 17th [September] he went to Dr. Tumblety again, and brought another bottle of medicine which looked like the former, and which he took in the same way. After he used this he vomited and grew so sick that he had to take to his bed. He could then eat nothing. She went for Dr. Tumblety to see him, and when he came to the house she charged him with having killed her husband by the medicine he had given him. She pointed to the bottles on the table, and said the medicine was there, and she meant to show it to the doctors. He said very well, and took a bottle up and smelled it, and then put it down again. He told her to apply hot water fomentations over her husband's kidneys, and she did so. He then went away, promising to send a balsam at 4 o'clock to settle his stomach, and immediately after he was gone she missed the bottles. She told her husband Tumblety had taken the bottles, and he said let the villain take them. She had not tasted the medicine, and had no idea what it was. No one was in the room during this time but her husband, herself and Dr. Tumblety. Dr. Tumblety did not send the balsam, nor did he return, but he sent word he was busy. Dr. Humphreys [sic] was then called in, and Dr. Botsford saw her husband some hours before he died. While sick at this time he did not suffer much from his old complaint, but chiefly from the pain in his stomach.[150]

Dr Humphrey, who had attended Potmore on a former occasion, was called in on the night of Wednesday 26 September and found him speechless and barely alive, suffering from acute inflammation of the stomach. Potmore died later that night and Mrs Mary Potmore called for the arrest of Tumblety for poisoning her husband. Dr Humphrey and Dr Botsford made a post-mortem examination the following day. They found the lungs sound but the kidneys 'disorganised', and evidence that the deceased had suffered from calculus or stone, but were left with the firm opinion that the immediate cause of death had been acute inflammation of the stomach.

The inquest opened before Coroner William Bayard MD on Thursday 27 September and was adjourned for making an analysis of the stomach. On Friday 28 the doctors reported that Potmore's death 'was not a necessary consequence of his old disease, and did not arise from it' and were careful to point out, 'according to the highest medical authorities, inflammation of the stomach is rarely or ever idiopathic, or arising from natural causes, but is the result of the introduction of some powerful irritant into the stomach'.[151]

Although satisfied that in this instance the inflammation was caused by some acid, or other irritant introduced into the stomach, the doctors would not swear to it; furthermore, they could find no such substance in the stomach when they made the examination. However, the coroner concluded to the jury that he agreed fully with the medical experts' opinion. The jury returned a verdict of manslaughter.

Tumblety was conspicuous by his absence from the inquest on Friday. Shortly after 9 p.m. the previous night Tumblety had left the American House where he lodged wearing a cloak, a cap, grey pantaloons and riding boots, and lit his cigar as he passed its proprietor. He strode away purposefully, and met up with his clerk, James Hamilton, in much the same way they had done many times for a house call before. Tumblety did not mention the inquest but gave Hamilton instructions to pay his bills and said he would telegraph him where to send his trunks, they then rode together to the suspension bridge that spanned the Reversing Falls near the mouth of the Saint John River. Here they parted. Tumblety told Hamilton was going to Calais, Maine, but told him to keep that information secret and, with a swish of the long white tail of his beautiful horse, he rode into the night never to return.[152] Tumblety would spend the rest of his life as a fugitive from the law.

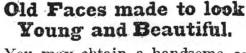

Dr. Tumblety's Pimple Banisher.

Old Faces made to look Young and Beautiful.

You may obtain a handsome complexion, exempt from Pimples, Blotches, &c., by using DR. TUMBLETYY'S PIMPLE BANISHER. Price One Dollar per Bottle. Sent by mail or Express to any address. Office 499 Broadway, New York.

Advert for Dr Tumblety's Pimple Banisher published in *Harper's Weekly*, 5 October 1861.

As the new decade of the 1860s emerged, Tumblety was to be found back in New York and using the popular magazines *Harper's Weekly*, *Frank Leslie's Illustrated Newspaper* and *New York Illustrated News* to advertise Dr Tumblety's Pimple Banisher, available at a $1 a time mail order from his office at 499 Broadway. War, especially civil war, is a time when popular fears can peak and trade on the black market is rife, and those who could exploit either or both can make a lot of money very quickly. So, in 1861, as the clouds of the American Civil War were gathering, Tumblety was drawn to Washington.

Tumblety would claim in his self-published accounts of his life he 'partially made up my mind to tender my professional services as surgeon in one of the regiments' when General George B. McClellan was appointed commander of the Army of the Potomac.[153] Having made enquiries, Tumblety stated he 'had the assurance from head-quarters that they would be cheerfully received' and was furnished by McClellan with passes 'to go and come where and when I pleased'[154] but, experiencing 'a decline of health of an alarming character',[155] Tumblety claimed he abandoned his attempts to enter the army. There is, however, evidence to suggest Tumblety did not entirely detach himself from the military. There may be some truth in this as General McClellan was himself known to subscribe to 'alternative medicine'.[156] Either way, it did not stop Tumblety wearing a style of clothing akin to a uniform. An article published in the *Rochester Daily Union and Advertiser* in 1881 recalled:

> when he was next heard from by Rochester men he was parading himself as one of General McClellan's staff at Washington. He was not on the staff, but dressed as near like an officer as he dare, and would follow the General's staff on horseback at a safe distance. When the Thirteenth Regiment was at Fort Corcoran, Tumblety came around mounted on a fine Arabian horse ...[157]

Similar recollections came from Edward Haywood:

> I saw him here in Washington and he was putting on great style. He wore a military fatigue costume and told me he was on General McClellan's staff. Lieutenant Larry Sullivan, who belonged to a Rochester regiment, came up to him one day. He tried to palm the same tale off upon Sullivan, but the latter being perfectly familiar with McClellan's staff, told the imposter plainly just how great a liar he was. During the war and for some time after Tumblety remained in Washington and played the 'doctor' as he had done in Detroit. He got up some sort of a patent medicine, and at one time the walls were covered with large posters advertising the virtues of the Tumblety Pimple Destroyer. He must have made money, for he was able to spend plenty and live in the most extravagant elegance.[158]

Tumblety also had a lucrative black-market sideline: selling forged discharge papers to soldiers at between $8 and $10 dollars a time. While in Washington Tumblety did make quite an impression but when his military-style attire led to the rumour that he was on McClellan's staff, and it was even reported he was his chief medical officer, this led to enquiries being made by the press. The rumours were quashed,[159] at least for the time being, and Tumblety became a figure of mockery, as reported in the *Weekly Despatch*:

DR. TUMBLETY IN TROUBLE AGAIN

Dr. Tumblety, who has been cutting large figures about Washington for the past six or eight months, and who was reported at one time to holding the position of Senior Surgeon on the staff of General McClellan – an idea that was probably created by the superb air of distinguished importance that the fellow knows how to wear – has come to grief, it appears, and is having his pretentious charlatanry exposed. The proprietor of a place of amusement in Washington called 'Canterbury Music Hall', has had the audacity, it seems, to make the 'eccentricities' of the Doctor a subject of dramatic ridicule, producing upon his stage a roaring farce entitled 'Dr. Tumblety's First Patient'. Such an outrage upon his magnificent dignity was not to be tolerated by Dr. T. of course, and he has brought suit against the presumptuous manager for libel.[160]

The article concluded with a brief portrait of Tumblety at that time:

It appears that Tumblety has been running a prosperous career in Washington. It will be strange if the present suit does not result in its being, as the slang phrase has it, 'played out'. The Doctor, who, by the way, is a very handsome man, is rather eccentric and odd in his manners, appearing at times on the streets dressed as an English sportsman, with tremendous spurs fastened to his boots, and accompanied by a pair of grey hounds lashed together, and at other times in full highland costume. His skill as a physician, however, is undoubted, his practice in Washington, being very extensive, and among the higher classes of society.

Wherever Tumblety went trouble was never far behind. The military authorities had begun an investigation into black-market discharge certificates: Tumblety got wind of the trail leading to him and fled Washington for Philadelphia in May 1863. Here a rather curious incident occurred. Tumblety went to the police and filed an affidavit claiming a man named St Clair had stolen a gold medal presented to him by the citizens of Montreal and worth $800 from his rooms. A warrant was issued and St Clair, who claimed his real name was Joseph Aspinwall, was arrested and brought into custody. Tumblety then turned up at the police station to claim the medal had been returned after someone slipped it under the door of his office. St Clair was released but Tumblety was not going to get off lightly. He had aroused suspicion since his arrival and he was rebuked by Police Chief Franklin for putting an innocent man behind bars. Franklin further considered Tumblety an imposter and perhaps even a rebel spy! The Philadelphia authorities were also dissatisfied with Tumblety's behaviour and a warrant for his arrest on a charge of perjury was issued by the mayor on 1 July.[161] But when the lawmen came looking for him Tumblety had fled again.

Tumblety had returned to his old stomping ground of New York by the time the draft riots erupted in mid-July 1863. The rioters were predominantly working-class men, many of them from the immigrant Irish population in the city, and there was much indignation among them that they should be compelled to fight for their new country. In the aftermath of the riots Tumblety, became conspicuous for his public stance as an Irish patriot and spoke before well-attended indignation meetings on East Broadway.

Tumblety was in Albany in September, and by October he had established offices in Brooklyn at 181 Fulton Street, near Nassau; his arrival did not go unnoticed:

> Fulton Street was put into a state of the most feverish excitement by the appearance of a very tall, muscular man, with a huge black moustache, who was in the habit of promenading the street every day between ten o'clock and twelve, and sometimes in the afternoon. What made his appearance so remarkable was the style of his habiliments, which were decidedly outré. On his first appearance, he generally wore nankeen pants, and in the course of a few days he came to be styled the 'nankeen swell', &c. He was generally accompanied in his perambulations by a huge greyhound, which was in the habit of taking the most of the walk by running against ladies and gambolling around the 'nankeen' individual, in a style which often resulted disastrously to the dresses of ladies whom the man and dog happened to meet. All this display, however, was made with a motive, and, in a few days, by copious posters, handbills, &c., the man in the 'nankeen pants' was merged in.[162]

Around a year after his arrival a disenchanted patient demanded a refund when the medicine did not have the desired effect, the *Brooklyn Daily Eagle* took up the story:

> THE INDIAN DOCTOR IN COURT. – The case of the Indian Doctor, Francis Tumblety, or as the Court spelled it, Tumbletoe, was called on before Justice Perry yesterday afternoon. The Doctor appeared in his usual resplendency, his mustache having a slight upward curl of defiance. He was accompanied by his cane and friend Parmenter. The 'yaller dorg' was still missing. Fenton Scully, the asthmatic complainant, being placed in the stand, swore that the Doctor promised to cure him complete for $20; that he paid $14 on account and received a liberal supply of medicine. He took the medicine home and applied it internally, but got worse instead of better; he then came to Brooklyn

to see the Doctor again, and told him that the medicine made him worse; that the Doctor refused to have anything at all to say to him, and finally kicked him several times in the ribs and knocked him down stairs. Per contra the Doctor produced two witnesses, who magnanimously swore that the Doctor never touched Scully, that the latter was disorderly in his behavior, drove several patients out of the office, and that the Doctor, after politely requesting him to leave, took him by the arm and led him out. The balance of the evidence being in favor of defendant, the Justice dismissed the case.[163]

Some say the only bad publicity is no publicity, but Tumblety was on the verge of proving that adage wrong. Even though the case against him had been dismissed, a reputation for assaulting dissatisfied patients was bound to impact upon trade, particularly when there were other similar providers available. To make matters worse, the back-street side of Tumblety's doctoring seemed to catch up with him as his closet trade of performing abortions became known to such a degree that the rumours were printed in the press – it was time for Tumblety to move on again.

After a few months in New York, Tumblety subsequently caught a steamer up the Mississippi River to St Louis, arriving there in January 1865. Initially working out of the prestigious Lindell Hotel, Tumblety then set up offices at 52 Third Street. As ever, his dress attracted the attention of the public and the authorities, particularly in a military area in a time of civil war, and he was arrested by members of the Provost Guard for impersonating a federal officer in March 1865; perhaps the local military had just had enough of him poncing about assuming the airs and graces of officers who were really were doing something for their cause. In *A Few Passages in the Life of Dr Tumblety* he wrote of the incident:

> I was informed of some eligible landed property for sale, near Carondelet, in Missouri, and one day I visited it with the intention, if it suited me, of making a purchase. While there, I was unceremoniously arrested and incarcerated for two days, for no other offense, that I could learn, than that I was 'putting on foreign airs', riding fine horses, dressing in a semi-military style, with a handsome robe, high patent leather boots, and spurs; that I kept a large greyhound, sported a black moustache; and, in short, as one of my gallant captors affirmed, 'You're thinking yourself another God Almighty, and we won't stand it.'
>
> However, as there was neither treason, murder, arson, or any other hanging or penitentiary crime in all this, and as I fortunately had an influential friend at hand, I was, after, as I have said, an imprisonment of a couple of days, set free, once again.[164]

It was, however, his rivals in medical practice, rather than the military, that Tumblety was to blame for occasioning his arrest.

Tumblety claimed he continued to move within military circles and even, in his 1866 memoir, that he had been introduced to Abraham Lincoln through 'a distinguished officer' with whom he had become acquainted in Boston, Massachusetts,[165] and was 'constant attendant at the President's levees' in

A poignant cartoon of the devil tempting John Wilkes Booth to carry out the assassination of President Abraham Lincoln, 14 April 1865.

Washington.[166] In later editions of his memoir, Tumblety's claim to friendship with Lincoln is enlarged upon and includes the reproduction of a letter of introduction allegedly written by Lincoln in 1863, in which he described Tumblety as 'an esteemed friend of mine'.[167] In contrast, in the fraught aftermath that followed Lincoln's assassination by John Wilkes Booth on 14 April 1865, Tumblety was far from being regarded as a friend of the president!

Booth had not acted alone – his actions had been part of a larger conspiracy whereby the top three members of the Federal government would all have been eliminated on the night of 14 April to help the Confederacy's cause. Booth's fellow conspirators were identified as George Andreas Atzerodt, who was to kill the vice-president Andrew Johnson, and Lewis Powell and David Herold, who had been assigned to kill William H. Seward, the secretary of state.

Atzerodt lost his nerve and did not attempt to kill Johnson, whereas Herold led Powell to Seward's residence. Seward had suffered painful injuries of a broken jaw and arm after suffering a carriage accident earlier in the month and was at home convalescing. Powell bluffed his way in, claiming he had brought medicine for Seward from Dr Verdi and, having gained entry to Seward's bedroom, stabbed him repeatedly. Seward was severely wounded but the splint to his jaw deflected what could have been a fatal blow to his neck. The noise of the attack and Seward's cries woke the household and hearing the commotion from within Herold rode off. Powell also made his escape but a manhunt for the assassins saw them all captured soon after. Then came the repercussions – as the search for any others involved in the conspiracy ensued.

It soon became known that Herold had worked as a pharmacist's assistant and as clerk to a doctor – this was to be the root of Tumblety's problems. An unidentified boy aged about 15, who was arrested in Brooklyn on a charge of theft, offered information pertinent to the Lincoln conspiracy in an attempt to lessen his punishment. The boy claimed that he had known Booth and had acted as an errand boy for David Herold, who had lived in Brooklyn and had been the attendant of a physician who formerly resided there.

The *Brooklyn Daily Eagle* ran 'The Assassination – An Accomplice Arrested in this City' and identified, 'this great "medicine man" who called himself Blackburn was in reality named DR. TUMBLETY, and that the change in his name was a matter not of choice, but of necessity, growing out of some matters which transpired before his arrival here'.[168] The article goes on to discuss the behaviour of Tumblety and two other men associated with him in Brooklyn:

Besides the doctor these rooms generally had two other occupants and it is of one of these that this article is written. These two men were the hangers on or dependents of the doctor, occupying different positions, however, in his esteem. The taller of them was treated by the doctor as a sort of confidential valet, while the other one, who was shorter and of a stouter build, performed the duties of hostler to the two stylish looking piebald horses, on which the doctor and his confidential valet were wont to excite the admiration of foolish females. The most remarkable thing about the doctor's establishment was the manner in which his wardrobe was distributed. Almost every day the doctor had on some new garment, and on the same day, the one which he had worn on the previous one would be seen on the back of his valet, and the next day from the valet to the hostler, and from thence for aught we know to the second hand clothes' dealers. Everybody who has been in the habit of travelling in Fulton street during the past year, will have a distinct recollection of the doctor and his valet, and it was at the time a general subject of remark, that the valet seemed to ape almost unconsciously all the airs of his master, and appeared to pay him the same deference which those who generally accompanied them did. This fact will be recalled with fearful distinctness now by many who formerly noticed it, for this accomplice of Booth and Harold [sic], who was arrested as above stated, and who knows the parties well, stated to the police that this soi-distant valet was none other than the notorious Harold who is now awaiting the just punishment of his horrible crime, and it would seem that he had attached himself to the Indian Herb Doctor in the same manner in which he subsequently attached himself to Booth from a womanish sort of admiration for his supposed cleverness.[169]

Tumblety certainly seemed to have the power to draw what the *Eagle* referred to as 'a womanish sort of admiration' from some men, and for anyone who had encountered Tumblety over the years the article would have had a ring of truth about it. The day after the *Eagle* published its story, the *New York Times* reported that the information supplied by the boy informant had been communicated to General Superintendent Kennedy of the Metropolitan Police but, having investigated the matter, he declared the claims to be 'bosh' and ordered the young man's release. He was still held, however, upon the charge for which he was originally arrested.[170]

The problem was that the damage was already done and a number of other newspapers from across America picked up the story and ran it in their own columns without the subsequent rebuttal. Consequently, a warrant for Tumblety's arrest was issued by Colonel James H. Baker, the Union Provost Marshal General of St Louis. Having attended Lincoln's funeral at Springfield, Illinois, on 4 May, the following day Tumblety was promptly arrested at his offices on Third Street and taken to the Provost Marshal where he was held while his offices and apartments were searched. No evidence was found to connect him to the conspiracy. After his captors consulted with Assistant Secretary Charles Dana, Tumblety was transported under escort to Washington for questioning.

No evidence was ever produced to connect Tumblety to the conspiracy, but the issue of his alleged use of the alias Blackburn would present him with another problem. Tumblety's protégé, who rode out from Brooklyn with him on those fine pair of piebald horses, had been a young man named Mark Blackburn, who had been known as J.H. Blackburn in St Louis. The press confused Tumblety with Blackburn but, like so many aspects of Tumblety, we cannot be sure he never used the name Blackburn as an alias.

The press certainly spoke of him in terms of 'the notorious Dr. Tumblety' and repeated the story that he used the alias of Blackburn in numerous reports after his arrest. The Blackburn alias was also mentioned in official correspondence. Colonel John P. Baker, the Provost Marshal General of Missouri, in a report to Assistant War Secretary Dana, having 'carefully examined all his papers … but found nothing in them tending to implicate him with the assassination', still referred to him as 'Dr. Tumblety, alias Blackburn'.[171]

The use of the Blackburn alias that had been ascribed to Tumblety compounded his problems; he was no sooner proved to have no connection with Herold and the Lincoln assassination conspiracy than he was mistaken for Dr Luke Pryor Blackburn, the man accused of what became known as the Yellow Fever Plot. Yellow fever was the scourge of nineteenth-century America: over the years outbreaks of the fever had claimed thousands of lives. The cause of the disease was not known but it was believed to be carried by either the 'fomites' (germs) of infected people or 'miasma' on the air (it was only discovered in 1900 that yellow fever was spread by mosquitos). Dr Blackburn had been praised for his work in the control of the fever in Mississippi and Louisiana, and had travelled to the American colony of Bermuda in September 1864 to assist the local doctors when the fever broke out on the island. On 14 April 1865, Charles M. Allen, the US Consul in Bermuda, gravely announced that he had received intelligence from a double agent that Blackburn had come to the colony not to help fight the disease but to use the opportunity to gather soiled clothes infected with the fever and ship them to cities of the north with the intention of spreading the disease to them. Soon after the announcement a number of trunks were found in St George in the care of Edward C. Swan. The cases were found to contain both clean and soiled clothing and bedding that bore coloured stains and dark spots akin to the distinctive 'black vomit' brought up by those suffering from the throes of yellow fever. At a hearing before a grand jury in St George, testimony from Swan and others revealed that Blackburn had promised to pay Swan $150 per month to store the trunks until the spring, when they were to be shipped to New York and Philadelphia. The American newspapers picked up on the story and soon the newly dubbed Yellow Fever Plot became big news and Blackburn was condemned as a 'vindictive traitor'.[172] Overzealous police in St Louis mistook Tumblety's widely reported alias of Blackburn to point to him as being the author of the plot; he was arrested and thrown into the Old Capitol Prison, and the *New York Tribune* brayed:

> Dr. Tumblety, alias Blackburn, Chief of the Rebel department for the importation of yellow fever, has been brought to this city and is lodged in the Old

Capitol Prison. He is just as vain, gaudy, dirty and disgusting as ever. He wears
the same stunning clothes and is widely suspected that by collusion with others,
he produced his own arrest in this singular allegation, in order to add a little to
his already disreputable notoriety.[173]

A number of other papers joined in, even in Canada the *Hamilton Evening Times*
ran with:

> Tumblety:– It is now stated that the arrest of Blackburn, alias Dr. Tumblety, is
> nothing but a smart advertising dodge on his part by which his 'infallible cures'
> will be better known. He has bamboozled Stanton into putting him into the
> Old Capitol, from which, of course, he will soon emerge innocent, a hero, and
> the demand for his nostrums will be increased at least a hundred fold.[174]

The real Dr Blackburn was arrested in Canada and, having stood trial in Toronto,
was acquitted for lack of evidence. Whether or not there was an actual yellow fever
plot is still being debated, but it was confirmed that Dr Luke Blackburn was a supporter of the Confederate cause. After his trial he did not return immediately to
the United States for fear of prosecution. He did eventually return to the US and
rescued his reputation by working to combat yellow fever outbreaks in Memphis,
Tennessee, Florida and Kentucky; he became governor of the latter in 1879.

Back in May 1865, after three weeks inside the Old Capitol Prison without
charge, Tumblety was also released – livid about what had happened to him. He
immediately set about getting repudiations published in newspapers such as the
Washington Star and the *New York Herald*, where the following appeared:

> After three weeks' imprisonment in the Old Capitol Prison in this city, I have
> been unconditionally and honourably released from confinement by the direc-
> tions of the Secretary of State for War, there being no evidence whatever to
> connect me with the yellow fever or assassination plot, with which some of
> the Northern journals have charged me with having some knowledge. My
> arrest appears to have grown out of a statement made in a low, licentious sheet,
> published in New York, to the effect that Dr. Blackburn, who has figured so
> unenviously in the hellish yellow fever plot, was no other person than myself. In
> reply to that statement, I would most respectfully say to an ever generous public
> that I do not know their fiend in human form named Dr. Blackburn; nor have
> I ever seen him in my life. For truth of this assertion I can bring hundreds of
> distinguished persons throughout the United States to vouch for my veracity,
> and, if necessary, can produce certificates from innumerable numbers of gentle-
> men in high official positions.
>
> While in imprisonment, I noticed in some of the New York and other
> Northern papers a paragraph setting forth that the villain Herold, who now

stands charged with being one of the conspirators in the atrocious assassination plot, was one time in my employment. This, too, is false in every particular, and I am at a loss to see how it originated, or trace it to its origin. For the past five years I have had but one man in my employment, and he is with me yet, his character being beyond reproach. I never saw Herold, to my knowledge, and I have no desire to see him.

Another paper has gone so far as to inform the public that I was an intimate acquaintance of Booth, but this too is news to me, as I never spoke to him in my life, or any of his family.

I do hope the persons which so industriously circulated these reports, connecting me with these damnable deeds, to the very great injury of my name and reputation, will do me the justice to publish my release and the facts of my having been entirely exonerated by the authorities here, who, after diligent investigation, could obtain no evidence that would in the least tarnish my fair reputation.

With these few remarks in justice to myself, I will close by submitting them to the public.

Tumblety left Washington for New York, then went back to St Louis, but he was soon to realise a new start was the best option for him. This time he made his way to Cincinnati where, in addition to his usual adverts in the press, Tumblety produced a booklet entitled *A Few Passages in the Life of Dr. Francis Tumblety*. It contained eighty-two pages of text primarily about his arrest in St Louis, which he embroidered with a dramatic drawing of his arrest on the cover, captioned, 'Kidnapping of Dr. Tumblety. By Order of the Secretary of State for the U.S.'. His narrative does not hold back about how he felt about the incident and, in doing so, affords us a glimpse of how anger and animosity manifested within him:

I cannot trust myself to reflect upon the cruel manner in which I have been treated and the indignity I have suffered, for at such times I feel the hot blood tingling to my finger ends, and it requires a strong effort to calm an indignation which, if allowed full scope, might lead the victim of a tyrannical despot to contemplate redress, by personal chastisement, upon the author of his misfortunes. Thank Heaven! there is considerable philosophy in my composition, and I can bear and forbear – or, at least, bide my time:

'For time at last sets all things even –
And, if we do but wait the hour,
There never yet was human power
Which could evade, if unforgiven,
The patient search and vigil long
Of him who treasures up a wrong.'[175]

The Langham hotel, Portland Place, London, 1865.

The booklet also contained accounts of his life from the beginning of his practice in Canada; his philosophy of medicine; and no less than eighteen pages of testimonials from Toronto, Quebec, Montreal, Boston, New York, St Louis and Cincinnati.

Tumblety made his first foray back across the Atlantic in 1869. He would claim in the new enlarged edition of his autobiographical memoir, published in 1872, 'My tour was not one of mere pleasure, but rather of research in behalf of my profession.' Tumblety's account of his trip is written more in terms of a travelogue, and he described the places he visited in verbose terms very much akin to a guidebook, too much so – in all probability he rehashed most of the accounts he published from guides he found along the way. It seems far more likely that Tumblety, having realised that there were increasing numbers of adverts for eccentric medical products and alternative medicines within the British magazines and newspapers he had seen, came to scout around Britain to essay how rich the pickings could be for the Indian Herb Doctor.

Leaving New York aboard the steamer *Nebraska* on 14 July, Tumblety landed in Queenstown[176] on 23 July.[177] At the time of Tumblety's arrival, Queenstown was one of the major transatlantic ports of Ireland – about a third of all those who immigrated to America in the 100 years or so after 1848, an estimated 2.5 million people, saw the last of Ireland from this port. From here, Tumblety embarked on a brief tour of Ireland, during which he claimed to have visited Cork, Killarney, the Wicklow Mountains and the Curragh of Kildare, and 'remained some time in Dublin, which is really a beautiful city'.[178] Curiously, Tumblety never made any reference in any of his autobiographical memoirs to the fact that he was visiting the country of his birth at this time.

He then went on to London, where he stayed in the prestigious Langham hotel in Portland Place. So far, so good; passenger lists confirm Tumblety had been in Ireland and once back in England a stay in one of the premier hotels of London fits well with Tumblety's *modus operandi*. And what a place The Langham was; built in the Italian style to be the height of elegance both inside and out, it was described as 'not a monster but a leviathan of its kind'. It rose to a commanding 156 feet and had ten floors in all — three underground, including the cellars — and upwards of 600 rooms if the public and hotel staff rooms were included.[179] The hotel employed over 160 staff to attend to its guests. Situated in what its adverts proudly boasted was 'the most healthy, convenient and fashionable position in London', The Langham commanded views of Regent's Park and was in the centre of London's vibrant West End, with Regent Street and Oxford Street, Hyde Park and the Houses of Parliament within easy distance.

The Langham was noted for being particularly popular among American businessmen looking for overseas trade due to the internal problems of their own country in the aftermath of the Civil War.[180] The manger was Captain James M. Sanderson, who had served as a Confederate officer and was described as having 'good social connections' in America. During the war he served as first quartermaster for the 22nd Massachusetts Volunteer Infantry; he published *Camp Fires and Camp Cooking; or Culinary Hints for the Soldier* in 1862 and was promoted to Lieutenant Colonel, Commissary of Subsistence of Volunteers to the First Army Corps, in 1863. Before joining The Langham, Sanderson had been managing hotels in the States for about twenty-five years, including the College Hotel, the Brevoort House on Fifth Avenue and the New York Hotel.[181]

In his autobiography, Tumblety claims that after his stay in London he toured mainland Europe, including Paris where he apparently performed an 'almost miraculous cure' for the advanced case of scrofula suffered by Emperor Louis Napoleon. For this service, Tumblety wrote, he was presented with a *Légion d'honneur*. He then proceeded to Berlin, where he claimed to have spent a week, during which time he was formally presented to King Wilhelm I:

> His Majesty at the first expressed a desire to consult me upon matter pertaining to the United States, and our subsequent converse was as free and affable as between two equals in rank, I was honoured with an appointment upon his medical staff, and the portrait upon the title page of this work is copied from a photograph taken in Berlin at that time, at the instance of the king, and represents me as I appeared in the uniform of the Imperial Guard.[182]

At first glance, the photograph shows Tumblety in the typical attitude of what appears to be a German army officer of the period, complete with pickelhaube, uniform and fur-trimmed coat. Anything more than a cursory look, however, particularly to a trained eye, shows a man in a theatrical costume rather than an authentic military uniform of 1870s Imperial Germany. Closer scrutiny of the image shows it has been retouched with a number of painted details. The badge upon his helmet is not recognisable as one from the continental armies of the period, and the spike appears to be slightly bent to one side; indeed it appears as if Tumblety is actually wearing one of his military-*style* costumes and one of his flamboyant coats with an old pickelhaube and faux badge popped on his head for the photo. On his chest he wears a *Légion d'honneur* – on a bow such as was usually worn by female recipients – along with the gold medallion he claimed had been presented to him by the citizens of Montreal.

Then, upon his return to London (in the conclusion to a tale more akin to the adventures of Baron Münchausen) Tumblety claimed to have encountered none other than Charles Dickens, who persuaded him to delay his return to America by a week to ten days so he may attend a gentleman suffering from 'an affection of the liver'.[183] If all of this does not stretch the bounds of credulity, simply consider the letter Tumblety published in his booklet, purporting to have been written from The Langham hotel in London on 23 August 1869.[184] In it he talks of his forthcoming visit to Paris, whereas the passenger list for the *Nevada* shows he departed homeward for America on 1 September 1869: the necessary travel and time he claimed to have spent in France would have been impossible in the time frame of just eight days.[185]

Tumblety's scouting mission had served him well, however; he knew if he set up as the Indian Herb Doctor in Britain people would read his adverts and think he was some fakir from colonial India, which would have been counterproductive for his purposes. Tumblety realised he would have to tweak his persona. As such, when he returned to England again in 1873 he did not stride down the gangplank and onto the pier at Liverpool as the Indian Herb Doctor; instead, the Great American Doctor had arrived!

6

AFFECTIONATELY YOURS

The Liverpool docks where Tumblety landed in 1873 were a hub of the British export industry. The great granite dock, fronted by imposing warehouses that housed every kind of commodity, stretched for 7¼ miles on the Lancashire side of the river alone. Here shipping from every nation could be found, echoing every tongue spoken on the seas. The dockside was littered with commodities from all over the world and bustled with all types of humanity: there were those who worked, manhandling cargos on and off the great ships; there were those who waited, the rich with their fine luggage and poor with brown parcels and battered cases seeking passage to the far-flung corners of the empire; and there were those who loitered, waiting perhaps for work or with some nefarious intent to pickpocket or steal, their eyes alert for the patrols of the dock police.

A bustling Prince's Landing Stage, Liverpool docks, 1872.

As his ship drew in, Tumblety could not have failed to notice the tide of bricks and mortar that spread for 8 miles on either shore to house the aggregation of human beings eking out their existence in the town; a dense mass of dwellings and long trenches of terraced houses over which seemed to hang a low, broad pall of dun-coloured smoke. The aesthetic and educated Liverpool that Hall Caine loved was a cloistered society, surrounded by these mean streets where poverty, disease and squalor were rife and violence, crime and despair were part of daily life. Liverpool had acquired the unenviable nickname, 'the black spot on the Mersey'.[186]

Tumblety had family near Liverpool; a short distance down the Mersey at Simms Cross in Widnes his sister Bridget lived with her husband, Thomas Brady. Tumblety may well have stayed with or near them upon his arrival in July 1871, before he made his way down to London and checked in to The Langham hotel.

During his stay in England an incident occurred that echoed the theft Tumblety accused young Mr St Clair (aka Joseph Aspinwall) of in Philadelphia ten years previously. In October 1873 Tumblety encountered 18-year-old Henry Carr, a presentable young man who described himself as a carpenter and who lived with his parents at 20 Chichester Road, Paddington. Tumblety told him he wanted a secretary and at a subsequent meeting asked Carr to go away with him. Carr's parents objected to this but he persisted and eventually went to Liverpool with Tumblety. While there, Carr's opinion of Tumblety changed. What passed between them is unclear, but Carr was to state he, 'not liking the gentleman's manner', left him and returned to London.

Back in London, Carr brought a gold chain into the pawnbroker's shop run by a Mr Parr on the Harrow Road, where he offered the chain in pledge. Parr asked how he had come by the chain, was unconvinced by the story and summoned the police. Carr was taken into custody and his case was brought before Marylebone Magistrates Court in December 1873. Carr testified that Tumblety had asked him to take charge of the chain. Henry Carr's father then took the stand. He confirmed his son's statement and produced Tumblety's pamphlet memoir bearing the portrait of Tumblety 'in the uniform of a Prussian officer', stating this was the person who had decoyed his son away. He pointed out that Tumblety 'had lately been stopping at The Langham hotel'. Mr Mansfield, the magistrate, remarked, 'the prisoner had no right to the chain' and that it was to be retained by the police. Carr was then discharged.[187]

The account of Carr's appearance in court probably did not tell the whole story, and the term 'decoyed away' that Carr's father used indicates a particular type of deceit in Victorian parlance. The term was used in newspapers and there had been reports of girls being 'decoyed' down to London by being promised employment as servants or nannies. When they arrived they were manipulated by a variety of devious means into prostitution. In an interview given a number of years later, American detective William Pinkerton's memories of the case endorse this view. Pinkerton stated he had been contacted by Superintendent Shaw of the

Metropolitan Police after Carr had made a counter-statement that Tumblety had attempted to procure him for homosexual purposes. Shaw enquired of Pinkerton if anything was known of Tumblety in the States, his reply was direct: 'I told him that the boy had undoubtedly told the truth, as the vile character the boy gave of the Doctor was just the character that he had a reputation for in the United States.'[188]

Tumblety had taken no part in the prosecution and with the counter-allegations made against him it is hardly surprising he didn't drop by the police station to pick up the chain. Nevertheless, Tumblety began advertising in the Liverpool newspapers from early September 1874, introducing himself with the following advert:

GOOD NEWS FOR THE AFFLICTED – The Great American Doctor, from British America, has arrived and can be consulted at 177, Duke Street. The doctor will describe disease and tell persons the nature of their complaints or illness without receiving any information from them. No charge for consultation or advice.

OUR MOTTO

We use such balms as have no strife
With nature or the laws of life:
With blood our hands will never stain,
Nor poison men to ease their pain.
Our Father – whom all goodness fills –
Provides the means to cure all ills:
The simple herbs beneath our feet,
Well used, relieve our pains complete.
A simple herb, a simple flower
Gulled from the dewy lea –
These, there shall speak with touching power
Of change and health to thee.

To be good looking! Old faces made to look young and beautiful. You may obtain a handsome complexion, exempt from pimples, blotches, &c., by using the Great American Doctor's Pimple Banisher.[189]

In 1874 Hall Caine was 21 years old and making some headway into the world or journalism and the arts. Standing just 5ft 3in tall and slender of build, he began affecting a bohemian dress of shepherd's plaid trousers, soft velvet or tweed jackets, waistcoat and loosely tied artist's cravat. He made the most of his slight resemblance to one of his heroes, Shakespeare, by cultivating his soft red-gold hair in a longer style, brushed back from his distinguished high forehead with a gentle wave, and trimming his darker red beard in the style of the Bard. His appearance would have drawn the eye, while his big, dark brown soulful eyes were particularly engaging. The problem was, Caine's biographer pointed out, 'The state of his health was Caine's constant preoccupation. By the time he reached his majority he was thoroughly psychoneurotic'.[190] From seeing such medical adverts in newspapers and moving in the cultural fringe of Liverpool, it is not surprising that Caine encountered Francis Tumblety and was drawn to him as other impressionable young men had been. Tumblety was around 6ft tall, he was well built, handsome and cultivated a large and impressive black moustache. Aged 43, he still dressed flamboyantly and had acquired a tough skin and years of experience to carry off such an image in a way he thought would add gravitas. Those who were worldly wise could usually see through the pastiche of this deluded and deceitful man, but other, younger men were impressed with his stories of adventure and claims of acquaintance and sway with influential people, and could, very soon, become mesmerised by him. Years later, New York lawyer William P. Burr was to remark of Tumblety, 'once he had a young man under his control, he seemed to be able to do anything with the victim'.[191] Tumblety took Caine into his confidence by showing him aspects of his medical preparations, he also involved him in his business, dictated letters to him and asked him to edit the new edition of his memoirs. However, the Great American Doctor was soon to encounter the first of a series of problems in Liverpool.

True to form, Tumblety's adverts published in the local newspapers were soon including testimonials, but clearly he had not obtained permission from all he named. On 2 November 1874, Tumblety's advert in the *Liverpool Mercury* published the statement, 'My face was covered with pimples and blotches and my blood was very impure. The Great American Doctor, of 177, Duke –street, has cured me.'[192] Attached to this was the name of William Carroll, a carpenter of 2 George's Road, West Derby Road, Liverpool. The testimonial was run again as part of a long list of similar letters of praise for a variety of complaints 'cured' by the Great American Doctor on 12 December, but Mr Carroll was outraged and sued Tumblety for libel, seeking damages of £200. The action was to be brought before a jury at Liverpool County Court in January 1875 but Tumblety's barrister, Mr Devey, had been granted a postponement of the hearing 'on the ground that at the present time, in consequence of a recent matter in which the defendant's name has figured prominently in the newspapers, there might be a prejudice in the public mind with respect to him'.[193] The case was adjourned for a month.

Thomas Armstrong of 1 Duke's Terrace, Duke Street, a client that lived only a short distance from Tumblety's offices, was also named among the testimonials as 'cured of congestion of lungs'; the fact he sent the following letter to Caine implies Caine was known to be associated with Tumblety's business in Liverpool:

Thursday Noon
Mr Cain
    Dear Sir I was rather surprised to find a letter from you stating you had made use of my name I have had Anoyance Enough Concerning the American Doctor and I told both Dr Tumilty [sic] and yourself that my letter should Not

be Published without my consent therefore I hope you will withdraw your reply as far as my name is concerned and oblige

Yours respy
T. Armstrong

In a later letter from Tumblety to Caine it appears Armstrong had threatened Tumblety with legal proceedings for financial compensation but did not see the matter through.[194]

January 1875 was not a good month for Tumblety, as well as the threats of legal suits for slander and libel that hung over him his problems were further compounded by a more serious matter, resonant of the death of James Potmore in 1860. Forty-five-year-old Edward Hanratty of 91 Athol Street, a 'sheeter' employed by the Lancashire and Yorkshire Railway, had been under the care of Dr John Bligh for about two years with congestion of the lungs and heart disease; the doctor would comment 'he had been exposed to cold and damp, and drank more liquor than was good for him'. Hanratty had made sufficient recovery that he had returned to work, but a short while later the old problem was back with a vengeance. Dr Bligh said there was nothing more that he could do and in desperation Hanratty's wife Ann arranged for a cab to take them to the Great American Doctor at his Duke Street rooms on Monday 11 January. Tumblety tapped Hanratty on the chest and said he would cure him for £2 10s, adding he was 'bad in breath'.[195] Pleading they were in reduced circumstances, the couple asked if Tumblety could provide the medicine for any less: he agreed to do so for £2. Tumblety told Ann that her husband would have no medicine until Wednesday. Mrs Hanratty returned on that day, paid him £2 and said her husband 'would require some nourishment'. He supplied a bottle of medicine, some herbs with a piece of paper attached that gave directions of how they should be used and a box of pills, of which he advised Mrs Hanratty to administer four to her husband that night. About 5 p.m. that evening Mrs Hanratty gave her husband a tablespoonful of the mixture. He died at 9 p.m. the same night.

The following day Mrs Hanratty went with her friend Mrs Johnstone to Tumblety and requested a death certificate. He replied he knew nothing about the case and left the room. When he returned about twenty minutes later Mrs Hanratty tackled him again stating 'I know you, if you don't know me.' Tumblety replied 'Oh, is that you?' and handed back 30s. But he did not want to get involved with signing the death certificate.

Hanratty's death was brought before an inquest on Monday 18 January and Tumblety was questioned. Asked if he had examined the deceased Tumblety replied he had sold him medicine, then asked if he knew what had afflicted the man Tumblety said he did not know, repeating he 'only sold medicine and did not know anything about disease' and adding he 'had only come to Liverpool for the purpose of bringing an action for the recovery of some property which he had in Canada'.[196] The post-mortem revealed Hanratty had died from natural causes and produced no evidence of erroneous treatment, but the inquest was adjourned for a week in order that the brain of the deceased be examined and the stomach contents analysed. The examinations revealed nothing more and at the resumed inquest the jury returned a verdict of death by 'natural causes'. However, they left it an open question as to whether death had been accelerated by unskilful treatment and strongly censured the conduct of Tumblety for 'administering medicine, he being in total ignorance of the condition of the patient'.[197]

True to form, Tumblety did not hang around: he fled to London and found lodgings at 58 Margaret Street, a respectable house not far from his usual haunt of The Langham hotel in the west of central London. Tumblety was long gone when the Carroll libel case was called on 23 February and as neither he nor Carroll, nor their lawyers presented themselves in court, the registrar, Mr Hime, directed the case should be struck out.[198]

Tumblety continued to correspond with Caine and we are fortunate that some of the correspondence survived and is preserved in the Hall Caine Papers, held in the library at Manx National Heritage. These letters allow us to gain some insight into the way Tumblety drew young men deep into his power, as well as his mood swings, opinions and rants. The earliest letter to survive from their correspondence reflects this; it is simply headed 'London 28/1/75':

Dear Friend
'There is a great deal done in friendships sacred name'
'It will be found that those that make the most parade of friendship are the least to be trusted.'

For instance, the one who told about my bank after pretended to be my very confidential friend but he has proved himself otherwise but you have proved yourself genuine and I feel under a great obligation and hope some time to be able to make some recompense.

I will correspond with Murphy about the other matter.[199] Will you please fix the book ready for publication and send it to me, also get an estimate for the cost of 10 thousand, when they could be ready etc from Matthews Bros. Or any other establishment in Liverpool as printing is much cheaper than in London.

I am dear friend
Yours sincerely
F Tumblety M.D.[200]

Over the next few letters, Tumblety supplied Caine with material to work from and copies of letters of endorsement he claimed to have received from notable persons including Napoleon III. Significantly, Tumblety's form of address soon become more familiar, with his letter of 1 February being addressed to 'My Dear

Friend' and on 8 February to 'Dear Caine'. Tumblety signed this latter letter with
what was to become his familiar parting words – 'Affectly Yours Francis Tumblety
M.D.'[201] In it, Tumblety also pointed out he had moved to 5 Glasshouse Street,
Regent Street, London. This was another smart address a short distance from
Piccadilly Circus, it was also a notorious cruising ground for picking up homosexuals in Victorian London.[202] Tumblety concluded his letter with an offer for
Caine to travel down to London, at Tumblety's expense, to discuss the publication. Clearly it was only a flying visit, as Tumblety later wrote, 'I am glad to hear
your trip to London has pleased you so much and especially glad to know you
arrived home quite safe. The next time you come here you must be prepared to
stay longer …'[203] The two had also discussed using Caine's old acquaintanceship
with Gladstone, possibly to get an testimonial or even an introduction. In his
letter of 23 February Tumblety enquired, 'I expect by this time you have received
a letter from Mr Gladstone. I suppose you have not forgotten it. It is now almost
two weeks once we had a talk over the matter and that was the principal subject
of conversation.'[204]

The Gladstone matter is not discussed after this, in his letter written the following day Tumblety instead claims his health has taken a sudden turn for the worse
– although this does not stop him from keeping abreast of the news of the Carroll
case or showing his displeasure at the handbill printed by one of his critics:

5 Glasshouse Street
Regent Street. W.
Feb. 24–75
My dear friend

I am so ill that I am not able to crawl out of bed. Enclosed please find some
more matter for the book. I think you are getting with it very well. I am quite
unable to correct proofs or anything else, so do the best you can. I am glad that
the Carroll affair has terminated as it has. It kept us back almost too long, yet
notwithstanding I think that you will agree that it has been the best plan. There
is now no obstruction whatever. As for Robinson's cowardly handbill it would
be well to find out who his printers are and to warn them that they will be
prosecuted for libel. There are some competing establishments! For instance:
the 'Leader' establishment. They would print any libellous hash. I have not been
so ill for 20 years as I am at the present time. I have not taken food of any kind
for over one week. If there any mistakes – attribute them to my illness. I think
you arranged Dr. Kenealy's letter & the rest very well. If you are let alone and
not tormented by anybody you will make the affair a great success. I must conclude wishing you success in this undertaking

Affectly Yours
Francis Tumblety M.D.[205]

Tumblety's booklet, entitled 'Passages from the Life of Dr Francis Tumblety', was advertised in the *Liverpool Mercury* as available from 'Temporary Offices of the Liverpool Lantern, Warrington Chambers, 2, South Castle Street' from mid-March. The subsequent letters to Caine for the reminder of March and April are filled with Tumblety's wrangling with printers over the booklet and handbills. His letter of 16 March was typical of this:

5 Glasshouse Street Regent St. W.

16 March 1875

Dear Friend Cain [sic]

I regret to learn by a letter this morning that the printers have acted so mean. I can't make them do anything. Mr Dunn the young man that was in my employ brought then back over 60,000 handbills that they printed wrong and they refused to take them they told him that if ~~you~~ he would not take them away that they would throw them in the street. I have already overpaid them. I here enclose you £2 to pay them or use it as you like. I hope before you get this that the books may be ready.

Yours Affectly

F. Tumblety M.D.[206]

By 24 March 1875 all was not well with his relationship with the *Liverpool Lantern* offices, who having not been paid by Tumblety ceased to forward letters to him and were concerned by the adverse articles published about him in the *Liverpool Leader* newspaper:

Dear Caine

Your kind letter and packet of books come to hand this morning for which accept my sincere thanks. I told Guion's people to forward my letters by post, you have had enough trouble that way it was not Mr Guion you saw he has a son in law there named Marsh and he manages the business. Mr Guion would not hesitate a moment to let you have my letters but his damned clerks have been reading the Leader so that's what is the matter. I did not mention the errors in the book to cause you pain far from it.

Enclosed you will find £1 which will assist in advertising the book. Posters will do no good the only thing is the newspapers the bill stickers are all rascals and cannot be depended on if you would insert that little paragraph you sent me in the Evening Express to occupy the same place as it did in the Mercury it will be a great victory over them fellows, if you see the manager of the Courier and make arrangements with him about it, anybody else connected with the establishment will do their utmost against it. The Evening Express has an immense circulation 2 pence a line they used to charge me for paragraphs among the reading matter.

I regret very much that you are not able to come to London so that we could have a good time. I hope you will be prepared by the 1st July to take your trip to America your sedentary occupation is enough to make you ill all the time you have so much of it a trip across the ocean will invigorate your muscular system any time you get tired of Liverpool let me know it. I will send you funds to come home here. I see some pleasure every day but I don't enjoy it a bit, if you were with me it would be quite different, now do tell me when you can come. Your advice about the letter I gave to McDevitt and other matters are consoling.

Affectionately Yours

F. Tumblety M.D.[207]

Caine never took criticism well and had been hurt by words from Tumblety and in the Liverpool press about the booklet. On 27 March he wrote to Tumblety doubting his own abilities. Tumblety consoled him:

Dear Friend Caine

Your last letter I received with much pleasure & am astonished at your thinking that there is nothing in yourself to esteem, I found all that was possible to find a man of brains a friend a genious [sic] in fact I will when I meet you next about that defrauder, I know the way you are situated & therefore will not advance further on that topic until you are free. I admire your love towards a mother a loving nature you rise more in my esteem every day, you think too much of the small error I have shown you I have not shown half enough, the person that writes to me I do not know their disease but will attend to them when I go to Liverpool by notifying my arrival there and then will arrange matters &c. I admire your political turn of mind it shows me that I have indeed picked up a Jewell where the Jewel imagines itself to be a stone, do not now heap on the throne small favors until & believe me to be

Your affectionate friend

F. Tumblety M.D.[208]

Tumblety wrote again on 29 March, buoyed up with excitement over the entertainments in London during the Easter holiday:

Dear Caine

I wrote you a hurried letter on Saturday last and it was not such an agreeable letter as I would write if I had time. Captain Boynton the American Swimmer and his friends were here in the room and I was considerably confused I wish you were here during the Holydays. I visited the Crystal Palace, Sanger's Circus, and the Cremorne Gardens in the evening. The last named place was exceedingly gay the weather was splendid. The Bank Holyday is a great institution here The carnivals at Rome are nothing compared with it, you have missed a rare treat.

I hope your health is good and I presume you have enjoyed yourself according
to the limited amusements in Liverpool. Hoping to hear from you soon
I remain,

Yours affectionately
F. Tumblety M.D.[209]

The 'Captain Boynton [sic]' Tumblety mentioned was Paul Boyton, a showman
and adventurer, well known for his feats of open-air swimming. He was in London
carrying out public demonstrations of the 'paddle your own canoe' at Wormwood
Scrubs. The way Tumblety crammed so much of his Easter holiday into the letter
reads rather like one of Tumblety's fanciful accounts from his published memoirs – one cannot but wonder if he did actually attend all the events or simply
copied them from a newspaper and imagined the visit of 'Captain Boynton' and
his friends. Tumblety did not return to Liverpool but sought to have Caine join
him in London and become his protégé, his very own Mark Blackburn in Britain:

5 Glasshouse St
31 March 1875.
Dear Caine,
    Your kind and welcome letter came to hand I received the 'Express' and I am
very much pleased with the paragraph I showed it to one of the reporters of
the 'Times' and he said that gentleman should be in London and I think so too
but I know how you are situated now I think of commencing business here and
I could manufacture better pills than Holloways and I would give all of them
the people a box free of charge in order to introduce them, and let the people
test them and judge for themselves, and all who were not satisfied with the
pills £10 worth given away to the people would break down Holloway's and
Brandreth's besides it would create a fresh sensation
    To do this I must have a partner who can share the profits, there is no place in
the world like England for good pills to make the enterprise a success the pills
must be just what they are purported to be and that's all that's necessary. The
English people all indulge in eating late suppers which produces caustiveness
and they ~~all most~~ must have cathartic pills. My plates are at Mathew Bros and
I shall want them right off, if I conclude to have my Printing done by them
I want no such promises as they made about the book I should like a written
agreement from them and then I could hold them to it, they used to and then
I will receive new life for I will furnish you with funds as fast as the money
comes in. You might talk with some prominent chemist of your acquaintance
as we must have a depot in a popular thoroughfare in Liverpool for the sale of
the pills and if you can negotiate with him or make terms with him in any way
I should like it. I want to hear what you say about that matter. You enclose me
a long advertisement I don't approve of long advertisements it would be a first

rate poster or a large bill to have hung up at the news stands. Shall I return it?
No more at present from

Yours affectionately
F. Tumblety M.D.
Per W.H.

P. S. Glad to hear that your health is better. How about the 'Post' people go for
them and let us gain a victory over them, it will torment the Leader fellow awfully
F.T. M.D.[210]

Tumblety even sent a telegram to Caine on 9 April: 'Come here tomorrow
evening I must see you.'[211] Despite the flack over the booklet, Caine wished to
stay in Liverpool to pursue his literary career and probably used sickness as an
excuse not to take up Tumblety's offer. Tumblety then tempted Caine (with notorious lack of punctuation) by offering a new start with him in America:

5 Glasshouse St
Regent St
Dear Caine
    You know that I got things mixed up a little in relation to the date of Kenealy's
letter half a dozen copies will be all I want
    I am sorry to hear of your illness I hope you will soon be better I do wish to
see you so much
    Now has the thing book is almost finished I hope you will be able to soon
pay a visit here again I have told you on more than one occasion to quit
Liverpool and come with me and I will guarantee you to make more money
by the operation than you will in Liverpool beside your health would be very
much improved I hope that you have been thinking of our anticipated trip
across the Atlantic you have accepted of my invitation and I hope you will have
yourself ready, in proper shape for the voyage it is something you need more
than anything else if you want to come with me soon come now if you like
I have means plenty and if you come with me to you shall everything you want
    It pains me to hear that you suffer. you have had to wrestle with adversity all
your life but you can congratulate yourself you have conquered thats something
that very few young men in England can say it amused me very much to read
your long letter how you can clue into the Details of anything is a caution
Murphy or 10000 such lawyers could not stand before you 5 minutes I must
close this letter hoping you will forgive all the mistakes I have made

I Remain Yours Affc
F Tumblety MD[212]

With plans to visit America afoot, Tumblety's letters suddenly stop and Caine was
concerned enough to write to Thomas Brady to enquire if he had heard from

him. Curiously, at the same time certain events were occurring in Liverpool that may have driven Tumblety into hiding – at least for a while.

On 12 March a 26-year-old named Margaret McKivett had visited Alfred Thomas Heap, a man who called himself a surgeon, at his rooms on Gorton Lane, Gorton Brook, Manchester, to obtain an abortion. McKivett's mother got wind of what her daughter had gone to do and went to the Heap residence where she ran upstairs and found Heap and his housekeeper, Julia Carroll, applying a bottle under Margaret's nose, trying restoring her to consciousness. The mother was alarmed but was quietened by Carroll who said: 'Don't make a noise, a constable might be passing.'

Returned to her home but still in great pain, Miss McKivett had a miscarriage after which she herself died a few days later. A post-mortem examination was carried out and the cause of her death was revealed as peritonitis. Heap was arrested on 17 March and was found to be practising as a 'surgeon' but in reality having neither diploma nor certificate of qualification. The instruments he had used in the abortion were found in a kitchen drawer. Carroll was also arrested and was due to be tried as an accomplice but the grand jury threw out the bill against her. Heap was brought before the Liverpool Assizes on Friday 3 April. In summing up, the learned judge stated 'if the prisoner acted in the way he was said to have done, with the intention of procuring abortion, although there was no intention on his part to cause the woman's death, and death resulted from such act, he was guilty or murder'. The jury retired for twenty minutes and returned a verdict of guilty – Heap was sentenced to death.[213] Heap was then executed at Kirkdale Gaol on the morning of Monday 19 April. The case received high-profile coverage in both local and national press with such headlines as 'Conviction of a Quack Doctor for Murder',[214] 'Murder by a Quack Doctor'[215] and 'Execution of the Manchester Sham Doctor'.[216] With so many aspects of the Heap case resonating with the darker aspects of his own practises it is no wonder Tumblety disappeared for a while.

A letter dated and postmarked 4 May 1875 restored communications between Tumblety and Caine. In it Tumblety wrote affectionately:

Regent Street W.
May 4th 1875
Dear Caine

Though I have been so long silent you have not been absent from my remembrance. The intimate friendship which has subsisted between us for so long a period has prompted me to feel lively interest in all that concerns your welfare and happiness It is not therefore in the mere observance of a cold and formal custom that I at present write but in obedience to the dictates of the truest friendship I mentioned in my last letter to you that unavoidable circumstances would prevent me from answering your communications regularly If you have an idea that I am going any great distance without seeing you first it is a mistake I wish to know how your health is.

Yours very affectionately

F. Tumblety MD[217]

The next letter to survive is undated but was in an envelope postmarked 'London E.C. 21 June 1875', and shows Tumblety was back at the Margaret Street lodgings. The London E.C. (East Central) cancellation rather than the previous London W. (West) cancellations is a curious feature of this subsequent correspondence up to August 1875, as neither Glasshouse Street nor Margaret Street are in the E.C. area, nor, if the suggestion that Tumblety had offices in Charing Cross is correct, would this address attract an E.C. cancel. We are left pondering where he was going on such a regular basis? Could it have been business in the city? Tumblety would later claim he knew London well; perhaps his travels took him to east London too.

Whatever Tumblety was up to, he had fallen out with the distributors of his book in Liverpool:

58, Margaret Street
Cavendish Square
London, W.
Mr T. H. H. Caine
Dear friend,

I have just returned from Brighton and got your kind letter. I am glad to hear that your health is good. I see by the London papers that one of the Liverpool Black Mailers has got himself into trouble, so every dog has his day.

It will be the Lantern fellows turn next, for as it is the stench of him goes up all over the land, and is an offence in the nostrils of all decent, cleanly people.

My address in future will be
58 Margaret Street
Cavendish Square

Yours Affect:

F. Tumblety, M.D.[218]

Whether Tumblety was actually in Brighton all the time between letters cannot be determined, but in his next letter he continued to express his disdain of the Liverpool press:

58 Margaret Street
Cavendish Square
July 13 1875
T. H. H. Caine Esq

Dear Friend

In consequence of being absent from London I could not answer your letter sooner. I am quite surprised to think that a gentleman of your exalted ideas would condescend to read such a sheet as the 'Leader'

I am much pleased to hear that your health is good

Affectly yours
Francis Tumblety MD[219]

Dispensing of his Liverpool distributors – more likely they wished to be rid of associations with him – the adverts for Tumblety's booklet in the Liverpool press changed to:

Passages in the Life of 'The Great American Doctor', Francis Tumblety, M.D. A sketch of an eventful career. With letters from the late Emperor Napoleon, Earls Derby and Granville, Right Honourable B. Disraeli, Right Honourable G. Ward Hunt, Right Honourable John Bright, Marquis of Ripon, Sirs Edward Thornton and C. W. Dike, Abraham Lincoln, Horace Greeley, J. Gordon Bennett, Generals Sherman and Lee, Mr. Fish, Secretary of State, USA, J. A. Roebuck M.P., Mr. Plimsoll, M.P., Sir Wilfrid Lawson, M.P. and others, Price sixpence, post free. All communications to 58, Margaret, Street, Cavendish Square, London.[220]

Tumblety moved shortly afterwards to the smart apartments of Devereux Court, off the Strand. The next surviving letter dates from 4 August when it appears Caine had been forwarding orders for the booklet to Tumblety:

16 Devereux Court
Strand
London
Augst. 4. 1875
My dear Caine
    Your telegram to hand as follows
'Been away from telegram just to'
'hand too late for order very sorry'
'will send first thing tomorrow'
'will this do'
    Yes this will do, I will explain the particulars when I see you
    Trusting you are quite well
    I am

Yours Affec
Francis Tumblety M.D.[221]

It was hardly surprising Tumblety's last missive was sent in such haste. Tumblety was under pressure: he would claim he was low on money and fled to Birmingham where he vented his frustrations upon Caine and, dare I suggest it, mooted a little blackmail about their relationship:

Midland Hotel
Birmingham
Augst. 6 1875
Dear Caine
    Don't trifle with my patience any longer, send me two pounds & our friendly correspondence shall go on independent of the little financial matter, nobody else knows anything about it, there is no fraud being committed on you, as I am not in the habit of telling people my private affairs.
    I got your letter this morning at 16 Devereaux Court, Strand. I felt a little surprised at finding an excuse in it instead of two pounds Matthew Bros have no claim on you I've paid them,
                                                            Yours in haste
                                                            F. Tumblety M.D.
P.S I am stopping here for 3 or 4 days don't fail to send P.O.O here at once[222]

The next letter shows how quickly Tumblety's mood could swing: he managed to sort out lodgings and explained himself, but did not apologise:

50 Union Passage
Birmingham
Augst. 10th 1875
My dear Caine
    Many thanks for the P.O.O which I received this morning, you may have thought my last note imperative but the fact is I really required the money. Invested what funds I had & I could not get a farthing of it out, I will do you a better favour before long
                                                            Yours Affec
                                                            Francis Tumblety M.D.[223]

Tumblety now vented his rage in a diatribe about the editor of the *Liverpool Leader*, in the process exposing his darker side:

50 Union Passage
Birmingham
Augst. 14 1875
Dear Caine
    The proprietor of that filthy sheet 'The Leader' is the Champion Black Mailer

of England. He is one of the most infamous scoundrels ever vomited upon the earth from the basement story of hell. He would do well to get himself out of the country as soon as possible, for as it is the stench of him goes up all over the land & is an offence in the nostril of all decent & cleanly people. He is worse than the Colorado potato beetle. When the villain shuffles off his mortal coil there will be a great rejoicing in Pandemonium. Since that eventful day when Adam & Eve manufactured clothes out of fig leaves there has been many large gatherings on earth and in hell, but the cavalcade that will turn out in the infernal regions to greet Richardson The Champion Black Mailer of England will be the largest ever paid to a congenial spirit, I think he is destitute of all belief in the Christian religion and his little soul steeped in sin will go straight to the devil, who has got a mortgage on him He is revengeful & malignant & so stubborn in opinion that he rarely changes his views or relinquishes a purpose. He is as remorseless & cruel as a Comanche Indian. It would be a libel on the dog to call him a brute. He hungers for blood & belongs eminently to the animals called cold bloods, so impulses ever stirred the feeble & sluggish currents of his moral or mental nature. The fiend sometimes bursts into wild demonic laughs, but thank God who would not permit the builders to occupy the impious tower on the plains of Shinah will punish this beastly Black mailer Richardson His hungry editor the gutter snipe who writes his diabolical articles looks like a superannuated bird-catcher. They may both exclaim like Dean Swifts two balls of horse dung – brother how we apples swim.

A portion of this I gave you before, I hope you don't still continue to read this filthy paper, I have a notion to have this printed and send a copy of it to the individuals who have subscribed to his relief fund, I have a list of their names only my valuable time is so important that I don't think it is worth while, what say you, I know it will amuse you and that is why I send it to you. I hope you are quite well & I hope the time will not be long before I shall have the pleasure of seeing you

I Remain

Yours affecly
Francis Tumblety M.D.[224]

Tumblety returned to Devereux Court about 22 August and, seeing the Californian banks in jeopardy, made swift plans to head back to America without Caine. However, it then appears Caine's heart was never keen on going to London and he may have been railroaded by Tumblety into agreeing to go to America with him:

16 Deveraux Court
Strand
London
Augst 31. 1875
My dear friend

I suppose you noticed the failure of some of the banks in California, I have just recd a despatch calling me there at once, answer this note and direct it to the National Hotel Courtland Street New York If you have concluded to go to the U.S.A. I hope it will not be long before you take your departure, I should be very pleased to see your over there I have just this moment got a ticket & will sail at 10 o'clock tomorrow morning from London by the 'Greece' of the National Line, again hoping soon to see you in New York.

I Remain

Your Affec friend
Francis Tumblety MD[225]

Shortly after his arrival in America, and settled into the National Hotel in New York, Tumblety wrote to Caine:

National Hotel
Courtlandt St., N.Y.
Sept. 24th 1875
Dear Friend Caine,

Your kind letter reached me this day. I would have written to you sooner, but fatigue resulting from the voyage prevented. I am glad to hear that you are well. Business, in New York, is rather dull. This letter will be necessarily brief, but as an apology for this one I will write you a much longer epistle in a few days.

Yours affectionately,
Francis Tumblety M.D.[226]

Once in America, Tumblety wrote more openly about his feelings for Caine and rather than dictating to an assistant he wrote in his own hand:

New York, Sept. 29/75.
National Hotel
Courtlandt St.
Dear Caine

I suppose you have heard of the devastation in Texas by both wind and water. There were many lives lost, and considerable property destroyed. We came in for the tale [sic] end of the gale. September is the month in which Old Sol performs his tight-rope feat here as we come in for a share of the fun. My dear friend though my pen has been inactive and though absent, you are dearly remembered and I long to see you. I send you a little something that I am certain will please you and your companions. Both are views of Niagara Falls in their summer and winter aspect, and I feel assured that a young gentleman of your literary culture, will readily imagine how grand, sublime and awe-inspiring they must be when viewed in reality. The sound of this magnificent fall of water can be heard for many miles away and the spray arising from it resembles a fall of rain to a visitor approaching. There can be no grander illustration of the power of the Almighty than this work of nature – so called – but really the handiwork of God. How deeply I regret your absence you can scarcely imagine, being perfectly aware that to a greater extent would I realize the beauty and sublimity of this wonderful cataract had you been with me to express in the language, peculiarly your own the feelings which I know would have inspired us both on viewing it. The first thing I know you would say, after a few moment's reflection is 'this is a success'. Much as I desire your company, however, I would not advise anyone to leave their homes for America at the present time, and business, in all its branches is extremely dull, both machined, and those who follow professions finding it difficult to live with any of the comforts suitable and necessary to their positions. Neither is there any hope for better times until a change takes place in the administration. Hoping that this letter will find you in good health as I am happy to say it leaves me,

I remain,

Yours Affectionately
Francis Tumblety M.D.[227]

The letters became less frequent, but the sexual emotions expressed by Caine heightened, notably with the line 'I should dearly love to see your sweet face and spend an entire night in your company', in this letter:

1875
San Francisco Cal
Dec 30
My Dear friend Caine

Your kind and welcome letter reached me this evening and although it makes me sad to hear that you are in such bad health still it gives me infinite pleasure to hear from you and I should dearly love to see your sweet face and spend an entire night in your company. I feel melancholy when I read your amiable letter and it brings back the pleasing reminiscences of the past and although eighteen thousand miles now separate up it only stimulates the affections I have for you.

I am stopping at the Palace Hotel, the great caravanery of the western world, California, the land of prodigies, of giantesses, or wonderful vegetable growth of stupendous enterprises and colossal skemes [sic], come forward once again to claim the championship, throws down the gauntlet to her sister states and challenges them to equal her in matters of hotel accommodations. This is the garden of the world, I saw them mowing hay on Christmas Day. I went to a picnic and there were as many strawberries in the field that I could not place my foot down without treading on them. I will continue to send you newspapers so that you can have an idea of the correctness of my remarks. I hope that by the time you receive this your health will be quite restored. I wish you would come out to the Centennial at Philadelphia and I will meet you there and escort you to the Niagera Falls [sic] and all other interesting places in the Eastern states. I hope God may take a liking to you but not too soon. Direct your letters to San Francisco P.O. Col. To be kept till called for. So no more at present.

From your affectionate friend Francis Tumblety M.D.[228]

Tumblety's letter from St Louis of 31 March 1876 began with a travelogue but was soon twisted into an attack upon Chinese immigrants, concluding with his disgust of Chinese prostitutes and how they 'decoy youths of the most tender age, into these dens, for the purpose of exhibiting their nude and disgusting persons to the hitherto innocent youth of the cities':

St. Louis Mar. 31st 76
My Dear Friend Caine
I left San Francisco on the first of March and am now on the banks of the Mississippi River the father of waters it is four thousand two hundred miles long and runs through all the most fertile valleys in the world. Indian corn is sold for one shilling a bushel according to how many, and everything else in proportion. The most lovely part of the world is California, that delightful country, is being overrun by the Asiatic hoards. The evils which the Asiatic influx is inflicting upon California is imperfectly understood in the Eastern States. They are beginning to be fully realized by all the classes, and all parties. The Chinese empire has a population of four hundred millions, United States has a white population of not excluding forty million. A stream of emigration from the land of the four hundred million is now steadily joining into the land of forty million. A stream which unless something is speedily done to check it will constantly increase until the country is overrun by the Asiatic hoards as the fields, as the farms and prairies of the Northwest where [sic] not long ago overrun by the Rocky mountain locust. The chinamen are as nasty as Locust, they devour everything they come across, rats and cats, and all sorts of decomposed vegetable matter, they are a species of the Digger Indian. Grass hopper is a luxury which they partake with delight. This is not all, the Chinese that are now being landed on the Pacific shelf are of the lowest order. In morals and obscenity they are far below those of our most degraded prostitutes. Their women are bought and sold, for the usual purposes and they are used to decoy youths of the most tender age, into these dens, for the purpose of exhibiting their nude and

disgusting persons to the hitherto innocent youth of the cities. I am on my way to the Centennial and by the first of July I think I shall be prepared to leave for England I have nothing more of information to relate at present. Hoping that you are enjoying good health I remain affectionately yours

Francis Tumblety M.D.

P.S. Direct to Philadelphia Per. U.S. American care of Post Officer until called for.[229]

And so as suddenly as it began, the correspondence between Tumblety and Caine stops; or at least, these are all the letters that have survived. Hall Caine squirreled away boxes of correspondence in no particular order, as well as storing heaps of letters in drawers and files. Through years of diligent sorting and cataloguing over the last ten years by Caine's biographer Vivien Allen and Manx National Archives, good runs of letters from numerous correspondents have been assembled. Still, there are clearly gaps and tranches of correspondence missing. Caine lived until 1931, no doubt meaning to do *something* with his letters one day; however, he never sorted them and, considering the volume of his letters and the fact he moved a number of times over the years, it is not surprising there were losses.

There is a chance that Caine and Tumblety continued to correspond, equally, there is the chance they did not. No evidence had been found to date to suggest either, but it should be noted that there is *no letter* in the Hall Caine Papers to show Tumblety and Caine split acrimoniously or grew to dislike one another in any way. The likely scenario is they just drifted apart like many people in long-distance relationships. If they did meet again during Tumblety's subsequent visits to London they could well have greeted each other as old friends.

7

DRAW BACK THE CURTAIN

London of the 1880s was a maelstrom of entertainments, distractions and shows that enjoyed the benefits of unprecedented numbers of visitors, who could now easily access the city by road and railway. Each of the major theatres established reputations by genre; as Ellen Terry's son Edward Gordon Craig recalled, there were seven distinct permanent playhouses:

Drury Lane Theatre for spectacular drama, under Augustus Harris; the Adelphi Theatre for light melodrama and farce, under the Grattis; the Savoy for light opera, under D'Oyle Carte; the Haymarket for light comedy under Bancroft and later under Tree; the Surrey for the very heaviest of melodrama, under Conquest; the St. James's for domestic drama, under Kendall and the Lyceum for tragedy, classic and comedy under Irving.[230]

From the triumphant success of the opening night under Irving's management the sense

Henry Irving as the demon Mephistopheles in *Faust*, 1885.

of occasion on an opening night at the Lyceum Theatre was not to be missed by London theatre-going society. Theatre writer J.B. Booth evocatively described a typical Irving premiere, when he was at the height of his popularity and powers:

> As we turn out of the Strand up Wellington Street the three braziers over the portico throw ruddy gleams over the surging crowds and the long lines of carriages whose gleaming panels bear the crests of half of Burke's peerage ... The finest horses and the finest 'turn-outs' in the world are on view, bringing the audience representative of all the strata of London Society – Royalty, the Peerage, Parliament, the Bench, the Bar, literature, art, music and folk who are merely 'in the swim'. Pit and gallery have been filled long ago by the sternest critics and keenest enthusiasts ... We ascend the steps and enter the heavily carpeted vestibule from which an immensely wide staircase, covered with thick, soft carpets, leads to the back of the circle, and on each side of the staircase stand the programme attendants – small boys in Eton suits, for the programme girl is not yet. And the programmes, almost innocent of advertisement, well and clearly printed in an artistic shade of brown, are free. We are still in the days of 'No Fees'! At the top of the staircase a tall, reddish bearded man in evening dress greets us. It is Bram Stoker, Irving's faithful friend and manager. To Bram his chief is a god who can do no wrong ... The audience slowly settles in its seats; the murmur of the voices dies and there is a curious hush of expectancy for one is assisting at an event. The overture finishes, the house lights die down and the curtain rises. At last the entrance of the well-known figure, the tones of the familiar voice – and the 'Lyceum roar' or greeting.[231]

In those glorious days Bram had found his métier; Horace Wyndham recalled:

> To see Stoker in his element was to see him standing at the top of the theatre's stairs, surveying a 'first-night' crowd trooping up them. There was no mistake about it – a Lyceum premiere did draw an audience that really was representative of the best of that period in the realms of art, literature and society. Admittance was a very jealously guarded privilege. Stoker, indeed, looked upon the stalls, dress circle and boxes as if they were annexes to the Royal enclosure at Ascot, and one almost had to be proposed and seconded before the coveted ticket would be issued. The rag-tag-and-bobtail of the musical comedy, theatrical, stock exchange and journalistic worlds who foregather at a present-day premiere would certainly have been sent away with a flea in their ear.[232]

Bram was far more than a front of house manager; as acting manager Bram's duties, as defined by theatrical convention, meant he had control of everything on the auditorium side of the curtain, but the services he performed went far above and beyond the conventional duties of the job. Irving was omnipotent,

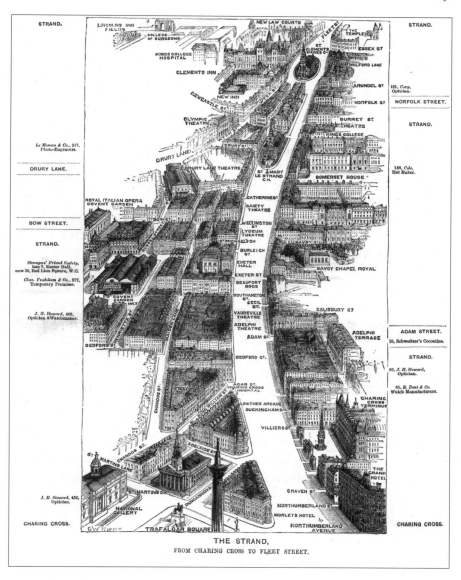

A map of the Strand and its theatres in the 1880s.

his word was law in the theatre and no one was left under any allusion that he was anything other than the name he was known by all employed by him – 'The Chief' – but Bram was his closest and staunchest ally; if you could get the ear of Bram, you had the ear of Irving. Bram served his master loyally, he would counter no criticism of Irving and was at his beck and call, day and night. Bram also deputised for Irving and worked with him on his speeches for the many public engagements and dinners where the great actor was asked to speak. Some of the speeches that survive are written entirely in Bram's handwriting; truth be known, Irving relied on Stoker to write most of his speeches, and even toasts – he was the great actor and Bram was his scriptwriter. Bram also scrutinised the plays submitted to the Lyceum; it was a demoralising and sometimes irksome task – he reckoned he had read over 1,000 and out of those he had only found two worthy of consideration.

It also fell to Bram to organise the travelling arrangements and advance publicity for tours both home and abroad, and even the programmes for the shows – proofs of which would be sent back to printers after Bram's keen eye had passed over them, with his corrections and annotations to the text and presentation observed to the minutest degree. It also fell to Bram to ensure the forty-eight retained staff were paid, oversee the box office and look after the comfort and welfare of the company of actors employed in the theatre. And all this for £22 per week; not a bad wage (it was almost three times his income as an Inspector of Petty Sessions) but, as the ghost of his father may have asked, was it commensurate with the effort he put in? Bram would not have thought of it that way, during those great years of the late 1870s and 1880s he was living the life he had worked for, dreamt of and aspired to since those trips to the Dublin theatre with his father all those years before. Bram shared Irving's implacable view that the theatre came first in all things. Being overworked did not matter a jot, Bram was supremely happy and truly in his element.

While he was a critic in Dublin actors and actresses grew to love and trust Bram and shared their uncertainties and innermost thoughts in letters to him. At the Lyceum Bram was similarly always on hand to provide a sensitive and understanding ear for the company of actors and actresses under his care; he was like a mother to them all but none more so than Irving's leading lady, Ellen Terry. Irving and Terry were a perfect pairing, for she was an actress of beauty, charm and immense stage presence, an actress whose greatness was the only worthy match for Irving at the height of his powers. Bram would treasure the memory of his first sight of her at the Lyceum:

The first time I saw Ellen Terry was on the forenoon of Monday, December 23, 1878. The place was the passage-way which led from the stage of the Lyceum to the office, a somewhat dark passage under the staircase leading to the two 'star' dressing-rooms up the stage on the O.P. side. But not even the darkness of that December day could shut out the radiant beauty of the woman to whom Irving, who was walking with her, introduced me. Her face was full of colour and animation, either of which would have made her beautiful. In addition was the fine form, the easy rhythmic swing, the large, graceful, goddess-like way in which she moved. I knew of her of course all the world did then though not so well as afterwards; and she knew of me already, so that we met as friends.[233]

They remained treasured friends for life; she would cry on his shoulder, they shared joys, sadness, her insecurities and doubts, and Bram's big heart never failed her. Despite being of the same generation, Terry just one year younger than Bram, in her own words, written with love, she described Bram as her 'Ma' and herself as 'her dutiful child'.[234]

The success of *Hamlet* was followed by a long run of *The Corsican Brothers* and a triumphal *Merchant of Venice* that ran for 250 nights in 1879. Also in 1879, on 30 December, Bram and Florence were blessed with a son. He was named after Bram's idol – Irving – with middle names Noel Thornley. The Stokers moved from their suite of six rooms on the top floor of 7 Southampton Street in Bloomsbury to the more commodious and fashionable 27 Cheyne Walk in Chelsea. The 1881 census records Bram as head of the household, stating his occupation as 'Theatrical Manager', Florence is shown as an 'artist' and Bram's brother George, who was living with them at the time, as a 'physician and surgeon'. There were three staff: Elizabeth Jarrald as nurse for baby Irving, Harriett Daw as cook and 15-year-old Emma Barton as housemaid.

Bram's daily routine would begin with breakfast in bed at about ten in the morning, he would then leave in the forenoon and return again about four in the afternoon. The family would dine together at six, then Bram would disappear off to the theatre again and not return until midnight at the earliest. Work in the theatre meant Bram was seldom at home, and as young Irving loved playing with his father and missed having him around, he grew jealous of the time his father spent there and felt as if he were second best. As he later recalled, his mother would despair at times and on one occasion challenged Bram, saying that he would be more troubled if Henry Irving died than his own son – to which Bram replied he could have another son but not another Irving![235] Florence and Bram would, however, only have one child. When he reached his maturity Irving Stoker dropped his first name in preference of Noel to demonstrate his resentment of Henry Irving for monopolising his father. Ironically, in time Bram would be made to feel second best and even face rejection from Irving but, unlike his own son's love, Bram's love for 'The Chief' never failed.

The year 1881 saw two major achievements for Bram: one was the publication of his first fiction book, *Under the Sunset*, a weird collection of fantasy stories supposedly for children that Bram dedicated to his little son. The second was his organisation of the first Lyceum Company tour of America. The schedule took in New York, Philadelphia, Boston, Baltimore, Brooklyn and Chicago with many stops along the way. Irving, Terry and Bram travelled in opulent first-class style with a private parlour car complete with maid, porter and cook; the rest of the company and baggage took up a further seven carriages. Wherever their train pulled in they were met by well-wishers and reporters. Bram lapped it all up: he thrived on the strenuous schedule and the romance of the travelling life of the theatrical company, and he was captivated by America. During this tour, as ever,

Bram cut a dash and left quite an impression; tall and genial, he strode into theatres and receptions with an easy, broad smile and basked in the glory of Irving.

The gallant rescues carried out by Bram and PC John Jenkins as illustrated in *Penny Illustrated Paper*, 4 November 1882.

Back in London, The Embankment near Stoker's home provided Bram with
an easy run to the Lyceum by cab, ferry or even bicycle in later years and also, due
to its close proximity to the river and Bram's regular use of river transport, occasioned a remarkable act of gallantry by Bram. On the evening of 14 September
1882 he was on a steamer from Chelsea bound for London Bridge when, as they
passed the steamboat *Twilight*, he saw an man aged between 60 and 70 climb
over the aft rails and throw himself into the water. Although it had been almost
a decade since he was a champion athlete, Bram had never lost confidence in his
abilities – he threw off his coat and dived in to rescue the drowning man. After
grappling with the man, he managed, with some difficulty, to get him onto the
deck of the steamer where attempts were made to resuscitate him, but sadly to
no avail. Bram did not give up, however, he had the body taken to his house
at Cheyne Walk where medical assistance was summoned, albeit in vain.[236] The
jury returned a verdict, 'That the deceased committed suicide, but there was no
evidence to show his state of mind.' A juryman remarked that 'to jump from a
boat when the tide was strong was a very brave act' and the jury went on to add
they 'wished to publicly recognise the gallant conduct of Mr. Bram Stoker'.[237] At
the express wish of the jury, the coroner communicated with the Royal Humane
Society and Bram was duly recognised with the award of their medal in bronze.

The second Lyceum Company tour of 1884 saw them play in both America
and Canada. It proved to be a great success but for Bram this was a bitter experience where he was left feeling rejected and used – Irving had taken on board
Louis Frederick Austin as his secretary and Austin Brereton, a rather pretentious
freelance writer, whom he entrusted with the advance planning for the tour in
New York. Bram would remain loyal to his master and still strove to please him
but his eyes were opened to another side of Irving, perhaps something of Irving's
performance as the scheming manipulator Iago to Edwin Booth's Othello back
in 1881 came to mind. Then, in 1885, there was *Faust*.

Based on Goethe's dramatic poem, the play was adapted for the Lyceum stage
by William Gorman Wills. W.G. Wills was both a skilled portrait painter and a
favourite dramatist of Irving's; Wills would write and adapt plays around Irving,
giving him the roles and set piece speeches he adored. Ellen Terry would recall
of Wills:

He was Irish all-over – the strangest mixture of aristocrat and the sloven. He
would eat a large raw onion every night like a peasant, yet his ideas were magnificent and instinct with refinement. A true Bohemian in money matters, he made
a great deal out of his plays – and never had a farthing to bless himself with.[238]

The appearance of W.G. Wills was invariably akin to a man who slept in his
clothes, and he probably did. His pockets were always stuffed with a strange mixture of artist's materials, rolls of manuscript and a host of smoking impedimenta

while his face, or at least what you could see of it over a tangled beard, was usually smeared with paint or charcoal. Irving was never keen on visiting Wills at his barn-like studio on the Fulham Road for, as Irving's grandson would record, it was, 'not only the rendezvous of fashionable sitter but the haunt of spongers, beggars and models, who camped upon his dilapidated furniture, ate his meals and pocketed the money with which absent minded generosity he gave to anyone who seemed to need it'.[239]

Wills did try to raise the tone of his premises and play the role of the fashionable portrait painter 'by engaging a liveried page to attend upon his sitters; but the page soon became infected by the pervading disorder and melted into the background of hangers-on, kittening cats and a monkey which swung from the gas bracket'.[240] One cannot avoid the thought that there was to be something about W.G. Wills that Bram drew upon in his creation of R.M. Renfield, Dr Seward's zoophagous patient in *Dracula*, for it was he who, having tempted the flies with his food and fed his spiders, then collected a colony of sparrows about him. Renfield would implore of Dr Seward 'Oh, yes, I would like a cat! I only asked for a kitten lest you should refuse me a cat. No one would refuse me a kitten, would they?'[241] His master, Dracula, did not rush to see him and only kept Renfield, the man he had possessed to become his obedient servant, alive as long as he was of use to him.

The Lyceum production of *Faust* had been much anticipated. Every year the sets at the Lyceum had become more magnificent and the special effects more spectacular; the numbers of staff involved were staggering as Irving would regularly employ between 450 and 600 personnel in a production. To prepare for *Faust*, Irving had travelled to Nuremberg with Hawes Craven, the scene painter, to observe the authentic setting while W.G. Wills obtained descriptions of the scenery and interiors from his friend Carl Ambruster. Nothing was left to chance, no expense was spared: an organ was installed for the cathedral scene as were a peal of bells, real electricity was connected to the foils in the duelling scene so they flashed with blue sparks on contact, real steam would hiss and billow and a small army of supporting artists would recreate the seething mass of demons and the damned upon the Brocken Mountain. Behind the scenes the mechanics of the piece were immense; the list of properties and instructions to the carpenters was so extensive it became a joke and once in place the set scenery and effects required over 400 ropes, each of them named to avoid confusion by the scene shifters. It was soon rumoured the whole production cost the fantastic sum of £15,000. In 1882 the theatre had been renovated; sixty seats were added to the dress circle and a further 200 to the pit – the theatre could now seat 2,000, and due to the rumours of this unprecedented production, every ticket was sold.

Even fifty years on, the gala opening night of *Faust* on 19 December 1885 was still remembered as the greatest of all Lyceum first nights and one of the most magnificent that London has ever seen. Actor and theatre historian W. Macqueen-Pope wrote in 1939:

His [Irving's] friends told him the play would fail. But there were enough applications to fill six theatres of the size of the Lyceum, and thousands of visitors came from Germany as well. People gathered outside the theatre at nine in the morning. By six o'clock the crowd was halfway along the Strand. Scores of fashionable women thronged the vestibule all day casting despairing glances at Hurst, the box office keeper, and attempting to rush the doors.[242]

W. G. Wills recalled, 'Never was there such a first night. Royalty was represented by the Prince of Wales, and even the top gallery was occupied by persons of distinction. Many thousands of applications for seats came from Germany, and people gathered at the pit doors from nine o'clock in the morning.'[243] Wills went on to evoke the opening of the fifth act, the vision of the Broken Mountain:

> The scene is in the Hartz Mountains, among which the zigzag lightning flashes. To the left, old dwarfed trees; to the right, practicable rocks, from which, in this region of cloudland, a huge white owl soars away on noiseless wing. Mephisto and Faust come toiling up the mountain, the former, in his red dress, the lurid centre of the picture. Lichened rocks seem to separate from themselves forms in grey, cobwebby robes, of sorcerers and witches and ape-like creatures, whose eldritch screeches greet the master Faust, spellbound, looking on at the diabolical revel. The plaints of the old bent sorcerer, who, for three hundred years, has been climbing up the mountain, and never reached the top, are chorused by wild shrieks of witches' laughter. Here as the apes fawn upon him, the electric flames burst from the rocks on which he seats himself among his familiars, or as he stands, like a lightning blasted tree in malignant majesty, upon the Brocken's summit – Mr. Irving's Mephisto rises to real grandeur ...[244]

At the centre of it all was a Machiavellian demon, a dark fiend who commanded elements and the spawn of hell. It was a vision that would linger in Bram's memory – a shape of things to come.

The Lyceum festivities after an opening night became a social event in their own right and an invitation to them carried considerable cachet. In his account of the opening night of *The Dead Heart* on 28 September 1889, Gordon Craig gives an idea of the notable society people who frequented the Lyceum and who would have received invites to the after party; they were truly among the crème de la crème of the *fin de siècle*:

> The doors of the Lyceum Theatre opened at 7.30 and Mr. Bram Stoker would be at his post, ready to receive the first comers. Every seat would have been allotted weeks beforehand – he would recognize all the guests. Coming into the theatre on this first night Mr. Stoker would see, maybe, Mr. and Mrs. George Lewis, Sir Morel and Lady Mackenzie, Mr. and Mrs. Jopling, Mr. and

A dramatic rendition of the Broken scene in the Lyceum production of *Faust*, as depicted in the *Illustrated Sporting and Dramatic News*, 16 January 1886.

Mrs. Linley Sambourne, the Tadema family, John Sargent, Max Beerbohm with Aubrey Beardsley, the Duke of Beaufort, William Rothenstein, and the family of Dr. Pryde. A while later as the clock pointed to five minutes to eight, Sir Edward Arnold, the Duchess of Teck, Pinero, Labouchere, would arrive: then Lord Londesborough, George du Maurier and his lovely family, and Dr. and Mrs. Todhunter. Some would drive up in carriages, some in Hansomes, some in four wheelers – other would arrive on foot. In they poured: Mr. and Mrs. Felix Moscheles, the Seligmanns, Mr. and Mrs. Comyns Carr, Lockwood, Walter Gilbey, Edmund Yates, Walter Palmer, Walter Dowdeswell, Mr. and Mrs. Perugini, Mrs. Bancroft, Mr. and Mrs. Walter Pollock … dozens of families known to Irving and Ellen Terry, and all welcomed there by the very able Bram Stoker.

… It was this able and delightful assistant who performed the part of deputy host on a first night, for Irving, until the curtain was lowered at the end of the evening. The general public then went off to their houses, but some few hundred of the invited friends would stay lingering in their places or in the corridors until a new scene was set upon the boards. Then the small door between auditorium and stage would be opened and everyone would drift through it and discover long tables laden with good things from Gunters [the Lyceum caterers] – a cold supper to be eaten standing up.

And amongst his friends came Irving, possibly in evening dress, maybe in his stage costume – it depended, I think, on how much time he had to change in – and for an hour or longer everyone enjoyed themselves.[245]

But the inner sanctum, the very heart of the Lyceum and the centre of Irving's circle of friends was to be found in the Beefsteak Room. The room had been rediscovered after a number of backstage 'lumber rooms' of the Lyceum had been, on Irving's instructions, cleared out during his sojourn in the Mediterranean in 1879. Behind the theatre armoury they came upon the old meeting place of the Sublime Society of Beefsteaks. The original society came about in the 1730s as George Lambert, a Covent Garden Theatre scene painter, was often too busy to leave his work to dine and contented himself with a simple beefsteak broiled upon the fire in his painting room. In this hasty meal Lambert was occasionally joined by others who were delighted to share the modest repast and witty conversation with him. The conviviality of these gatherings inspired the notion that they should create their own club and the famous harlequin and friend of Lambert, John Rich, saw to it that in 1735 the Sublime Society of Beefsteaks was founded.[246] Among its first twenty-four members were numerous characters from the theatre and arts, including the great pictorial satirist William Hogarth. The society originally met in Covent Garden Theatre until it was destroyed by fire and then removed to the Bedford Coffee House in 1808, and to the Lyceum Theatre in 1809. The society had a president who wore the badge of a silver gridiron on his breast, the other officers were the bishop, the recorder, the secretary, the laureate and the boots. Laurence Irving describes the experience of dining at the society:

> Beyond the supper room, which could seat some thirty members, and in full view of them all, was the kitchen equipped solely with a huge gridiron upon which beefsteaks, the staple diet of the Society, were grilled. The steaks, cut from the rump, were introduced 'hot, hot' into the dining room through an aperture in the wall and were laid before the President, who carved for his members delicate and succulent cuts so that their plates were never overloaded and could be returned for a second or third time. The only vegetable served was a delicious salad in which beetroot predominated. Porter and port slaked the thirst and loosened the tongues of these carnivorous, noble and intellectual gentlemen whose number included those most distinguished in the arts, the law and the medical sciences.[247]

They could speak freely too, for in the best traditions of the very best gentlemen's clubs they observed their society's motto emblazoned upon the gridiron, suspended from the ceiling and on the wall:

> Let no one bear beyond this threshold hence
> Words uttered in confidence

The Sublime Society of Beefsteaks continued to meet at the Lyceum until 1830, when it too suffered from a fire. It then adjourned to the Lyceum Tavern and the Bedford Coffee House, before returning to the Lyceum in 1838. Its new room was magnificently trimmed out with English oak panelling, portraits of past and present members bedecked the walls and nearly everything in the place from the wainscoting, picture frames and chairs to the silver, glass and cutlery bore the gridiron and motto of the society. Even the cook could still be seen; through the bars of a huge gridiron at the eastern side of the room. Sadly the membership slowly evaporated, and when the society folded in 1867, its furniture, portraits and appointments were sold at Christies to defray the debts it had incurred.[248]

However, when Irving returned from the Mediterranean, the rediscovered room had been restored to something of its former glory. The panelling had been restored by the carpenters, the walls were repainted and appropriate drapery and curtains fitted, the old gridiron hung once more over the table and, over the chimney-piece, the motto was displayed in Latin:

> *Ne fidos inter amicos*
> *Sit, qui dicta foras eliminet*

The walls were hung with the collection of pictures Irving had begun to acquire. In a recess near the supper table was a large conversation piece by Clint, showing

What stories those walls could have told: the Beefsteak Room in the Lyceum Theatre, as featured in the *English Illustrated Magazine*, September 1890.

one of Irving's favourite actors, Edmund Kean, 'at the climax of his performance of A New Way to Pay Old Debts. Near it was a study which Clint had made for this picture, a superb head of Kean which was believed to be the only portrait for which the volatile actor had ever been persuaded to sit. Among the rest was Whistler's portrait of Irving as Philip and a fine head of the young Napoleon which he had used as a model for his make-up as Claude Melnotte.' Over the years this collection would be joined by pictures of David Garrick, William Charles Macready, John Singer Sargent's striking full-length portrait of Ellen Terry in her beetle-wing gown holding a crown aloft as Lady Macbeth (now in the Tate), and a version of the statue of Irving as Hamlet by E. Onslow Ford. A new kitchen range and a chef were also installed that afforded a greater selection of dishes than were ever indulged in by the old society, as well as a cellar stocked with fine wines, brandy and champagne. This was to be Irving's inner sanctum for his most honoured guests and work colleagues and it was here that Stoker and Irving would spend many nights discussing plays, plans for future productions, the esoteric and all manner of matters that interested them through the night; for time flew here and there were no windows to show the light of dawn.

It was here, after many performances, that there would be little supper parties for Irving and his friends. Bram wrote in his *Personal Reminiscences*:

The history of the Lyceum Theatre was for a quarter of a century a part of the social history of London. A mere list of Irving's hospitalities would be instructive. The range of his guests was impossible to any but an artist. As he never forgot or neglected his old friends there were generally at his table some present who represented the commonplace or the unsuccessful as well as the famous or the successful sides of life. The old clays and the new came together cheerily under the influence of the host's winning personality, which no amount of success had been able to spoil.

Sometimes the Beefsteak Room, which could only seat at most thirty-six people, was too small; and at such times we migrated to the stage … On the hundredth night of The Merchant of Venice, February 14, 1880, there was a supper for three hundred and fifty guests. On March 25, 1882, ninety-two guests sat down to dinner to celebrate the hundredth night of Romeo and Juliet.

As Bram would recall in *Personal Reminiscences*, it was, however, at the smaller, more intimate gatherings, which would be held around the table, that the company could be very diverse and intriguing and the conversation at its most scintillating:

The ordinary hospitalities of the Beefsteak Room were simply endless. A list of the names of those who have supped with Irving there would alone fill chapters of this book. They were of all kinds and degrees. The whole social scale has been represented from the Prince to the humblest of commoners. Statesmen, travellers, explorers, ambassadors, foreign princes and potentates, poets, novelists, historians, writers of every style, shade and quality. Representatives of all the learned professions; of all the official worlds; of all the great industries. Sportsmen, landlords, agriculturists. Men and women of leisure and fashion. Scientists, thinkers, inventors, philanthropists, divines. Egotists, ranging from harmless esteemers of their own worthiness to the very ranks of Nihilism. Philosophers. Artists of all kinds. In very truth the list was endless and kaleidoscopic.

Royalty from around the world would occasionally grace the Beefsteak Room but there was always an extra

HRH Edward, Prince of Wales (later King Edward VII) *c.* 1872.

frisson when members of the British royal family arrived. Bram would recall with affection the time when the Duke of Teck, Princess Mary, their three sons and Princess May Victoria, whose birthday it was, came to supper. The Prince of Wales (later Edward VII) would, on occasion, arrive unannounced and join those gathered for supper but would prefer the nights when the table had more adventurers, influential businessmen, high-flyers and pretty women rather than the intelligentsia and literati whose conversation bored the playboy prince. Those who knew him would dread the sight of his fingers drumming on the table, a sure sign His Royal Highness's patience was wearing thin.

Some guests were more mysterious and exotic than others and one night particularly stuck in Bram's memory. It was the evening of 8 July 1892, after the play *Faust*, and Irving had some friends to supper in the Beefsteak Room:

> I think that, all told, it was as odd a congeries of personalities as could well be.
>   Sarah Bernhardt, Darmont, Ellen Terry and her daughter, Toole, Mr. and Mrs. T. B. Aldrich of Boston, two Miss Casellas and Stepniak. It was odd that the man was known only by the one name; no one ever used his first name, Sergius. Other men have second names of some sort; but this one, though he signed himself S. Stepniak, I never heard spoken of except by the one word. I sat next to him at supper and we had a great deal of conversation together, chiefly about the state of affairs in Russia generally and the Revolutionary party in especial. He, who had presumably been in the very heart of the Revolutionary party and in all the secrets of Nihilism, told me some of his views and aspirations and those of the party or rather the parties of which he was a unit.[249]

Bram recalled others who graced the table over the years: there were those skilled in the world of haute finance such as Major Ricarde-Seaver; the great coal owner and Member of Parliament Sir George Elliott; the popular song writer Henry Russell, author of the song *Cheer, boys, cheer*; while Charles Dickens the younger, Kate Dickens (Mrs Kate Perugini) and their brother Henry Fielding Dickens, described by Stoker as 'closest of them all', were frequent visitors. The painter Burne-Jones had, as Bram would remember with affection in *Personal Reminiscences*: 'an endless collection of stories of all sorts': 'In our meetings on the stage or at supper in the Beefsteak Room, or on those delightful Sunday afternoons when he allowed a friend to stroll with him round his studio, there was always some little tale breathing the very essence of human nature.'

A friend of both Bram and Irving, Hall Caine was a regular guest at the Beefsteak Room for gatherings large and small; particularly as Caine's books' popularity grew and 'Irving had a strong desire that Caine should write some play that he could act'. As a result, Caine was often part of the most exclusive suppers in the room with Irving and Bram; on one occasion, when the guests for supper were just Caine and the composer Alexander Mackenzie, Caine flaunted the general taboo of no children in the Beefsteak Room and brought his son Ralph with him, but nobody seemed to mind. Indeed, it was recalled by Bram as 'a delightful evening, a long, pleasant, home-like chat'.

Even Caine's old friend Francis Tumblety may have been a guest on occasions. The gatherings at the Beefsteak Room had the atmosphere of a very special club, indeed the room was often referred to by infrequent visitors and the uninitiated simply as 'The Beefsteak Club', an easy error as it was, quite correctly, and often referred to as The Beefsteak Club Room. This has led to confusion over the years as there was an independent Beefsteak Club extant in London at the same time. The mistake is even repeated in Ellen Terry's *The Story of My Life*, where the index refers to The Beefsteak Club but the text only mentions The Beefsteak Room. I suspect, in this instance, Bram corrected the error in her manuscript or proof copy from the publishers but it was not transcribed to the index. I would argue that this common misunderstanding was also the case when Tumblety gave an interview to *The New York World*, published on 29 January 1889, in which he mentioned he was 'a frequenter of some of the best London clubs, among others the Carleton Club and the Beefsteak Club'. It was to the exclusive gatherings at The Beefsteak Club Room at the Lyceum that he was alluding. Tumblety was known to frequent theatres, and it is precisely the sort of gathering he would have loved to be invited to. As a man who used testimonials as he did, he would have hesitated to have used his old friend Hall Caine's name as an entrée. If they had remained in contact Caine may even have arranged an inivitation for him.

Whatever else can be suggested about Tumblety he was, without doubt, a teller of stories and could be very convincing – not to mention, in 1888, he dressed well and was quite wealthy. But there had to be something more to attract an invitation to the Room, and with Tumblety there were the stories he was known to tell about his personal acquaintance with President Lincoln: of being a guest at his levees, of being recognised by members of the president's staff and of being present at his funeral. Bram had a passionate interest in Lincoln. He had read widely and corresponded with Walt Whitman on the subject and would present lecture on 'Abraham Lincoln: how the Statesman of the People saved the Union, and abolished Slavery in the American Civil War' for the Sunday Lecture Society at St George's Hall on 9 December 1888. Bram presented further, occasional lectures on Lincoln in both Britain and in the US over the ensuing years. Moreover, Bram and Irving were among the twenty men who joined to purchase the moulds for the life mask and hands of Lincoln by Volk and presented them to the American nation. Each of the subscribers received casts in bronze of the face and hands with his name in each case cut in the bronze. Bram's casts were sold with his library books and manuscripts at Sotheby's in 1913 (see Appendix 5).

Irving entrusted Bram to deal with the invitations to the Beefsteak Room and, as in so many matters of correspondence from the Lyceum, the invitations, notes, letters and memos would be in Bram's hand and bear only the signature of Irving. All of these factors could well have been the key to an invitation for Tumblety to be a guest at the old Beefsteak Club Room after a show. In the light of subsequent events, however, it is not surprising his visit is not mentioned by Bram among the numerous other intriguing characters that graced the table over the years.

The hospitality at Beefsteak suppers was superb, as one of the menus from a dinner held there on 9 July 1888 demonstrates:

Dressed Crab

Consommé à la Brunoise

Filets de Soles frits au Beurre

Suprême de Volaille à l'Ecarlate

Côtelettes d'Agneau grillé

Pommes de Terre.   Champignons grille.

———————————

Jambon au Madère

Petit Pois.   Salade.

———————————

Soufflé Glacée aux Fraises

Croustade de Laitance de Harengs

Bram often bit his knuckles when he saw Irving's expenditure on hospitality, but it was the wish of 'The Chief' that it would be so. Ultimately, Bram's *Personal Reminiscences of Henry Irving* was written as a great eulogy to Irving by a man who loved him, no matter how he was treated.

Those closest to Irving and Stoker would comment on the deeper natures of their personalities. Hall Caine said of his dear friend:

Bram was a man of the theatre only by the accident of his great love for its leader and his true self was something quite unlike the personality which was seen in that environment. Those who knew him there only hardly knew him at all. Some hint of this world would occasionally reveal itself among the scarcely favourable conditions of a public dinner, when as speaker (always capable of the racy humour which is considered necessary to that rather artificial atmosphere), he would strike, in the soft roll of his rich Irish tongue, a note of deep and almost startling emotion that would obliterate the facile witticisms of more important persons.

Whereas, poignantly, despite being the public figure that he was, despite all those friends and thousands spent on hospitality, Ellen Terry said of Irving:

Stoker and Irving were daily, nay hourly, associated for many years with Henry Irving; but after all, did they or any one else really know him? And what was Henry Irving's attitude? I believe myself that he never wholly trusted his friends, and never admitted to them his intimacy, although they thought he did, which was the same thing to them.[250]

8

THE WHITECHAPEL VAMPIRE

'Do something – do something!' Lord Salisbury cried
'We've done all we can!' Worried Warren replied;
'We keep on arresting as fast as we can,
And we hope soon or late we shall get the right man.'
Then, goaded by taunts to the depths of despair,
The poor First Commissioner tore at his hair,
And fell upon Matthews's breast with a sob –
But the Whitechapel Vampire was still on the job. [251]

Dagonet, George R. Sims

As the crowds poured out on to the portico and into the cold night beyond the warm glow of the theatre, the streets of 1880s London were suffering from an intensifying climate of fear.

The old fires of the Young Ireland movement, which had agitated for rebellion in Ireland, had been rekindled with the creation of the Irish Republican Brotherhood (IRB) in Dublin in 1858. In 1859, the American wing of the IRB, the Fenian Brotherhood, was founded to raise funds and muster volunteers for the cause. Many of the Irish driven to America to escape the potato famines in the 1840s were resentful that they had been conscripted to fight in the American Civil War and were drawn to the Fenians; the more extreme element formulated a plan of military action. A daring raid was attempted on Canada in 1866 whereby Fenian forces attempted to seize the transport systems of the British province and hold it for ransom in exchange for Ireland's freedom. The Fenian force contained many battle-hardened soldiers of the Civil War but the size of the force doomed it to failure. Nevertheless, fundraising and fear of further actions in America and against Britain were very much alive into the 1880s.

The IRB began to stockpile weapons and planned a rebellion in 1865 but British authorities, forewarned by their spies within the Fenian movement, were able to move rapidly to emasculate the rising by shutting down their newspaper

'After the Play – Under the Lyceum Portico', *The Graphic*, 21 May 1881.

and arresting most of the leadership. Early in 1867 a group of Irish-American officers landed at Cork intent on raising an army against England but were doomed by bad organisation, lack of support and British intelligence, and yet again the leaders were rounded up and imprisoned.

In November 1867 American Civil War veteran and Fenian arms agent Captain Richard O'Sullivan Burke was arrested and held on remand in Clerkenwell Prison, London. An attempt to rescue him, by blowing a hole in the prison wall, was attempted on 13 December. However, the amount of dynamite was grossly overestimated and the ensuing blast destroyed a prison wall, wrecked many of the nearby houses, caused the deaths of twelve people and injured over 120. Michael Barratt, the man responsible for the bombing, was captured, tried, found guilty and hanged at Newgate on 26 May 1868. He has the grim distinction to have been the last man publicly executed in Britain.

In the aftermath of the failed rising, the Fenians reorganised and adopted a new constitution in 1873. The new policies eschewed armed rebellion and physical force unless they had mass backing from the Irish people. Instead they set about building a new nationalist movement and gave their support to the Irish Land League in their campaign to abolish landlordism in Ireland.

A number of Fenians did not agree with the change of policy and several radical splinter groups who wished to maintain militant action emerged. Two factions – one sponsored by IRB activist Jeremiah O'Donovan Rossa, who had been tried and sentenced to penal servitude for his part in the Fenian Rising, released as part of the Fenian Amnesty in 1870 and was now operating in America; the other was the Irish-American Clan na Gael (successor to the Fenian Brotherhood). Both began a bombing campaign on the British mainland. Another group, the Irish National Invincibles, usually known simply as the 'Invincibles', adopted assassination and terror as their bloody code.

In January 1881 Fenian bombs exploded at military barracks in Salford and Chester. Another device exploded at Hatton Garden police station in Liverpool, and yet another was discovered at Liverpool Town Hall but removed by a police officer before it detonated. On 15 March the attacks moved to London and a bomb was discovered at the Mansion House in London and defused.

After the arrest of Charles Stewart Parnell, president of the newly formed Irish National Land League, in October 1881, a number of abortive attempts were made by the Invincibles to assassinate the Irish Chief Secretary, William Edward Forster. Renewing their efforts, they turned their attentions upon Thomas Henry Burke, the Permanent Undersecretary at the Irish Office. Invincibles leader Patrick Carey decided a knife attack would be most practical and would maximise terror, and long surgical knives (manufactured by the reputable surgical knife and instruments maker John Weiss & Son, 287 Oxford Street, London) were smuggled in for the purpose. On Saturday 6 May 1882 Lord Frederick Cavendish, the newly appointed Chief Secretary for Ireland, was spending his first day in the country and was walking with Burke in Phoenix Park, Dublin. As they approached the Viceregal

Persons and places associated with the Phoenix Park assassination trials from the supplement published with the *Weekly Freeman*, 2 June 1883.

Lodge a cab pulled up beside them, four men leapt out and, in a frenzied attack, stabbed both Cavendish and Burke to death. Leaving the bodies bleeding where they fell, the assassins scrambled back into their cab and sped off.

News of the assassinations rocked the British government in London and newspapers howled outrage and demanded the 'Phoenix Park Murderers' be tracked down and brought to justice. Concerns about the escalating actions of the Fenians led to the formation of the Special Irish Branch or SIB (later known

Premature detonation of the Fenian bomb on London Bridge, *Illustrated London News*, 20 December 1884.

as Special Branch when the unit's remit widened), the first specialist operational subdivision of the CID. The man appointed to head this new unit was Chief Inspector John G. Littlechild. A large number of suspects were arrested and eventually James Carey, the Invincibles' leader, and group members Joe Hanlon and Michael Kavanagh agreed to testify against the assassins. After due trial, five conspirators were sent to the gallows at Kilmainham Gaol between 14 May and 4 June 1883; six others were sentenced to long prison terms.[252]

The Fenian bombing campaign continued in London throughout 1883 with explosions at government buildings in Whitehall, at the offices of *The Times* newspaper and on the London Underground. In February 1884 bombs were planted in four London stations but only the device in the left-luggage room at Victoria station exploded. The most audacious of the attacks occurred on 30 May 1884 when a Fenian bomb tore through the gable end of the CID and Special Irish Branch headquarters in Great Scotland Yard. Smashed glass and brick rubble was strewn across the road and a 30ft-high hole was blasted out. Fortunately, no one was injured but the damage to the reputation of the police, having had a bomb go off literally under their noses, was inestimable.

Matters were compounded with other bombs being exploded at the Junior Carlton Club and outside Sir Watkin-Wynne's house; there was even an unexploded device found at the foot of Nelson's Column. Luckily the fuse, attached to sixteen sticks of dynamite that would almost certainly have brought the great monument down, proved to be defective. Another attempt to attack a London landmark on 13 December 1884 saw three Fenian bombers killed when the bomb they were planting on London Bridge exploded prematurely. Nevertheless, despite the efforts of the SIB, the Fenian bombing campaign opened again early in 1885 when a bomb exploded at Gower Street station on 2 January, and later that same month, on the 24th, Fenian bombs were set off in some of the most significant and historic buildings of London. One exploded in the Tower of London, scattering stands of arms and armour and creating havoc in the Old Banqueting Hall. A second bomb was discovered on the steps going down to St Stephen's Crypt in the Palace of Westminster and was reported to PCs Cole and Cox of A (Whitehall) Division. Lifting the parcel with its burning envelope, PC William Cole carried the device up the stairs into Westminster Hall; unfortunately, his hands were by then so badly burnt he was forced to drop the bomb and it exploded. Bravely tended by PC Cox who was on duty in the hall, Cole, who incredibly survived, was later awarded the Albert Medal for his gallantry. A third bomb was detonated in the House of Commons; luckily the House was not in session at the time but extensive damage was caused to the Division Hall and Strangers' and Peers' galleries. Two men were convicted of complicity in the bombings and were sentenced to penal servitude for life.

Just two years on, in 1887, newspapers reported that a plot to assassinate Queen Victoria had been foiled. It was claimed the Fenian plotters intended to blow

Charles Stewart Parnell, the head of the Irish National Land League, depicted as a vampire bat sweeping down on slumbering Erin in a cartoon from *Punch*, 24 October 1885.

up Westminster Abbey, killing half the British Cabinet and Her Majesty in the process. The 'plot' was later revealed to be a sting whereby Francis Millen, a spy in the service of British authorities who had infiltrated the Fenians, would draw in brother Fenians to join the plot; they would then be captured. The general public were not, however, privy to this information and were not made any more comfortable on the streets of London by this report.

The situation was further inflamed by an undercurrent of fear as the troubles of the East End spilled over into the city. Immigrants, especially those from central Europe, were subject to xenophobic fears and mistrust, socialist activism was on the rise and the huge numbers of unemployed workers were being mobilised to take part in demonstrations and rallies on the streets of the capital, in Hyde Park and Trafalgar Square.

Previously, on 8 February 1886, two rival radical movements, The London United Workmen's Committee and H.F. Hyndman's pro-revolution Social Democratic Federation held rallies in Trafalgar Square on the same day. Gladstone's newly appointed Home Secretary Hugh Childers was still finding his feet in office and both meetings had been approved in error. The meetings went without incident in the square but the mob, fired up by the speeches, began to cause mayhem along Pall Mall. Unfortunately, a garbled message was sent to the police that there was trouble in the *Mall* rather than *Pall Mall*. The police reserves rushed to defend Buckingham Palace and the mob was left to run amok in Pall Mall and St James's. Another (unofficial) rally in Hyde Park saw the mob whipped into a frenzy of window smashing and looting along Oxford Street. Inspector James Cuthbert was routinely parading his sergeant and constables ready for their duties when he heard the mob. His actions were swift, brave and decisive. He marched his men – seventeen in number – to Oxford Street, and with truncheons drawn they charged the crowd and ended the riot. Two days later rumours of a large mob assembling to attack Oxford Street saw businesses barricade themselves and fear for the worst. The mob did not materialise, however, and was probably only ever a paranoid overreaction by police officials dependent on unreliable information. An enquiry into the day's incidents, dubbed 'Black Monday', was called for and Metropolitan Police Commissioner Sir Edmund Henderson took the only option open to him and resigned. A man with a strong military background was needed to head the police and deal decisively with such incidents so he was replaced by General Sir Charles Warren. It was a time of change in politics as well, as the general election in August 1886 saw the Liberal government trounced by the Conservatives led by Lord Salisbury; he appointed Henry Matthews as Home Secretary.

By November 1887 unemployment and poverty had grown to such proportions in London that jobless agitators started camping in Trafalgar Square, in a desperate attempt to draw attention to their plight. Political meetings began to be held in the square with increasing regularity, with the speeches delivered there becoming more and more inciteful and impassioned. Sir Charles Warren saw the warning signs and successfully pressured Home Secretary Matthews to declare such meetings in and around the square illegal. A meeting to challenge this prohibition was called on the afternoon of 13 November, a day that would become known as 'Bloody Sunday'.

Commissioner Warren personally took 2,000 of his men to Trafalgar Square and had two squadrons of Life Guards on standby at Horse Guards Parade with two magistrates to read the Riot Act if necessary. When an unruly mob, armed with sticks, iron bars, knives, stones and bricks approached the square intent on storming it the police lines held but, concerned with the escalating violence, Warren ordered the Life Guards in. In all, 4,000 constables, 300 mounted police, 300 Grenadier Guards and 300 Life Guards were deployed to quell the riot. Over 150 of the crowd were treated for injuries and over 300 were arrested. Most were dismissed with warnings or fines, although some got imprisonment with hard labour varying between one to six months.

Warren had acquitted himself well but 1888 was to bring the greatest challenge any police commissioner had ever faced as the streets of London would be gripped with fear by a series of increasingly horrific murders in the East End of London. Harold Furniss evocatively recreated the atmosphere, when he looked back on those crimes in his magazine *Famous Crimes* the early twentieth century:

> In the long catalogue of crimes which has been compiled in our modern days there is nothing to be found, perhaps, which has so darkened the horizon of humanity and shadowed the vista of man's better nature as the series of mysterious murders committed in Whitechapel during the latter part of the year 1888. From east to west, from north to south the horror ran throughout the land. Men spoke of it with bated breath, and pale-lipped, shuddered as they read the dreadful details. A lurid pall rested over that densely populated district of London, and people, looking at it afar off, smelt blood. The superstitious said the skies had been of deeper red that autumn, presaging desperate and direful deeds, and aliens of the neighbourhood, filled with strange phantasies brought from foreign shores, whispered that evil spirits were abroad.

The evening of Thursday 30 August 1888 saw busy houses in the London theatres: the Theatre Royal, Covent Garden, was staging Freeman Thomas's seventh annual series of promenade concerts; the Adelphi presented William Terriss in *Union Jack*; the Haymarket had a double bill of *Captain Swift*, preceded by *That Dreadful Doctor*; and Richard Mansfield strode out upon the Lyceum stage in his disturbing portrayal of *Dr Jekyll and Mr Hyde*. As the patrons left the theatres they stepped out into heavy downpours of rain punctuated by deep rolls of thunder and occasional flashes of lightning. The sky was blood red, a vast pall of smoke darted by tongues of blue flames was seen over the East End and horse-drawn fire appliances with polished brass boilers and brass-helmeted fireman clinging on for dear life flew past the crowds. The streets of east London were abuzz with people making their way to observe the drama of the Shadwell Dry Dock fire for themselves. The *East London Advertiser* described the scene:

> In the enormous docks, crammed with goods of incalculable value, with vast buildings on every side, and with great vessels in the wet docks, firemen,

policemen and dock officers were either watching or aiding in endeavouring to extinguish the fire, while an enormous crowd gathered round the great gates and gazed at the progress of the fire from a distance. In a great shed building close to the fire the steamers had been drawn up in little clusters of twos and threes, and were pumping continuously with a deafening noise, while the horses, which had been unharnessed, stood quietly in couples in every corner. The water poured over the granite stones of the docks in torrents, and the whole scene was brilliantly illuminated by the fire above.

Tragic 42-year-old Mary Ann Nichols was seen on the Whitechapel Road that night, probably prostituting herself to earn a few coins for food, bed or, more likely, a drink. Mary, known on the streets as 'Polly' Nichols, had been living in a room she shared with four other women in a doss house at 18 Thrawl Street but had recently moved to another, known as the White House, at 56 Flower and Dean Street in an area of Spitalfields that, along with nearby Thrawl Street, was known as the 'evil quarter mile'. 'Flowery Dean' was one of the most foul and dangerous streets in the whole metropolis.

At 12.30 a.m. on 31 August 1888, Polly Nichols turned up at her old lodging house after drinking at the Frying Pan Public House on the corner of Brick Lane and Thrawl Street. After about an hour there Polly was turned away by the deputy because she had not got the 4d to stay the night.

Described as being 'worse for drink, but not drunk', as she left Polly turned to the deputy, saying, 'I'll soon get my "doss" money; see what a jolly bonnet I've got now.' Polly was next seen by her room-mate Emily Holland, outside a grocer's shop on the corner of Whitechapel Road and Osborn Street, nearly opposite the parish church, where the clock had just struck the half hour of 2.30 a.m. Emily had been watching the Shadwell Dry Dock fire and she recalled Polly was, by then, much the worse for drink and staggering against the wall. Emily tried to persuade her to come home with her, but Polly declined, telling Emily that she had had her doss money three times that day and had drunk it away, and declared confidently, 'It won't be long before I'm back.' All Emily could do was watch as Polly staggered off eastward down Whitechapel Road.

Less than an hour and a quarter later and just under three-quarters of a mile distant, her mutilated body was discovered on Buck's Row, in the gateway entrance to an old stable yard, by Charles Cross,[253] who was on his way to work as a carman for Messrs. Pickford & Co. Initially he thought it was a tarpaulin sheet but walking into the middle of the road he saw it was the body of a woman. He then heard the footsteps of another man (a carman named Robert Paul) going up Buck's Row. Cross rushed over to him and said, 'Come and look over here; there is a woman lying on the pavement.' The pair crossed over to the body, Cross took hold of the woman's hands, which he found were to be cold, limp and lifeless. Cross thought she was dead but Paul placed his hand on her chest, thought

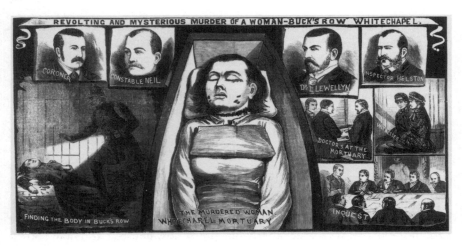

The murder of 'Polly' Nichols on the cover of *The Illustrated Police News*, Saturday 8 September 1888.

he detected some breathing and went to seek a policeman. They encountered PC Mizen on Baker's Row and reported that they had found a woman lying dead or drunk on Buck's Row. The street was dark and neither man noticed her throat had been slashed across.

At more or less the same time, PC John Neil 97J was on patrol on Buck's Row. The *Daily Mail* reported that at the inquest held on the following day he stated:

> I was proceeding down Buck's-row, Whitechapel, going towards Brady-street. There was not a soul about. I had been round there half an hour previously, and I saw no one then. I was on the right-hand side of the street, when I noticed a figure lying in the street. It was dark at the time, though there was a street lamp shining at the end of the row. I went across and found deceased lying outside a gateway, her head towards the east. The gateway was closed … Deceased was lying lengthways along the street, her left hand touching the gate. I examined the body by the aid of my lamp, and noticed blood oozing from a wound in the throat. She was lying on her back, with her clothes disarranged. I felt her arm, which was quite warm from the joints upwards. Her eyes were wide open. Her bonnet was off and lying at her side, close to the left hand. I heard a constable passing Brady-street, so I called him. I did not whistle. I said to him, 'Run at once for Dr. Llewellyn', and, seeing another constable in Baker's-row, I sent him for the ambulance. The doctor arrived in a very short time. I had, in the meantime, rung the bell at Essex Wharf, and asked if any disturbance had been heard. The reply was 'No'. Sergeant Kirby came after, and he knocked. The doctor looked at the woman and then said, 'Move her to the mortuary. She is dead, and I will make a further examination of her.' We placed her on the ambulance, and

moved her there. Inspector Spratling came to the mortuary, and while taking a description of the deceased turned up her clothes, and found that she was disembowelled.

Curiously, despite Polly's body being found almost underneath the window of the end terrace house known as the 'New Cottage', the inhabitants, a widow named Mrs Green, her two sons and a daughter, all claimed they had not heard a thing until the police arrived.

Dr Llewellyn conducted the post-mortem and reported his findings at the inquest:

Five of the teeth are missing, and there is a slight laceration of the tongue. On the right side of the face there is a bruise running along the lower part of the jaw. It might have been caused by a blow with the fist or pressure by the thumb. On the left side of the face there was a circular bruise, which also might have been done by the pressure of the fingers. On the left side of the neck, about an inch below the jaw, there was an incision about four inches long and running from a point immediately below the ear. An inch below on the same side, and commencing about an inch in front of it, was a circular incision terminating at a point about three inches below the right jaw. This incision completely severs all the tissues down to the vertebrae. The large vessels of the neck on both sides were severed. The incision is about eight inches long. These cuts must have been caused with a long-bladed knife, moderately sharp, and used with great violence. No blood at all was found on the breast either of the body or clothes. There were no injuries about the body till just about the lower part of the abdomen. Two or three inches from the left side was a wound running in a jagged manner. It was a very deep wound, and the tissues were cut through. There were several incisions running across the abdomen. On the right side there were also three or four similar cuts running downwards. All these had been caused by a knife, which had been used violently and been used downwards. The wounds were from left to right, and might have been done by a left-handed person. All the injuries had been done by the same instrument.[254]

The press leapt on the story and reports rapidly drew together previously unconnected murders in the East End, among them Elizabeth Smith and Martha Tabram. Soon headlines were announcing that Polly Nichols was *another* victim of the killer the press dubbed, 'The Whitechapel Murderer' or 'Fiend'. *The Star* was typical in its reportage and also reflects the trend to at least partly dehumanise the killer, talk of 'a thirst for blood', and decry the efforts of the police, who appeared to be powerless in their efforts to track down the monster:

HORROR UPON HORROR.
WHITECHAPEL IS PANIC-STRICKEN AT ANOTHER FIENDISH
CRIME.
A FOURTH VICTIM OF THE MANIAC.
A Woman is Found Murdered Under Circumstances Exceeding in Brutality
the Three Other Whitechapel Crimes.

London lies to-day under the spell of a great terror. A nameless reprobate –
half beast, half man – is at large, who is daily gratifying his murderous instincts
on the most miserable and defenceless classes of the community. There can be
no shadow of a doubt now that our original theory was correct, and that the
Whitechapel murderer, who has now four, if not five, victims to his knife, is
one man, and that man a murderous maniac. There is another Williams in our
midst. Hideous malice, deadly cunning, insatiable thirst for blood – all these are
the marks of the mad homicide. The ghoul-like creature who stalks through
the streets of London, stalking down his victim like a Pawnee Indian, is simply
drunk with blood, and he will have more. The question is, what are the people
of London to do? Whitechapel is garrisoned with police and stocked with
plain-clothes men. Nothing comes of it. The police have not even a clue. They
are in despair at their utter failure to get so much as a scent of the criminal.[255]

Soon the press announced that the police were questioning slaughtermen and
were actively seeking a man known in the Whitechapel area as 'Leather Apron'
for questioning in connection with murders because of his reputation for
'ill-using prostitutes'. A Polish Jew named John Pizer was well known to the
police and people of his locale as 'Leather Apron' because he wore his work apron
on the street. On 10 September 1888 Pizer was arrested by Sergeant Thick and
several sharp, long-bladed knives were found on his premises at 22 Mulberry
Street – but that is hardly surprising as his trade was that of boot finisher. Pizer
was taken to Leman Street police station; fearing for his life his friends joined
him, confirmed his alibis and he was released the following day. However, the
broadsheets still demanded the capture of 'Leather Apron' – no longer a name
just for Pizer but transposed into a generic term for the Whitechapel Murderer,
who was thought to be a slaughterman or tradesman skilled with his knife, such
as a cork worker or cobbler. But we must not get ahead of ourselves because, by
the time Pizer had been arrested, there had been another murder.

The next horribly mutilated body was discovered in the early hours of Saturday
8 September 1888 in the backyard of 29 Hanbury Street, Spitalfields, a secluded
spot known to be occasionally used by prostitutes and their clients. The body was
identified as 47-year-old Annie Chapman. Investigations revealed she had once
enjoyed a good standard of living, was married and had three children but the
'demon drink', indulged to excess by both Annie and her husband John, split the
family. John paid Annie some money each week but this stopped when he died in

1886. Up to that time she had been living with another man on Dorset Street, but he too left her, probably because the regular money dried up. Annie was then left to fend for herself; destitute and ill and with no family to support her, she turned to prostitution and became known on the streets as 'Dark Annie'.

At 1.35 a.m. on Saturday 8 September, Annie had arrived at Crossingham's, the lodging house she usually resided at, at 35 Dorset Street, Spitalfields. She had been in and out of the lodging house a number of times during the evening, and was sporting a black eye after a fight with another woman a few days earlier. She had been drinking and witnesses reported that she had been eating a baked potato. John 'Brummy' Evans, the lodging house's elderly night watchman, was sent to collect her bed money but she went upstairs to see Timothy Donovan, the deputy in charge, in his office. Annie pleaded, 'I haven't sufficient money for my bed, but don't let it. I shall not be long before I'm in.' But Donovan chastised her, 'You can find money for your beer and you can't find money for your bed.' Nonplussed, Annie stepped out of the office and stood in the doorway for two or three minutes, then she said, 'Never mind, Tim, I'll soon be back' and left peaceably. Donovan recalled, 'She walked straight. Generally on Saturdays she was the worse for drink.' As Annie left she saw Watchman Evans again and said, 'I won't be long, Brummy. See that Tim keeps the bed for me'; he watched her wander up the road, enter Little Paternoster Row going in the direction of Brushfield Street, and finally lost sight of her as she turned towards Spitalfields market.

The last witness to see Annie alive was Mrs Elizabeth Long, who passed her when she was few yards from 29 Hanbury Street; she would testify at the inquest:

> On Saturday 8 September, about half past five o'clock in the morning, I was passing down Hanbury Street, from home, on my way to Spitalfields Market. I knew the time, because I heard the brewer's clock strike half-past five just before I got to the street. I passed 29, Hanbury-street. On the right-hand side, the same side as the house, I saw a man and a woman standing on the pavement talking. The man's back was turned towards Brick-lane, and the woman's was towards the market. They were standing only a few yards nearer Brick Lane from 29, Hanbury Street. I saw the woman's face. Have seen the deceased in the mortuary, and I am sure the woman that I saw in Hanbury Street was the deceased. I did not see the man's face, but I noticed that he was dark. He was wearing a brown low-crowned felt hat. I think he had on a dark coat, though I am not certain. By the look of him he seemed to me a man over forty years of age. He appeared to me to be a little taller than the deceased.

When questioned by the coroner, Dr Wynne Baxter, about the appearance of the man she said he 'looked like a foreigner' and when asked if he looked like a dock labourer or a workman she replied, 'I should say he looked like what I should call shabby-genteel.' The couple were talking loudly, and Mrs Long stated she overheard him say to Annie, 'Will you?' and she replied, 'Yes'. Mrs Long confirmed, 'That is all I heard, and I heard this as I passed.' Long walked on and did not look back to see where the couple went next.

The body of Annie Chapman was discovered at 6.00 a.m. by elderly John Davis who occupied the top front room on the third floor of 29 Hanbury Street

Cover of *The Illustrated Police News*, 22 September 1888, with the lead illustrations and story of the murder of Annie Chapman – 'The Hanbury Street Horror'.

Bram Stoker (seated centre), with the officers of the Trinity College Dublin Historical Society, 'the Hist', for the season 1872/73. (*The Board of Trinity College Dublin*)

Front gate, Trinity College Dublin, viewed from College Green as Bram would have known it in the early 1870s.

Walt Whitman *c.* 1870.

Professor Edward Dowden, *c.* 1874–75,
Bram's most influential tutor at Trinity
College Dublin.

Police armed with batons wade in to break up the Fenian Amnesty meeting at Dublin's
Phoenix Park in August 1871.

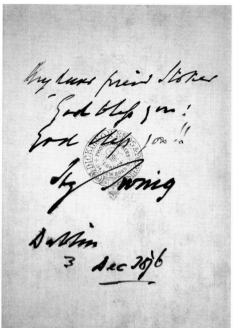

The photograph and the effusive message, hastily inscribed on its reverse by Henry Irving after his powerful rendition of Hood's *The Dream of Eugene Aram*, and presented to Bram Stoker on the evening of 3 December 1876.

The Shelbourne Hotel, St Stephen's Green, Dublin, *c.* 1875.

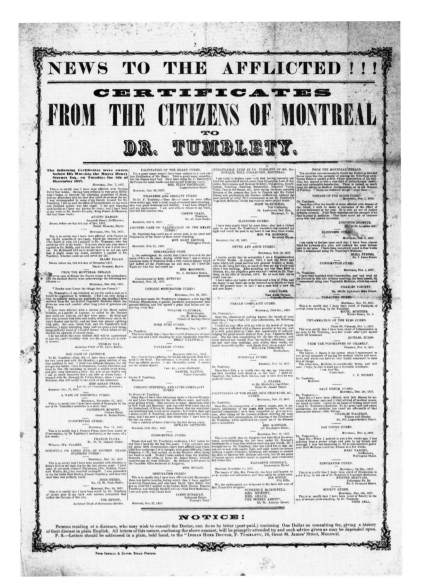

Dr Tumblety's broadside of testimonial certificates from the citizens of Montreal, 1857. (*Bibliothèque et Archives Nationales du Québec*)

Advert for 'Dr Tumblety's Pimple Banisher' that appeared in *Harper's Weekly*, 20 July 1861.

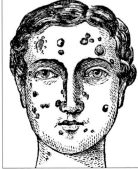

South Castle Street, Liverpool as Hall Caine and Francis Tumblety would have know it *c.* 1875. (*Colin Wilkinson, Bluecoat Press*)

Photograph of Francis Tumblety, which he claimed showed him in the uniform of a member of the Prussian Imperial Guard in 1869. (*Collection of the New York Historical Society*)

Francis Tumblety, 'The Great American Doctor', pictured at the time of his correspondence with Hall Caine *c.* 1875. (*Private Collection*)

WHO IS THE GREAT AMERICAN DOCTOR?

TO THE
TOWNSPEOPLE OF LIVERPOOL.

A few weeks ago I was the subject of an attack which would have merited the lash, or, a legal, rather than a literary chastisement, if it had not been perpetrated by men whose powers and position were beneath serious consideration. The puny efforts I allude to were made with the sanguinary effectiveness of ours yelping at the heels of a war horse, and yet such, unhappily, is the gullibility of certain sections of the public, and such the mighty and much to be lamented power to check, guide, and control public opinion exercised by the public press (even when conducted by men for whose motives no guarantee my be given, and at whose education every mountebank may fairly grin), that I now find myself compelled to recognize, to challenge, and confute statements which would otherwise have passed by me, with the multitude of gnats, beetles, wasps, and butterflies, and the whole tribe of ephemerals and insignificants, which hum and buzz and jar, and shrill their tiny pipes, unchased and unnoticed.

Very frequent in their occurrence have been the occasions upon which, though discharged by law of every impeachment laid against me, I have been compelled to endure to the judgment, an addendum at once stupid and damaging and appended at the caprice of some petty court governor, of whom it might always have been said that if his motives were pure, his judgment and education were at least questionable. The old faculty have ever entertained a deep rooted prejudice against the advanced principles I espouse, and that circumstance, when added to the other fact of my demanding a large share of public attention, will be found to account for the sly, childish, waspish, acrimonious attacks made upon me.

I have thought fit to prepare under the title of

PASSAGES IN THE LIFE OF
DR. FRANCIS TUMBLETY

some history of my past experiences. The pamphlet will be issued at a low price, and the date of publication, and all particulars concerning it, will be made known in due course by the publishers. It is hoped, and confidently believed, that this pamphlet will re-instate me into public favour amongst the inhabitants of Liverpool. As to my professional reputation elsewere, there are few practitioners who can produce such gratifying evidence of successful treatment as myself, and when I say that I am daily adding valuable testimony to the efficacy of my labours, and further that I am yearly enlarging my acquaintance with a really distinguished circle of people, such as are not merely of national, but also of cosmopolitan reputation, the reader will pardon any occasional show of impatience I may manifest when replying to queries of respectability emanating from persons of whom society knows little, or that little not of the best.

Your obedient servant,
Dr. FRANCIS TUMBLETY.
(The American Doctor.)

February 10th, 1875.

Published at the Temporary Offices of the

"LIVERPOOL LANTERN"
WARRINGTON CHAMBERS.
2, SOUTH CASTLE STREET, LIVERPOOL.

Poster produced by Francis Tumblety as he set about repudiating allegations against him in Liverpool, February 1875. (*Papers of Sir Thomas Henry Hall Caine (1853–1931), Manx National Heritage MS 09542*)

Thomas Henry Hall
Caine (1853–1931),
pictured *c.* 1890.

Bram Stoker (1847–1912),
pictured in 1890.
(*Getty Images*)

One of the envelopes of the letters sent by Francis Tumblety to Hall Caine, 4 August 1875, showing the London East Central postmark. (*Papers of Sir Thomas Henry Hall Caine (1853–1931), Manx National Heritage MS 09542*)

Midland Hotel
Birmingham
Aug.st 6. 1875

Dear Caine

Don't trifle with my patience any longer,

Send me two pounds to the above address no more nor no less a paltry amount than two pounds & our friendly correspondence shall go on. independent of the little financial matters, Nobody else Knows anything about it, there is no fraud being committed on you, as I am not in the habit of telling people my private affairs

I got your letter this morning at 16 Devereux Court Strand & felt a little surprised at finding an excuse in it instead of two pounds Matthew Bros have no claim on you I've paid them,

Yours in haste
F. J. Tumblety

P.S. I am stopping here for 3 or 4 days don't fail to send P.O.O here at once

A flare of aggression displayed in the Tumblety letter to Hall Caine on 6 August 1875. (*Papers of Sir Thomas Henry Hall Caine (1853–1931), Manx National Heritage MS 09542*)

Henry Irving, the young actor, in 1868.

Eleanora 'Nelly' Moore, the love that Irving lost. She died of typhoid fever at her house on Soho Square on 22 January 1869, aged just 24. (© *Victoria and Albert Museum, London*)

The photograph of Zaré Thalberg, pasted back-to-back with the 1868 photo of Henry Irving and found in Irving's pocketbook after his death in 1905. (© *Victoria and Albert Museum, London*)

Ellen Terry (1847–1928). Bram Stoker's 'dutiful child' pictured as Lucy Ashton in the Lyceum production of *Ravenswood*, 1891.

The Royal Lyceum Theatre, Wellington Street, Strand, London, 1891 – as proclaimed on the programmes – Sole Lessee and Manager: Mr Henry Irving; Stage Manager: Mr. H. J. Loveday; Acting Manager: Bram Stoker.

American actor, Edwin Booth (1833–93), the brother of John Wilkes Booth, the assassin of President Abraham Lincoln. Booth and Irving alternated in the roles of Othello and Iago during the 1881 production at the Lyceum.

A clever double exposure of Richard Mansfield in his double roles of Dr Jekyll and Mr Hyde at the Lyceum in 1888. His portrayal was so disturbing it was seen as influencing the crimes of Jack the Ripper.

The East Cliff and ruins of Whitby Abbey photographed from the East Pier lighthouse, Whitby, *c.* 1891.

The wreck of the Russian Schooner *Dimitry* of Narva (that became the *Demeter* of Varna in *Dracula*) on Tate Hill Sands, Whitby, October 1885. (*The Sutcliffe Gallery*)

Whitby Abbey as Bram Stoker would have seen it in 1891.

The ruins of St Mary's Abbey Church, York, c. 1891. The only two remaining photographs in Bram Stoker's notes for *Dracula* were assumed to have shown Whitby Abbey but actually show these ruins.

Explorer Henry Morton Stanley (1841–1904), described by Bram as looking 'more like a dead man than a living one'.

Richard Francis Burton (1821–90), explorer, adventurer, spy, translator of *The Arabian Nights* and self-confessed murderer.

Poet Laureate Alfred, Lord Tennyson (1809–1902), whose occasional lifting of the upper lip to show the canine tooth 'marked an indication of militant instinct in him'.

Painter and playwright William Gorman 'W.G.' Wills whose strange bohemian behaviour and appearance could well have inspired the creation of R.M. Renfield.

William F. 'Buffalo Bill' Cody (1846–1917), the embodiment of all that fascinated Bram in America and the inspiration for the Texan Quincey P. Morris.

Genevieve Ward, an amour of Bram's youth and a lifelong friend, pictured in the character of Rebecca in *Ivanhoe* at Drury Lane Theatre in 1875.

Swedish operatic soprano Christina Nilsson (1843–1921), who, it was suggested, was Gaston Leroux's inspiration for Christine Daaé in *Phantom of the Opera*. (© *Victoria and Albert Museum, London*)

Hortense Catherine Schneider (1833–1920), one of the greatest operetta stars of the nineteenth century. (© *Victoria and Albert Museum, London*)

Hall Caine, pictured shortly before his death in 1931.

The Tumblety family grave and monument, Holy Sepulchre Cemetery, Rochester, New York. (*Rusty Clark*)

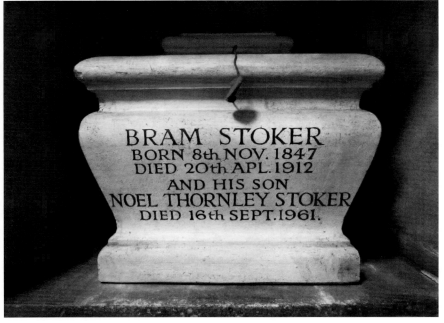

The urn containing the ashes of Bram Stoker at Golders Green Crematorium, London. When Noel died in 1961 his ashes were mixed with those of his father.

with his wife and three sons. At the inquest, held at the Working Lads' Institute, Whitechapel Road, on Monday 10 September 1888 before Mr Wynne Baxter, Mr Davis recounted the circumstances of his grim discovery:

Directly I opened the door I saw a woman lying down in the left hand recess, between the stone steps and the fence. She was on her back, with her head towards the house and her legs towards the wood shed. The clothes were up to her groins. I did not go into the yard, but left the house by the front door, and called the attention of two men to the circumstances. They work at Mr. Bailey's, a packing-case maker, of Hanbury Street. I do not know their names, but I know them by sight. Mr Bailey's is three doors off 29, Hanbury Street, on the same side of the road. The two men were waiting outside the workshop. They came into the passage, and saw the sight. They did not go into the yard, but ran to find a policeman.[256]

Police were soon on the scene and Mr George Bagster Phillips, the divisional surgeon, was summoned to the murder site. Annie's body could be seen from the back windows of the adjacent terraced houses and enterprising occupants charged the grimly curious a penny a time for a look. Even after the body was removed hundreds still came to see the murder site and were still happy to pay for the experience, though all that could be seen by that time were a couple of packing cases beneath which the stain of a blood track was still visible.[257]

The inquest jury viewed the corpse at the mortuary in Montague Street, but all evidence of mutilations to which the deceased had been subjected had been concealed. Her clothing and few tragic effects were also inspected and listed as:

A long black figured coat that came down to her knees
A black skirt
Brown bodice
Another bodice
Two petticoats
A large pocket worn under the skirt and tied about the waist with strings (empty when found)
Lace-up boots
Red-and-white striped woollen stockings
Neckerchief, white with a wide red border
Scrap of muslin
One small-tooth comb
One comb in a paper case
Scrap of envelope containing two pills bearing the seal of the Sussex Regiment post, marked 'London, 28, Aug., 1888'; inscribed was a partial address consisting of the letter M, the number 2 as if the beginning of an address, and an S.

Curiously, Annie was known to have worn two brass rings on her ring finger, these were missing after her murder, and the marks left by the rings were noted by Mr George Bagster Phillips, the divisional police surgeon, but no one could have anticipated the further revelations he would present when he gave his evidence at the resumed inquest on Thursday 13 September:

> On Saturday last I was called by the police at 6.20 a.m. to 29, Hanbury Street, and arrived at half-past six. I found the body of the deceased lying in the yard on her back, on the left hand of the steps that lead from the passage. The head was about 6in in front of the level of the bottom step, and the feet were towards a shed at the end of the yard. The left arm was across the left breast, and the legs were drawn up, the feet resting on the ground, and the knees turned outwards. The face was swollen and turned on the right side, and the tongue protruded between the front teeth, but not beyond the lips; it was much swollen. The small intestines and other portions were lying on the right side of the body on the ground above the right shoulder, but attached. There was a large quantity of blood, with a part of the stomach above the left shoulder. I searched the yard and found a small piece of coarse muslin, a small-tooth comb, and a pocket-comb, in a paper case, near the railing. They had apparently been arranged there. I also discovered various other articles, which I handed to the police. The body was cold, except that there was a certain remaining heat, under the intestines, in the body. Stiffness of the limbs was not marked, but it was commencing. The throat was dissevered deeply. I noticed that the incision of the skin was jagged, and reached right round the neck. On the back wall of the house, between the steps and the palings, on the left side, about 18in from the ground, there were about six patches of blood, varying in size from a sixpenny piece to a small point, and on the wooden fence there were smears of blood, corresponding to where the head of the deceased laid, and immediately above the part where the blood had mainly flowed from the neck, which was well clotted. [258]

Once the body had been removed to the mortuary Bagster Phillips carried out a further, detailed examination:

> The body had been attended to since its removal to the mortuary, and probably partially washed. I noticed a bruise over the right temple. There was a bruise under the clavicle, and there were two distinct bruises, each the size of a man's thumb, on the fore part of the chest. The stiffness of the limbs was then well-marked. The finger nails were turgid. There was an old scar of long standing on the left of the frontal bone. On the left side the stiffness was more noticeable, and especially in the fingers, which were partly closed. There was an abrasion over the bend of the first joint of the ring finger, and there were distinct markings of a ring or rings – probably the latter. There were small sores

on the fingers. The throat had been severed. The incisions of the skin indicated that they had been made from the left side of the neck on a line with the angle of the jaw, carried entirely round and again in front of the neck, and ending at a point about midway between the jaw and the sternum or breast bone on the right hand. There were two distinct clean cuts on the body of the vertebrae on the left side of the spine. They were parallel to each other, and separated by about half an inch. The muscular structures between the side processes of bone of the vertebrae had an appearance as if an attempt had been made to separate the bones of the neck. There are various other mutilations of the body, but I am of opinion that they occurred subsequently to the death of the woman and to the large escape of blood from the neck.

(The witness, pauses)

I am entirely in your hands, sir, but is it necessary that I should describe the further mutilations. From what I have said I can state the cause of death.

BAXTER: The object of the inquiry is not only to ascertain the cause of death, but the means by which it occurred. Any mutilation which took place afterwards may suggest the character of the man who did it. Possibly you can give us the conclusions to which you have come respecting the instrument used.

PHILLIPS: You don't wish for details. I think if it is possible to escape the details it would be advisable. The cause of death is visible from injuries I have described.

BAXTER: You have kept a record of them?

PHILLIPS: I have.

BAXTER: Supposing any one is charged with the offence, they would have to come out then, and it might be a matter of comment that the same evidence was not given at the inquest.

PHILLIPS: I am entirely in your hands.

BAXTER: We will postpone that for the present. You can give your opinion as to how the death was caused.

PHILLIPS: From these appearances I am of opinion that the breathing was interfered with previous to death, and that death arose from syncope, or failure of the heart's action, in consequence of the loss of blood caused by the severance of the throat.

BAXTER: Was the instrument used at the throat the same as that used at the abdomen?

PHILLIPS: Very probably. It must have been a very sharp knife, probably with a thin, narrow blade, and at least six to eight inches in length, and perhaps longer.

BAXTER: Is it possible that any instrument used by a military man, such as a bayonet, would have done it?

PHILLIPS: No; it would not be a bayonet.

BAXTER: Would it have been such an instrument as a medical man uses for post-mortem examinations?

PHILLIPS: The ordinary post-mortem case perhaps does not contain such a weapon.

BAXTER: Would any instrument that slaughterers employ have caused the injuries?

PHILLIPS: Yes; well ground down.

BAXTER: Would the knife of a cobbler or of any person in the leather trades have done?

PHILLIPS: I think the knife used in those trades would not be long enough in the blade.

BAXTER: Was there any anatomical knowledge displayed?

PHILLIPS: I think there was. There were indications of it. My own impression is that that anatomical knowledge was only less displayed or indicated in consequence of haste. The person evidently was hindered from making a more complete dissection in consequence of the haste.

BAXTER: Was the whole of the body there?

PHILLIPS: No; the absent portions being from the abdomen.

BAXTER: Are those portions such as would require anatomical knowledge to extract?

PHILLIPS: I think the mode in which they were extracted did show some anatomical knowledge.

BAXTER: You do not think they could have been lost accidentally in the transit of the body to the mortuary?

PHILLIPS: I was not present at the transit. I carefully closed up the clothes of the woman. Some portions had been excised.

BAXTER: How long had the deceased been dead when you saw her?

PHILLIPS: I should say at least two hours, and probably more; but it is right to say that it was a fairly cold morning, and that the body would be more apt to cool rapidly from its having lost the greater portion of its blood.

BAXTER: Was there any evidence of any struggle?

PHILLIPS: No; not about the body of the woman. You do not forget the smearing of blood about the palings.

BAXTER: In your opinion did she enter the yard alive?

PHILLIPS: I am positive of it. I made a thorough search of the passage, and I saw no trace of blood, which must have been visible had she been taken into the yard.[259]

In his summing up, Coroner Wynne Baxter, added some startling revelations of his own:

The object of the murderer appears palpably shown by the facts, and it is not necessary to assume lunacy, for it is clear that there is a market for the object of the murder. To show you this, I must mention a fact which at the same time proves the assistance which publicity and the newspaper press afford in the detection of crime. Within a few hours of the issue of the morning papers containing a report of the medical evidence given at the last sitting of the Court, I received a communication from an officer of one of our great medical schools, that they had information which might or might not have a distinct bearing on our inquiry. I attended at the first opportunity, and was told by the sub-curator of the Pathological Museum that some months ago an American had called on him, and asked him to procure a number of specimens of the organ that was missing in the deceased. He stated his willingness to give £20 for each, and explained that his object was to issue an actual specimen with each copy of a publication on which he was then engaged. Although he was told that his wish was impossible to be complied with, he still urged his request. He desired them preserved, not in spirits of wine, the usual medium, but in glycerine, in order to preserve them in a flaccid condition, and he wished them sent to America direct. It is known that this request was repeated to another institution of a similar character. Now, is it not possible that the knowledge of this demand may have incited some abandoned wretch to possess himself of a specimen. It seems beyond belief that such inhuman wickedness could enter into the mind of any man, but unfortunately our criminal annals prove that every crime is possible. I need hardly say that I at once communicated my information to the Detective Department at Scotland Yard. Of course I do not know what use has been made of it, but I believe that publicity may possibly further elucidate this fact, and, therefore, I have not withheld from you my knowledge. By means of the press some further explanation may be forthcoming from America if not from here. I have endeavoured to suggest to you the object with which this offence was committed, and the class of person who must have perpetrated it.

If your views accord with mine, you will be of opinion that we are confronted with a murder of no ordinary character, committed not from jealousy, revenge, or robbery, but from motives less adequate than the many which still disgrace our civilisation, mar our progress, and blot the pages of our Christianity. I cannot conclude my remarks without thanking you for the attention you have given to the case, and the assistance you have rendered me in our efforts to elucidate the truth of this horrible tragedy.[260]

A verdict of wilful murder against a person or persons unknown was returned and the newspapers went wild with even more lurid descriptions and depictions of the 'Hanbury Street Horror'. Within hours of the murder – such was the speed the horror travelled – a broadsheet of doggerel verses entitled 'Lines on the Terrible Tragedy' was being hawked on the streets by long-song sellers who cried out the verses to the hardly appropriate tune of *My Village Home*.

The Whitechapel Murderer was again depicted in the *Daily Telegraph* on Monday 10 September 1888:

… no wild beast in its fury could have displayed a fiercer rage to rend and destroy than the again unknown perpetrator of this latest enormity. The

A fanged demon bill poster feeds the frenzy of penny dreadfuls, broadsides and gutter press
cashing in on the Jack the Ripper murders in *Punch*, 13 October 1888.

circumstances under which the fourth victim of so shocking a series of murders was seen weltering in her blood and disembowelled are fully given in another portion of our columns, and we may, therefore, spare ourselves and the public a repetition here of the ghastly details. Assuredly no surprise can be felt that with the recurrence of such startling crimes in a circumscribed space, committed upon miserable women of the same sad category, and with reiterated evidence of the existence of some perfectly fiendish being, possessed with a murderous frenzy, as cunning as he is cruel – no surprise, we say, can be felt that the whole quarter of London wherein these frightful acts have been perpetrated is at present in a state of consternation and horror, and that the attention of the Capital itself should be concentrated upon them.

The account went on to suggest:

Moreover, if the monster in human form whom we have imagined be captured, it must not be too lightly advanced or admitted that he is insane and irresponsible. There are natures 'mad' only in being immeasurably bad – beings who look like men, but are rather demons, vampires, of whom society has the right to be quickly rid, without too much attention to the theories of mental experts. It may be trusted that, if no clue be found to the perpetrator of this latest horror, his own cunning will eventually fail him, and that the villain will, by some garrulity or imprudence betray his guilty knowledge.

The editorials and coverage of the Whitechapel Murderer, the climate of fear they invoked and the description of the murderer as a vampire in the *Daily Telegraph* could well be significant for our story because it was the paper most likely to be read by Bram Stoker. The *Daily Telegraph's* influential drama critic was Clement Scott, a man who provided effusive and consistently good reviews for the Lyceum; Stoker biographer Barbara Belford was to describe him as 'the Lyceum's main praiser' and a man 'so inextricably involved with a specific theatre objectivity was impossible'.[261] Bram assiduously collected the good reviews of Irving and detested any against him, so the *Telegraph* would have been among his essential newspaper reading. Indeed, Bram loved to code compliments that would be recognised by his friends in his books and it may be why he chose the name of *The Dailygraph* for the newspaper that carried the news of the terrible storm heralding the Count's arrival aboard the *Demeter* at Whitby, and whose cutting Mina Murray was to paste into her journal.[262] The news that a vampire may have been at large on the streets of the East End may just have been a very inspirational cutting that Bram squirreled away, perhaps in a collection now lost or just in the back of his mind, either way, *something* was stirring.

Back on the streets of London, rumours became rife. One said the killer had scrawled 'Five, fifteen more and then I give myself up' on the fence above his handiwork on poor Annie. A leather apron had been found at the scene of the Hanbury Street murder, and although not connected with the crime word had got out and thus suspicion fell upon anyone who used a knife or wore a leather apron for their trade. In addition, after the revelations of Dr Phillips', even more horrifying fears were aroused that the murderer was a man of medical learning, perhaps even a gentleman.

Following the repeated assertions in the press and on the streets that 'no Englishman could have perpetrated such a horrible crime', there were numerous cases of assault upon 'foreign types' especially members of the East End Jewish population. The *Echo* expanded the story to claim that Divisional Police Surgeon George Bagster Phillips and his assistant 'were out of their beds nearly all Saturday night in attendance on cases of assault, some of them of the most serious character, arising directly or indirectly out of the intense excitement occasioned by the discussion of this affair'.[263] The *Daily News* picked up on the story and was drawn to sensationally conclude:

> The public are looking for a monster, and in the legend of 'Leather Apron' the Whitechapel part of them seem to be inventing a monster to look for. This kind of invention ought to be discouraged in every possible way, or there may soon be murders from panic to add to murders from lust of blood. A touch would fire the whole district, in the mood which it is now.[264]

On 10 September 1888 Detective Inspector Abberline, who was leading the hunt for the Whitechapel Murderer on the ground, drew a crowd at Commercial Street police station. He had arrived hotfoot from Gravesend with a suspect, one William Piggott. Piggott was apprehended for being seen drinking in a pub wearing a blood-stained shirt. He was known in Gravesend for his strange behaviour but he was not identified by police witnesses, and within two hours his speech had become so garbled a doctor was sent for to assess his sanity. Piggott was pronounced insane and immediately removed to the asylum at Bow.

On the evening of 10 September, dissatisfied with police progress and concerned for the safety of the people of the East End, a disparate body of interested parties from tradesmen to labourers gathered at The Crown, a public house on Mile End Road, to form the Whitechapel Vigilance Committee. At the meeting local vestryman George Lusk was appointed their chairman and Joseph Aarons, the licensee of The Crown, their treasurer.

Meanwhile, following concerns expressed to the authorities by Dr Cowan and Dr Crabb about a certain Jacob Isenschmid, the police at Holloway succeeded in making an arrest and Detective Inspector Styles was sent to investigate this potential suspect for the murders. After Isenschmid was brought into custody he was soon certified a lunatic and was sent under restraint to Islington Workhouse and later Grove Hall Lunatic Asylum.

On 18 September 1888 PC John Johnson (No. 866 of the City force), was on duty in the Minories at about 3 a.m. when he heard loud screams of 'Murder' from a dark court. Running towards the screams, Johnson found they led to Butcher's Row and some railway arches near Whitechapel Road where he found a man behaving in threatening manner with a prostitute named Elizabeth Burns. Asked what he was doing the man replied, 'nothing,' but the distressed unfortunate begged, 'Oh, policeman, do take me out of this.' PC Johnson sent the man on his way and walked with the woman, who was too shaken to speak properly, to the end of his beat, when she blurted out, 'Dear me, he frightened me very much when he pulled that big knife out.' The constable set out in pursuit of the man but he could not be found. The man was apprehended, later that same day, after an altercation at a coffee stall where he drew a knife and threatened Alexander Finlay (also known as Freinburg), who threw a dish from the stall at the threatening man. PC John Gallagher 221H intervened and arrested the man, who was subsequently identified as German immigrant Charles Ludwig. Ludwig was held for a fortnight until his hearing at Thames Magistrates' Court. Being in custody at the time of the subsequent murders of Stride and Eddowes, Ludwig was thus provided with solid alibis for the latest Ripper killings. Magistrates considered he had been incarcerated long enough for his crimes and released him.

On 19 September Sir Charles Warren sent a report to the Home Office discussing the suspect Isenschmid (which Warren spelled Isensmith) and a certain Oswald Puckeridge who had been released from an asylum on 4 August. Puckeridge had been educated as a surgeon and had been known to threaten to rip people up with a long knife. In the report Warren stated, 'He is being looked for but cannot be found yet … A brothel keeper who will not give her address or name writes to say that a man living in her house was seen with blood on him on the morning of the murder … when the detectives came near him he bolted, got away and there is no clue to the writer of the letter.'

Never one to miss a chance to publicise the plight of his flock, Canon Samuel Barnett of St Jude's and a founder warden of Toynbee Hall wrote an extended letter to *The Times*, which was published on 19 September 1888. His arguments were clear: 'There should be a national effort to rehouse the poor because such was degradation in which many in the End End lived, especially Spitalfields, crime was an inevitability.' Part of his letter stated, 'Whitechapel horrors will not be in vain, if "at last" public conscience awakes to consider the life which these horrors reveal. The murders were, it may also be said, bound to come; generation could not follow generation in lawless intercourse.'

Canon Barnett then made four practical suggestions to avoid the perpetuation of the situation:

1. Efficient police supervision
2. Adequate lighting and cleaning

3. The removal of slaughter houses (sights such as blood on the streets from the butchers and slaughter houses brutalise ignorant natures)

4. The control of tenement houses by responsible landlords

There was no groundswell from government or the people of Britain to improve the lot of the poverty-stricken in the East End but Canon Barnett never lost hope and, tirelessly working with local councils, charities and benevolent individuals and organisations, he did much to improve the life of many in the hardest quarters of the East End.

The 27 September 1888 was a red-letter day for the Whitechapel murders, literally, for this was the date postmarked on the letter received at the offices of the Central News Agency, 5 New Bridge Street, Ludgate Circus. Posted in EC1 (east London), it read:

Dear Boss.

I keep on hearing the police have caught me but they wont fix me just yet. I have laughed when they look so clever and talk about being on the right track. That joke about Leather Apron gave me real fits. I am down on whores and I shant quit ripping them till I do get buckled. Grand work the last job was, I gave the lady no time to squeal. How can they catch me now. I love my work and want to start again. You will soon hear of me with my funny little games. I saved some of the proper red stuff in a ginger beer bottle over the last job to write with but it went thick like glue and I cant use it. Red ink is fit enough I hope ha ha. The next job I do I shall clip the ladys ears off and send to the police officers just for jolly wouldn't you. Keep this letter back till I do a bit more work then give it out straight. My knife's so nice and sharp I want to get to work right away if I get a chance. Good luck.

  Yours truly

  Jack the Ripper

Don't mind me giving the trade name. Wasn't good enough to post this before I got all the red ink off my hands curse it. No luck yet. They say I'm a doctor now ha ha.

This lurid missive, known as the 'Dear Boss' letter, is more likely to have been penned by an unscrupulous journalist hoping to add yet another twist to the tale than the actual murderer. In either case, the theme took off and soon hundreds of letters were being sent to London and provincial police forces and civic officials purporting to come from the Whitechapel Murderer. This letter will, however, remain unique and would go down in infamy as the first appearance of the name 'Jack the Ripper'.

The Whitechapel Vigilance Committee and many people of the East End felt great indignation that the Home Office had not taken more proactive steps in the matter, so wrote to the Home Secretary on two occasions with regard to putting up a reward for the capture of the killer. Both requests were turned down but the committee did manage to raise a subscription and wrote to the editor of *The Standard* on 29 September:

Sir, – As Chairman of the Whitechapel Vigilance Committee, who communicated, without result, with the Home Secretary, with the view of obtaining, on behalf of the public at large, the offer of a Government reward for the apprehension and convictions of the assassin or assassins in the recent East-end atrocities, we shall be glad if you will allow us to state that the Committee do not for one moment doubt the sincerity of the Home Secretary in refusing the said offer, as he apparently believes that it would not meet with a successful result.

If he would, however, consider that, in the case of the Phoenix Park murders, the man Carey – who was surrounded by, we may say, a whole society steeped in crime – was tempted by money to betray his associates, in our opinion, Mr. Matthews might see his way clear to coincide with our views, and the Government offer would be successful.

The reward should be ample for securing an informer from revenge, which would be a very great inducement in the matter, in addition to which such an offer would convince the poor and humble residents of our East-end that the Government authorities are as anxious to avenge the blood of these unfortunate victims as they were the assassination of Lord Cavendish and Mr. Burke. The whole British nation are as much in favour of a reward now as they were then. Apologising for troubling you,

> We are, Sir, your obedient servants.
> GEORGE LUSK.
> JOSEPH AARONS.
> 1, 2, and 3, Alderney-road, Mile-end, E.,
> September 29.

On the same day, *Punch* magazine published an eerie cartoon showing a spectre stalking the mean streets of the metropolis, the word 'CRIME' emblazoned the forehead of the shroud it was wearing. The accompanying script contained this poem:

Foulness filters here from honest homes
And thievish dens, town-rookery, rural village.
Vice to be nursed to violence hither comes,
Nurture unnatural, abhorrent tillage!
What sin so ever amidst luxury springs,
Here amidst poverty finds full fruition.
There is no name for the unsexed foul things
Plunged to their last perdition
In this dark Malebolge, ours – which yet

We build, and populate, and then – forget!
Dank roofs, dark entries, closely-clustered walls,
Murder-inviting nooks, death-reeking gutters,
A boding voice from your foul chaos calls,
When will men heed the warning that it utters?
There floats a phantom on the slum's foul air,
Shaping, to eyes which have the gift of seeing,
Into the Spectre of that loathly lair.
Face it – for vain is fleeing!
Red-handed, ruthless, furtive, unerect,
'Tis murderous Crime – the Nemesis of Neglect!

At 12.45 a.m. in the early hours of 30 September 1888, Israel Schwartz, a Hungarian Jew, followed a man who appeared to be drunk into Berner Street from Commercial Road. As the man walked along the road he was seen by Schwartz to stop and speak with a woman later identified as Elizabeth Stride. Stride was born Elisabeth Gustafsdotter near Gothenburg, Sweden; on the streets of the East End she was commonly known as 'Long Liz'. Schwartz saw the man throw her to the ground and attempt to pull her onto the path outside Dutfield's Yard beside the International Workmen's Club. She screamed three times, but not very loudly. Schwartz wanted no part of this strife and crossed to the other side of the road where he saw a man lighting his pipe. The man who threw the woman down could see Schwartz was staring and he shouted the typical abusive name for East End Jews at the time – 'Lipski' – after the convicted and executed murderer of Miriam Angel in 1887.

The man began to follow Schwartz, so Schwartz ran off. About fifteen minutes later, at 1.00 a.m., Louis Diemshitz was returning to Dutfield's Yard with his coster-monger's barrow but as his pony entered it shied and would not walk on. Diemshitz went to investigate and saw what he thought was a pile of old clothes laying in the yard. He struck a match and, although it was almost instantly blown out by the wind, he had seen enough. It was the body of a woman, later identified as Long Liz Stride. Her throat had been slashed across, but she had not been mutilated; many drew the conclusion that Jack had been disturbed. Furthermore, Jack had not had his hideous appetite for mutilation sated – he soon found his second victim.

Forty-three-year-old Catherine Eddowes had been arrested by City Constable Lewis Robinson for being drunk and disorderly at 8.30 p.m. outside 29 Aldgate High Street on the evening of 29 September. Catherine was described by her contemporaries as an educated woman but one with a fierce temper. Her marriage to George Eddowes had failed on account of her drinking. Catherine Eddowes soon fell on hard times and took to living in doss houses, drinking and turning to prostitution as an occasional means of earning money.

Held in a cell at Bishopsgate police station, when PC Robinson asked her name she replied 'Nothing'. Eddowes was then put into a cell until she sobered

The infamous *Nemesis of Neglect* cartoon published in *Punch* on 29 September 1888, the day before Jack the Ripper's 'Double Event'.

up, and therein lay her fate. If she had been arrested for drunk and disorderly behaviour in the Metropolitan Police area she would have been put in the cells until the following morning. However, the City Police discharged drunks when they had sobered up.

City Constable George Henry Hutt, the gaoler at Bishopsgate station, took over the cells at 9.45 p.m. and as per regulations visited Eddowes in her cell several times, roughly every half hour. At 12.30 a.m. on 30 September Eddowes asked when she would be able to get out. Hutt replied: 'Shortly'. To which she said,

The Illustrated Police News graphically reports the 'Double Event' of 30 September 1888.

'I am capable of taking care of myself now.' At 12.55 a.m. Hutt was directed to see if any of the prisoners were fit to be discharged and, finding Eddowes sober, allowed her to leave. As Hutt was taking her out of the cell, she asked him what time it was, Hutt answered, 'Too late for you to get any more drink.' To which Eddowes replied, 'Well, what time is it?' Hutt replied, 'Just on one.' Thereupon she said, 'I shall get a — fine hiding when I get home, then.' Hutt reprimanded her, 'Serve you right; you have no right to get drunk.' Hutt then pushed open the swing door leading to the passage, saying, 'This way, missus.' As Eddowes departed Hutt called to her, 'Please, pull it to' and she replied, 'All right. Good night, old cock.' She pulled the door to within a foot of being closed, and he watched her turn to the left towards Houndsditch.

Just 400 yards from Bishopsgate police station is Mitre Square and there, at 1.45 a.m. on 30 September, PC Edward Watkins discovered the hideously mutilated body of Catherine Eddowes.

Major Henry Smith, Police Commissioner for the City of London force, recalled what happened next in his memoirs *From Constable to Commissioner*, published in 1910:

> The night of Saturday, September 29, found me tossing about in my bed at Cloak Lane Station, close to the river and adjoining Southwark Bridge. There was a railway goods depot in front, and a furrier's premises behind my rooms; the lane was causewayed, heavy vans were going constantly in and out, and the sickening smell from the furrier's skins was always present. You could not open the windows, and to sleep was an impossibility. Suddenly the bell at my head rang violently.
>
> What is it?' I asked, putting my ear to the tube.
>
> 'Another murder, sir, this time in the City.' Jumping up, I was dressed and in the street in a couple of minutes. A hansom – to me a detestable vehicle – was at the door, and into it I jumped, as time was of the utmost consequence. This invention of the devil claims to be safe. It is neither safe nor pleasant. In winter you are frozen; in summer you are broiled. When the glass is let down your hat is generally smashed, your fingers caught between the doors, or half your front teeth loosened. Licensed to carry two, it did not take me long to discover that a 15-stone Superintendent inside with me, and three detectives hanging on behind, added neither to its comfort nor to its safety.
>
> Although we rolled like a 'seventy-four' in a gale, we got to our destination – Mitre Square – without an upset, where I found a small group of my men standing round the mutilated remains of a woman … The approaches to Mitre Square are three – by Mitre Street, Duke Street, and St. James's Place. In the south-western corner, to which there is no approach, lay the woman.

Dr Frederick Gordon Brown, City Police surgeon, arrived at Mitre Square around 2 a.m. His report contained a description of the most hideous and extensive mutilations inflicted by the Ripper to date:

> The body was on its back, the head turned to left shoulder. The arms by the side of the body as if they had fallen there. Both palms upwards, the fingers slightly bent. The left leg extended in a line with the body. The abdomen was exposed. Right leg bent at the thigh and knee. The throat cut across.

The intestines were drawn out to a large extent and placed over the right shoulder – they were smeared over with some feculent matter. A piece of about two feet was quite detached from the body and placed between the body and the left arm, apparently by design. The lobe and auricle of the right ear were cut obliquely through.

Body was quite warm. No death stiffening had taken place. She must have been dead most likely within the half hour. We looked for superficial bruises and saw none. No blood on the skin of the abdomen or secretion of any kind on the thighs. No spurting of blood on the bricks or pavement around. No marks of blood below the middle of the body. Several buttons were found in the clotted blood after the body was removed. There was no blood on the front of the clothes. There were no traces of recent connexion.

When the body arrived at Golden Lane, some of the blood was dispersed through the removal of the body to the mortuary. The clothes were taken off carefully from the body. A piece of deceased's ear dropped from the clothing.

The face was very much mutilated. There was a cut about a quarter of an inch through the lower left eyelid, dividing the structures completely through. The upper eyelid on that side, there was a scratch through the skin on the left upper eyelid, near to the angle of the nose. The right eyelid was cut through to about half an inch.

There was a deep cut over the bridge of the nose, extending from the left border of the nasal bone down near the angle of the jaw on the right side of the cheek. This cut went into the bone and divided all the structures of the cheek except the mucous membrane of the mouth.

The tip of the nose was quite detached by an oblique cut from the bottom of the nasal bone to where the wings of the nose join on to the face. A cut from this divided the upper lip and extended through the substance of the gum over the right upper lateral incisor tooth.

About half an inch from the top of the nose was another oblique cut. There was a cut on the right angle of the mouth as if the cut of a point of a knife. The cut extended an inch and a half, parallel with the lower lip.

There was on each side of cheek a cut which peeled up the skin, forming a triangular flap about an inch and a half. On the left cheek there were two abrasions of the epithelium under the left ear.

The throat was cut across to the extent of about six or seven inches. A superficial cut commenced about an inch and a half below the lobe below, and about two and a half inches behind the left ear, and extended across the throat to about three inches below the lobe of the right ear.

The big muscle across the throat was divided through on the left side. The large vessels on the left side of the neck were severed. The larynx was severed below the vocal chord. All the deep structures were severed to the bone, the knife marking intervertebral cartilages. The sheath of the vessels on the right side was just opened.

The carotid artery had a fine hole opening, the internal jugular vein was opened about an inch and a half – not divided. The blood vessels contained clot. All these injuries were performed by a sharp instrument like a knife, and pointed.

The cause of death was haemorrhage from the left common carotid artery. The death was immediate and the mutilations were inflicted after death.

The intestines had been detached to a large extent from the mesentery. About two feet of the colon was cut away. Right kidney was pale, bloodless with slight congestion of the base of the pyramids.

There was a cut from the upper part of the slit on the under surface of the liver to the left side, and another cut at right angles to this, which were about an inch and a half deep and two and a half inches long. Liver itself was healthy.

The peritoneal lining was cut through on the left side and the left kidney carefully taken out and removed. The left renal artery was cut through. I would say that someone who knew the position of the kidney must have done it.

The lining membrane over the uterus was cut through. The womb was cut through horizontally, leaving a stump of three quarters of an inch. The rest of the womb had been taken away with some of the ligaments. I believe the wound in the throat was first inflicted. I believe she must have been lying on the ground.

The wounds on the face and abdomen prove that they were inflicted by a sharp, pointed knife, and that in the abdomen by one six inches or longer.

I believe the perpetrator of the act must have had considerable knowledge of the position of the organs in the abdominal cavity and the way of removing them. It required a great deal of medical knowledge to have removed the kidney and to know where it was placed. The parts removed would be of no use for any professional purpose.

I think the perpetrator of this act had sufficient time, or he would not have nicked the lower eyelids. It would take at least five minutes.

I cannot assign any reason for the parts being taken away. I feel sure that there was no struggle, and believe it was the act of one person.

The throat had been so instantly severed that no noise could have been emitted. I should not expect much blood to have been found on the person who had inflicted these wounds.

This night of macabre events was concluded with a discovery made by PC Alfred Long of A Division (on attachment to H Division) in the doorway of 108–19 Wentworth Model Dwellings, Goulston Street. It was a piece of material, torn from Catherine's apron, smeared with blood and faeces upon which the murderer had wiped his knife and hands. Dr Brown commented:

My attention was called to the apron, particularly the corner of the apron with a string attached. The blood spots were of recent origin. I have seen the portion of an apron produced by Dr. Phillips and stated to have been found in Goulston Street. It is impossible to say that it is human blood on the apron. I fitted the piece of apron, which had a new piece of material on it (which had evidently been sewn on to the piece I have), the seams of the borders of the two actually corresponding.

Above the apron fragment, written 'in a good schoolboy hand' was the statement 'The Juwes are the men that will not be blamed for nothing'. Two schools of thought enshroud this message: one suggests it was a coincidence, that the rag was simply cast away by the murderer and just happened to land under the message; the other suggests it was a message left by the killer himself. Sir Charles Warren, the Commissioner of the Metropolitan Police, attended the scene in person. No doubt fearing riots and reprisals against the Jewish population in the East End if such an inflammatory statement became public knowledge, he overruled the other officers on the scene and, rather than wait until there was enough light to photograph the message, only had it copied down, personally giving a direct order to 'obliterate the writing at once'. Some accounts even claim Warren erased the message himself. It was a controversial decision that was ultimately a contributing factor to his later resignation. Warren recorded his reasons in a confidential letter to the Undersecretary of State on 6 November 1888:

Sir,
     In reply to your letter of the 5th instant, I enclose a report of the circumstances of the Mitre Square Murder so far as they have come under the notice of the Metropolitan Police, and I now give an account regarding the erasing the writing on the wall in Goulston Street which I have already partially explained to Mr. Matthews verbally.
     On the 30th September on hearing of the Berner Street murder, after visiting Commercial Street Station I arrived at Leman Street Station shortly before 5 a.m. and ascertained from the Superintendent Arnold all that was known there relative to the two murders.
     The most pressing question at that moment was some writing on the wall in Goulston Street evidently written with the intention of inflaming the public mind against the Jews, and which Mr. Arnold with a view to prevent serious disorder proposed to obliterate, and had sent down an Inspector with a sponge for that purpose, telling him to await his arrival.
     I considered it desirable that I should decide the matter myself, as it was one involving so great a responsibility whether any action was taken or not.
     I accordingly went down to Goulston Street at once before going to the scene of the murder: it was just getting light, the public would be in the streets in a few minutes, in a neighbourhood very much crowded on Sunday mornings by Jewish vendors and Christian purchasers from all parts of London.

There were several Police around the spot when I arrived, both Metropolitan and City.

The writing was on the jamb of the open archway or doorway visible in the street and could not be covered up without danger of the covering being torn off at once.

A discussion took place whether the writing could be left covered up or otherwise or whether any portion of it could be left for an hour until it could be photographed; but after taking into consideration the excited state of the population in London generally at the time, the strong feeling which had been excited against the Jews, and the fact that in a short time there would be a large concourse of the people in the streets, and having before me the Report that if it was left there the house was likely to be wrecked (in which from my own observation I entirely concurred) I considered it desirable to obliterate the writing at once, having taken a copy of which I enclose a duplicate.

After having been to the scene of the murder, I went on to the City Police Office and informed the Chief Superintendent of the reason why the writing had been obliterated.

I may mention that so great was the feeling with regard to the Jews that on the 13th ulto. the Acting Chief Rabbi wrote to me on the subject of the spelling of the word 'Juwes' on account of a newspaper asserting that this was Jewish spelling in the Yiddish dialect. He added 'in the present state of excitement it is dangerous to the safety of the poor Jews in the East to allow such an assertion to remain uncontradicted. My community keenly appreciates your humane and vigilant action during this critical time.'

It may be realised therefore if the safety of the Jews in Whitechapel could be considered to be jeopardised 13 days after the murder by the question of the spelling of the word Jews, what might have happened to the Jews in that quarter had that writing been left intact.

I do not hesitate myself to say that if that writing had been left there would have been an onslaught upon the Jews, property would have been wrecked, and lives would probably have been lost; and I was much gratified with the promptitude with which Superintendent Arnold was prepared to act in the matter if I had not been there.

I have no doubt myself whatever that one of the principal objects of the Reward offered by Mr. Montagu was to shew to the world that the Jews were desirous of having the Hanbury Street Murder cleared up, and thus to divert from them the very strong feeling which was then growing up.

I am, Sir,

Your most obedient Servant,
Charles Warren

Shortly after the Ripper's 'Double Event' on 30 September, a lurid pamphlet entitled 'The Curse of Mitre Square' began to be circulated on the streets of the East
End. It stated the square had been damned since the murder of another woman
on exactly the same spot by a mad monk known as Brother Martin in 1530. It
is true to say that Mitre Square *was* the site of the Priory of the Holy Trinity,
founded in 1108 and dissolved in 1540, but the broadsheet went on to claim that
a woman praying before the high altar had been attacked by the insane monk, his
knife 'descended with lightening rapidity, and pools of blood deluged the altar
steps. With a demon's fury the monk then threw down the corpse and trod it out
of recognition.' Brother Martin then plunged the knife into his own heart, thus
the spot remained unhallowed, and thus the Ripper simply fulfilled the ancient
curse – so the author of the broadsheet argued. In the meantime, the police made
door-to-door enquiries regarding the murder, and posters were pasted up:

Police Notice:
To the Occupier.
    On the mornings of Friday, 31st August, Saturday 8th, and Sunday, 30th
September 1888, Women were murdered in or near Whitechapel, supposed by
some one residing in the immediate neighbourhood. Should you know of any
person to whom suspicion is attached, you are earnestly requested to commu-
nicate at once with the nearest Police Station.

Metropolitan Police Office
30th September 1888

On 1 October 1888 a postcard smeared with blood and written in red ink was
received by the Central News Agency; its contents would immortalise the previous night's atrocities as the 'Double Event':

I was not codding dear old Boss when I gave you the tip. You'll hear about
saucy Jacky's work tomorrow. Double event this time. Number one squealed a
bit. Couldn't finish straight off. Had not time to get ears for police. Thanks for
keeping back the last letter till I got to work again
– Jack the Ripper.

On 2 October 1888 private investigators Grand and Batchelor (employed by
the Whitechapel Vigilance Committee) found a blood-stained grape stalk in a
drain near where the body of Elizabeth Stride was found. This information was
not widely broadcast but, when combined with the account of Matthew Packer
(who ran a small greengrocer's through a street window at 44 Berner Street) that
he had served a man accompanied by Stride with half a pound of black grapes,
the sale of the fruit entered into East End folklore. The grapes have taken on yet
greater significance in recent years as imaginative theorists suggest the Ripper

laced the grapes with laudanum to stupor his victims prior to his attack. On the same day Robert James Lees, a medium, offered his powers as a psychic to assist the police. Lees indignantly records in his diary he was sent away and '... called a fool and a lunatic'.

With little or no concept of forensic clues to assist with the detection of the murderer and mounting pressure coming from all quarters for progress in tracking Jack the Ripper, new ideas and any new method which may have some merit were considered. Sir Charles Warren personally oversaw the trials of bloodhounds in Regent's Park on 9 and 10 October. Two hounds, Barnaby and Burgho, were brought down to London from Scarborough by well-known breeder Mr Brough. Sir Charles even acted as quarry in one of the trials and expressed himself satisfied with the result. The incident did, however, acquire a certain mythology whereby both the hounds and Sir Charles got lost in the London smog.

As time passed, more and more suggestions of how the police could catch the Ripper or protect the women of London from the fiend were related in the letter columns of the press. Typical of the tenor and logic employed in the correspondence is the following from the *Pall Mall Gazette*: 'There are numbers of well-trained pugilists in Shoreditch and Whitechapel who are, many of them, young, and in the custom in their profession, clean shaved ... Twenty game men of this class in women's clothing loitering about Whitechapel would have more chance than any number of heavy-footed policemen.'[265]

That said, the police did start to experiment, with 'decoys' being used in attempts to draw out and capture Jack the Ripper. Among the small number were two clearly recorded decoys. One was Detective Sergeant Robinson, who took to the streets in 'veil, skirt and petticoats' with Detective Sergeant Mather, who remained in his plain clothes. Ironically, while observing a man behaving in a strange manner with a woman in a doorway near Phoenix Place, St Pancras, the detectives were accused of being voyeurs by a passing cab washer named William Jarvis. Challenged with 'Wot yer muckin' about 'ere for?' the policemen identified themselves. 'Oh a rozzer, eh?' Jarvis replied sceptically and belted Robinson in the eye. Another decoy was a volunteer named Amelia Brown of Peckham who, although kept under close observation by policemen, had only a police whistle for her personal protection. Further ingenious suggestions for the apprehension of Jack the Ripper and appliances to be worn about the neck to prevent his deadly attack were proffered; Mr W.H. Spencer summed up this theme in a letter printed in *The Star*:

a few young men of somewhat feminine appearance should be got up in disguises as females. They should wear around their necks steel collars made after the style of a ladies' collaret, coming well down the breast and likewise well down the back. My reason for this is ... that the assassin first severs his victim's windpipe, thereby preventing her raising an alarm.

During the month of October 1888 the Victorian philanthropist Dr Thomas John Barnardo was to become involved in the story of Jack the Ripper. Writing an impassioned letter about the suffering of the children in common lodging houses to *The Times*, published on 9 October 1888, he revealed:

> Only four days before the recent murders I visited No. 32 Flower and Dean Street, the house in which the unhappy woman Stride occasionally lodged … In the kitchen of No 32 there were many persons, some of them being girls and women of the same unhappy class that to which poor Elizabeth Stride belonged. The company soon recognised me, and the conversation turned upon the previous murders. The female inmates of the kitchen seemed thoroughly frightened at the dangers to which they were presumably exposed … One poor creature, who had evidently been drinking, exclaimed somewhat bitterly to the following effect:– 'We're all up to no good, and no one cares what becomes of us. Perhaps some of us will be killed next!' I have since visited the mortuary in which were lying the remains of the poor woman Stride, and I at once recognised her as one of those who stood around me in the kitchen of the common lodging-house on the occasion of my visit last Wednesday week.

While little progress had been made in finding Jack the Ripper, the newspapers continued to condemn the murderer for his crimes, spoke in fearful terms of his 'thirst for blood', of him being a 'blood sucker' or vampire, and even made attempts to psychologically profile him, as illustrated by this remarkable article published in the *East London Advertiser*:

A THIRST FOR BLOOD.

The two fresh murders which have been committed in Whitechapel have aroused the indignation and excited the imagination of London to a degree without parallel. Men feel that they are face to face with some awful and extraordinary freak of nature. So inexplicable and ghastly are the circumstances surrounding the crimes that people are affected by them in the same way as children are by the recital of a weird and terrible story of the supernatural. It is so impossible to account, on any ordinary hypothesis, for these revolting acts of blood that the mind turns as it were instinctively to some theory of occult force, and the myths of the Dark Ages rise before the imagination. Ghouls, vampires, bloodsuckers, and all the ghastly array of fables which have been accumulated throughout the course of centuries take form, and seize hold of the excited fancy. Yet the most morbid imagination can conceive nothing worse than this terrible reality; for what can be more appalling than the thought that there is a being in human shape stealthily moving about a great city, burning with the thirst for human blood, and endowed with such diabolical astuteness, as to enable him to gratify his fiendish lust with absolute impunity? The details of the two last crimes make it morally certain that they were committed by the same being who took the lives of the other unfortunate women. The victims belonged to the same class – wretched wanderers in the streets of the lowest type; they were killed under circumstances of a similar nature, and although mutilation did not occur in the case of the woman who was first killed, there is good reason for supposing that this was only because the murderer was interrupted in his ghastly task. It is owing to this fact, in all probability, that a second murder was perpetrated on the same night. Stopped before he could gratify his fiendish mania, and with fierce desire coursing through his veins, the ghoul slunk off to find another victim. When everything is shrouded in such impenetrable mystery it is impossible to advance a theory which can bear examination. But it is obvious that these new crimes go far to upset the theory advanced by the coroner, Mr. Baxter, that the murders were committed in order to supply an American publisher with specimens of internal female organs. There was, indeed, something intrinsically absurd about parts of Mr. Baxter's theory. It was, for instance, incredible that any medical book should be issued with portions of the human body attached in bags, or in some other manner. Booksellers do not sell books in this fashion. Moreover, no rational object would have been attained. A diagram would have answered the purpose equally well for medical use, and except as a ghastly and sensational means of advertisement the enormous sum paid for the actual organ would have been thrown away. There still remained the possibility, however, that part of Mr. Baxter's theory might have been false, and part true. The American might have required these organs, although not for the purpose suggested. But the murders of Sunday render any further conjectures on the theory superfluous. No man in his senses would have risked his life, while the attention of the whole of London was still aroused, by committing a similar crime in order to earn a paltry sum of £20. A man may be ready to kill a person for the first time to gain a much smaller sum, but he would certainly not do so when he knew that in consequence of the notoriety of the first crime he would certainly be arrested if he tried to sell his ghastly booty. We are, therefore, forced to return to the maniac theory as the only one which at all fits in with the barbarous circumstances attending the murders, and the complete absence of motive.

THE SUPERNATURAL ELEMENT.

ALL the circumstances connected with the terrible East End murders are of a nature to stir up people's imagination in an exceptional degree. But even amid so much that is awe-inspiring and dramatic one fact that was elicited at the inquest on the unfortunate woman Stride or Watts was of a peculiarly thrilling nature. If anything were wanted to heighten the horrors of these tragedies it was the introduction of the supernatural element. This was supplied by the evidence of the murdered woman's sister. The coroner had evidently been informed that the witness had received what for want of a better word we will call an occult warning of her sister's death. He, therefore, pressed her closely on the point. At first she was disposed to deny the fact, but finally she admitted it, and stated its nature. She was lying awake in bed, when, to give her own words: 'About twenty minutes past one on Sunday morning I felt a pressure on my breast and heard three distinct kisses.' Now, this was just about the time at which the sister was giving up her life under the hands of the awful being in Berner-street. It was more than probable that Judas-like he first betrayed his victim with a kiss, and the pressure on the breast is what would naturally occur as he knelt over to cut her throat. Here then we have a representation of what was happening to the murdered woman reproduced at the same time in the mind of her sister. Of course it is quite possible that the circumstances she related only came into the mind of the witness after she had heard of her sister's death. But it could easily be ascertained whether she spoke of her presentiment to any of her neighbours prior to the news of the murder having reached her. If it could be satisfactorily proved that she did a very interesting case would be ready for the investigation of the Psychical Research Society. The late Mr. Edmund Gurney, in his 'Phantasms of the Living', gives several instances of telepathy, or thought-transference, occurring at the moment of a person's death. At such a moment, according to the theory he advances, the sensations of a person are most likely to be transferred to any one with whom they have been closely connected during life. That thoughts can pass between two people during life by other channels than those at present recognised is now fairly well established. It would be interesting if a distinct case of thought-transference taking place at the moment of a person's demise could be authenticated. But the value of the evidence all depends upon whether Stride's sister related her experiences before she knew of her unfortunate sister's death. We shall be surprised if this proves to be the case.

THE COMMON LODGING-HOUSE DANGER.

MR. MONTAGU WILLIAMS has done well to call public attention to the infamous conditions under which 'common lodging-houses' are allowed to exist. A more appalling description than that which he elicited of these dens of infamy cannot well be imagined. It is a disgrace to civilisation that to use the magistrate's own words, these haunts of robbers, homes of pickpockets, and hotbeds of prostitution should be permitted to flourish in the midst of what we boastfully call the capital of the civilised world. Fourpence, it appears, is the price of a single bed; eightpence, of what is technically known as a double. For those respective sums of money a single person, or a man and woman together, can pass the night. As many as ninety or a hundred people sleep under the same roof, numbers of them huddled together in the same room.

No surveillance is exercised, and a woman is at perfect liberty to bring any companion she likes to share her accommodation. Well might Mr. Williams' remark that those lodging-houses are about as unwholesome and unhealthy, as well as dangerous to the community, as can well be. There are places among them where the police dare not enter, and where the criminal hides all day long. Is it any wonder that vice should ride rampant in such slums and that, bred and fostered by the hideous contagion, crimes of the most ghastly nature should spring from time to time into life to horrify society. The practical question is – What can be done to clean this Augean stable? Even the criminal classes must have places where they can lay their heads at night. It would, moreover, be a hard case if an honest, respectable couple, who perhaps have come up to London to seek work, should be refused a lodging. To insist that a lodging-house keeper should demand the 'marriage lines' of every man and woman who seek shelter beneath his roof, would be, of course, ridiculous. But without demanding that any farfetched fads should be adopted, reforms of a practical nature might be introduced. The keepers of these lodging-houses know full well the character of the people who frequent their establishments and the police have an equally accurate knowledge on the point. It could be easy, therefore, to cancel the licences of all such houses, and the law should be stringently carried out in this direction. If loose women were to be prevented from frequenting 'common lodging-houses', their companions, the thieves, burglars, and murderers of London, would speedily give up resorting to them.

HOMICIDAL MANIA.

DR. SAVAGE'S article on 'Homicidal Mania' in the Fortnightly Review for October will attract universal interest at the present moment. Dr. Savage gives us an exhaustive classification of the various mental states which lead to murder, and draws a marked line between 'an insane tendency to kill and a tendency to kill as met with in the insane'. People who have the education of children entrusted to them will do well to note that the former tendency often results from careless bringing-up. Thus Dr. Savage gives a ghastly instance of a child who commenced his career – the story reads like an extract from Miss Edgeworth's 'Moral Tales' – by pulling off the wings of flies. After a time this amusement palled, and the pleasing child took to baking frogs. He next turned his young intelligence to capturing birds and boring out their eyes. And later on nothing would satisfy him but ill-treating other children. Altogether Dr. Savage's reminiscences of childhood do not tend to increase our confidence in these imps, a love for whom is supposed to be the index of every well-regulated mind. 'I have known children,' he writes, 'kick cats and dogs to death, or set light to them, or pour boiling water over them, the fiend-ish pleasure being increased if the young of the animals were thus reduced to starvation.' Who, after reading this, will not feel a hidden qualm as he fondles some blue-eyed flaxen-haired little urchin, that stands at his knee and looks as though it were a gentle little angel newly arrived from the soft fleecy regions of the sky? As might be expected we find that natural heredity has much to do with these bloodthirsty propensities. Professor Benedikt of Vienna, it appears, has been for some time making an exhaustive comparison of the brains of criminals, and has devoted especial attention to the cerebral development of murderers. He has weighed, measured, and done everything but taste the brains of scores of malefactors. The result of his experience is that he has demonstrated satisfactorily that the brain of a murderer frequently resembles that of a lower animal 'in certain definite ways'. There is a strong similarity between the convolutions of a monkey's brain and those of some criminals. What the particular class of criminal may be we are not told, but it is fair to suppose that thieving and a monkey like convolution of brain go together. It is a terrible thought, though no new one, to feel that one's chance of spending half one's life in prison depends on an extra twist or so in the internal organs of the head. According to Professor Benedikt murderers brains have a special likeness to those of bears. A man with a bear-shaped brain should therefore be avoided – unfortunately there is considerable difficulty in telling the shape of your friend's brain while he is alive. The number of interesting, though blood-curdling theories, brought forward by Dr. Savage, are enough to form the material for a score of 'shilling dreadfuls'.[266]

In the light of such events and graphic reportage, it was hardly surprising that in October 1888 reports circulated of the curious circumstances surrounding the death of Mrs Mary Burridge, a floor cloth dealer on the Blackfriars Road. It was stated by some she had been so overcome by reading a particularly lurid account of the Whitechapel murders in *The Star* she fell dead '… a copy of the late final in her hand'. Tom Cullen, in *Autumn of Terror: Jack the Ripper: His Crimes and Times* (London: Bodley Head, 1965), suggested this passage may have caught her eye: 'A nameless reprobate – half beast, half man – is at large … Hideous malice, deadly cunning, insatiable thirst for blood – all these are the marks of the mad homicide. The ghoul-like creature, stalking down his victim like a Pawnee Indian, is simply drunk with blood, and he will have more.'

Ever since the Jack the Ripper letter was sent to the Central News Agency the floodgates opened for a torrent of letters claiming to know, have knowledge of or even purport to be from Jack the Ripper. Some were illustrated with lurid drawings and lots of red ink. Then George Lusk, Chairman of the Whitechapel Vigilance Committee, received a small parcel in the form of a cardboard box wrapped in brown paper on 16 October 1888. To Lusk's horror, upon opening the parcel he found the box contained a blood-stained letter and half a human kidney:

From Hell
Mr Lusk
Sor
   I send you half the
Kidne I took from one woman
presarved it for you tother piece I
fried and ate it was very nise. I
may send you the bloody knif that
took it out if you only wate a whil
longer.

signed Catch me when
you can
Mishter Lusk.

The kidney was examined by Dr Openshaw at The London Hospital, who confirmed it was a longitudinally divided human kidney. Major Smith of the City Police added in his memoirs that 2 inches of the renal artery (which averages about 3 inches long) remained in Eddowes' body where her kidney had been removed – 1 inch of artery was all that was attached to the organ sent to Lusk.

Then there were other fears: fears that it was not just lurid broadsides and chap books that could have turned the head of the killer but even theatrical performances! American actor Richard Mansfield was performing his own stage adaptation of Robert Louis Stevenson's *Dr Jekyll and Mr Hyde*. Victorian sensibilities were outraged by the premise that every human being (even the respectable ones) had a demon imprisoned within them, which the right concoctions of chemicals could release on society, and which could gorge themselves on an orgy of debauchery and malevolence. Mansfield's transformation from the upright Dr Jekyll to hideous Mr Hyde 'in all his blood-curdling repulsiveness' was remarked upon for the convincing and complete transformation of man to half-human beast, a transformation made more shocking and horrible because it was done in full view of the audience without screens, gauzes or traps. Due to accusations that the play was responsible in some way for the Jack the Ripper murders (on the grounds of his performance, some even suspected Mansfield himself of being the Ripper) its run was terminated in its tenth week.

So the investigation for Jack the Ripper rolled on, through October into November. With no convincing suspect in sight the police were facing ever increasing barrages of criticism and loss of public confidence, the streets of London were gripped by the terror, and many across the nation were on tenterhooks, not wondering if, but when, Jack the Ripper would strike again. Nothing happened. Then, just as the height of fear began to diminish, the murder of Mary Jane (or Marie Jeanette) Kelly occurred. Mary Jane Kelly was remembered as a striking figure in the East End; at 25 she was younger than most of the prostitutes, blue-eyed, tall with a fine head of hair almost reaching to her waist. She had come to London in 1884 and after a short period working as a domestic servant she worked as a high-class prostitute in a West End brothel. This life saw her turn more and more to drink and she soon found herself out of the brothel and down in the East End working as a common prostitute out of a dingy little room, about 12ft square, at 13 Miller's Court, 26 Dorset Street. This property was colloquially known as one of 'McCarthy's Rents', named after John McCarthy, who owned a chandler's shop at 27 Dorset Street and rented out a number of properties around the locale. Miller's Court itself was accessed through a narrow opening about 3ft wide, the first archway on the right off Dorset Street when approaching from Commercial Street.

Mary Jane had been living from rent to rent and at a few lodging houses with her male friend, Joe Barnett, since 1887. While at Miller's Court Joe lost his job as a fish porter and Mary Jane returned to the streets. She brought girls back to the room out of the cold but, as Joe told a newspaper, he could not tolerate any more after 'Marie allowed a prostitute named Julia to sleep in the same room; I objected: and as Mrs. Harvey afterwards came and stayed there, I left and took lodgings elsewhere.' At the inquest Barnett stated he and Kelly separated on 30 October 1888, but they did stay in friendly contact and Barnett sometimes visited Mary Jane. He last saw her at Miller's Court on the night of Thursday 8 November, when he stayed for a quarter of an hour, leaving at about 8 p.m.

At about 11.45 p.m. on the same night Mary Jane was seen with another man, probably a client, in Miller's Court by fellow resident and prostitute Mary Ann Cox. Kelly and the man were standing outside Kelly's room as Mrs Cox passed and said 'Goodnight'. Somewhat incoherently, Kelly replied, 'Goodnight, I am going to sing.' A few minutes later Mrs Cox heard Kelly singing *A Violet from Mother's Grave*. Cox went out again at midnight and heard Kelly singing the same song:

Well I remember my dear old mother's smile,
As she used to greet me when I returned from toil,
Always knitting in the old arm chair,
Father used to sit and read for all us children there,
But now all is silent around the good old home;
They all have left me in sorrow here to roam,
But while life does remain, in memoriam I'll retain
This small violet I pluck'd from mother's grave.

The last witness to have claimed to see Mary Jane Kelly alive was an old acquaintance of hers named George Hutchinson. In a statement he gave to the police after the inquest, Hutchinson recounted this sighting: at about 2 a.m. Hutchinson was walking on Commercial Street and passed a man at the corner of Thrawl Street but paid no attention to him. At Flower and Dean Street he met Kelly who asked him to lend her sixpence. Hutchinson replied he could not, having spent all his money 'going down to Romford'. Mary Jane replied, 'Good morning, I must go and find some money.' And she went away towards Thrawl Street. Hutchinson continued:

> A man coming in the opposite direction tapped her on the shoulder and said something to her, they both burst out laughing. I heard her say 'All right?' to which the man replied 'You will be alright for what I have told you. The man then placed his right hand around her shoulders. He also had a kind of small parcel in his left hand with a kind of strap around it. I stood against the lamp of the Queens Head Public House and watched him. They both then came past me the man hid down his head with his hat over his eyes. I stooped down and looked him in the face. He looked at me stern. They both went into Dorset Street. I followed them. They both stood at the corner of Miller's Court for about three minutes. He said something to her, she said 'Alright my dear, come along, you will be comfortable.' He then placed his arm on her shoulder and gave her a kiss, then she said 'I've lost me handkerchief.' He then pulled his handkerchief, a red one, out and gave it to her. They both then went up the court together. I then went to the court to see if I could see them but could not. I stood there for about three quarters of an hour to see if they came out but they did not and so I went away.

Did George Hutchinson get a good look at Jack the Ripper and if he did was the description he gave accurate? It must be commented that for the short period of time he saw the man the following description Hutchinson provided is remarkably detailed. The accuracy of Hutchinson's statement will no doubt be debated for years to come; if it is to be believed then it is probably the best description we have of Jack the Ripper:

> Aged about 34 or 35, height 5' 6", complexion pale, dark eyes and eye lashes, slight moustache curled up each end and hair dark very surly-looking, dressed in a long dark coat, collar and cuffs trimmed with astracan [sic], and a dark jacket under, light waistcoat, dark trousers, dark felt hat, turned down in the middle, button boots and gaiters with white buttons. Wore a very thick gold chain and had a white linen collar, black tie with horse shoe pin, respectable appearance, walked very sharp, Jewish appearance. I think I would be able to identify him again.

But what happened to Mary Jane? At about 4 a.m. on Friday 9 November Elizabeth Prater was awakened by her pet kitten walking on her neck. She heard a faint cry of 'Oh, murder!' but could not be sure where it came from and, as the cry of murder was common in the district, she paid no attention to it. Sarah Lewis, who was staying with friends in Miller's Court, also heard the cry.

Later that morning ex-soldier Thomas Bowyer (known on the street as Indian Harry) was sent round to 13 Miller's Court by McCarthy to chase up Mary Jane Kelly – she was behind with her rent money to the tune of 29s and was facing eviction. At the inquest into the death of Mary Jane Kelly held at Shoreditch Town Hall before Dr Macdonald, MP, the coroner for the north-eastern district of Middlesex, Bowyer revealed what he had discovered:

'At a quarter to eleven a.m., on Friday morning [9 November], I was ordered by McCarthy to go to Mary Jane's room, No. 13. I did not know the deceased by the name of Kelly. I went for rent, which was in arrears. Knocking at the door, I got no answer, and I knocked again and again. Receiving no reply, I passed round the corner by the gutter spout where there is a broken window – it is the smallest window.' Charles Ledger, an inspector of police, G Division, produced a plan of the premises. Bowyer pointed out the window, which was the one nearest the entrance. Bowyer continued: 'There was a curtain. I put my hand through the broken pane and lifted the curtain. I saw two pieces of flesh lying on the table … in front of the bed, close to it. The second time I looked I saw a body on this bed, and blood on the floor. I at once went very quietly to Mr. McCarthy. We then stood in the shop, and I told him what I had seen. We both went to the police-station, but first of all we went to the window, and McCarthy looked in to satisfy himself. We told the inspector at the police-station of what we had seen. Nobody else knew of the matter. The inspector returned with us.

Inspector Frederick Abberline picked up the story with his inquest testimony:

I arrived at Miller's-court about 11.30 on Friday morning … I had an intimation from Inspector Beck that the bloodhounds had been sent for, and the reply had been received that they were on the way. Dr. Phillips was unwilling to force the door, as it would be very much better to test the dogs, if they were coming. We remained until about 1.30 p.m., when Superintendent Arnold arrived, and he informed me that the order in regard to the dogs had been countermanded, and he gave orders for the door to be forced …

The sight that met them was simply beyond normal human imagination – the walls were splashed up like an abattoir and on the blood-soaked mattress was a raw carcass, a mass of human evisceration that was once Mary Jane Kelly. Those who saw this horror – Inspector Walter Beck, Inspector Frederick Abberline, George Bagster Phillips (the H Division surgeon) and even young DC Walter Dew (the man who would later become world famous as the man who arrested Crippen) – would never forget it.

The Illustrated Police News graphically recreates scenes from the murder of Mary Jane Kelly and depicts the 'supposed Whitechapel Monster' based on the description of the suspect provided by George Hutchinson.

Dr Thomas Bond also attended the scene and recorded the state of the body of poor Mary Jane Kelly:

The body was lying naked in the middle of the bed, the shoulders flat but the axis of the body inclined to the left side of the bed. The head was turned on the left cheek. The left arm was close to the body with the forearm flexed at a right angle and lying across the abdomen.

The right arm was slightly abducted from the body and rested on the mattress. The elbow was bent, the forearm supine with the fingers clenched. The legs were wide apart, the left thigh at right angles to the trunk and the right forming an obtuse angle with the pubes.

The whole of the surface of the abdomen and thighs was removed and the abdominal cavity emptied of its viscera. The breasts were cut off, the arms mutilated by several jagged wounds and the face hacked beyond recognition of the features. The tissues of the neck were severed all round down to the bone.

The viscera were found in various parts viz: the uterus and kidneys with one breast under the head, the other breast by the right foot, the liver between the feet, the intestines by the right side and the spleen by the left side of the body. The flaps removed from the abdomen and thighs were on a table.

The face was gashed in all directions, the nose, cheeks, eyebrows, and ears being partly removed. The lips were blanched and cut by several incisions running obliquely down to the chin. There were also numerous cuts extending irregularly across all the features.

The neck was cut through the skin and other tissues right down to the vertebrae, the fifth and sixth being deeply notched. The skin cuts in the front of the neck showed distinct ecchymosis. The air passage was cut at the lower part of the larynx through the cricoid cartilage.

Both breasts were more or less removed by circular incisions, the muscle down to the ribs being attached to the breasts. The intercostals between the fourth, fifth, and sixth ribs were cut through and the contents of the thorax visible through the openings.

The skin and tissues of the abdomen from the costal arch to the pubes were removed in three large flaps. The right thigh was denuded in front to the bone, the flap of skin, including the external organs of generation, and part of the right buttock. The left thigh was stripped of skin fascia, and muscles as far as the knee.

The left calf showed a long gash through skin and tissues to the deep muscles and reaching from the knee to five inches above the ankle. Both arms and forearms had extensive jagged wounds.

The pericardium was open below and the heart absent.

During his inquest deposition Abberline also commented, 'I agree with the medical evidence as to the condition of the room. I subsequently took an inventory of the contents of the room. There were traces of a large fire having been kept up in the grate, so much so that it had melted the spout off a kettle. We have since gone through the ashes in the fireplace; there were remnants of clothing, a portion of a brim of a hat, and a skirt, and it appeared as if a large quantity of women's clothing had been burnt.'

The coroner enquired if Abberline could give any reason why the clothing had been burnt. Abberline replied, 'I can only imagine that it was to make a light for the man (the killer) to see what he was doing.'

Mary Jane Kelly is widely regarded by crime historians as the last of the canonical five victims of Jack the Ripper. Poignantly, the resignation (tendered on 8 November) of Sir Charles Warren, the man many held responsible for the failure of the police to capture Jack the Ripper, was accepted and announced on that day. But the investigation carried on and the following notice was issued:

MURDER-PARDON. Whereas on November 8 or 9, in Miller Court, Dorset Street, Spitalfields, Mary Jane Kelly was murdered by some person or persons unknown, the Secretary of State will advise the grant of her Majesty's pardon to any accomplice not being a person who contrived or actually committed the murder who shall give such information and evidence as shall lead to the discovery and conviction of the person or persons who committed the murder – (Signed) CHARLES WARREN, the Commissioner of Police of the Metropolis, Metropolitan Police Office, 4, Whitehall, November 10, 1888.

Even Queen Victoria sent a telegram to the Marquis of Salisbury, the prime minister, from Balmoral, expressing her concern and giving suggestions for actions to apprehend Jack the Ripper: 'This new most ghastly murder shows the absolute necessity for some very decided action. All courts must be lit, & our detectives improved. They are not what they should be ...'

The killer known as Jack the Ripper was never brought to justice but the case remained open and a few suspects contemporary to the crimes were named by senior police officers in the years immediately after.

In 1891 a certain Thomas Henry Cutbush was taken into Lambeth Infirmary and detained as a lunatic. He escaped within hours and over the following four days, until he was captured again, he stabbed Florrie Johnson in the buttocks and attempted to repeat the deed on Isabelle Anderson. Charged with malicious wounding, Cutbush spent the rest of his life in Broadmoor Criminal Lunatic Asylum, where he died in 1903. In February 1894 *The Sun* newspaper made the suggestion that Cutbush and Jack the Ripper were one and the same. This matter was thoroughly investigated and Cutbush was not considered a likely suspect at all. This investigation did, however, result in Sir Melville Macnaghten, Chief Constable CID, writing his confidential and now infamous report. Although not in post in 1888, he was appointed in 1889 when the crime and the available evidence was still fresh. He stated:

The Whitechapel Murderer had 5 victims – & 5 victims only, – his murders were (1) 31st August, '88. Mary Ann Nichols – at Buck's Row – who was found with her throat cut – & with (slight) stomach mutilation.
(2) 8th Sept. '88 Annie Chapman – Hanbury St.; – throat cut – stomach & private parts badly mutilated & some of the entrails placed round the neck.
(3) 30th Sept. '88. Elizabeth Stride – Berner's Street – throat cut, but nothing in shape of mutilation attempted, & on same date
Catherine Eddowes – Mitre Square, throat cut & very bad mutilation, both of face and stomach.
9th November. Mary Jane Kelly – Miller's Court, throat cut, and the whole of the body mutilated in the most ghastly manner –

The last murder is the only one that took place in a room, and the murderer must have been at least 2 hours engaged. A photo was taken of the woman, as she was found lying on the bed, without seeing which it is impossible to imagine the awful mutilation.

With regard to the double murder which took place on 30th September, there is no doubt but that the man was disturbed by some Jews who drove up to a Club, (close to which the body of Elizabeth Stride was found) and that he

then, 'mordum satiatus', went in search of a further victim who he found at
Mitre Square.

It will be noted that the fury of the mutilations increased in each case,
and, seemingly, the appetite only became sharpened by indulgence. It seems,
then, highly improbable that the murderer would have suddenly stopped in
November '88, and been content to recommence operations by merely prod-
ding a girl behind some 2 years and 4 months afterwards. A much more rational
theory is that the murderer's brain gave way altogether after his awful glut in
Miller's Court, and that he immediately committed suicide, or, as a possible
alternative, was found to be so hopelessly mad by his relations, that he was by
them confined in some asylum.

No one ever saw the Whitechapel Murderer; many homicidal maniacs were
suspected, but no shadow of proof could be thrown on any one. I may mention the cases of 3 men, any one of whom would have been more likely than
Cutbush to have committed this series of murders:

(1) A Mr M.J. Druitt, said to be a doctor & of good family – who disappeared
at the time of the Miller's Court murder, & whose body (which was said to
have been upwards of a month in the water) was found in the Thames on
31st December – or about 7 weeks after that murder. He was sexually insane and
from private information I have little doubt but that his own family believed
him to have been the murderer.

(2) Kosminski – a Polish Jew – & resident in Whitechapel. This man became
insane owing to many years indulgence in solitary vices. He had a great hatred
of women, specially of the prostitute class, & had strong homicidal tendencies:
he was removed to a lunatic asylum about March 1889. There were many circumstances connected with this man which made him a strong 'suspect'.

(3) Michael Ostrog, a Russian doctor, and a convict, who was subsequently
detained in a lunatic asylum as a homicidal maniac. This man's antecedents were
of the worst possible type, and his whereabouts at the time of the murders could
never be ascertained.

Macnaghten also went on to discuss other murdered women who had been
alleged to have been victims of Jack the Ripper:

(1) The body of Martha Tabram, a prostitute was found on a common staircase
in George Yard buildings on 7th August 1888; the body had been repeatedly
pierced, probably with a bayonet. This woman had, with a fellow prostitute,
been in company of 2 soldiers in the early part of the evening: these men were
arrested, but the second prostitute failed, or refused, to identify, and the soldiers
were eventually discharged.

(2) Alice McKenzie was found with her throat cut (or rather stabbed) in Castle
Alley on 17th July 1889; no evidence was forthcoming and no arrest were made

in connection with this case. The stab in the throat was of the same nature as in the case of the murder of

(3) Frances Coles in Swallow Gardens, on 13th February 1891 – for which Thomas Sadler, a fireman, was arrested, and, after several remands, discharged. It was ascertained at the time that Saddler had sailed for the Baltic on 19th July '89 and was in Whitechapel on the nights of 17th idem. He was a man of ungovernable temper and entirely addicted to drink, and the company of the lowest prostitutes.

Another suspect was later advanced by Chief Inspector Frederick Abberline. Abberline, who led the Ripper investigation 'at ground level' in Whitechapel, retired in 1892 and a few of his reminiscences were recorded to mark the occasion in *Cassell's Saturday Journal*. He summed up his views on the Ripper murders with: '… we were lost almost in theories; there were so many of them.' But in 1903 Abberline recorded his own theory for the first time in the *Pall Mall Gazette*. With George Chapman (aka Severin Klosowski) 'The Borough Poisoner' under sentence of death, when the reporter called on Abberline he found him about to write to Metropolitan Police Commissioner Sir Melville Macnaghten '… to say how strongly I was impressed with the opinion that "Chapman" was also the author of the Whitechapel murders'. Drawing on a sheaf of papers and cuttings Abberline passed his conclusions, which he had intended to send to Macnaghten, directly to the reporter. The letter covered a page and a half of foolscap paper and it outlined the coincidences (especially the fact that the murders had continued in America after Chapman had emigrated to New Jersey in 1891), Chapman's movements and how struck Abberline was with how well Chapman fitted the descriptions they had of the Ripper at the time. Sadly, most of Abberline's thoughts about Chapman as the Ripper do not withstand close scrutiny. Chapman was a killer but he was a poisoner and probably was not Jack the Ripper. However, if it gave Abberline peace of mind in his declining years to think that his old comrade Detective Sergeant Godley had been the man to catch Jack the Ripper, who are we to judge?

Then there is the Littlechild letter. Discovered by crime historian Stewart Evans in 1993, it is a letter written on 23 September 1913 to the noted author, playwright and journalist George R. Sims from ex-Chief Inspector John Littlechild, the man who had headed Special Branch from 1883 to 1893. In the letter Littlechild discusses the infamous Jack the Ripper letter sent to the Central News Agency in 1888, which gave the murderer the most notorious nom de plume in history:

With regard to the term 'Jack the Ripper' it was generally believed at the Yard that Tom Bullen [sic – Bulling] of the Central News was the originator, but it is probable Moore, who was his chief, was the inventor. It was a smart piece of journalistic work. No journalist of my time got such privileges from Scotland

Yard as Bullen. Mr James Munro when Assistant Commissioner, and afterwards Commissioner, relied on his integrity. Poor Bullen occasionally took too much to drink, and I fail to see how he could help it knocking about so many hours and seeking favours from so many people to procure copy.

Most significantly, however, Littlechild named another suspect:

Knowing the great interest you take in all matters criminal, and abnormal, I am just going to inflict one more letter on you on the 'Ripper' subject. Letters as a rule are only a nuisance when they call for a reply but this does not need one. I will try and be brief.

I never heard of a Dr D. in connection with the Whitechapel murders but amongst the suspects, and to my mind a very likely one, was a Dr. T. (which sounds much like D.) He was an American quack named Tumblety and was at one time a frequent visitor to London and on these occasions constantly brought under the notice of police, there being a large dossier concerning him at Scotland Yard. Although a 'Sycopathia Sexualis' subject he was not known as a 'Sadist' (which the murderer unquestionably was) but his feelings toward women were remarkable and bitter in the extreme, a fact on record. Tumblety was arrested at the time of the murders in connection with unnatural offences and charged at Marlborough Street, remanded on bail, jumped his bail, and got away to Boulogne. He shortly left Boulogne and was never heard of afterwards. It was believed he committed suicide but certain it is that from this time the 'Ripper' murders came to an end.

9

DRACULA AND THE UNDEAD

The 'Autumn of Terror' in 1888 rolled on into winter and, although there had been no capture of Jack the Ripper, there had also been no more murders quite like the Ripper attacks. Nevertheless, there were still many who considered it just a matter of time before he struck again, and the press were quick to resurrect the Ripper as the perpetrator of any murder or serious assault with a knife if there was no known suspect, as evinced by the coverage of the murder of Frances Coles at Swallow Gardens in Whitechapel on 13 February 1891. The lack of mutilation and the method of throat cutting did not point to this being a Jack the Ripper crime, even if he was disturbed, but it is true to say that many officers involved in the case, particularly the beat policemen, really did believe they were on the trail of Jack the Ripper. Tales of their exploits have passed down as family legends over the years and, because Coles's murderer was never caught, we can never know with absolute certainty that they were not actually on the trail of the Ripper. As a postscript, it may be of interest to note that the murder of Frances Coles is

Desmodus Rotundus: the common vampire bat as shown in a nineteenth-century encyclopaedia of nature.

the last case included in the extant police and Home Office files concerning the Whitechapel murders.

London theatreland was filled with stories, suspicions and rumours about who the killer might be, and with tales of fearful walks home at night when some young actress believed she saw '*him*' on the streets. Even years later, actresses like Ada Reeve, who was appearing at the Cambridge Music Hall on Commerical Street, Bishopgate, would recall the climate of fear:

> My father was one of the original Vigilance Committee set up to patrol the streets during the time of these murders … and how nervous mother used to be when he was out night after night, with only a stick and a whistle as protection. Afterwards, when the series of crimes could be seen as a whole, it was realised that the 'Ripper's' victims were all street-walkers, but at the time no one felt safe.
>
> It used to be eleven at night before I got home, walking through the long, winding Hanbury Street, which led from the direction of Bishopsgate past the stage door of the Pavilion. Usually our maid was sent to fetch me, but on the night of September 29th, 1888, she could not come and I had to make the journey alone. I have reason to remember that date – for next morning we heard that not one but two murders had been committed – the first in Berner Street, off the Commercial Road, and the second in Mitre Square, Aldgate. To get from the one place to the other, the 'Ripper' must have passed along streets very close to my own route. I still feel cold when I realise that he may have been lurking in the shadows within reach of me that night.[267]

Ellen Terry would observe that, 'Irving's mind was always stirred by the queer and the uncanny' and that 'he always took a deep interest in crime (an interest that his sons have inherited) and often went to the police court to study the faces of the accused'.[268] It would have been a lost opportunity not to recognise the public's heightened intrigue in the macabre and, catching a certain *zeitgeist* among the *fin de siècle* to gain some insight into the mind of a killer, Irving decided that the Lyceum would see out 1888 with *Macbeth*.

Ada Reeve.

Bram was to recall 'of all the plays of which Irving talked to me in the days of our friendship when there was an eager wish for freedom of effort, or in later times when a new production was a possibility rather than an intention, I think *Macbeth* interested me most'.[269] As ever, the high production standards, the sheer spectacle of the piece and the realistic battle scenes made the Lyceum production of *Macbeth*, which opened on 29 December 1888, a sight and spectacle to behold. It was a great success and ran for 151 continuous performances.

Bram had seen the play years before with Barry Sullivan in the lead, '*He had great strength, great voice, great physique of all sorts; a well-knit figure with fine limbs, broad shoulders, and the perfect back of a prize-fighter. He was master of himself, and absolutely well versed in the parts which he played. His fighting power was immense.*' Although Irving was tall he had nothing of Sullivan's great physique, but, in the role of Macbeth, he still demonstrated immense power; a power beyond that of his physique. Bram was to recall how easily he accepted the powerfully built Sullivan's entrance through the massive double doors of a Gothic archway into the Castle of Dunsinane, '*That Castle with the massive gates thrown back on their hinges by the rush of a single man came back to me vividly when I saw the play as Irving did it in 1888 … None of us ever questioned its accuracy to nature.*'

It was something about the supernatural aspect of this power in Irving's performance that caught Bram's imagination, mingled with Sullivan's words that echoed back from all those years before, perhaps as a voice from the crypt as he thundered out his speech, '*They have tied me to a stake; I cannot fly.*'[270]

Bram would have been only too aware of the palpable climate of fear that existed upon the streets of London in 1888. He had seen the impact of the crimes from within the prism of London and from without, for he had been in London when the first two murders were committed and, while tour with the Lyceum Company in Scotland and the north of England during September and November, read about them in the papers from a distance. He had the opportunity to read the accounts in more detail on the long train journeys to and from London during this period – accounts brimming with references to 'a thirst for blood' and spattered with allusions to vampires and demons. Then, back in the metropolis, Bram had the chance to observe the city under the cloud of the Ripper with stranger's eyes as he walked abroad.

Bram had been fortunate to have his dear friend Hall Caine living a short distance from him in Bexley Heath until he moved to the Lake District in 1888. Caine's move meant that their meetings would be less frequent but the times they spent together would often be a powerful concentration of literary and esoteric discussion about their latest writing projects or ideas. Bram had also moved, and Caine came to stay with him at 17 St Leonard's Terrace in January 1890;[271] Bram would conjure up an evocative image of Caine one afternoon:

At that time he was staying with me, and on the afternoon of Sunday, January 26, 1890, he said he would like to give his idea of the play. He had already had

a somewhat trying morning, for he had made an appointment with an inter-
viewer and had had a long meeting with him. Work, however, was always a
stimulant to Hall Caine. The use of his brain seems to urge and stimulate it 'as
if increase of appetite had grown by what it fed on'. Now in the dim twilight
of the late January afternoon, sitting in front of a good fire of blazing billets of
old ship timber, the oak so impregnated with salt and saltpetre that the flames
leaped in rainbow colours, he told the story as he saw it. Hall Caine always
knows his work so well and has such a fine memory that he never needs to look
at a note. That evening he was all on fire. His image rises now before me. He
sits on a low chair in front of the fire; his face is pale something waxen looking in the changing blues of the flame. His red hair, fine and long, and pushed
back from his high forehead, is so thin that through it as the flames leap we can
see the white line of the head so like to Shakespeare's. He is himself all aflame.
His hands have a natural eloquence something like Irving's; they foretell and
emphasise the coming thoughts. His large eyes shine like jewels as the firelight
flashes. Only my wife and I are present, sitting like Darby and Joan at either side
of the fireplace. As he goes on he gets more and more afire till at the last he is
like a living flame. We sit quite still; we fear to interrupt him. The end of his
story leaves us fired and exalted too …

Bram shared a fascination with the occult and the strange with Caine: both were
fascinated by table turners, spiritualist mediums and spirit photography, and found
kinship in this with numerous other luminaries of the day including Alfred Lord
Tennyson, and Sherlock Holmes creator Arthur Conan Doyle. In such an atmosphere it is difficult to dismiss the idea that something of the Count had not stirred
in Bram's imagination. Caine had inspired Bram on such matters before. During
his close friendship with the Pre-Raphaelite painter and poet, Dante Gabriel
Rossetti (who lived in Cheyne Walk, not far from the house Bram would move
to), Rossetti had confided to Caine a dark tale and a doom warning for those
who would disturb the resting dead that would inspire Bram's writings. Rossetti's
wife, Elizabeth Siddal, best remembered as the model for Sir John Everett Millias's
portrait of the death of Ophelia, was one of the most popular models of the Pre-
Raphaelite's; she was eulogised by Rossetti's brother William as, 'a most beautiful
creature with an air between dignity and sweetness with something that exceeded
modest self-respect and partook of disdainful reserve; tall, finely-formed with a
lofty neck and regular yet somewhat uncommon features, greenish-blue unspar-
kling eyes, large perfect eyelids, brilliant complexion and a lavish heavy wealth of
coppery golden hair'.

Rossetti adored her and was beside himself with grief when, suffering from
chronic tuberculosis, she accidentally took her own life with an overdose of laudanum in February 1862. As Rossetti gazed at her in the open coffin, he reached
for the book of manuscript poems he had written for her and gently nestled it

between her cheek and the tresses of red-golden hair and let it be buried with her at Highgate Cemetery. Grief did not leave Rossetti: a year later he completed his ethereal vision of her in his painting *Beata Beatrix*.

Tragically, as the years passed Rossetti consoled himself with drugs and alcohol and became chronically addicted. Convinced that he was going blind and could no longer paint he began to write poetry again but, before publishing his newer poems, struggled with his conscience over the idea that he should retrieve the poems he had buried with his beloved Elizabeth. Rossetti's agent, Charles Augustus Howell, had no compunction in the matter; indeed, it was believed he was an astute conniver and blackmailer. Burne-Jones minced no words in describing him as, 'a base, treacherous, unscrupulous and malignant fellow', neither did Algernon Swinburne who posited Howell as 'the vilest wretch I ever came across'. Howell gained Rossetti's assent and applied to the Home Secretary for an order to have Siddal's coffin exhumed to retrieve the manuscript. The permission was granted and by dead of night, to avoid public curiosity, the neo-resurrectionists wove their way through the cemetery and by lamplight set their spades to the grave of Elizabeth Siddal. Rossetti waited at home, consumed with guilt, 'in a state of agitation and torturing suspense'. Howell reported to Rossetti that the deed was done and although a little worm-eaten, the book of poems was successfully recovered. But what of Elizabeth? Howell assured him Elizabeth's corpse was remarkably well preserved and her delicate beauty remained intact. A legend also arose that her hair had continued to grow after death and the coffin had been filled with long, flowing coppery-golden strands.

The poems were published in a volume entitled *Poems by D. G. Rossetti* in 1870 but were damned by the critics as too 'fleshy' and erotic, and were not a great success. The criticism of his work was the major cause of Rossetti's mental breakdown in 1872, and he died in 1882, after spending the majority of the last decade of his life as a recluse at Cheyne Walk. In 1890 Charles Augustus Howell was found with his throat slit near a Chelsea pub. A 10s coin had been pushed in his mouth – a final payment for a slanderer.

It has been speculated that Rossetti found a suicide note with his wife, but destroyed it to ensure she could receive a Christian burial and avoid a public scandal. The inquest held after the day of her death returned a verdict that she, 'Accidentally and casually and by misfortune came to her death.' Caine, who had stayed with Rossetti through the last twelve months of the artist-cum-poet's life, alluded to this in *My Story*:

> All I knew of Rossetti, all he had told me of himself, all he had revealed to me of the troubles of his soul, all that seemed so mysterious in the conduct of his life, and the moods of his mind, became clear and intelligible and even noble and deeply touching in the light of his secret.[272]

By the time Bram wrote his first dated notes on *Dracula* on 8 March 1890, his ideas and concept for the novel were already developed to such a degree that he was able to draft out four distinct 'books' entitled *Book I Styria to London, Book II Tragedy, Book III Discovery* and *Book IV Punishment*. By 14 March, each had seven chapters and chapter headings.[273]

The concept of the book had clearly been in Bram's mind for some considerable time, probably years. Bram drew on his own interests, experiences and knowledge for the original draft of the tale, most notably his love since boyhood of the strange and the macabre.

As Bram was beginning to draw his notes together he was fortunate to encounter Arminius Vámbéry, the Professor of Oriental Languages at the University of Budapest in Austria-Hungary. Vámbéry was an adventurer with many stories to tell – he had travelled widely across Persia in the 1860s, on journeys that had never before been undertaken by any Western European.[274] When he came to see *The Dead Heart* on 30 April 1890, he was invited to supper in the Beefsteak Room. Bram described him as one of their most interesting visitors:

> He had been to Central Asia, following after centuries the track of Marco Polo and was full of experiences fascinating to hear. I asked him if when in Thibet he never felt any fear. He answered:
>
> 'Fear of death no; but I am afraid of torture. I protected myself against that, however!'
>
> 'How did you manage that?'
>
> 'I had always a poison pill fastened here, where the lappet of my coat now is. This I could always reach with my mouth in case my hands were tied. I knew they could not torture me; and then I did not care!'
>
> He was a wonderful linguist, wrote twelve languages, speaks freely sixteen, and knows over twenty. He told us once that when the Empress Eugenie remarked to him that it was odd that he who was lame should have walked so much, he replied:
>
> 'Ah, Madam, in Central Asia we travel not on the feet but on the tongue.'[275]

Vámbéry's visit to the Beefsteak Room was described by Ludlam in his 1962 biography of Bram Stoker – 'He was full of experiences, fascinating to hear, and spoke of places where mystery and superstition still reigned. Places like Transylvania' – but there is no written evidence he actually spoke to the gathering or directly to Stoker about Transylvania, nor, as others would suggest, that he was the first to mention the name 'Dracula' to Bram.[276] But Vámbéry's stories did inspire Bram to write about him in *Personal Reminiscences* and accord him the honour of a mention in *Dracula* in the character of a reliable factotum of knowledge of strange lands, customs and history, who is called upon by Van Helsing to provide him with further information about the history of the Count:

Thus when we find the habitation of this man-that-was, we can confine him to his coffin and destroy him, if we obey what we know. But he is clever. I have asked my friend Arminius, of Buda-Pesth University, to make his record, and from all the means that are, he tell me of what he has been.

According to Bram's version of the history of the Count's ancestry in *Dracula*:

The Draculas were, says Arminius, a great and noble race, though now and again were scions who were held by their coevals to have had dealings with the Evil One. They learned his secrets in the Scholomance, amongst the mountains over Lake Hermanstadt, where the devil claims the tenth scholar as his due. In the records are such words as 'stregoica' witch, 'ordog' and 'pokol' Satan and hell, and in one manuscript this very Dracula is spoken of as 'wampyr', which we all understand too well.

Viewing this passage and the mention of 'Wampyr' in context with Vámbéry does inspire a thought worthy of consideration. Bram was always interested in the use of language to evoke a sense of place and authenticity in his stories; in his notes for *Dracula* there are pages on words in the Yorkshire dialect.[277] As Vámbéry's pronunciation of vampire would have, phonetically, been 'Wampyr', this may have been why Bram adopted it as his first attempt as name for the Count. This would fit in well with the original location of Styria in the south-east of Austria, a place believed by Stoker to be 'where belief in vampires survived longest and with most intensity'.[278] It was also the location of J. Sheridan Le Fanu's story of *Carmilla*, one that Bram appears to have known and drawn upon, particularly in *Dracula's Guest*.

The next step in Stoker's research would prove to be the most influential for the entire book and took place during a three-week family holiday for Bram, Florence and Noel in the north-east Yorkshire fishing port and resort of Whitby. Arriving during the second week in August 1890, the Stokers stayed at Mrs Veazey's house at 6 Royal Crescent on Whitby's West Cliff; they had the second floor as their sitting room and their bedroom on the third, both of which commanded magnificent sea views. Beneath them, on the first floor, were three ladies from Hertford: Isabel and Marjorie Smith and their older friend Miss Stokes, stated by Cordelia Stamp in *Dracula Discovered* to be 'the prototypes of Lucy and her friend Mina, whilst the older Miss Stokes did duty as Mrs. Westernra'.[279]

Why the Stokers chose Whitby is not recorded but their friend, the novelist and illustrator George du Maurier, was staying around the corner and it may have been he who recommended the place. George du Maurier (father of the actor Gerald and grandfather of author Daphne) was an old friend of the Stokers and regarded Florence as one of the three most beautiful women he had ever seen (the other two were Mrs Stillman and Mrs John Hare). Du Maurier had been on the staff of *Punch* since 1861 and found the affected manners of Victorian society easy

The George du Maurier cartoon 'A Filial Reproof', featuring Noel, Florence and Bram. *Punch*, 11 September 1886.

targets for his humour and satires; some of them even involved his friends, not excluding the Stokers. In a cartoon published in *Punch* on 11 September 1886, he featured Bram, Florence and young Noel in a cartoon entitled 'A Filial Reproof'. Florence and Bram are pictured seated in chairs a short distance apart, facing one another and relaxing at a garden party. Noel stands behind his mother's chair, the caption reads: '[Noel] "Mamma"

([Mamma] to Noel, who is inclined to be talkative) "Hush, Noel! Haven't I told you often that little boys should be seen and not heard?"

[Noel] "Yes, Mamma! But you don't look at me!"'

The question is, was she concentrating on something in her gently raised and clasped hands – or was she looking at Bram when she made the comment? Was it just good humour or was there something more to the comment? Something revealing about Bram's relationship with his wife or perhaps their parenting? Du Maurier appears to have also used Florence as one of the subjects in his cartoon the following month, on 23 October 1886, where he depicts two attractive women sat on a beach a distance apart. One lady has a little boy (younger than Noel) beside her, he looks at the woman sat on her own. Entitled 'A Troubled Conscience' the little boy is captioned as saying, 'Mummy, I've got a wicked thought.' Mother asks, 'What is it darling?' To which the boy replies, 'I used to think you were the most lovely woman in the world – and now I don't!'

Despite du Maurier poking fun at the Stokers, Bram and he had much to talk about, notably their shared interest in mesmerism. Du Maurier's second novel,

Trilby, would explore the theme in depth; it was published as a part-work in *Harper's Monthly* in 1894 and in book form the following year. The story involved a poor artist's model named Trilby O'Farrell who was transformed into a diva after being mesmerised by evil musical genius Svengali.

Bram was inspired by and soaked up the atmosphere of Whitby, and the notes he took of the views he saw and things he gleaned are used almost verbatim in the text of *Dracula*, right down to the weather conditions. Bram transposes the fine views he enjoyed from the West Cliff into Mina Murray's journal:

> This is a lovely place. The little river, the Esk, runs through a deep valley, which broadens out as it comes near the harbour. A great viaduct runs across, with high piers, through which the view seems somehow further away than it really is. The valley is beautifully green, and it is so steep that when you are on the high land on either side you look right across it, unless you are near enough to see down. The houses of the old town – the side away from us, are all red-roofed, and seem piled up one over the other anyhow, like the pictures we see of Nuremberg. Right over the town is the ruin of Whitby Abbey, which was sacked by the Danes, and which is the scene of part of 'Marmion', where the girl was built up in the wall. It is a most noble ruin, of immense size, and full of beautiful and romantic bits. There is a legend that a white lady is seen in one of the windows. Between it and the town there is another church, the parish one, round which is a big graveyard, all full of tombstones. This is to my mind the nicest spot in Whitby, for it lies right over the town, and has a full view of the harbour and all up the bay to where the headland called Kettleness stretches out into the sea.[280]

George du Maurier considered Florence Stoker one of the three most beautiful women he had ever seen and depicted her in 'A Troubled Conscience', *Punch* 23 October 1886.

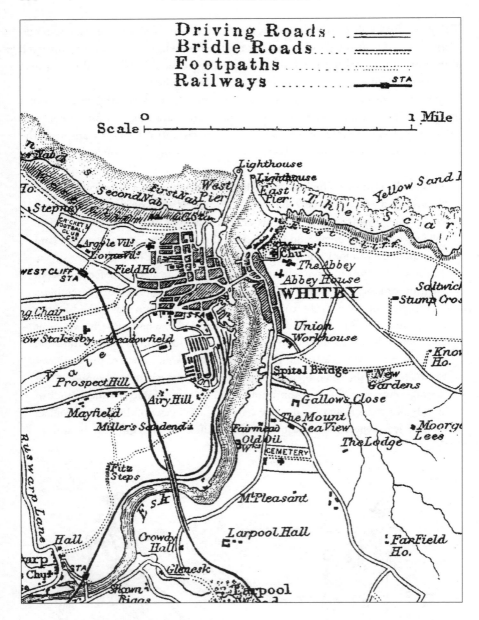

Map of Whitby from *Horne's Guide to Whitby* (1891).

Bram collected all manner of material while at Whitby: history, dialect, folklore, legends, geographical and location details, in fact more material than any other topic in his notes.[281] He even typed up ten pages of details from the inscriptions he found to mariners and those drowned at sea on the headstones in St Mary's churchyard on the East Cliff, from which he drew a number of names he used in the book.[282] A curious addition to Bram's *Notes for Dracula* are the only two pho-tographs among them, for they do not show Whitby Abbey but the ruins of the Abbey of St Mary in York, a place that is not mentioned in any way.

Bram talked to local fishermen and the local Coast Guard William Petherick, and it could well be in Petherick's neat hand that the notes about the wrecks of the British ship *Mary and Agnes* and the Russian schooner *Dimitry*, which occurred on 24 October 1885, were written. The *Whitby Gazette* of 31 October 1885 details the story:

A little later in the afternoon a schooner was descried to the south of the harbour, outside the rocks. Her position was one of great danger; for being evidently unable to beat off, there seemed nothing for it but to be driven among the huge breakers on the scar. Her commander was apparently a man well acquainted with his profession, for with consummate skill he steered his trim little craft before the wind, crossing the rocks by what is known as the 'sledway' and bringing her in a good position for the harbour mouth.

The piers and the cliffs were thronged with expectant people, and the life-boat 'Harriot Forteath' was got ready for use in case the craft should miss the entrance to the harbour and be driven on shore. When a few hundred yards from the piers she was knocked about considerably by the heavy seas, but on crossing the bar the sea calmed a little and she sailed into smooth water. A cheer broke from the spectators on the pier when they saw her in safety.

Two pilots were in waiting, and at once gave instruction to those on board, but meanwhile the captain not realising the necessity of keeping on her steerage, allowed her to fall off and lowered sail, thus causing the vessel to swing towards the sand on the east side of the harbour. On seeing this danger the anchor was dropped, but they found no hold and she drifted into Collier's Hope and struck the ground. She purported to be the schooner 'Dmitry' [sic] of Narva, Russia, Captain Sikki, with a crew of seven hands, ballasted with silver sand. During the night of Saturday the men worked incessantly upon her that her masts went by the board and on Sunday morning, she lay high and dry a broken and complete wreck, firmly embedded in the sand. In the mean while the lifesaving brigade by a well-directed rocket threw a line over the brigantine which now was seen to be the 'Mary and Agnes', of Scarborough. It seemed a long time before the crew on board fixed the apparatus, but eventually this was done, and the young-est of them, a lad of about fifteen years, was sent ashore in the breeches. In being dragged towards the shore the poor little fellow was struck by many seas and considerably buffeted about. There were, however, many ready and willing among those on shore to rush into the water and bring him to land.

Bram dramatically recreates the story in *Dracula*, retaining many of the facts about the wrecking of the *Dimitry*, and simply changing her name to the *Demeter* and her sailing port to Varna. Of course, the fate of the crew and their cargo in *Dracula* was a very different matter. The crew of the *Demeter* disappeared one by one, a story Bram probably based on a tale recorded on a memo in his notes dated 30 July 1890, when three old fishermen encountered on the cliff told him of a whaler named *The Esk* whose captain would not slacken his sail, cursing that he would be in 'Hell or Whitby tonight', and who knocked down the crew one by one as they implored him to change his mind. *The Esk* was wrecked and all bar three of the crew were lost. In another memo dated 15 October 1890, after his return to London, Bram recalls a few extra notes from Whitby and mentions, 'When ship ran in to Collier's Hope, big dog jumped off bow & ran into church-yard';[283] with an imaginative leap from the mind of Bram, this is the way the shape-shifting Count arrives in England.

As for the cargo, the *Demeter* carried silver sand and fifty 'cases of common earth for experimental purposes'[284] (for the Count to secrete as his required rest-ing places at his hideaways in Britain). The latter were consigned to fictional Whitby solicitor Samuel F. Billington; a letter of instruction was sent to him at No. 7, The Crescent, Whitby (next door to where the Stokers stayed).

Perhaps it was the discovery of the story of the *Dimitry* that inspired Bram to seek out more information about the Black Sea and the Danubian ports the schooner could have come from, or perhaps a casual browse at the Whitby Library, that led Bram's hand to alight upon *An Account of the Principalities of Wallachia and Moldavia with Various Political Observations Relating to Them* written by retired diplomat William Wilkinson, and published in 1820. Within the 320 pages of the volume, Bram came across a name that would change the entire tenor of his book. Its first appearance is on page 17 where Wilkinson talks of how the Voïvode fought the Turks and were defeated after a bloody battle and, as a consequence, compelled to become a tributary of the Turk and ordered to pay an annual tribute of 3,000 paisters:

> Wallachia continued to pay it until the year 1444; when Ladislas King of Hungary, preparing to make war against the Turk engaged the Voïvode Dracula to form an alliance with him. The Hungarian troops marched through the prin-cipality and were joined by four thousand Wallachians under the command of Dracula's son.[285]

The name crops up again two pages later in an account of the Wallachians' attempt to shake off the yoke of Sultan Mahomet II in 1460: 'Their Voïvode, also named Dracula, did not remain satisfied with mere prudent measure of defence; with an army he crossed the Danube and attacked the few Turkish troops that were stationed in his neighbourhood'[286]

In a footnote on the same page, Wilkinson explains that, 'Dracula in Wallachian language means Devil. Wallachians were at that time, as they are at present, used to

A late nineteenth-century map of Transylvania. Klausenburg, Bistritz and the Borgo Pass are located in the northern section, while the Carpathian Mountains are to the south.

give this as a surname to any person who rendered himself conspicuous either by courage, cruel actions, or cunning.'[287]

The name impressed itself upon Stoker, he clearly liked it, it sounded 'right' and just seemed to fit his character. No longer would Count Wampyr feature in the notes, his name was resolutely discarded – enter Count Dracula!

Bram drew selectively from a number of books and articles to flesh out the characteristics of Count Dracula, the folk beliefs he could attach to him and his kind, his history and his country. Bram borrowed many of his distinguishing features of Dracula such as canine teeth, pointed nails, hair in the palm of the hand

and the ability to shape-shift from the Reverend Sabine Baring-Gould's *The Book of Were-Wolves*, and for more about vampires and their folklore Bram found an article on 'Transylvanian Superstitions' by fellow nineteenth-century contributor Emily Gerard particularly fruitful, notably her passage:

> More decidedly evil, however, is the vampire, or nosferatu, in whom every Roumenian peasant believes as firmly as he does in heaven or hell. There are two sorts of vampires – living and dead. The living vampire is in general the illegitimate offspring of two illegitimate persons, but even a flawless pedigree will not ensure anyone against the intrusion of a vampire into his family vault, since every person killed by a nosferatu becomes likewise a vampire after death, and will continue to suck the blood of other innocent people till the spirit has been exorcised, either by opening the grave of the person suspected and driving a stake through the corpse, or firing a pistol shot into the coffin. In very obstinate cases it is further recommended to cut off the head and replace it in the coffin with the mouth filled with garlic, or to extract the heart and burn it, strewing the ashes over the grave. That such remedies are often resorted to, even in our enlightened days, is a well-attested fact, and there are probably few Roumenian villages where such has not taken place within the memory of the inhabitants.

A point well made by Elizabeth Miller is the error Emily Gerard made when she ascribed the word 'nosferatu' as a synonym for 'vampire'; Bram copied it directly into his notes and from there perpetuated the error in *Dracula*.[288] Other notes made by Bram prove more elusive when attempts are made to trace them in the published sources listed in his *Notes*. Only one paper cutting survives in them, an undated article from the *New York World* entitled 'Vampires in New England', based on a paper entitled 'The Animistic Vampire in New England', which was presented to a meeting of the Anthropological Society of Washington by Mr George Rochford Stetson on 17 December 1895.[289] There may well have been more cuttings that have not survived, as Bram employed the services of newspaper cutting agencies to obtain articles and reviews about Irving, such as Romeike & Curtice's Press Cutting Agency of 359 Strand, London, who proudly claimed, 'Newspaper Cuttings from the Press of the World. Files Searched, Translations, Reporting and all Press work. Special Information on all subjects.' Bram also used them to search out the reviews of his books[290] and could have used them for his research. However, he was not short on personalities to help him develop the character and features of Dracula himself.

Both Bram and Hall Caine had tried to create theatrical pieces for Irving and it has been suggested that this may have been the original stimulus for Bram to create Dracula, but the imagery of the Count was more likely to have been an amalgam drawn from a variety of Irving's theatrical characters over the years: from his 'impression of a dead man fictitiously alive' and glistening red eyes that 'seemed to shine like cinders of glowing red from out the marble face'[291] to his masterful performances as the demon Mephistopheles in *Faust* and as the tall and gaunt Macbeth with his supernatural powers. In the creation of such a loathsome character as Dracula, Bram may have intended a side swipe at 'The Chief' for sucking the life blood of his best years, drawing on the skills of Bram to make himself look good, and for not always appreciating him. As Irving would remark 'There is no general sympathy on the stage for tall old men!'

Other features and characteristics could have come from any number of people Bram had encountered over the years but his *Personal Reminiscences* produce a few likely candidates. First, there was the explorer Henry Morton Stanley, whom Bram first met upon his return from his expedition to Africa in October 1882 at the small dinner party Irving had arranged for him at The Garrick Club. Everyone present was anxious to hear of his adventures and held the guests entranced until the chimes of four in the morning when the group finally dispersed. In *Personal Reminiscences*, Bram was to observe of Stanley on that night:

> He was slow and deliberate of speech; the habit of watchful self-control seemed even then to have eaten into the very marrow of his bones. His dark face, through which the eyes seemed by contrast to shine like jewels, emphasised his slow speech and measured accents. His eyes were comprehensive, and, in a quiet way, without appearing to rove, took in everything. He seemed to have that faculty of sight which my father had described to me of Robert Houdin, the great conjurer. At a single glance Stanley took in everything, received facts and assimilated them, gauged character in its height, and breadth, and depth, and specific gravity; formed opinion so quickly and so unerringly to the full extent of his capacity that intention based on what he saw seemed not to follow receptivity but to go hand in hand with it. [When he laughed is was] a strange thing to see in that dark, still face, where toil and danger and horror had set their seals. But it seemed to light up the man from within and show a new and quite different side to his character … Henry Stanley had a look of the forest gloom as marked as Dante's contemporaries described of him: that of one who had traversed Heaven and Hell.

When they met again six years later Stanley had returned from more adventures:

> Stanley looked dreadfully worn, and much older than when I had seen him last. The six years had more than their tally of wear for him, and had multiplied themselves. He was darker of skin than ever; and this was emphasised by the whitening of his hair. He was then under fifty years of age, but he looked nearer to eighty than fifty. His face had become more set and drawn had more of that look of slight distortion which comes with suffering and over-long anxiety. There were times when he looked more like a dead man than a living one. Truly the wilderness had revenged upon him the exposal of its mysteries.

Then there was Alfred Lord Tennyson, the poet laureate, now best remembered for his poem *The Charge of the Light Brigade*. Bram met Tennyson for the first time soon after he arrived in London, when the great man came to the Lyceum to see *Hamlet* on 20 March 1879, and was to meet him on numerous occasions afterwards. Bram observed, 'Tennyson had at times that lifting of the upper lip which shows the canine tooth, and which is so marked an indication of militant instinct.' But he went on to state, 'Of all the men I have met the one who had this indication most marked was Sir Richard Burton.' Burton was a tough ex-soldier, explorer, Orientalist and cartographer who had conducted extensive explorations, penetrating deep into Asia, Africa and the Americas. His knowledge of the language and cultures in his field were extraordinary and his literary output, based on his travels and studies of the mystic East, was prodigious. He is, however, best remembered for his ten-volume translation of *A Thousand Nights and a Night*, often referred to as *The Arabian Nights*. Bram had first met Burton in August 1878 when they were introduced by Irving. Bram was impressed by the mettle of the man and when he had the opportunity to meet Burton at a number of suppers while he and Lady Burton were in London during 1879 he did not miss the opportunity of observing him more closely:

> The first supper was at Irving's rooms in Grafton Street ... The subdued light and the quietude gave me a better opportunity of studying Burton's face; in addition to the fact that this time I sat opposite to him and not beside him. The predominant characteristics were the darkness of the face – the desert burning; the strong mouth and nose, and jaw and forehead the latter somewhat bold and the strong, deep, resonant voice. My first impression of the man as of steel was consolidated and enhanced.[292]

Bram met Burton again in July 1886 when they were in London; on this occasion the discussion over the dinner table became a lot darker, but Bram remained fascinated:

> Burton was looking forward to his retirement and was anxious that there should not be any hitch. He knew well that there were many hands against him and that if opportunity served he would not be spared. There were passages in his life which set many people against him. I remember when a lad hearing of how at a London dinner-party he told of his journey to Mecca. It was a wonderful feat, for he had to pass as a Muhammedan; the slightest breach of the multitudinous observances of that creed would call attention, and suspicion at such a time and place would be instant death. In a moment of forgetfulness, or rather inattention, he made some small breach of rule. He saw that a lad had noticed him and was quietly stealing away. He faced the situation at once, and coming after the lad in such a way as not to arouse his suspicion suddenly stuck his knife

into his heart. When at the dinner he told this, some got up from the table and left the room. It was never forgotten. I asked him once about the circumstance not the dinner-party, but the killing. He said it was quite true, and that it had never troubled him from that day to the moment at which he was speaking. Said he: 'The desert has its own laws, and there supremely of all the East to kill a man is a small offence. In any case what could I do? It had to be his life or mine!'

As he spoke the upper lip rose and his canine tooth showed its full length like the gleam of a dagger.[293]

The other members of dramatis personae of Dracula were also amalgams of a name taken here, and characteristics and features taken there, such as Jonathan Harker's surname from Joseph Harker (probably some of his features and personality too), an amiable and talented Lyceum scenery painter whose father had befriended Irving in his young years on the stage. Mina reflects aspects the strength and vulnerability of Ellen Terry known only too well by Bram, blended with the empowered and resourcefulness of the 'New Women' emerging in Victorian society. In contrast, Lucy reflects the susceptible and the sensual; as Clive Leatherdale points out, Lucy 'by being both dead and erotic, she defies not only the law of nature, but also the unwritten law of Victorian moral behaviour'.

Quincey P. Morris, the Texan armed with his bowie knife and supplier of the Winchester rifles to the mission to destroy Dracula, embodied the America that had so captivated Bram and may well have been based on the iconic frontiersman William Frederick Cody, known to history as 'Buffalo Bill', who brought the people of the American plains to nineteenth-century Britain in his 'Wild West Show'. Bram first encountered Cody while on tour in America and met him again in Britain on a number of occasions when Cody was touring. Bram even helped arrange a special event at the Athenaeum Dramatic Club in Glasgow in November 1891 where Irving was being entertained to supper, and introduced Colonel Cody to the company as 'a man who he respected and loved for his simplicity and indomitable courage'. Cody was delighted and proud to say it was Irving 'who was first to suggest that he should bring the "Wild West Show" to Britain, and the first to extend him goodwill after his arrival'.[294]

Bram could have drawn on so many legal, medical and learned men for Van Helsing, whose character owes no little inspiration to Bram's own father and his esteemed university professor Edward Dowden. I am drawn to imagine how Bram and Dowden prepared to defend Walt Whitman, drawing on his works and the knowledge they had amassed about him to armour themselves against and to slay the 'vampires' that were his critics at the debating society.

Dr Seward was probably drawn from doctors Bram had encountered through his own life and his interest in pseudo-science such as mesmerism and phrenology. Knowing Bram's fascination with the Lincoln assassination, it is tempting to suggest he drew the name from William H. Seward, the US Secretary of State whose splint, fixed to his jaw after a recent accident, deflected the potentially fatal stab to the neck and allowed him to fend off the assassin and raise a commotion that brought others running to his aid. The assassin disappeared into the dark night just like Dracula, and just like the vampire Count he too was pursued and eventually destroyed.

He would have met possible characters through his physician brothers, too, and no doubt used a liberal dash of personality from the brothers themselves; be it his adventurous brother George who had served as a surgeon in the Imperial Ottoman Army and in both the Zulu War (1870–80) and the Turko-Russian War (1876–78) or Bram's older brother Thornley, a distinguished surgeon who received a knighthood for his services to medicine and helped with notes on medical details for *Dracula*.

It is apparent from his earliest notes for *Dracula* that Bram wanted to include vampire women, and to do this he revisited a scene from his story *The Chain of Destiny*, published over four editions of *The Shamrock* back in 1875 (see p. 52). However, this time they would be beautiful and sensual, there was to be no equiv-ocation in this as the passage that read, 'How right was Shakespeare, no one could believe that after three hundred years one could see in this fastness of Europe the counterpart of the witches of Macbeth' was deleted from Bram's typescript.[295]

The origins of the vampire women in *Dracula* may have been very close to Bram's heart, for he would record in *Personal Reminiscences* that he had only seen three actresses whose eyes could 'blaze':

> Miss Ward has one great stage gift which is not given to many: her eyes can blaze. I can only recall two other actresses who had the same quality in good degree: Mdlle. Schneider who forty years ago played the Grand Duchess of Gerolstein in Offenbach's Opera; and Christine Nilsson. The latter I saw in London in 1867, and from where I sat high up in the seat just in front of the gallery I could note the starry splendour of her blue eyes. Ten years later, in Lohengrin at Her Majesty's Opera House, I noticed the same this time from the stalls. And yet once again when I sat opposite her at supper on the night of her retirement, June 20, 1888.[296]

Each of these women that Bram admired and desired married continental counts. His dear friend, actress Genevieve Ward, while still in her teens, had been caught up in a whirlwind romance and married the Russian Count de Gerbel of Nicolaeiff in Nice in 1855. It did not end well; Bram picks up the story:

> [Nicolaeiff] declared that by a trick of Russian law which does not acknowl-edge the marriage of a Russian until the ceremony in the Russian church has been performed, the marriage which had taken place was not legal. His wife and her father and mother, however, were not those to pass such a despicable act. With her mother she appealed to the Czar, who having heard the story

was furiously indignant. Being an autocrat, he took his own course. He summoned his vassal Count de Gerbel to go to Warsaw, where he was to carry out the orders which would be declared to him. There in due time he appeared. The altar was set for marriage and before it stood the injured lady, her father, Colonel Ward, and her mother. Her father was armed, for the occasion was to them one of grim import. De Gerbel yielded to the mandate of his Czar, and the marriage with all needful safeguards this time was duly effected. Then the injured Countess bowed to him and moved away with her own kin. At the church door husband and wife parted, never to meet again.[297]

Hortense Catherine Schneider was one of the greatest operetta stars of the nineteenth century and left the stage when she married the Emile, Count de Brionne in 1881; newspapers bemoaned her parting:

> Hortense Schneider has taken the veil – not the conventnal but the hymeneal one. Had she sought refuge in a Carmelite convent and devoted herself entirely to the mortification of the flesh and the salvation of her soul, her retirement from the world would not have been more complete. Yes, the Grand Duchess has become Mdme. La Comtesse de Bionne. Her real title closes over her like a tomb. Her operatic title gained for her more worldly glory than falls to the lot of most princesses of Royal blood.[298]

It did not end well, Bionne seemed more interested in Schneider's money than her; he refused to move to Paris with her and the couple went through an acrimonious divorce. Hortense retained the title of comtesse and withdrew from society, living nearly thirty years of her life more or less a recluse, with only her son of mysterious origin for company.

Only one of the three, the Swedish operatic soprano Christine Nilsson, appears to have found an enduring relationship when she married Ramon Maria Vallejo y Miranda, Count de Casa Miranda, in 1887. It is interesting to note, however, that it has been suggested Gaston Leroux based his character Christine Daaé in *Phantom of the Opera* (1910) on her. In Leroux's story Christine is a character that drew a hideously deformed man to her with her voice, he falls in love with her and despite his appearance and that fact he tries to force her to marry him, she does grow to love the 'Phantom'.

All three of these women had distinctive features, they were not typical 'beauties' but there was *something* about them. If Bram did use these three as the models for his trio of female vampires he could have done so without too much imagination.

Bram loved to incorporate real people and events within his work, but he also liked to incorporate secrets and darker truths: could it be that encoded within *Dracula* are secrets and allusions to the most notorious serial killer of all time – Jack the Ripper?

The idea the Ripper crimes had influenced Bram's creation of *Dracula* was hotly debated and even dismissed out of hand until a rare copy of the first foreign language edition of *Dracula* was uncovered. Published in 1901, the new, heavily abridged book had been translated into Icelandic, was given the new title of *Makt Myrkranna* (*Powers of Darkness*), and was given a new preface by Bram:

> When he reads this story, the reader will see for himself how these papers have been arranged to create a unified text. I have not had to do anything except eliminate a few unnecessary minor details and let the participants tell their stories in the same unadorned fashion in which they were originally written. For obvious reasons, I have altered the names of people and places. Other than that, I have left the handwritten manuscript unchanged, in accordance with the wishes of those who consider it important to place it before the eyes of the public.

> There is no doubt that the events described herein actually took place, no matter how incredible or unbelievable [sic] they may seem to the general public. I am aware that many people will continue to be sceptical to some degree. However, it is not inconceivable that continuing research in psychology and natural sciences will eventually explain certain mysteries, that to date neither scientists nor undercover policemen have been able to solve.

> I must repeat that the strange and eerie tragedy which is portrayed here is completely true, as far as all external circumstances are concerned. Naturally, I have come to different conclusions on several points than those involved in the story; but the facts are indisputable and so many people know of them that they cannot be denied. Many people remember the strange series of crimes that comes into the story a little later – crimes which, at the time, appeared to be supernatural and seemed to originate from the same source and cause as much revulsion as the infamous murders of Jack the Ripper.

> Many will remember the extraordinary group of foreigners who, for a season, played a spectacular role in the lives of the nobility here in London; and some will recall that one of them disappeared suddenly, in a puzzling and bizarre manner, without leaving a trace. Everyone who participated in this remarkable story is well-known and respected. Jonathan Harker and his wife, who is a respectable woman, and Dr. Seward have been my friends for many years, and I have never doubted their word; while the highly respected scientist and scholar, who is presented under a pseudonym, is too famous throughout the civilized, educated world for his identity to be completely hidden – especially from those who have learned to appreciate his genius and virtues and who, like myself, admire his philosophy of life.

> In our times it should be clear to all serious-minded men that:
> 'There are more things in heaven and earth/than are dreamt of in your philosophy.'
> London, _____ Street
> August 1898

B.S.[299]

Bram's notes have no reference to Jack the Ripper within them but they are also light on references about London; arguably Bram knew the city well enough to have written from his own knowledge and imagination, and revealed something of his knowledge of the crimes of Jack the Ripper in the text.

London always had inner sanctums, clubs and societies, some public, some secret where only those from the elite or a select and interested group would meet. There were the clubs for darker pursuits such as drug dens and brothels, but while prostitutes both male and female of all classes were visited by a varied clientele, as a general rule the prettier, high-class prostitutes were visited by a better class of client, who would be only too keen to keep their practices discreet, if not secret. We may never find out if Bram visited any of these but his contacts through the theatre could gain him access almost anywhere. More than one of Bram's biographers have suggested his love life with Florence was moribund[300] – she has been described 'as frigid as a statue' and allegedly refused to indulge in sexual relations with Bram after the birth of Noel in 1879 had left her with 'bad menstrual disturbances'.[301] But perhaps the problems arose because Bram struggled with his sexual identity; his letters to Walt Whitman, written while at university, suggest this. It is also intriguing to recall that Florence's only amour prior to Bram was Oscar Wilde.

To the outside world, Bram and Florence appeared to obey the Victorian conventions of marriage and marital life; they wrote in terms of endearment to each other throughout their lives and their arrangements behind closed doors suited them both. There was always a gentleman willing to escort Florence to the theatre or events, notably the librettist and dramatist half of Gilbert and Sullivan, W.S. Gilbert,

DRACULA

6d.

BY

BRAM STOKER

6d.

WESTMINSTER
Archibald Constable & Co Ltd
2 WHITEHALL GARDENS

The jacket cover of the sixpenny abridged paperback edition of *Dracula* (1901).

who was frequently mentioned in the social pages of newspapers as attending balls, events and the theatre with Mrs Stoker.

Bram was always a club man and he was able to indulge as member or guest as often as he could be spared by Irving without too many repercussions from home. Both Irving and Bram were freemasons. Irving had been initiated into Jerusalem Lodge No. 197, London, in April 1877 and remained a member until his death in 1905, and Bram was initiated into Buckinghamshire and Chandos Lodge No. 1150, London, on 21 February 1883. The pair attended over forty meetings together before Bram resigned in June 1889. Bram also moved in the circle and was friends with a number of senior members of the Hermetic Order of the Golden Dawn, such as the actress Florence Farr (Chief Adept in Anglica); the lawyer John W. Brodie-Innes (Second Order, Sixth Degree); and Oscar Wilde's wife, Constance Wilde (First Order, Fourth Degree). The Order met at a house in Chelsea, not far from Bram, but no evidence, as yet, has been unearthed to confirm Bram was actually a member.

So if there was some inside knowledge of the Ripper crimes – fact, speculation or lie presented as fact – Bram could have picked it up from his friends in one of the secret societies, and wove it into *Dracula* to add a little spice for his friends 'in the know'. Darker still, there could have been a terrible secret, a burden of suspicion or knowledge shared between close friends, which Bram saw fit to include. In the spirit of Bram's love of codes and mysteries, it is intriguing to consider the following scenario.

Bram Stoker and Hall Caine were close friends, perhaps, as Caine would later write of Bram and Irving, they too shared 'the strongest love that man may feel for man'. While Bram was on a provincial tour with Irving, Terry and the Lyceum Company, which was appearing at Edinburgh Lyceum, Caine was due to guest at the Edinburgh Garrick Club and arranged to stay on a few days, sharing rooms with Bram. From Friday 14 November until the company departed for Glasgow on 22 November they stayed together at Mrs Martins's lodgings at 118 Princes Street, working together on literary matters:

> I well remember the occasion of our talking over his sketch of the novel on the night of Tuesday 17 Nov. and how at night often 'til light we proceeded to write it down. My sitting room was a very big room often the manner of old Scots houses and had big windows looking out on the castle. I sat at the table and wrote whilst Caine walked about the room with equal footsteps dictating the chapter headings as he had decided them in the morning. He had the whole project in his mind – 'in the back of my head' was his own phrase.[302]

Thus the chapter headings and even the number of words per chapter of *The Manxman*, a book that was to prove to be one of Caine's most popular, were drafted out on one side of 1891 Lyceum-headed notepaper.[303]

The Scott Memorial and Princes Street, Edinburgh, *c.* 1891. Bram stayed with Hall Caine at Mrs Martins's lodgings, 118 Princes Street, in a room with a fine view of the castle; perhaps another inspiration for Castle Dracula.

On the night of Wednesday 18 November Irving, Bram and Caine all took supper with their old friend, the scientist Dr Andrew Wilson, at the Northern Club. Bram recorded in *Personal Reminiscences*:

> That night both Irving and Caine were in great form and the conversation was decidedly interesting. It began with a sort of discussion about Shakespeare as a dramatist on the working side; his practical execution of his own imaginative intention. Hall Caine held that Shakespeare would not have put in his plays certain descriptions if he had had modern stage advantages to explain without his telling. Irving said that it would be good for moderns if they would but take Shakespeare's lesson in this matter. Later on the conversation tended towards weird subjects. Caine told of seeing in a mirror a reflection not his own. Irving followed by telling us of his noticing an accidental effect in a mirror, which he afterwards used in the Macbeth ghost: that of holding the head up. The evening was altogether a fascinating one; it was four o'clock when we broke up.

Bram tells us something of what passed on the night of 18 November in his introduction to *The Last Confession*, published in the three-volume *The Works of Hall Caine* in 1905:

> It may be interesting to the reader to know the first exposition of the tragedy, The Last Confession … we went to a breakfast given by Mr. and Mrs. Carlaw

Martin, he being the then Editor of the Scottish Leader. A day or two before
Hall Caine had been telling me an idea for a short story founded on an episode
told by Sir Richard Burton, and in which was involved the ethical point of a
murder necessary for self preservation. At breakfast was a large and delightful
company, all of whom were deeply interested in, if not concerned in, literary
matters. During breakfast we, at our end of the table, noticed that all eyes and
ears were being concerned with Hall Caine, who was at the other end. He was
telling of a case lately come to his notice of a man who had murdered a 'saint'
in a shrine in Morocco. We all listened enthralled, for Hall Caine is a wonderful story-teller. I myself was not the least interested of the party; for though
familiar with the bones of the story, I saw now the palpitating flesh put on
them. When the story was done we discussed freely the ethics of the question
with varying result.

The consequent story written by Caine was *The Last Confession* and it is a strange
one. Elements of Burton's story are certainly there, for as the tale shifts from
London to Morocco and involves a killing with clear resonances of the murder
Burton claimed he committed, but the tale revolves around another element, a
surgeon who had developed a 'surgical procedure' on the throat, one that only he
can perform, and the troubled conscience he has over a murder he committed in
the firm belief it was to save his own life. The story begins with the confession:

> Father, do not leave me. Wait! only a little longer. You cannot absolve me? I am
> not penitent? How can I be penitent? I do not regret it? How can I regret it?
> I would do it again? How could I help but do it again?
>
> Yes, yes, I know, I know! Who knows it so well as I? It is written in the
> tables of God's law: Thou shall do no murder! But was it murder? Was it crime?
> Blood? Yes, it was the spilling of blood. Blood will have blood, you say. But is
> there no difference? …
>
> … It is less than a year since my health broke down, but the soul lives fast,
> and it seems to me like a lifetime. I had overworked myself miserably. My life as
> a physician in London had been a hard one, but it was not my practice that had
> wrecked me. How to perform that operation on the throat was the beginning
> of my trouble. You know what happened. I mastered my problem, and they
> called the operation by my name. It has brought me fame; it has made me rich;
> it has saved a hundred lives, and will save ten thousand more … My work pos-
> sessed me like a fever. I could neither do it to my content nor leave it undone.[304]

Could this be the voice of a deluded crusader who sought to rid the streets of
the prostitutes and save many from the diseases they carried? In the story there
is also an encounter with an American surgeon who justifies some murders. The
surgeon narrates:

Then coming to closer quarters we talked of murder. The American held to the doctrine of Sterne. It was a hard case that the laws of the modern world should not have made any manner of difference between murdering an honest man and only executing a scoundrel. These things should always be rated ad valorem. As for blood spilt in self-defence, it was folly to talk of it as crime. Even the laws of my own effeminate land justified the man who struck down the arm that was raised to kill him; and the mind that reckoned such an act as an offence was morbid and diseased.

These opinions were repugnant to me, and I tried to resist them. There was a sanctity about human life which no man should dare to outrage. God gave it, and only God should take it away. As for the government of the world let it be for better or for worse, it was in God's hands, and God required the help of no man.

My resistance was useless. The American held to his doctrine: it was good to take life in a good cause, and if it was good for the nation, it was good for the individual man. The end was all.[305]

Could Caine's story have been influenced by an American doctor know to him in a similar position? Indeed could Tumblety, no less, have used this justification to Caine in real life? The surgeon commits his murder in a secluded alleyway, holding the victim's throat so they made no noise, and using a knife for the killing. He recalled to his confessor, as he left the scene:

I was no criminal to mask my crime. In a dull, stupid, drowsy, comatose state I tottered down the alley and through the crowd. They saw me; they recognised me; I knew that they were jeering at me, but I knew no more. Father, they called me a drunkard. I was a drunkard indeed, but I was drunk with blood.[306]

There is nothing in the surviving Hall Caine letters to suggest his friendship with Francis Tumblety, a man who had almost certainly been his homosexual lover, did not extend beyond where the letters suddenly cease; it is perfectly feasible that there were more letters but they were lost, mislaid or even expunged from the collection of correspondence by Caine himself. It is also possible the two could have met by chance or arrangement in 1888, and that what passed between them left Caine with some hideous revelation or deep-rooted suspicion that his old friend was Jack the Ripper.

Tumblety had a dreadful reputation for notoriety dating back to the American Civil War, newspapers got wise to him and were already branding him the 'notorious Dr. Tumblety' in the 1860s,[307] reporting how he would 'bamboozle' authorities into accusing and even jailing him, then emerge as the offended 'innocent' and gain free publicity for his business. Some thought it was all a publicity stunt for Tumblety[308] – but was it all a sham? Wherever Tumblety went trouble soon followed, but would Tumblety dare to associate himself with the Ripper crimes? He had always tried to attract high-class clientele – with such an accusation hanging about him such clientele would be driven from his door.

It is more likely Caine had encountered Tumblety in 1888 and, as a result of the meeting, had conceived a deep conviction he was the killer. Tumblety was hardly mentioned as a Ripper suspect in British papers but he was all over the American press and a number of those who claimed to have known him in the past freely expressed their opinion that, 'Knowing him as I do I should not be the least surprised if he turned out to be Jack the Ripper'[309] or 'hear his name mentioned in connection with the Whitechapel murders'.[310]

Among them was attorney William P. Burr, of 320 Broadway, New York, who stated:

I met him [Tumblety] in July 1880. He brought a suit against a Mrs. Lyons, charging her with the larceny of $7,000 worth of bonds, and I was retained to defend her. It seems that several years before he met the son of Mrs. Lyons while walking on the Battery. The lad had just come from college and was a fine looking young man. He was out of employment. Tumblety greeted him and soon had him under complete control. He made him a sort of secretary in the management of his bonds, of which he had about $100,000 worth, mostly in governments, locked up in a downtown safe deposit company. He employed the youth as an amanuensis, as he personally was most illiterate. On April 28, 1878, the 'Doctor', as he was called, started for Europe by the Guion line steamer Montana. See, here is his name on the passenger list, 'Dr. Tumblety'. He gave a power of attorney to the young man, and under that some South Carolina railroad bonds were disposed of, as it was claimed and shown, under an agreement that they were to be taken as compensation. When Tumblety got back the young man had disappeared and the mother was arrested, charged by the 'Doctor' with having taken the bonds. I remember the examination to which I subjected him at the Tombs Police Court.

James D. McClelland was his lawyer, and I went into a history of the doctor's life. I remember well how indignant he became when I asked him what institution had the honor of graduating so precious a pupil. He refused to answer, and was told that the only reason for which he could refuse was that the answer would tend to humiliate of criminate him. He still refused to answer, and I thought he would spring at me to strike. There was quite a commotion in court. The case fell through and the old lady was not held. The son returned and brought a suit against the doctor, charging atrocious assault, and the evidence collected in this case was of the most disgusting sort. The lawyer who had the matter in hand is now dead, but I remember that there was a page of the Police Gazette as one exhibit, in which the portrait of the doctor appeared, with several columns of biography about him. This suit was not pushed, and then came another suit brought by this Tumblety against William P. O'Connor, a broker, for disposing of the bonds. Boardman & Boardman defended and gathered up a great mass of evidence against the doctor. Charles Frost and Charles Chambers, detectives of Brooklyn, had evidence against him. At this time he kept an herb store, or something of that sort, at No. 77 East Tenth Street. The suit did not come to anything, and I do not know of any other law matters in which this notorious man was concerned … I had seen him before that time hovering about the old Post Office building, where there were many clerks. He had a seeming mania for the company of young men and grown up youths. In the course of our investigations about the man we gathered up many stray bits of history about him, but nothing to make a connected life story. He had a superabundance of cheek and nothing could make him abashed. He was a coward physically, though he looked like a giant, and he struck me as one who would be vindictive to the last degree. He was a tremendous traveller, and while away in Europe his letters to young Lyon showed that he was in every city in Europe. The English authorities, who are now telegraphing for samples of his writing from San Francisco, ought to get them in any city in Europe. I had a big batch of letters sent by him to the young man Lyon, and they were the most amazing farrago of illiterate nonsense. Here is one written from the West. He never failed to warn his correspondent against lewd women, and in doing it used the most shocking language. I do not know how he made his money. He had it before he became acquainted with the Lyon family, and was a very liberal spender. My own idea of this case is that it would be just such a thing as Tumblety would be concerned in, but he might get one of his victims to do the work, for once he had a young man under his control, he seemed to be able to do anything with the victim.[311]

As it is likely Caine did not see the accounts published in the American press in 1888, he would not have realised he was not alone in his concerns. When Caine stayed with Bram in Edinburgh they talked through the night on a number of occasions and, burdened with his knowledge or suspicions about Tumblety, it would have been logical for Caine to share these with his closest friend.

Perhaps *The Last Confession* is Caine's attempt at exploring his own struggle with his burden of suspicion. Although he could have reported his ideas, or even an intimation of guilt given to him by Tumblety, to the authorities, he could offer no proof. Caine was also beginning to make a name for himself as a published author in the Victorian romantic genre – any danger of taint or association with the Ripper could seriously damage his popularity. Then there was the danger of exposure if Caine informed on Tumblety; he feared what the Great American Doctor would have dredged up about their relationship.

The odd compendium of *Capt'n Davy's Honeymoon*, *The Last Confession* and *The Blind Mother*, originally published in 1893, were dedicated to Bram, four years before Bram's own enigmatic dedication to Caine in *Dracula*. Caine's remarkable dedication truly reflects the intimate friendship between these two men:

To Bram Stoker.

When in dark hours and in evil humours my bad angel has sometimes made me think that friendship as it used to be of old, friendship as we read of it in books, that friendship which is not a jilt sure to desert us, but a brother born to adversity as well as success, is now a lost quality, a forgotten virtue, a high partnership in fate degraded to a low traffic in self-interest, a mere league of pleasure and business, then my good angel for admonition or reproof has whispered the names of a little band of friends, whose friendship is a deep stream that buoys me up and makes no noise; and often first among those names has been your own.

Down to this day our friendship has needed no solder of sweet words to bind it and I take pleasure in showing by means of this unpretending book that it is founded not only on personal liking and much agreement, but on some wholesome difference and even a little disputation. 'The Last Confession' is an attempt to solve a moral problem which we have discussed from opposite poles of sympathy – the absolute value and sanctity of human life, the right to fight, the right to kill, the right to resist evil and set aside at utmost need the letter of the sixth commandment ... [312]

Was *The Last Confession* a version of the stories related over the table during the Edinburgh visit of 1891 or did Caine, the master storyteller, 'cloak the bones' of the terrible knowledge or suspicions he had of the Whitechapel murders with the 'palpitating flesh' of his story?

Curiously, Bram also wrote a similar tale to *The Last Confession* entitled *The Dream of Red Hands*. This was a short story of a man whose dreams were haunted by visions of a murder, his hands 'crimson with blood' that welled from the throat of the man he killed. Found among the papers of Bram's literary estate, along with a number of other works, *The Dream of Red Hands* was first published in *Sketch* magazine on 11 June 1894. Perhaps, rather than just trying to explore how the crime of murder could, in the mind of the killer, be justified, Bram thought he could better explore Caine's secret or suspicion by weaving it into his long-term book project – *Dracula*.

So, is it possible that Caine and Tumblety could have met during the period of the Ripper crimes? Tumblety was in London in 1888 while Caine was living at Aberleigh Lodge in the London suburb of Bexley Heath and was, at that time, often 'running in to town' by train to visit the author Wilkie Collins, with whom he was developing a friendship, or to call at his publishers, Chatto & Windus, at their offices on Piccadilly. Tumblety had been known to frequent that area in the past; he had been staying on Glasshouse Street, just off Piccadilly, during some of his correspondence with Caine and had sent telegrams to him from the GPO Telegram Office on Piccadilly Circus.[313] In 1888 Piccadilly was still a popular cruising ground for picking up homosexuals,[314] perhaps even more so, for it had become known as 'the heart of modern Babylon', and it was in Piccadilly

Piccadilly, London – 'The heart of modern Babylon', *c.* 1890.

Circus that the controversial figure of Anteros, popularly known as Eros, a symbol not only of unrequited but homoerotic love was erected upon the Shaftesbury Memorial in 1885. In this vein, it is in Piccadilly that, shortly after his return from his terrible experiences in Transylvania, Jonathan Harker happens to spot Dracula staring at another potential victim and, later, discovers he has a house nearby.[315] Bram gives the address of this 'mansion' as No. 347, Piccadilly, and locates it to the west of Piccadilly Circus, beyond the Junior Constitutional Club.[316]

In *Dracula*, the great wooden boxes of earth recovered from the *Demeter* were delivered to the Count's newly purchased fictional estate 'Carfax' in Purfleet, Essex, and deposited in 'the old chapel'. A Carter Paterson carrier was then employed to take a cartload of:

> six boxes left at 197 Chicksand Street, Mile End New Town, and another six which he deposited at Jamaica Lane, Bermondsey. If then the Count meant to scatter these ghastly refuges of his over London, these places were chosen as the first of delivery, so that later he might distribute more fully. The systematic manner in which this was done made me think that he could not mean to confine himself to two sides of London. He was now fixed on the far east on the northern shore, on the east of the southern shore, and on the south. The north and west were surely never meant to be left out of his diabolical scheme, let alone the City itself and the very heart of fashionable London in the south–west and west.[317]

Bermondsey is an interesting choice for Dracula's first lair south of the River Thames, it is evocative because it was a rough old dock area and had an interesting Ripper connection, as revealed by the following account published during 'The Autumn of Terror' in the *Morning Advertiser*, 19 October 1888:

The City Police have in hand a very important piece of information, and have under observation a man whose movements in Whitechapel, Mile-end, and Bermondsey, seem to indicate that he is likely to be the murderer of at least one of the women found slaughtered in the streets of East London. A man supposed to be an American was arrested in Bermondsey at one o'clock yesterday morning, and taken to the police station. His conduct, demeanour, and appearance gave rise to great suspicion, and his apprehension and general particulars were wired to the City Police. Following this episode, a very important conference took place yesterday afternoon between a young man named John Lardy, of 31, Redman's-road, Mile-end, and the head of the Detective Department at the Old Jewry, at which he stated as follows :- 'At 10:30 last night I was with a friend and a young woman outside the "Grave Maurice" Tavern, opposite the London Hospital, when I noticed a man whom I had never seen before come across the road, look into each compartment of the tavern, and enter the house. He came out again directly, and carefully looked up and down the road, and then walked over the road to the front of the hospital, where two women were standing talking. Those women were, I believe, unfortunates. The man said something to them, but I did not hear his words. The women shook their heads and said "No". I said to my friend, "What a funny-looking man; I wonder if he is the murderer." My friend replied, "Let us follow him." We said good night to our lady friend, and followed the man. When opposite the Pavilion Theatre he drew himself up in an instant, and looked carefully round. We believe that he saw us following him, and he disappeared into a doorway. We stopped for a moment or two, and he came out of his hiding-place, and went into a newspaper shop next door. During the whole time we saw him his right hand was in his overcoat pocket, apparently clutching something. He bought a paper at the shop and folded it up on his chest with his left hand, and then left the shop, looking up and down the road as he did so, and carefully reading the placard boards outside the shop windows. He afterwards started off towards Aldgate, and we followed him. When he got to the corner of Duke-street (the street leading to Mitre-square) he turned, and seeing that we were following him recrossed the road and walked back to Leman-street and went down it. When he reached Royal Mint-street he went into King-street, which is very narrow, and my friend and I ran round to the other end of that street, hoping to see him come out there. Just as we got to the other end of King-street, we heard a door close, and we waited to see if the man re-opened it, for we felt sure that he was the man, although we had not seen him go into the house. We both waited for twenty-five minutes, when we saw the same man come out of a house. He came up the street, and we stepped back and allowed him to pass, and he went in the direction of the Whitechapel-road. He went away so quickly that we lost sight of him in the fog, which was then very thick. The time then was a few minutes after twelve. When he reappeared from the house we noticed that he was very differently dressed to what he was when we first saw him, the most noticeable being his overcoat. At first he was wearing a sort of short frock coat reaching to his knees only, but when he came out of the house in King-street he had on a large overcoat which reached to within three inches of the ground. From what I could see he appeared to be between 40 and 45 years of age, and from 5 feet 11 inches to 6 feet high (a man 5 feet 11 inches was placed before Lardy, who said, "My man was a little taller than you"). He wore a low hat with a square crown, but I cannot describe either his trousers or boots. He had the appearance of an American; his cheek bones were high and prominent, his face thin, cheeks sunken, and he had a moustache only, his cheeks and chin being clean shaven. The moustache was, I believe, a false one, for it was all awry, one end pointing upward and the other towards the ground. His hair, was dark, apparently black, and somewhat long.'

The narrator, having finished his statement, was asked, 'Have you seen the man now in custody?' and replied in the negative. The police subsequently ascertained the truth of this statement, and Lardy left Old Jewry.

From what has subsequently come to the knowledge of the police, it is inferred that on leaving King-street, the stranger made his way over London-bridge into Bermondsey, where he was apprehended, and there is no doubt that the descriptions of the Bermondsey and King-street men tally in every particular.[318]

Historically, Bermondsey was also a worthy choice for the Count to have a hideaway for it was there that one of the most infamous murders of the early nineteenth century took place – 'The Bermondsey Horror'.

Husband and wife Frederick and Maria Manning had murdered Maria's former lover, Patrick O'Connor, and buried his body under the kitchen floor. Hanged atop Horsemonger Lane Gaol on 13 November 1849, their execution drew a large crowd, which included Charles Dickens. Maria Manning became known as 'the woman who murdered black satin' because she wore a black satin dress for her own hanging; such material was shunned by English women for years thereafter.[319]

Bram talks of another woman in black, the risen undead Lucy Westenra – 'the bloofer lady':

The neighborhood of Hampstead is just at present exercised with a series of events which seem to run on lines parallel to those of what was known to the writers of headlines as 'The Kensington Horror', or 'The Stabbing Woman', or

'The Woman in Black'. During the past two or three days several cases have occurred of young children straying from home or neglecting to return from their playing on the Heath. In all these cases the children were too young to give any properly intelligible account of themselves, but the consensus of their excuses is that they had been with a 'bloofer lady'. It has always been late in the evening when they have been missed, and on two occasions the children have not been found until early in the following morning.[320]

This account has clear parallels with a real case of murder, a mysterious 'woman in black' and even Jack the Ripper in both London and provincial newspaper reports published in early December 1894, carrying such headlines as 'The Kensington Horror'[321] and 'Mysterious Outrages in Kensington';[322] it even made the pages of *The Graphic*.[323]

A typical account of the case ran:

TWO WOMEN STABBED IN KENSINGTON

Two cases of assault of a mysterious nature on women have occurred in Stanhope Gardens, South Kensington. The assailant, a woman, is believed to be the same in both cases. The second assault took place on Saturday night during the fog and exaggerated rumours got into circulation, one account being that another 'Jack the Ripper' murder had been committed. It appears that a fortnight ago a Mrs. [Sarah] Haynes, the wife of a coachman, was returning to her home in Southwell Gardens, Gloucester Road late on Saturday night, when a well dressed woman in black, her features disguised by a thick spotted veil asked her way to Cromwell Road. Before she could answer, however, she received a stab on the face which necessitated a serious operation and resulted in the loss of the eyes. Since that time the police have kept a look-out for a closely veiled lady in the neighbourhood; but the affair had almost been forgotten when the outrage of last Saturday occurred. It is stated that a servant girl made a statement to the police which tallies exactly with that of the person previously assaulted. She also appears to have been accosted by a short woman, who asked for directions, and imme- diately followed up her question with a blow which knocked the girl down and cut the skin of the face. The blow, it is said, was given with a knife. The woman made no great haste to escape, but walked slowly towards Queen's Gate.[324]

The culprit of the Woman in Black stabbings was never brought to justice, and all of this came in the wake of the murder of Augusta Dawes (aka Augusta Dudley), an 'unfortunate' who had been found lying in a pool of blood with her throat cut on Holland Park Road, Kensington, on 25 November 1894. The murder weapon, a sharp shoemaker's knife, was found a short distance away.[325]

On 27 November 1894 a letter arrived at Kensington police station bearing a Dublin postmark:

Dear Sir,

The murder that was committed I did it. I did it just to the right of the door of a gentleman. I got her by the throat and tried to choke her, but without success. I got her on the ground and cut her knife with a Sloyd knife. It was a very good cut. When I had cut her a fellow was coming along, so I flew for my life, but left the stick, and the knife was thrown away in the back lane in a back street. I did the murder at 12 30. So good bye. On the job.

From Jack the Ripper

The handwriting was identified by Francis Rollison, one of the masters at Eastcote (a private institution for mentally affected gentlemen) in Hampton Wick, Kingston upon Thames in Surrey, as belonging to one of his patients, one Reginald Treherne Bassett Saunderson, the son of a good family. Saunderson had been an inpatient at Eastcote for six years and had previously absented himself from the institution without permission and had been missing for a few days. Saunderson, a handsome and athletic young man of 21, was arrested and taken into custody. Examined by Dr Forbes Winslow and other experts he had initially been found fit but his mental condition had rapidly deteriorated. He became liable to great excitement and paroxysms of violence so was put into a straitjacket and placed in a padded cell. Brought before Mr Justice Wills on 30 January 1895 he was tried for his sanity, the jury found the prisoner insane and not in any condition to plead and he was ordered to be 'detained until Her Majesty's Pleasure be known'.[326]

Bram's most overt reference to the Ripper crimes in the text is the location where Dracula sends, 'six boxes left at 197 Chicksand Street, Mile End New Town'.[327]

Observe the map on p. 231, the murder sites of the 'canonical five' women accepted as the five victims of Jack the Ripper are marked on the map, then consider, based on this mapping, the killing ground of Jack Ripper and you will see Chicksand Street at its heart. Furthermore, although Bram was probably not aware of this, the house-to-house search that was conducted by the Metropolitan Police Force investigating the Ripper murders in October 1888 included Chicksand Street. Chicksand Street becomes Osborne Place, cross over Brick Lane and you are in Flower and Dean Street where three of Jack the Ripper's victims are known to have lodged.

In the book, Dracula has five 'brides': three in his castle, and Lucy and Mina. Four he possesses entirely; the fifth – Mina – he manages to bite but not fully possess. Jack the Ripper also has five 'canonical' victims: four of them, Polly Nichols, Annie Chapman, Catherine Eddowes and Mary Jane Kelly, had their throats cut across and escalating amounts of mutilation inflicted upon their bodies; but the one in the middle of it all, Elizabeth Stride, only suffered a slash to the throat as Jack was disturbed and could not carry out his mutilations. Like Dracula with Mina, Jack did not fully 'possess' Elizabeth either.

10

THE KEEPERS OF THE SECRET

Francis Tumblety jumped bail in Britain and initially fled to France under the assumed name of Frank Townsend, but when he arrived back in New York aboard the *Bretagne* at 1.30 p.m. on Sunday 2 December 1888, the authorities and the press were waiting for him. Tumblety walked down the gangplank into a maelstrom of interest in him as a 'London police' prime suspect for the Whitechapel murders. The *Evening Star* warned, 'WATCH HIM The American Suspected of Whitechapel Butcheries Arrives in New York' and went on to state 'a reporter called upon Inspector Byrnes this morning and asked if there was anything for which Tumblety could be arrested in this country. The Inspector replied that although Tumblety was a fugitive from justice under $1,500 bail for a nominal offence in England, he could not be arrested there. The Inspector added that in case the doctor was wanted he knew where to lay his hands on him. Two Central office detectives were on the dock when the steamer arrived and followed Tumblety to a boarding house, the number of which will not be made public.'[328]

Byrnes concluded with the promise, 'The doctor will be kept under strict surveillance.'

The newspapers ran feature after feature, some of them tracing people who had recollections of Tumblety's eccentric and notorious behaviour over the years, and dredged up old accounts of his troubled past, filling long columns and features about his past misdemeanours; these were all reported as fact or based on strong suspicion in newspapers across the United States.

In one now infamous article, published in the *New York World* on Sunday 2 December 1888, Colonel Charles A. Dunham provided some startling revelations:

HIS CAREER IN WASHINGTON.

Colonel C. A. Dunham, a well-known lawyer who lives near Fairview, N.J., was intimately acquainted with Twomblety [sic] for many years, and, in his own mind, had long connected him with the Whitechapel horrors. 'The man's real name,' said the lawyer, 'is Tumblety, with Francis for a Christian name. I have

1.	Mary Ann Nichols, Buck's Row, 31 August 1888
2.	Annie Chapman, 29 Hanbury Street, 8 September 1888
3.	Elizabeth Stride, Berner Street, 30 September 1888
4.	Catherine Eddowes, Mitre Square, 30 September 1888
5.	Mary Jane Kelly, Miller's Court, 9 November 1888
A to B.	Chicksand Street

here a book published by him a number of years ago, describing some of his strange adventures and wonderful cures, all lies, of course, in which the name Francis Tumblety, M.D., appears. When, to my knowledge of the man's history, his idiosyncrasies, his revolting practices, his antipathy to women, and especially to fallen women, his anatomical museum, containing many specimens like those carved from the Whitechapel victims – when, to my knowledge on these subjects, there is added the fact of his arrest on suspicion of being the murderer, there appears to me nothing improbable in the suggestion that Tumblety is the culprit.

He is not a doctor. A more arrant charlatan and quack never fastened on the hopes and fears of afflicted humanity. I first made the fellow's acquaintance a few days after the battle of Bull Run. Although a very young man at the time I held a colonel's commission in the army, and was at the capital on official business. The city was full of strangers, 90 per cent of them military men. All the first-class hotels resembled beehives. Among them were many fine-looking and many peculiar-looking men, but of the thousands there was not one that attracted half as much attention as Tumblety. A Titan in stature, with a very red face and long flowing mustache, he would have been a noticeable personage in any place and in any garb. But, decked in a richly embroidered coat or jacket, with a medal held by a gay ribbon on each breast, a semi-military cap with a high peak, cavalry trousers with the brightest of yellow stripes, riding boots and spurs fit for a show window, a dignified and rather stagy gait and manner, he was as unique a figure as could be found anywhere in real life. When followed, as he generally was, by a valet and two great dogs, he was no doubt the envy of many hearts. The fellow was everywhere. I never saw anything so nearly approaching ubiquity. Go where you would, to any of the hotels, to the war department or the navy yard, you were sure to find the 'doctor'. He had no business in either place, but he went there to impress the officers whom he would meet. He professed to have an extensive experience in European hospitals and armies, and claimed to have diplomas from the foremost medical colleges of the Old World and New. He had, he declared, after much persuasion accepted the commission of brigade surgeon at a great sacrifice pecuniarily; but, with great complacency, he always added that, fortunately for his private patients, his official duties would not, for a considerable time, take him away from the city.

WHY HE HATED WOMEN.

At length it was whispered about that he was an adventurer. One day my lieutenant-colonel and myself accepted the the [sic] 'doctor's' invitation to a late dinner – symposium, he called it – at his rooms. He had very cosy and tastefully arranged quarters in, I believe, H. street. There were three rooms on a floor, the rear one being his office, with a bedroom or two a story higher. On reaching the place we found covers laid for eight – that being the 'doctor's' lucky number, he said – several of the guests, all in the military service, were persons with whom we were already acquainted. It was soon apparent that whatever Tumblety's deficiencies as a surgeon, as an amphitryon he could not easily be excelled. His menu, with colored waiters and the et ceteras, was furnished by one of the best caterers in the city. After dinner there were brought out two tables for play – for poker or whist. In the course of the evening some of the party, warmed by the wine, proposed to play for heavy stakes, but Tumblety frowned down the proposition at once and in such a way as to show he was no gambler. Some one asked why he had not invited some women to his dinner. His face instantly became as black as a thunder cloud. He had a pack of cards in his hand, but he laid them down and said, almost savagely: 'No, Colonel, I don't know any such cattle, and if I did I would, as your friend, sooner give you a dose of quick poison than take you into such danger.' He then broke into a homily on the sin and folly of dissipation, fiercely denounced all woman and especially fallen women.

Then he invited us into his office where he illustrated his lecture, so to speak. One side of this room was entirely occupied with cases, outwardly resembling wardrobes. When the doors were opened quite a museum was revealed – tiers of shelves with glass jars and cases, some round and others square, filled with all sorts of antomical [sic] specimens. The 'doctor' placed on a table a dozen or more jars containing, as he said, the matrices of every class of women. Nearly a half of one of these cases was occupied exclusively with these specimens.

THE STORY OF HIS LIFE.

Not long after this the 'doctor' was in my room when my lieutenant-colonel came in and commenced expatiating on the charms of a certain woman. In a moment, almost, the doctor was lecturing him and denouncing women. When he was asked why he hated women, he said that when quite a young man he fell desperately in love with a pretty girl, rather his senior, who promised to reciprocate his affection. After a brief courtship he married her. The honeymoon was not over when he noticed a disposition on the part of his wife to flirt with other men. He remonstrated, she kissed him, called him a dear, jealous fool – and he believed her. Happening one day to pass in a cab through the worst part of the town he saw his wife and a man enter a gloomy-looking house. Then he learned that before her marriage his wife had been an inmate of that and many similar houses. Then he gave up all womankind.

Shortly after telling this story the 'doctor's' real character became known and he slipped away to St. Louis, where he was arrested for wearing the uniform of an army surgeon.

Colonel Dunham was asked whether there was any truth in the statement of a city paper that Harrold [sic], who was hanged as one of Booth's confederates in the assassination of Lincoln, was at one time the 'doctor's' valet. The reply was that it was not true. The gentleman added that he could speak positively on the subject, as he knew the valet well.

Colonel Dunham also said that Tumblety had not been arrested on suspicion of having guilty knowledge of the assassination conspiracy. 'He was arrested in St. Louis,' said the Colonel, 'on suspicion of being Luke P. Blackburn, lately governor of Kentucky, who had been falsely charged with trying to introduce yellow fever into the northern cities by means of infected rags. It is perfectly clear that

Tumblety purposely brought about his own arrest by sending anonymous letters to the federal authorities to the effect that Blackburn and himself were identical. His object, of course, was notoriety. He knew he was too well known in Washington, whither he felt certain he would be sent, to be kept long in custody.

Recent research into Colonel Charles A. Dunham (Sanford Conover) has exposed him as a perjurer and a fabricator of stories; unsurprisingly, as he was a spy and a chameleon with many faces. Motivated by both politics and money, during the American Civil War he 'systematically and ingeniously faked stories' that were damaging to Confederates and northern Peace Democrats.[329] Carman Cumming points out that Dunham created at least nine identities for himself, 'working brilliantly in his journalism to craft and deploy them throughout the war and in the years after'.[330] But one theme does recur: that he was not a pathological liar. Furthermore, there is no evidence that Charles A. Dunham accepted payment for his Tumblety story. The world of covert operations and black propaganda is, by the nature of the work, one of smoke and mirrors. Evidence is thin but if Dunham had continued his covert activities for the government after the war it may provide a motive for the story he gave to the New York World and would thus have been founded on grains of truth or strong suspicions so should not be dismissed out of hand. Dunham was no saint but what he did is believed to have been done 'for the better good'.[331] Joe Chetcuti has made a specialised study of Francis Tumblety over a number of years and here kindly shares his thoughts on the Dunham/Conover account published in the New York World:

Tumblety may have been the Ripper and still not owned an 'anatomical collection'. And Tumblety may have indeed owned an anatomical collection and not have been the Ripper. Either way, Tumblety's guilt or innocence in Whitechapel will not be determined by the validity or lack of validity of Conover's accusation. People who wish to use Conover to assess Tumblety's worth as Ripper suspect can only go a limited distance with him.

With that said, what do I personally think of Conover's story about Tumblety having owned an anatomical collection in his Washington DC closet? I think it was a hypothetical story that tried to convey a truthful and legitimate suspicion.

I believe Conover wrote his story for the New York World because on Oct 6, 1888 a member of English Parliament, Colonel Francis Hughes-Hallett, had shared some information with a New York World reporter. The Parliament member was quoted in saying that the Ripper has stored the confiscated body parts of his victims. Hughes-Hallett then declared that the Ripper preserves the body parts in alcohol and dances around the sacrifice in some dark ritual. Hughes-Hallett's words were printed in the New York World on Oct 7, 1888. Two weeks later on Oct 16th, the Lusk letter was received in London, and it contained a half kidney that had been preserved in alcohol. The kidney came with a letter signed 'From Hell'. This development gave Hughes-Hallett's words a strong jolt of validity to the journalists at the *New York World*. I believe Conover's 'anatomical collection' story was printed in the paper for the enhancement of Hughes-Hallett's Oct 6th testimony that he gave to the *New York World* about the Ripper's preservation of the body parts he took.

Hughes-Hallett also declared that he suspected the Ripper of being a dubious medical man who studied anatomy 'as a fad'. He claimed the Ripper was a man of leisure who indulges in the Pall Mall club scene. Tumblety fits Hughes-Hallett's assessment amazingly well.

I think Conover's tale reads more like a parable than a historical account. It was printed in the New York World because that newspaper had the inside track on Hughes-Hallett's Pall Mall suspect. The dubious doctor who preserves anatomical specimens. I have no doubt that Hughes-Hallett's suspect was Francis Tumblety.

It is also worth considering a possible motive for Dunham's statement. There is evidence of communication between Robert Anderson, head of Scotland Yard's Criminal Investigation Department, and the police authorities in Brooklyn and San Francisco, requesting an investigation of Tumblety. There were strong suspicions in Special Branch that Tumblety was a suspect for the Whitechapel murders, as confirmed in the letter from Chief Inspector Littlechild to George R. Sims in 1913.[332] Scotland Yard had a 'large dossier' concerning Tumblety but there was not enough evidence to justify his arrest for the murders. Such a high level of interest in Tumblety may have led to co-operation from Washington, who could have used their old contact, Colonel Dunham, to create the story based on what material they had against Tumblety in an attempt to shake the tree and see what apples fell.

To find a reason why Special Branch had taken such an interest in Tumblety, consideration must be given to the roots of the climate of fear in 1880s London. The Fenian 'Dynamite Outrages' had rocked the government and shocked the public, as had the horrible murders of Lord Cavendish and Undersecretary Thomas Henry Burke by the Fenian Invincibles at Phoenix Park, Dublin, in May 1882. During the Whitechapel murders the spectre of the Phoenix Park murders rose again as press reportage frequently spoke of an 'assassin'.[333] The Phoenix Park murders were even mentioned in the appeals of the Whitechapel Vigilance Committee to the Home Secretary for a government reward for the capture of the killer so that he might 'convince the poor and humble residents of our East-end that the Government authorities are as anxious to avenge the blood of these unfortunate victims as they were the assassination of Lord Cavendish and Mr. Burke'.

The Phoenix Park murders had been carried out to devastating and bloody effect with Weiss surgical knives and the Ripper was believed to have used something similar, as Dr Phillips pointed out in his testimony at the Annie Chapman inquest: 'It must have been a very sharp knife, probably with a thin, narrow blade, and at least six to eight inches in length, and perhaps longer.'[334] Senior officers in Scotland Yard were concerned some 'secret society' was at work in the Ripper crimes; Sir Charles Warren commented in a confidential memo, 'As Mr Mathews [the Home Secretary] is aware I have for some time past inclined to the idea that the murders may possibly be done by a secret society, as the only logical solution to the question, but I would not understand this being done by a Socialist ...'[335]

Sensationally, it was suggested by Stephen Knight in *Jack the Ripper: The Final Solution* in the 1970s that the 'secret society' responsible for the murders was the Freemasons. While this has been repeated, ad nauseam, in numerous books, articles, television programmes and films ever since, a more considered approach to the situation in the 1880s presents the Fenians as far more likely candidates for his comment. There is no direct evidence to prove Tumblety was a Fenian activist but he was Irish by birth, had lived through the famine and, having started a new life in America, had seen many of his countrymen compelled, unwillingly, by the draft to serve during the Civil War. He had also made speeches as an Irish patriot in the aftermath of the New York draft riots in 1863. Furthermore, there is no evidence of a clear reason why Tumblety went to London in 1888; unusually, adverts promoting his business did not spring up in the newspapers to herald his arrival. While in London Tumblety was arrested on a charge of indecency, there were witnesses to testify against him and a date for the case to be heard had been set. It therefore seems incredible that the Chief of CID would have gone to so much trouble to gather more evidence against Tumblety on this charge after he had skipped bail and fled to America. There had to be something more to it.

Tumblety kept his head down and eventually emerged to give an interview to the *New York World*, published on 29 January 1889, in which he repudiated the allegations against him:

Dr. Francis Tumblety, the celebrated Whitechapel suspect, after two months' silence has given his version of why he was accused of being Jack the Ripper. He says it was owing to the stupidity of the London Police, who arrested him because he was an American and wore a slouch hat. He is preparing a pamphlet defending himself and giving a history of his life.

After months of profound silence Dr. Francis Tumblety, whose name in connection with the Whitechapel crimes has become a house-hold word, has at last consented to be interviewed and give his version of how he came to figure so prominently in the most remarkable series of tragedies recorded in the long list of crimes.

The doctor landed in New York on the 3rd of last December, and from the moment that he set foot in New York he was under surveillance. An English detective, whose stupidity was noticeable even among a class not celebrated for their shrewdness, came over especially to shadow him, and scores of reporters tried in vain to see him. As soon as he got off the ship Dr. Tumblety went direct to the house of Mrs. McNamara, No. 79 East Tenth Street, and he has been there ever since. Mrs. McNamara is an old Irishwoman whose fidelity to the doctor is remarkable, and it was due to her vigilance that all efforts to see him personally failed. She was able to throw reporters and detectives completely off the scent, and if it were not for the fact that the doctor voluntarily came forward and made his own statement no one would have known whether he was in New York or New Zealand.

The police long since ceased to take any interest in the case, as it became evident that the English authorities had no evidence to hold the doctor. Finding himself no long pursued, the doctor concluded to satisfy the public by making a complete statement himself. With this object in view he has carefully prepared a pamphlet giving a history of his life.

It will be a refutation of all the charges that have been made against him.

The pictures that have been published of Dr. Tumblety in London and New York give a very good idea of him. He is a powerfully built man and stands 6 feet 2 inches in his stockings. His long black mustache has been trimmed close and reaches down in the shape of a thick growth of beard around his chin, which he keeps smooth shaven. His face is ruddy and he has blue eyes. If he ever dressed sensationally in the past, he does not do so now. Yesterday he wore a dark suit which was by no means new, and a little peaked traveling cap. Altogether, he gave the appearance of a prosperous Western farmer. He wore no jewelry.

Dr. Tumblety talks in a quick, nervous fashion, with a decidedly English accent, and at times, when describing his treatment by the English police, he would get up from his chair and walk rapidly around the room until he became calm.

'My arrest came about this way,' said he. 'I had been going over to England for a long time – ever since 1869, indeed – and I used to go about the city a great deal until every part of it became familiar to me.

I happened to be there when these Whitechapel murders attracted the attention of the whole world, and, in the company with thousands of other people, I went down to the Whitechapel district. I was not dressed in a way to attract attention, I thought, though it afterwards turned out that I did. I was interested by the excitement and the crowds and the queer scenes and sights, and did not know that all the time I was being followed by English detectives.'

'Why did they follow you?'

'My guilt was very plain to the English mind. Someone had said that Jack the Ripper was an American, and everybody believed that statement. Then it is the universal belief among the lower classes that all Americans wear slouch hats; therefore, Jack the Ripper, must wear a slouch hat. Now, I happened to have on a slouch hat, and this, together with the fact that I was an American, was enough for the police. It established my guilt beyond any question.'

The doctor produced from an inside pocket two magnificent diamonds, one thirteen carats and the other nine carats, both of the purest quality, and a superb cluster ring set in diamonds. He said that, in his opinion, his arrest was due, in a measure, to the police desiring his diamonds and thinking they could force him to give them up.

'How long were you in prison?'

'Two or three days; but I don't care to talk about it. When I think of the way I was treated in London, it makes me lose all control of myself. It was shameful, horrible.'

'What do you think of the London police?'

'I think their conduct in this Whitechapel affair is enough to show what they are. Why, they stuff themselves all day with potpies and beef and drink gallons of stale beer, keeping it up until they go to bed late at night, and then wake up the next morning heavy as lead. Why, all the English police have dyspepsia. They can't help it. Their heads are as thick as the London fogs. You can't drive an idea through their thick skulls with a hammer. I never saw such a stupid set. Look at their treatment of me. There was absolutely not one single scintilla of evidence against me. I had simply been guilty of wearing a slouch hat, and for that I was charged with a series of the most horrible crimes ever recorded.

Why, if Inspector Byrnes was over in London with some of his men they would have had the Whitechapel fiend long ago. But this is all very unpleasant to me, and I would prefer talking about something else.'

'You are accused of being a woman-hater. What have you to say to that?'

This seemed to amuse the doctor a great deal. He laughed loud and long. Then he said:

'I don't care to talk about the ladies, but I will show you one little evidence that I am not regarded with aversion by the sex. I will first explain how it came to me. I had received a letter of introduction to a lady of rank, a duchess, who was then at Torquay, which is several hundred miles from London. I presented my letter and was invited to breakfast with her. When I came I presented her with a bouquet of flowers and she picked up a quill which was lying on the table near by and dashed off the following stanzas extempore:

To Dr. Francis Tumblety, M.D.:
Thanks for the lovely rosebuds sent.
Its beauty may be fleeting,
But not its sentiment.
And its charming beauty
Nor colour cannot last,
It will be a pleasant duty,
In memory of the past,
To guard the faded flower,

When you have gone from me,
In memory of the hour
You came to sweet Torquey (pronounced Tork-kee).
Mary.

'Now that doesn't look like a woman-hater, does it?' said the doctor, with a look of pride.

The doctor then exhibited a number of letters from well-known people certifying to his character and integrity. One general endorsement was signed by A.L. Ashman, proprietor of the Sinclair House; Dr. E.P. Miller, C.T. Ryan, Dr. Alfred Wynkoop, and J.C. Hughes, of 753 Broadway. He had any number of letters from merchants, physicians, lawyers, bankers, and business men. Some of the letters he showed were from patients in England. One was from a gentleman named Bowers, connected with the Midland Railroad, who told him that his former medicines had done his father a great deal of good, and who urgently requested the doctor to forward some more. Another letter was from W.H. Eccleston, of Finsbury Park, who wrote him a glowing letter of thanks for his services, and said that all his friends looked upon the doctor as having saved his life. In talking about his standing in England, the doctor said:

'If it were necessary I could show you letters from many distinguished people whom I have met abroad. I am a frequenter of some of the best London clubs, among others the Carleton Club and the Beefsteak Club. I was the victim of circumstances when this horrible charge was first brought, and since then I have been attacked on all sides and no one has had a good word to say for me. It is strange, too, because I don't remember ever to have done any human being harm, and I know of a great many I have helped.'[336]

No conclusive evidence to prove Tumblety was the Whitechapel Murderer emerged in the States although, as Tumblety seemed to have lost his alleged 'power' over young men, he was brought in for questioning after attempting to proposition boys on the streets of New York on no less than three occasions between June 1889 and November 1890.[337] The words of a *Washington Post* reporter paint a telling image of Tumblety at that time:

Dr Tumblety is an enormous man over six feet in height, with broad shoulders. His hair is black, tinged with gray, and his skin red and course. His moustaches is a rather large affair, evidently dyed black, and extends around the corners of his mouth. His eyes are steely blue, and he gazed steadily at nothing, as he spoke in a weak, effeminate voice. He was dressed in a big black overcoat and wore a German cap, and had on rubber boots.[338]

Tumblety retired from his medical practice soon after, he probably had little other option in the light of the adverse publicity he had received in the press. During his retirement Tumblety made a number of benevolent donations and public acts of charity, prominent among them his generous payment for thousands of New York newsboys and girls to have a free 'real soap and hot water bath' in September 1891.[339] He spent the rest of his days living in New York and visiting American spa resorts. In 1893 Tumblety published another version of his biography. Larger than any previous versions, it was his usual mix of his own experiences, medical philosophy, testimonials (some authentic and some fabricated) and travel features (lifted from other publications) about places around the world that he claimed to have visited but, as ever, in reality had probably not. He included a few feature articles on such topics as 'Causes of Heart Disease', 'Physiognomy', 'Poisonous Drinks', 'Great Men Who Died from Overwork' and, perhaps most significantly from the point of view of this book, in a chapter entitled 'A Few Remarks on Two Leading Diseases viz Paralysis and Bright's Disease'. In it, he dealt with paralysis in little over a half page, spending the rest of the chapter discussing Bright's Disease with special attention to its effects on the kidneys. While this may have been a correct emphasis for such a condition, no matter who the physician was, it seems tinged with blood when recalling the parcel containing 'half the Kidne I took' sent to George Lusk, and the comments of Major Smith of the City Police.

The final chapter is 'Dr. Tumblety as Orator' in which he reproduced a speech he claimed to have given at Boston in response to the toast 'Irish Soldiers in America'. In it he discussed the history of great commanders of Irish birth and descent in America during the Civil War and, focusing on and giving emphasis to the victories over the hated British during the War of Independence, he concludes the speech, and his book, with the battle call:

Vive la the old brigade
Vive la the new one, too:
Vive la the rose shall fade,
And the shamrock bloom forever true![340]

Modern criminal profilers state serial killers often take trophies. The Ripper's second victim, Annie Chapman, was known to wear two brass rings – they were noted as missing when her body was found in the backyard of 29 Hanbury Street in 1888. When Tumblety finally died of a heart condition at St John's Hospital, St Louis, in 1903 he left a considerable amount of money in his will. It is, therefore, strange to note among the few effects that he kept on him to the very end were listed 'two imitation rings worth $3'.

But what of Bram? The Stokers had moved from Cheyne Walk to 17 St Leonard's Terrace in 1886, Florence was happy to go; it is said she had not liked the atmosphere of the place since Bram brought the man he rescued from drowning into the house and he died on the dining table. Later, in 1895, when the lease came up on No. 18, the larger house opposite, Bram snapped it up. These changes of address are all marked in the correspondence between Bram and his dear friend Hall Caine. From the earliest days and throughout the years of their correspondence, despite predominantly exchanging letters about business matters and legal issues in publishing (clearly their more esoteric and creative exchanges were made on the occasions when they stayed with one another and were embodied in their books), Bram and Caine always addressed one another with terms of great affection: Bram would begin his letters, 'My dear Hall Caine' and Caine, 'To my dear Bram'. By 1896 this had changed to an even deeper and meaningful greeting of 'My Dear Hommy Beg',[341] the name Caine's Manx grandmother had called him when he was a boy, and the name that appeared in the enigmatic dedication of *Dracula*, 'To My Dear Friend Hommy-Beg'. In 1896 Bram was in straitened circumstances, the purchase of the lease at 18 St Leonard's Terrace was expensive and the money he had invested in a publishing venture with William Heinemann had not earned out. Bram had to write to Caine and ask for the favour of a loan; in doing so he revealed a little more about his affection for Caine and the regard in which he held him. Although written on Lyceum Theatre-headed notepaper, Bram disassociated himself from the theatre by scoring a line through the heading. Addressed from the Adelphi Hotel, Liverpool, on 3 June 1896, it read:

My dear Hommy Beg

There is a matter which I want to ask you about and I write instead of speaking as I wish you to be quite free in the matter. Though I would like to make it a matter of business it is a matter entirely between friends also, and I would rather if I might, ask you than any one I know. I have to borrow some money – £600 – as I have to pay an old debt which I intended some time ago and which in my case I would have cleared off in the immediate future had not the call come rather sooner than I expected and I want to know if you would care to lend me the amount. The Heinemann & Balestier enterprise took so much more than I intended investing – £800 in all – it left me rather short, and a year ago I bought the lease on my house leaving me with a rental of only £10 a year for the next eleven years. This cost me £600 which I got from Coutts giving them a security some £800 worth of stocks all good paying things which it would not be wise to sell … I am glad to hear Heinemann & Balestier is getting all right but at present the money is laid up & is not available.

Now my dear old fellow if you would rather not do this do say so freely for I would not for all the world have you get anything to do with money (of all things) come in any way between us. I only mention this matter to you at all because you are closer to me than any man I know, and I prefer to ask my own kind who are workers like myself rather than rich men who do not understand. Any time within a month (or even longer) would do me to have the money but I like to be in time in such matters and if the matter is settled it will be a certain ease to me in the midst of much work and after a long and trying year. Of course if the new book comes out well at all the first money I get will go to pay the debt ...

This is a long letter but I want you to quite understand and honestly hope that if you do not care to go into the matter you will treat me as a friend and say so frankly – as frankly as all things have been – and please God ever shall be between you and me. In any case you must not let the matter worry you by a hair's breadth.

Yours always
Bram Stoker [342]

Caine was pleased to oblige his dear friend. The book Bram alluded to was to be *Dracula*, published the following year. Much has been made about the initial response to *Dracula* being negative or poor. Admittedly, the first theatrical reading of *Dracula or, The Undead* at the Lyceum was not well attended – but it was not meant to be. The function of putting on the play was to establish its copyright in that form. Thus, the unprepossessing green posters with bold black lettering advertising the play were only put up an hour before it began and the box office opened at 10 a.m. on the morning of Tuesday 18 May 1897 – a most inappropriate time for theatre! The price of 1 guinea for entrance was also inflated beyond the usual price of admission.[343] The cast was made from a few members of the Lyceum Company and Ellen Terry's daughter Edith Craig played Mina, while small-part actors and friends of Bram took the minor roles. Harry Ludlam records:

> The fantastic 'performance' was watched by other friends and the Lyceum staff and cleaners as well as a few regular patrons. Among those who turned up to pay their money at the box office was Bram's devoted cook, Maria Mitchell. The story goes that after the play extraordinary Bram asked Irving what he thought of it, and the actor replied, with characteristic brevity, 'Dreadful'. He probably did and it probably was.[344]

Dracula, the book, was published on 26 May 1897 and, contrary to the widely held belief that it was not well received, the contemporary reviews tell a different story. Yes, it was seen as an 'eerie and gruesome tale'[345] but the critics also picked up on many of its subtleties and how Bram skilfully breathed new life into long-dead legend. The *Daily Telegraph* was to remark:

> there are two things which are remarkable in the novel – the first is the confident reliance on superstition as furnishing the groundwork of a modern story; and the second, more significant still, is the bold adaptation of the legend to such ordinary spheres of latter-day experience as the harbour of Whitby and

Hampstead Heath. What is the good of telling us that romance is dead, or dying, when we see before our eyes its triumph and survival in ghost stories from the Highlands, and scientific mysticism of the Psychical Society? How absurd to suppose that even the old gloomy and awe-inspiring melodrama of the Castle of Otranto has disappeared when Mr. Bram Stoker invites us to sup on horrors not only in the Carpathian mountains, but in the more cheerful and common-place precincts of our metropolis! [346]

Wry praise also came from the *Pall Mall Gazette*, who offered it as 'Midnight Reading' with the warning:

Mr. Bram Stoker should have labelled this book 'For Strong Men Only', or words to that effect. Left lying carelessly around , it might get into the hands of your maiden aunt, who believes devoutly in the man under the bed, or of the new parlour maid with unsuspected hysterical tendencies Dracula to such would be manslaughter … there is a creep in every dozen pages or so. For those who like that, this is a book to revel in. We did it ourselves, and are not ashamed to say so. [347]

Dracula was not a blockbuster in its day but it was a popular page-turner filled with suspense, intrigue and the supernatural; an evergreen with enough demand for it to have a second printing and an American edition in 1899, and a paperback issued in 1901. It got Bram back on track with his money and he repaid his debt to Hall Caine. The tragedies that followed, however, would inspire some to speak of a 'curse' brought about by Bram's evocation of the undead Count.

The first tragedy came on 14 December 1897 when the Strand was rocked by the murder of one of the leading actors of the day, William Terriss, a man who had been a popular member of the Lyceum cast for a number of years. Terriss had been stabbed to death at his private entrance to the Adelphi Theatre in London by Richard Archer Prince. Prince, known to acquaintances as 'Mad Archie', was an inveterate letter writer who sent high-handed missives to theatrical managers who offended him, or fawning letters of commiseration or congratulations to royalty or celebrities, depending on the occasion. He was thought harmless enough by most. During the run of *The Harbour Lights*, in which Prince had a minor role, Terriss took offence at a comment Prince made about him and had him dismissed. Terriss did, however, send small sums of money to Prince, via the Actors' Benevolent Fund, and continued to try to find him acting engagements. By the end of 1897, Prince was destitute and desperate for work but he had become unemployable. On 13 December, Prince attempted to get a complimentary ticket to the Vaudeville Theatre which adjoined the Adelphi – he was turned down and forcibly ejected. Prince brooded on this event and, fired by jealousy of Terriss's success and blaming him for the rotten situation he was in, Prince

stepped out of the shadows the following evening and carried out his revenge.
Convicted of the murder but found insane, Prince spent the rest of his life at
Broadmoor Criminal Lunatic Asylum.

At 5.10 a.m. on Friday 18 February 1898 the news reached Bram of another
tragedy: the Lyceum storage on Bear Lane in Southwark was on fire. Stepping
out into that bitterly cold morning Bram found a 'four wheeler' was waiting for
him and they made haste to the scene. When Bram arrived his heart sunk:

> I found Bear Lane a chaos. The narrow way was blocked with fire-engines pant-
> ing and thumping away for dear life. The heat was terrific. There was so much
> stuff in the storage that nothing could possibly be done till the fire had burnt
> itself out; all that the firemen could do was to prevent the fire spreading.[348]

The storage had held over 2,000 pieces of scenery for 260 scenes from 44 plays,
many of them expensive and elaborate creations. These had been intended as
Irving's wealth spring: a stock of scenery, sets and bulky properties he had planned
to draw upon rather than create anew for each show. All was lost. It was estimated
the contents had been worth more than £30,000, a fantastic sum in its day. The
situation was made all the more bitter as Irving had instructed Bram to reduce
the insurance cover the previous year from £10,000 to £6,000. Irving was devastated and rather than confide in his dear friend Bram he withdrew into himself.

Irving was not a well man. In December 1896 he had 'slipped a foot' on the
narrow upper stairs of his home on Grafton Street, causing him to hit his knee
against a large oak chest on his landing and rupture the ligaments under his knee-
cap. The Lyceum had to close for three weeks as he recuperated and the injury
left its mark upon the great actor; his ability to move on stage was never quite
the same again. Irving's judgement was also faltering, he had lost something of
that instinct for what the audience wanted and what productions would prove
popular. As an example, Irving turned down an offer from Conan Doyle to write
a Sherlock Holmes play for him, an almost guaranteed success, preferring to
open the 1898 season production with *Peter the Great*, a play written by his son
Laurence. It was not a success, neither was his next production *Medicine Man* and
Irving became even more introspective. Bram did his best to keep the Lyceum
running – 'business as usual' – but the debts amassed by Irving's lavish productions
and hospitality in the Beefsteak Room were becoming unsustainable. During
October 1898 Irving's health was further undermined by a bout of pleurisy and
pneumonia he contracted when performing at Glasgow.

He had no other option but to convalesce and soon became depressed and
vulnerable. He had not consulted Bram when he appointed Austin Brereton to
be his press secretary in the aftermath of the fire, and when he was approached by
Joe Comyns Carr during his convalescence with plans for a syndicate to take over
the Lyceum he transferred his interests over to them without any consultation

with Loveday or Bram. Upon hearing the deal, Bram examined the figures and his advice was frank: the deal with the Lyceum Company was very good for the Lyceum Company but unfavourable for Irving. Irving went ahead anyway. Loveday and Bram stuck with 'The Chief' but Bram was to bemoan that he saw far less of Irving than he had in the past. The Lyceum Theatre Company lasted from 1899 to the end of the 1902 season. Irving's plays, even the revivals such as *Faust*, simply did not do well; the only notable success was *Sherlock Holmes* in 1901, with William Gillette in the lead as the master detective. Irving was declining rapidly, the Company cancelled its contract with him and the Lyceum was sold to become a music hall.

Perhaps something of the supposed 'curse' manifested itself in Bram's writing from that time too, particularly the tale of *The Jewel of Seven Stars*, published in 1903 – a dark tale of ancient powers evoked in the modern world with an Egyptologist's attempts to reanimate Queen Tera, an ancient Egyptian mummy. It helped establish the mummy genre in English literature and inspired the film *Blood from the Mummy's Tomb* (1972), *The Awakening* (1980) and *Legend of The Mummy* (1997). It enjoyed reasonable success in its day but Bram's novels did not soar to mass popularity.

In the meantime, Irving needed his old ally. He was tired, his powers were fading fast and he asked Bram to plan the first of what were to be two provincial farewell tours, beginning in the winter of 1904. Travel in the snow and bitterly cold weather during that winter caused Irving to develop a chest infection that rapidly progressed to acute bronchitis. He collapsed in the hallway of a hotel in Wolverhampton in February 1905 and it was only then his doctor found out he had been coughing up pus from an unhealed lung since his attack of pleurisy. The Company was disbanded and the tour resumed the following October. All went well at Sheffield, then they went on to the Theatre Royal Bradford. Bram was concerned as Irving 'seemed tired, tired; tired not for an hour but for a lifetime',[349] and implored him not to play *The Bells* as it would be too much for him. However, play it he did; as Bram knew only too well, 'His will was the controlling power of his later as of his earlier days. He could, not stop. To do so would have been final extinction.'[350]

On 13 October Irving took the lead in Tennyson's *Becket*. He played well but was exhausted. Irving would usually appear after his performances and deliver a speech to his audience. There was no speech that night. The last words he spoke on the stage were Becket's last words in the play, *'Into Thy hands, O Lord! Into Thy hands!'*

Bram sat in Irving's room while he dressed and sincerely hoped, in a way that only a loving friend or close family member can, that his marvellous recuperative powers would bring him back to health again. As Bram took his leave Irving did something unusual, he took Bram's hand and shook it and after advising Bram he should muffle his throat against the cold on that bitterly cold night he bade him farewell, as he had done so many nights throughout their friendship with, 'Goodnight! God bless you!'

Later that night one of Bram's assistants came to rush him to the Midland Hotel: Irving had suffered another collapse, just like the one at Wolverhampton. When Bram arrived a crowd had gathered, finding his way through it he discovered Walter Collinson, Irving's valet, sitting on the floor beside him. He looked at Bram with a tear-stained face and simply said, 'He died in my arms.' Bram reached down and gently closed Irving's eyes.

British theatre went into mourning, the columns of the Lyceum were wrapped in crépe and, after a quiet cremation at Golders Green, the ashes of 'The Chief' were laid to rest in Westminster Abbey, with the honours befitting the first knight of the British theatre.[351] Despite all those years of dedication Irving left no tokens of appreciation to Bram, Loveday or even his valet Collinson in his will. What few souvenirs Bram wanted from Irving he had to buy. Yet still there was no bitterness, Bram remained loyal to his master even after his death and set to work on his remarkable two-volume eulogy, *Personal Reminiscences of Henry Irving*, which was published in 1906. Bram's life, his energy and his world had revolved around and was entwined with that of Irving's – and now Irving was gone.

Bram turned to journalism, wrote more books, even tried his hand at theatrical management again, but nothing was the same. He was lost and one can but wonder how such grief manifested in him; it may have been at this time he sought some escape in sexual exploits away from the marital home. It seems that suddenly the years of devotion and the grief at losing Irving hit Bram and, in 1906, he suffered a paralytic stroke. Bram did return to work but the stroke was to mark the beginning of the decline in his health and the Stokers moved to a smaller flat at 4 Durham Place, just around the corner from St Leonard's Terrace, in 1907.

Free from the beck and call of Irving, Bram took a more active role in the literary affairs of Hall Caine. No matter how ill he was, as long as he was physically able Bram wrote to Hall Caine – he even rushed over to be with him at Greeba Castle on the Isle of Man after Caine, suffering from nervous prostration and forced to endure complete rest, had apparently suffered a decline that was 'causing some anxiety' in September 1907.[352] Caine recovered; it was Bram who continued to decline.

Work was slow coming in, it did not pay well and Bram was unsuccessful in a number of his applications for work. Finances had become tight again and Bram petitioned the Royal Literary Fund for a grant, explaining his situation:

> At the beginning of 1906 I had a paralytic stroke. Fortunately the stroke was not a bad one and in a few months I resumed my work. Just a year ago I had another break-down from overwork which has incapacitated me ever since. The result of such a misfortune shows at its worst in the case of one who has to depend on his brain and his hands.

Bram's claim was supported by Henry Dickens, a son of the great author Charles Dickens, and W.S. Gilbert, the trusted friend who had been Florence's gallant escort so many times when Bram was at the beck and call of Irving. Bram was granted an award of £100.

Bram had enjoyed trips to Port Errol (the name was changed to Cruden Bay in 1924) since the 1880s when he first came across it during a Lyceum research trip for *Macbeth*. The backdrop of the distant Braemar Mountains and the baronial Slains Castle, then the home of the Earls of Errol, inhabited by Charles Gore Hay, 20th Earl of Erroll, high upon its jagged stone cliffs may have been another inspiration for Castle Dracula.[353] Port Errol was certainly the inspiration for Bram's spirited tales *The Watter's Mou* (1895) and *The Mystery of the Sea* (1902). Bram would stay there a number of times over the years and after the loss of Irving it became a place of solace for him. A little cottage overlooking the sea known as The Crookit Lum had become Bram's regular summer retreat during what would sadly prove to be the last years of his life; he made his last stay there in 1911. His behaviour was marked by the locals as rather strange; his walks across the sands looked odd, unsteady, as if he was stamping his feet. He shouted at the sea, and his voice was drowned by the crash of the waves.[354] Bram not only acted oddly, his books became decidedly weird and one can but wonder at the troubled dreams and visions that inspired the creation of his last book, *The Lair of the White Worm*, published in 1911.

The year 1911 also saw the Stokers move to 26 St George's Square, Pimlico. By this time Bram's health had seriously deteriorated, walking was difficult and he began to spend most of his time in bed reading the books he had always meant to read and revisiting some of his old manuscripts. Bram died quietly in that bed on 20 April 1912 with Florence and Noel at his bedside. Dr James Browne, who certified his death, listed three causes: 'Locomotor Ataxy 6 months, Granular Contracted Kidney and Exhaustion'. Hidden in the medical terminology is a darker secret, for locomotor ataxy was understood in late nineteenth-century medicine as a late form of syphilis, a condition usually passed through sexual intercourse.[355] Florence Stoker did not suffer from syphilis; she lived an active life and finally passed away in 1937.

A fine obituary of Bram was published in *The Times* on Monday 22 April, but a more moving and personal one came from his dear friend Hall Caine. It was published two days later in the *Daily Telegraph*:

Bram Stoker: The Story of a Great Friendship
By Hall Caine

Bram Stoker is to be buried today. The remains will be cremated at Golders Green Crematorium. Only the friends (and they are many) who knew and loved him will be there when the last offices are done, and that will be enough. He could have desired no more and no better. The big, breathless, impetuous hurricane of a man who was Bram Stoker had no love of the limelight.

A few days ago I stood, for the twentieth time or more, at the foot of that sloping stone, under the shadow of the pyramid of Caius Cestius, which bears the inscription 'Cor Cordium'. And nothing else, and nothing less, will be necessary to tell the few friends who really and truly knew Bram Stoker (fully conscious that he had no other claim to greatness) that all that was mortal of his big heart has been committed to the dust.

In one thing our poor Bram, who had many limitations was truly great. His was indeed the genius of friendship. I speak as perhaps the oldest of his surviving associates, outside the immediate circle of his family, when I say that never in any other man have I seen such capacity for devotion to a friend.

Much has been said of his relation to Henry Irving, but I wonder how many were really aware of the whole depth and significance of that association. Bram seemed to give up his life to it. It was not only his time and his services that he gave to Irving – it was his heart, which never failed for one moment in loyalty, in enthusiasm, in affection, in the strongest love that man may feel for man. I remember what all this was in those far-off first days of their relation, when Irving said one night in Liverpool, 'Bram is going to join me'; I follow it in memory through the triumphant times of dazzling success, and the dark days of sickness, failing powers and financial misfortune, down to the last great but tragic hour (and after it), and I say without any hesitation that never have I seen, nor do I expect to see, such absorption of one man's life in the life of another. If Bram's body had its rightful resting-place it would be at Irving's feet; and yet he was a man of himself, a strong and stalwart separate being who in his best days might have stood alone.

Never, I am certain, had he any thought of sacrifice but while always rewarded with the gratitude of that other heart, what a price he paid for the devotion to his chief! We who were very close to him realised this fact when the time of the asundering came and we saw that with Irving's life poor Bram's had really ended. It was too late to begin afresh. The threads that had been broken thirty years before could not be pieced together. There could be no second flowing of the tide. It was the ebb and though Bram made a brave fight for a new life, he knew well, and we knew well, that his chances were over.

I am partly conscious that in the world of the theatre there were those (and perhaps they were not a few) who attributed to Bram every misfortune that overtook them in their connection with his principal; but I wonder if they gave a thought to the inevitable difficulties of the place he filled. Into the life of nearly all great men (especially such a man as Irving was) there come moments when it is necessary to do disagreeable things and yet not seem to do them. Someone must stand between, assuming the responsibility, taking the blame, accepting the blow. It would not be a gracious thing to say how often during the score of years I saw Bram in that position. It is sweeter to remember that Irving himself always knew and never forgot.

Thinking of this reminds me how miserably mistaken was the estimate of Bram's personal character which prevailed at that period. He had to steel himself to say 'No', and to shirk no painful duty, but his real nature was of the tenderest. When I think how tender it was there come crowding upon me incident after incident in which his humanity shone out as a bright light, though the scene of it was only the front of a box-office, the door to the gallery, the passageway to the pit. But it was not there that his best qualities appeared. Bram was a man of the theatre only by the accident of his great love for its leader and his true self was something quite unlike the personality which was seen in that environment. Those who knew him there only hardly knew him at all.

Some hint of this world would occasionally reveal itself among the scarcely favourable conditions of a public dinner, when as speaker (always capable of the racy humour which is considered necessary to that rather artificial atmosphere), he would strike, in the soft roll of his rich Irish tongue, a note of deep and almost startling emotion that would obliterate the facile witticisms of more important persons.

I cannot truly say that this deeper side of the man ever expressed itself in his writings. He took no vain view of his efforts as an author. Frankly, he wrote his books to sell and except in the case of one of them (his book on Irving) he had no higher aims. But higher aims were there, and the power of realising them had not been denied to him.

When I think of his literary output I regret the loss of the one book with which he might have enriched the literature of autobiography. The multitude of interesting persons with whom his position brought him into contact – Tennyson, Disraeli, Gladstone, Randolph Churchill, Archbishop Benson, Henry Ward Beecher, President Cleveland, Walt Whitman, Rénan – had left him with a vast store of memories which the public would have welcomed if he had written them down. He never did write them, and the world is poorer for want of his glimpses, however brief and casual, of some of its great souls in their happiest hours.

In concluding this little and imperfect tribute to the memory of a massive and muscular and almost volcanic personality that must have been familiar by sight to many thousands in Great Britain and America, I could wish to end where I began with the warmest and most affectionate recognition of his genius for friendship. No one knows better than the friend to whom, under various disguises (impenetrable to all except themselves) he dedicated in words of love some of his best-known books ('Dracula' in particular) how large was the heart that was not entirely exhausted even by its devotion to the great man with whom his name is generally associated. There were moments during the last twenty-odd years when I felt ashamed that anybody should give me his time, his energy and his enthusiasm as Bram gave them and the only way in which I could reconcile myself to his splendid self-sacrifice was to remember he loved

The letter from Bram to Hall Caine of 3 June 1896. Note also the unusual way Bram often used three sides of a folded piece of paper. (*Papers of Sir Thomas Henry Hall Caine, Manx National Heritage MS 09542*)

to make it. I can think of nothing – absolutely nothing – that I could have asked Bram Stoker to do for me that he would not have done. It is only once in a man's life that such a friendship comes to him and when the grave is closed on the big heart which we are to bury to-day, I shall feel that I have lost it.

Of the devotion to his wife during these last dark days, in which the whirl-wind of his spirit had nothing left to it but the broken wreck of a strong man, I cannot trust to speak. That must always be a sacred memory to those who know what it was. If his was the genius of friendship, hers must have been a genius of love.[356]

Bram's funeral was conducted by the Revd Herbert Trundle in the chapel at Golders Green Crematorium on Wednesday 24 April 1912. It was a quiet affair; beyond Bram's family, the friends who attended included Henry Irving's son Laurence, Hall Caine, Ford Maddox Heuffer and Genevieve Ward. Wreaths were sent by Ellen Terry, Sir Arthur Pinero, Mrs Maxwell and Mr and Mrs Frederick Watson.[357]

Hall Caine, the last of the three great friends, had been one of the greatest and most popular authors of the late nineteenth century, he was the first English language author to sell over 1 million copies of his works, his fame and acclaim can be equated with that of Dickens in his heyday. Caine would realise his dream of a home on the Isle of Man when he finally agreed a price for Greeba Castle in 1896. As the years passed, however, Caine and his wife Mary seemed to grow apart. Mary did not like Greeba, it was too grim and distant from the London social life she loved and she would spend much of her time in the capital, leaving

Caine alone at Greeba. Caine did not seem to mind and would frequently have male visitors from the literary circles in which he moved. In later years historical research and biographers have revealed a number of them to have been gay, but they were not widely known to be so at the time; homosexuality was a criminal offence and could not only result in a custodial sentence but exposure to public humiliation and revulsion. Yet the comings and goings of so many men at Greeba Castle still led to rumours about Caine's own sexuality. His known friendship and outrage at the 'unspeakable' treatment of Oscar Wilde did not help his case in the eyes of locals.[358]

Despite continued bouts of his illness Caine lived on until 31 August 1931, when he died quietly in his bed at Greeba Castle. His wife Mary and grand-daughter Elin were with him, along with Dr Marshall, who was to record the cause of death as 'cardiac syncope'.[359] Hall Caine was 78.

After the death of Caine's son Derwent in 1971, his will bequeathed the papers of Sir Thomas Henry Hall Caine to the Manx Museum and National Trust. The deposit was presented in September 1976 but, conscious of the concerns of the Trustees of Derwent Hall Caine's estate that any sensitive content should not be circulated to the public, and mindful of the feelings of living relatives, Librarian Archivist Ann Harrison proposed a closure period for the papers that would expire on 1 January 2000. The closure period was accepted. After over ten years' sorting and cataloguing the papers, the work is still ongoing. One can but wonder if more papers will emerge with time, or what secrets Hall Caine took to the grave with him.

Hall Caine was buried in Kirk Maughold churchyard on his beloved Isle of Man. A finely carved slate obelisk and pediment featuring characters from his stories was designed by Archibald Knox and erected over his grave, and a well-attended memorial service was held for him in St Martin-in-the-Fields in London. Six months after Hall Caine's death his wife, Mary, died from pneumonia and was reunited with him in this grave in March 1932.

The passage of time can bring many ironies. In his own lifetime Hall Caine became one of the most famous authors of his day but his books, so loved for their comfortable, predictable plots, based mostly around love triangles and extolling the best Christian values and religious themes, have failed to endure and have little appeal for modern audiences. Just one book by Bram Stoker has endured above all others, something beyond the horror, the weird and the strange, something that continues to capture the imagination; a mesmerising and intriguing power that draws each new generation to *something* they know will scare them – *Dracula*. That same something continues to exert a fascination of murders so horrible London was gripped by an autumn of terror in 1888, the murders of five East End prostitutes by the killer known to history as Jack the Ripper – the Whitechapel vampire.

APPENDIX 1

An Expert Witness: Character Profile Based on the Expert Analysis of the Letters of Francis Tumblety

Ruth Myers is an internationally respected forensic handwriting analyst who has specialised in the examination of documents and handwriting for almost twenty years. She has experience in the presentation of expert evidence in courts of law in England and Northern Ireland and is a member of the UK Register of Expert Witnesses. Ruth also holds a diploma in Document Examination awarded by the American Board of Forensic Handwriting Examiners and a diploma in Document Examination awarded by the World Association of Document Examiners.

Ruth is equipped to carry out a number of techniques used in forensic document examination as encountered in investigation and litigation. These include the identification of handwriting, genuineness or otherwise of signatures, comparison of typescript and the investigation of altered documents.

Criminal profiling can play a very important part in identifying a criminal suspect. A competent profile is always grounded firmly on physical evidence. In the event of there being handwriting present, the analysis of this handwriting can support, confirm and possibly add to a criminal profile. Ruth has experience in the presentation of expert evidence in cases of murder, abduction and ransom, where the speedy identification of likely suspects has been of prime importance.

As a regular consultant to national newspapers, magazines and journals, Ruth has applied her range of skills to produce character profiles for infamous killers Fred and Rosemary West, Peter Sutcliffe 'the Yorkshire Ripper', Dr Harold Shipman, Ian Huntley and the serial prostitute killer Steve Wright. Now, in a specially commissioned character profile, Ruth has applied her years of expertise to the letters written in the hand of Francis Tumblety. The summary of her findings are transcribed verbatim:

Francis Tumblety was a man of intellect, perception, analytical and investigative ability. He was a strong-minded individual who resented intrusion into his affairs. At times he welcomed opposition since it gave him a chance to impose his will on other people.

A man of mood swings who had difficulty controlling his emotions and could act without any consideration of others and of the consequences. Impatient, easily irritated he had the potential of losing control under intense pressure and could resort to physical action in extreme situations.

He was highly motivated, ambitious with a ruthless desire to dominate. Assertive and alert to challenges, and any ideas that conflicted with those of his own would be resisted, rejecting and defending his case strongly. He could argue heatedly on opposition that differed from his own to the point of arrogance.

Overly domineering and dominating to the extent of unbalance he could alienate many with his unreasonable behaviour. He had enduring determination and a need to be obeyed. Outwardly pleasant but touchy when criticised.

A demanding man with an autocratic air having extreme persistence never to admit defeat or failure. He craved importance and recognition but deep down feared humiliation of being judged which indicated an actual insecurity.

Strongly acquisitive, narrow-minded, thrifty and unforgiving in attitude. Dissatisfied with status quo he sought to impress and mislead and change his image. He scattered his energies which reduced his efficiency and involved himself in many interests and projects.

He could resist authority and feared loss of autonomy and was always alert to any injustices. Unforgiving, inflexible in opinion, he would have caused disharmony in any relationship and was unreasonably obstinate.

Francis Tumblety was not truthful and deliberately misrepresented. He connived and hedged issues; consequently his word was not to be taken as he always found excuses and he allowed no intrusion into his inner life and presented a deceitful image.

Very few people reached his inner circle of friends. He had cultural leanings, literary qualities and expressed himself by the pen rather than being overly communicative.

Ruth Myers ABFHE WADE CGA
Forensic Handwriting Analyst
12 December 2011

APPENDIX 2

Published Sources Listed by Bram Stoker in his Research Notes for *Dracula*

★ Denotes those the books from which notes are known to have been taken.
★★ This may refer to *The Spottiswoode Miscellany* compiled by James Maidment (1844). Published in two volumes, it is a collection of original papers and tracts, illustrative chiefly of the civil and ecclesiastical history of Scotland.

Baring-Gould, Rev., *The Book of Were-Wolves* (London: Smith, Elder & Co., 1865).★
Baring-Gould, Rev., *Curious Myths of the Middle Ages* (London: Rivingtons, 1877).
Baring-Gould, Rev., *Germany, Present and Past* (London: Kegan Paul, Trench & Co., 1879).
Bassett, Fletcher S., *Legends and Superstitions of the Sea and Sailors – In All Lands and at All Times* (London: Sampson Low, Marston, Searle & Rivington, 1885).
Bird, Isabella A., *The Golden Chersonese and the Way Thither* (London: Murray, 1883).★
Boner, Charles, *Transylvania: Its Products and its People* (London: Longmans, Green, Reader & Dyer, 1865).★
Browne, Sir Thomas, *Pseudodoxia Epidemica or Enquries into Very Many Received Tenets and Commonly Presumed Truths* (London, 1646).★
Cross, Andrew F., *Round About the Carpathians* (Edinburgh and London: William Blackwood & Sons, 1878).★
A Fellow of the Carpathian Society [Nina Elizabeth Mazuchelli], *Magyarland: Being the Narrative of our Travels through the Highlands and Lowlands of Hungary* (London: Sampson Low, Marston, Searle & Rivington, 1881).★
Gerard, Emily, 'Transylvanian Superstitions', *Nineteenth Century* (London, 1885), pp. 128–44.★
Johnson, Major E.C., *On the Track of the Crescent: Erratic Notes from the Piraeus to the Pesth* (London: Hurst and Blackett, 1885).★

Jones, John, *The Natural and the Supernatural: Or Man – Physical, Apparitional and Spiritual* (London: H. Bailliere, 1861).

Jones, William, *Credulities Past and Present: including the sea and seamen, miners, amulets and talismans, rings, word and letter divination, numbers, trials, exorcising and blessing of animals, birds, eggs, and luck* (London: Chatto & Windus, 1880).

Jones, William, *History and Mystery of Precious Stones* (London: Richard Bentley & Son, 1880).

Jones, Rev. W. Henry and Kropf, Lewis L. (trs and eds), *The Folk Tales of the Magyars* (London: Elliott Stock, 1889).

Lea, Henry C., *Superstitions and Force – Essays on The Wager of Law, The Wager of Battle, The Ordeal – Torture* (Philadelphia: Henry C. Lea, 1876).

Lee, Rev. Frederick George (ed.), *The Other World: Or Glimpses of the Supernatural: Being Facts, Records and Traditions Relating to Dreams, Omens, Miraculous Occurrences, Apparitions, Wraiths, Warnings, Second-Sight, Witchcraft, Necromancy, Etc.* (London: Henry S. King & Co., 1875).

Lee, Henry, *Sea Fables Explained* (London: William Clowes & Sons, 1883).

Lee, Henry, *Sea Monsters Unmasked* (London: William Clowes & Sons, 1883).

Lee, Mrs R. [Sarah Bowditch Lee], *Anecdotes of Habits and Instincts of Birds, Reptiles and Fishes* (London: Grant and Griffith, 1853).

Maury, L.F. Alfred [No titles cited by Stoker].

Mayo, Herbert, *On the Truths Contained in Popular Superstitions with an Account of Mesmerism* (Edinburgh and London: William Blackwood & Sons, 1851).

Pettigrew, Thomas Joseph, *On Superstitions Connected with the History and Practice of Medicine and Surgery* (London: John Churchill, 1844).

Reville, Rev. Albert, *The Devil: His Origin, Greatness and Decadence* (London: Williams & Norgate, 1871).

Rivington, F.C. and J., *The Theory of Dreams* (London: F.C. and J. Rivington, 1808).★

Robinson, F.K., *A Glossary of Words Used in the Neighbourhood of Whitby* (London: English Dialect Society, 1876).★

Scott, Robert H., *Fishery Barometer Manual* (London: HMSO, 1887).★

Spottiswoode, W., 'Miscellany'.★★

Spottiswoode, W., *A Tarantasse Journey Through Eastern Russia in the Autumn of 1856* (London: Longman, Brown, Longmans & Roberts, London 1857).

Thiers, Jean-Baptise, *Traité des superstitions qui regardent les sacrements selon l'Ecriture sainte, les décrets des conciles, et les sentiments des Saints Pères, et des théologiens,* 3 vols (Paris: Dezallier et de Nully, 1697–1704).

Wilkinson, William, *An Account of the Principalities of Wallachia and Moldavia: With Various Political Observations Relating to Them* (London: Longman, Hurst, Rees, Orme & Brown, 1820).★

APPENDIX 3

Jonathan Harker's Journey to Castle Dracula – Klausenburg to Bistritz – A Suggested Source

The late nineteenth-century maps of the Austro-Hungarian Empire show Transylvania (or Siebenbürgen, it's name in the German tongue) as the farthest flung of all the colonies; it veritably hangs over the neatline of the eastern reaches of the map. When researching the arduous journey Jonathan Harker would have to make from Britain to Transylvania, Bram Stoker would have found no finer vade mecum than a Baedeker's *Southern Germany and Austria, Including Hungary and Transylvania. Handbook for Travellers*. This transcription is taken from the 1887 edition that was current into the early 1890s when Bram began his notes for *Dracula*:

From Klausenburg to Bistritz
74½ M. Railway in 7 hrs

The Train follows the course of the Little Szamos, running at first on the rails of the Klausenberg and Kronstadt route (R.76) – 8M. Apahida (State Railway-station). The State Railway turns to the S., while our line continues to follow the Szamos to the N.- 8½ M. Aphida, a Rumanian village with about 1000 inhab.

The railway now crosses the river and skirts the left bank, between low ranges of barren hills, dotted here and there with villages. – 18 M. Válasút-Boncichida; then, to the left of the railway, Keudi-Lóna, all with châteaux and parks. – Beyond (22½ M.) Nagy-Iklod, and Dengeleg, we recross the Szamos and reach - 28½ M. Szamos Ujvár (Town Hotel; Grüner Baum), a royal free town with regular streets, a handsome main square, and 5500 inhab., chiefly Armenians, who are, however, completely 'Magyarised'. The fort at the N. end of the town, erected on the 17th cent., is now a prison; Rosza Sàndor, the notorious bandit chief, died in confinement here. – On the left bank of the Szamos, ¾ M. To the W., lie the small baths of

Kerö, with springs containing sulphur and Epsom salts. – Mikula, on a hill to the S. of the Szamos Ujvár, is a resort of pilgrims of the Greek church.

The Szamos is now crossed for the third time; the valley contracts and woods begin to cover the hills. To the left diverges the branch-line to the salt works of Deésakna (see below). Szent-Benedek, on the right, has a pilgrimage-church, and a châteaux belonging to Count Kornis, at one time strongly fortified and afterwards converted into a monastery. – At the foot of the wooded Rosenberg lies – 37½ M. Deés (Europa, R. from 80kr., well spoken of), a royal free town with 6200 inhab., capital of the district of Szolnok Doboka, situated at the confluence of the Grosse and Kleine Szamos. The Protestant church, a tasteful Gothic edifice, dates from the 15th century. In the upper promenade is a tower (16th cent.) dating from the old fortifications. Opposite is the Béla-Berg, with a rifle-range, and fine views. – The village of Deésakna, with its salt-works and salt-baths, lie 1½ M. To the S., the old mine, explored since the 15th cent., is worth a visit.

From Deés a diligence plies daily to Nagy Bánya in Hungary, viâ Somkút (57 M. in 12½ hrs., for 4 fl. 60 kr.): and another through the valley of the Lápos to Magyar Lápos (26 M. in 4½ hrs., for 2 fl.).

The railway curves towards the N.E., cross the Grosse Szamos, and leads on the left bank to Kozárvar, with the remains of a Roman fortress, Baca, and (44½ M.) Rettég. Among the hills, a little way to the left of the next station, (46½ M.) Csicsó Keresztur, are the picturesque ruins of the rocky fastness of Csicsó, built in the 15th cent. And destroyed in 1544, which command a magnificent view. The railway crosses the Szamos, and reaches (51½ M.) Bethlen (1800 inhab.), the ancestral residence of the Bethlen family. – A road leads hence northwards to Naszód and Rodna in the upper Szamos valley.

Beyond Bethlen the railway continues to follow the course of the Szamos, partly on embankments in the river-bed, but at the junction of the Sajó, enters the valley of the latter (to the E,). Fune view of the snow-peaks of the Czibles and Kuhorn, and of the maountains on the N. border. At (57 M.) Somkerék, the line bends to the S. and crosses the Sajó. To thr right lie the villages of Kentelka and Kerlés, where Prince Ladislaus, afterwards King of Hungary, defeated the Kumanes in 1070. The strife was most hotly contested on an oak-clad knoll, called Cserhalom, now occupied by a château and park of the Bethlen family, and has been celebrated by the Hungarian poet Vörosmarthy in his poem of that name. – The Sajó is again crossed. Beyond (67½ M.) Szeret-falva are the ruins of Szent-László (to Szász Regen on the Maros). The train once more returns to the left bank of the Sajó, and at the junction of the Bistritz turns N.E. into the valley of that river, in which we soon come in sight of the Saxon village of Heidendorf, Hungar. Bosenyö, with numerous vineyards.

74½ M. Bistritz, Hungar. Besztercze (Town Hotel: König von Ungarn, R. from 1 fl.), a royal free town and capital of the district Bistritz_naszod, with 8063 inhab., chiefly Germans of a still earlier immigration than the other 'Saxons'. It was

formerly called Nösen, and gave its name to the Nösner Land. The town which
lies on the river Bistritz, formerly carried on a considerable trade, particularly in
the 15th and the beginning of the 16th cent., but has long since lost its commercial importance. The walls and towers, with which it is still surrounded, give the
town a quaint and medæval air, but it possesses no other attractions. The Gothic
Protestant Church, finished in 1563, has lost almost the whole of its external
embellishments in consequence of repeated conflagrations. The Burgberg, above
the town, with the castle of John Hunyady, affords a beautiful view of Bistritz,
embedded among orchards and vineyeards, and of the Carpathians on the frontier
of the Bukowina.

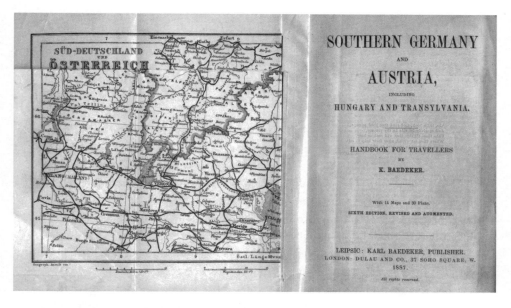

Baedeker's Southern Germany and Austria, Including Hungary and Transylvania.
Handbook for Travellers (1887).

APPENDIX 4

Mr Bram Stoker – A Chat with the Author of *Dracula*

Bram Stoker's extended interview with 'Lorna', (Jane Stoddard) published in *British Weekly*, 1 July 1897, p. 185. This is the only interview, discovered to date, given by Bram about his new book *Dracula*.

One of the most interesting and exciting of recent novels is Mr. Bram Stoker's "Dracula." It deals with the ancient mediaeval vampire legend, and in no English work of fiction has this legend been so brilliantly treated. The scene is laid partly in Transylvania and partly in England. The first fifty-four pages, which give the journal of Jonathan Harker after leaving Vienna until he makes up his mind to escape from Castle Dracula, are in their weird power altogether unrivalled in recent fiction. The only book which to my knowledge at all compares with them is "The Waters of Hercules," by E.D. Gerard, which also treats of a wild and little known portion of Eastern Europe. Without revealing the plot of the story, I may say that Jonathan Harker, whose diary first introduces the vampire Count, is a young solicitor sent by his employer to Castle Dracula to arrange for the purchase of a house and estate in England.

From the first day of his starting, signs and wonders follow him. At the "Golden Krone" at Bistritz the landlady warns him not to go to Castle Dracula, and, finding that his purpose is unalterable, places a rosary with a crucifix round his neck. For this gift he has good cause to be grateful afterwards. Harker's fellow-passengers on the stage-coach grow more and more alarmed about his safety as they come nearer to the dominions of the Count. Kindly gifts are pressed upon him: wild rose, garlic, and mountain ash. These are meant to be a protection against the evil eye. The author seems to know every corner of Transylvania and all its superstitions. Presently in the Borgo Pass a carriage with four horses drives up beside the coach. "The horses were driven by a tall man with a long brown beard, and a great black hat which seemed to hide his face from us. I could only see the gleam of a pair of very bright eyes, which seemed red in the lamplight as he turned to us … As he spoke he smiled, and the lamplight fell on a hard-looking mouth, with very red lips and sharp-looking teeth as white as ivory. One of my companions whispered the line from Burger's 'Lenore': 'Denn die Todten reiten schnell' ('For the dead travel fast')."

This is the famous king vampire, Count Dracula, in ancient times a warlike Transylvanian noble. Jonathan Harker is conscious from the first that he is among ghostly and terrible surroundings. Even on the night journey to the Castle, wolves which have gathered round the carriage disappear when the terrible driver lifts his hand. On his arrival the guest is left waiting, and presently a tall old man, whom he suspects from the beginning to be none other than the driver himself, bids him welcome to his house. The Count never eats with his guest. During the day he is absent, but during the night he converses, the dawn breaking up the interview. There are no mirrors to be seen in any part of the ancient building, and the young solicitor's fears are confirmed by the fact that one morning, when the Count comes unexpectedly to his bedroom and stands looking over his shoulder, there is no reflection of him in the small shaving glass Harker has brought from London, and which covers the whole room behind. The adventures of Jonathan Harker will be read again and again; the most powerful part of the book after this is the description of the voyage of the Demeter from Varna to Whitby. A supernatural terror haunts the crew from the moment that they leave the Dardanelles, and as time goes on one man after another disappears. It is whispered that at night a man, tall, thin, and ghastly pale, is seen moving about the ship. The mate, a Roumanian, who probably knows the vampire legend, searches during the day in a number of old boxes, and in one he finds Count Dracula asleep. His own suicide and the death of the captain follow, and when the ship arrives at Whitby, the vampire escapes in the form of a huge dog. The strange thing is that, although in some respects this is a gruesome book, it leaves on the mind an entirely wholesome impression. The events which happen are so far removed from ordinary experience that they do not haunt the imagination unpleasantly. It is certain that no other writer of our day could have produced so marvellous a book.

On Monday morning I had the pleasure of a short conversation with Mr. Bram Stoker, who, as most people know, is Sir Henry Irving's manager at the Lyceum Theatre. He told me, in reply to a question, that the plot of the story had been a long time in his mind, and that he spent about three years in writing it. He had always been interested in the vampire legend. "It is undoubtedly," he remarked, "a very fascinating theme, since it touches both on mystery and fact. In the Middle Ages the terror of the vampire depopulated whole villages."

"Is there any historical basis for the legend?"

"It rested, I imagine, on some such case as this. A person may have fallen into a death-like trance and been buried before the time. Afterwards the body may have been dug up and found alive, and from this a horror seized upon the people, and in their ignorance they imagined that a vampire was about. The more hysterical, through excess of fear, might themselves fall into trances in the same way; and so the story grew that one vampire might enslave many others and make them like himself. Even in the single villages it was believed that there might be many such creatures. When once the panic seized the population, their only thought was to escape."

"In what parts of Europe has this belief been most prevalent?"

"In certain parts of Styria it has survived longest and with most intensity, but the legend is common to many countries, to China, Iceland, Germany, Saxony, Turkey, the Chersonese, Russia, Poland, Italy, France, and England, besides all the Tartar communities."

"In order to understand the legend, I suppose it would be necessary to consult many authorities?"

Mr. Stoker told me that the knowledge of vampire superstitions shown in "Dracula" was gathered from a great deal of miscellaneous reading.

"No one book that I know of will give you all the facts. I learned a good deal from E. Gerard's 'Essays on Roumanian Superstitions,' [sic] which first appeared in The Nineteenth Century, and were afterwards published in a couple of volumes. I also learned something from Mr. Baring-Gould's 'Were-Wolves.' Mr. Gould has promised a book on vampires, but I do not know whether he has made any progress with it."

Readers of "Dracula" will remember that the most famous character in it is Dr. Van Helsing, the Dutch physician, who, by extraordinary skill, self-devotion, and labour, finally outwits and destroys the vampire. Mr. Stoker told me that Van Helsing is founded on a real character. In a recent leader on "Dracula," published in a provincial newspaper, it is suggested that high moral lessons might be gathered from the book. I asked Mr. Stoker whether he had written with a purpose, but on this point he would give no definite answer, "I suppose that every book of the kind must contain some lesson," he remarked; "but I prefer that readers should find it out for themselves."

In reply to further questions, Mr. Stoker said that he was born in Dublin, and that his work had laid for thirteen years in the Civil Service. He is an M.A. of Trinity College, Dublin. His brother-in-law is Mr. Frankfort Moore, one of the most popular young writers of the day. He began his literary work early. The first thing he published was a book on "The Duties of Clerks of Petty Sessions." Next came a series of children's stories, "Under the Sunset," published by Sampson Low. Then followed the book by which he has hitherto been best known, "The Snake's Pass." Messrs. Constable have published in their "Acme" library a fascinating little volume called "The Watter's Mou," and this with "The Shoulder of Shasta," completes Mr. Stoker's list of novels. He has been in London for some nineteen years, and believes that London is the best possible place for a literary man. "A writer will find a chance here if he is good for anything; and recognition is only a matter of time." Mr. Stoker speaks of the generosity shown by literary men to one another in a tone which shows that he, at least, is not disposed to quarrel with the critics.

Mr. Stoker does not find it necessary to publish through a literary agent. It always seems to him, he says, that an author with an ordinary business capacity can do better for himself than through any agent. "Some men now-a-days are making ten thousand a year by their novels, and it seems hardly fair that they should pay ten or five percent of this great sum to a middleman. By a dozen letters or so in the course of the year they could settle all their literary business on their own account." Though Mr. Stoker did not say so, I am inclined to think that the literary agent is to him a nineteenth century vampire.

No interview during this week would be complete without a reference to the Jubilee, so I asked Mr. Stoker, as a Londoner of nearly twenty years standing, what he thought of the celebrations. "Everyone," he said, "has been proud that the great day went off so successfully. We have had a magnificent survey of the Empire, and last week's procession brought home, as nothing else could have done, the sense of the immense variety of the Queen's dominions."

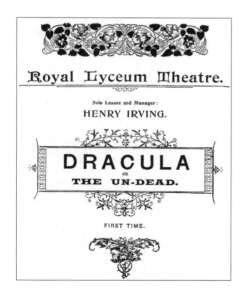

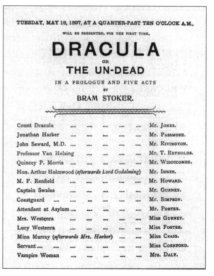

Cover and cast list from the programme of the first stage performance of *Dracula or The Un-Dead*, at the Lyceum, Tuesday 18 May 1897.

APPENDIX 5

Catalogue of the Library of the Late Bram Stoker, Esq (Deceased)

Sold by Auction by Messrs. Sotheby, Wilkinson & Hodge
No. 13 Wellington Street, Strand, W.C.
On Monday 7 July 1913 Commencing at One O'Clock Precisely
OCTAVO ET INFRA.
LOT

1. Budge (E.A. Wallis) History of Egypt from the End of the Neolithic Period to the Death of Cleopatra VII, 9 vol. *illustrations* 1902

2. Budge (E.A. Wallis) Egyptian Ideas of the Future Life, Egyptian Magic, Easy Lessons in Egyptian Hieroglyphics, 3 vol. Illustrations, 1899–1902 – The Mummy, Chapters on Egyptian Funereal Archæology, 88 *illustrations*, *Cambridge*, 1893: etc. (7)

3. Guhl and Koner: Life of the Greeks and Romans, translated by F. Hueffer, *illustrations*, n. d. – Leggo (Wm.) History of the Administration of the Earl of Dufferin in Canada, Montreal, 1878 – Raumer (F. von) America and the American People, translated by W. W. Turner, *New York*, 1846: etc.

Cover of the Sotheby's auction catalogue for the sale of the Library of the Late Bram Stoker, Monday 7 July 1913.

CATALOGUE
OF VALUABLE
PRINTED BOOKS
AUTOGRAPH LETTERS
AND
Illuminated and other Manuscripts
INCLUDING
THE LIBRARY OF THE LATE BRAM STOKER, ESQ.
AND OTHER PROPERTIES.

A VERY IMPORTANT COLLECTION OF LETTERS & MANUSCRIPTS OF DAVID GARRICK, AND LETTERS OF CELEBRATED PERSONAGES WRITTEN TO HIM;
NUMEROUS HORAE, PRINTED AND MANUSCRIPT;
RARE PAMPHLETS RELATING TO GEORGE WASHINGTON;
COPYRIGHTS OF DISTINGUISHED AUTHORS OF THE 18TH CENTURY;
PERSIAN AND INDIAN PAINTINGS AND MINIATURES;
COLLECTION OF ARMORIAL BINDINGS OF FRENCH MONARCHS FROM HENRI II TO NAPOLEON III;
THE HUGE COLLECTION OF PRINTED AND PICTORIAL MATTER OF THE LATE HENRY SOUTHGATE, ARRANGED AND BOUND IN 196 THICK QUARTO VOLUMES, INCLUDING A SERIES OF 700 ENGRAVED TRADESMEN'S CARDS OF THE 17TH AND 18TH CENTURIES;
The Bryden Copy of the First Folio Shakespeare;
A COPY OF THE SECOND FOLIO EXPURGATED BY THE INQUISITION OF SPAIN;
HAZLITT'S LIFE OF NAPOLEON, WITH NEARLY 2000 EXTRA ILLUSTRATIONS;
A FINE ILLUMINATED MANUSCRIPT OF VALERIUS MAXIMUS; ETC.

WHICH WILL BE SOLD BY AUCTION
BY MESSRS.
SOTHEBY, WILKINSON & HODGE
Auctioneers of Literary Property & Works illustrative of the Fine Arts,
AT THEIR HOUSE, No. 13, WELLINGTON STREET, STRAND, W.C.
On MONDAY, the 7th of JULY, 1913, and following Day,
AT ONE O'CLOCK PRECISELY.

4. Browning (E.B.) Poetical Works, 6 vol. *portraits* 1890

6. Jefferson (Joseph) Autobiography, *portrait, character portraits and plates, red cloth, uncut, t.e.g. with inscription on title: 'To Bram Stoker, with kind regards from the Author's daughter, Margaret J. Farjion'* 1890

7. Shakespeare (Wm.) Works, edited by Howard Staunton, EDITION DE LUXE, 15 vol. *portrait, and illustrations by Sir John Gilbert, original cloth, uncut imp. 8vo.* 1881

8. MEREDITH (GEORGE) Works, with Poems, Essays, Miscellaneous Prose, etc. EDITION DE LUXE, 35 vol. *and the illustrations prepared for this edition in a case, portrait on Japanese paper, original linen boards, uncut, with autograph signature of author on fly-leaf of vol. I*

9. Herriot (Edouard) Madame Récamier, translated by Alys Hallard, 2 vol. *15 portraits in photogravure, blue cloth, uncut, t.e.g.* 1906

10. Shelley (P.B.) Life, by Edward Dowden, 2 vol. *portrait, brown cloth, uncut* 1886

11. Blauchan (N.) Nature's Garden, an Aid to Knowledge of our Wild Flowers and their Insect Visitors, *coloured plates and illustrations, green cloth, uncut imp. 8vo. New York,* 1900

12. Carleton (Wm.) Traits and Stories of the Irish Peasantry, edited by D.J. O'Donoghue, 4 vol. *portrait and illustrations, green cloth, uncut, t.e.g.* 1896

13. Ruskin (J.) Works, 12 vol. *blue cloth New York,* 1887

14. Ruskin (J.) Works, vol. XVI–XX (Arrows of Chace, Miscellanea, and Fors Clavigera), 5 vol. *ib.* 1886

15. Sherman (Gen. Wm. T.) Memoirs, 2 vol. portrait and maps, New York, 1887 – Macmullen (J.) The Hudson from the Wilderness to the Sea, *frontispiece, engravings, cloth gilt, g.e. n.d.* (4)

16. Burton (Isabel) Arabia, Egypt, India, *2 maps and 15 illustrations, presentation copy, with autograph inscription: 'Bram Stoker, with Isabel Burton's kind regards, Feb. 21st, 1879'* 1879

17. Newfeld (Chas.) A Prisoner of the Khaleefa, Twelve Years' Captivity at Omdurman, *portraits and plans,* 1899 – Macquoid (G.S.) Up and Down Sketches of Travel, 29 illustrations by T.R. Macquoid, presentation copy, with autograph inscription: *'To Bram Stoker, Esq. With the kind regards of Gilbert S. Macquoid, April 1890',* brown cloth, t.e.g. 1890

18. America. The George Catlin Indian Gallery in the U.S. National Museum, with memoir and Statistics by Thomas Donaldson, *maps and numerous illustrations Washington,* 1887

19. Craik (G.L.) History of English Literature and the English Language from the Norman Conquest, 2 vol. 1866 – Molloy (J.F.) The Faiths of the People, 2 vol. *presentation copy, with autograph inscription: 'To Mrs. Bram Stoker, with kind regards from J. Fitzgerald Molloy',* 1892

20. Bernhardt (Sarah) Memoirs, *portraits and illustrations, blue cloth, uncut, t.e.g.* 1907 – Fitzpatrick (W.J.) Life of Charles Lever, portrait presentation copy, with

autograph inscription: 'To Bram Stoker, Esq, with the Author's kindest regards', *n.d.* – Ernst (W.) Memoirs of the Earl of Chesterfield, *portrait,* 1893 (3)

21. Hibbert Journal (The), vol. I, no.1–3, vol. III, no. 1 and 4, vol. IV, vol.V, no. 2 and 3, vol.VI, no. I; together 12 parts *as issued* 1902–7

22. Cervantes (M. De) History of Don Quixote, translated by Thomas Shelton, with Introductions by J. Fitzmaurice Kelly, 4 vol. half buckram, uncut, with inscription: 'To Bram Stoker, with very kind regards of W. B. Blaikie, Edinburgh, 16 June 1896' 1896

23. Shakespeare (Wm.) Works, New Varvorum Edition, edited by H.H. Furness, vol. II–V, etc. 5 vol. *portrait, cloth, t.e.g. presentation copy, with autograph inscription: 'Bram Stoker, in return for many courtesies and with the regards of Horace Howard Furness, Jr. September, 1908'* Philadelphia, 1874–1908

24. Gallup (Mrs. E.W.) Bi-literal Cypher of Sir Francis Bacon discovered in his Works and deciphered, portraits and facsimiles, 1900 – Marston (E.) After Work Fragments from the Workshop of an old Publisher, *portraits and plates, presentation copy, with autograph inscription: Bram Stoker, with the kind regards of E. Marston, March 15/05',* 1904 (2)

25. Herkomer (Prof. Sir Hubert von) My School and my Gospel, *illustrations, uncut, presentation copy, with pencil autograph inscription 'To Bram Stoker from the Author, 1908'* imp.8vo. 1908

26. Barrie (J.M.) The Little Minister, 'Maude Adams Edition', *illustrations, some extra included, white buckram, uncut, t.e.g. in case New York,* 1898

27. Caine (Hall) The Manxman, a Novel, LARGE PAPER, 2 vol. *one of 250 copies, illustrations selected by the Author, and portrait, vellum, uncut, t.e.g. presentation copy from the Author, with autograph inscription: 'To my dear friend Bram Stoker, with love and greeting, Hall Caine, New York, Dec. 3rd, 1895', in case New York,* 1895

28. Blackburn (Henry) Randolph Caldecott: A Personal Memoir of his Early Art Career, *portrait and illustrations,* 1887 – Blackburne (E. Owens) Illustrious Irishwomen from the Earliest Ages to the Present Century, 2 vol. *presentation copy, with autograph inscription: 'Bram Stoker, Esq. With E. Owens Blackburne's Compts. London, Oct. 1877'* 1877 (3)

29. Ellwanger (G.H.) The Pleasures of the Table. Account of Gastronomy from Ancient Days to Present Times, *illustrations, uncut, t.e.g. New York,* 1902 – Wilson (A.) Glimpses of Nature, *illustrations, presentation copy from the Author, with autograph inscription,* 1891: etc. (3)

30. Ward (H.) Five Years with the Congo Cannibals, *illustrations by the Author, etc., presentation copy,* 1891 – Hatton (F.) North Borneo with Biographical Sketch and Notes, *portrait and illustrations, presentation copy, with autograph inscription: 'Bram Stoker, M.A., from his friend Joseph Hatton, 1886'* (2)

31. Walker (F.A.) History of the Second Army Corps in the Army of the Potomac, *portraits and map New York,* 1886

32. Winter (Wm.) Shakespeare's England, *illustrations, presentation copy, with autograph inscription: 'To Mr. and Mrs. Bram Stoker from their old friend William Winter, September 1910'*, New York, 1910 – Life and Writings of William Law Symonds, *portrait and plate*, 1908 (2)

33. Sikes (W.) British Goblins: Welsh Folklore, Fairy Mythology, etc. *Illustrations*, 1880 – O'Donnell (E.) *Byways of Ghost-Land*, 1911 – MacRitchie (D.) Fians, Fairies and Picts, *illustrations*, 1893: etc. (6)

34. Waliszewski (K.) Story of a Throne (Catherine II of Russia), *portrait*, 1895 – Romance of an Empress, *portrait*, 1895 – Cushman (Charlotte) Her Letters and Memories of her Life, edited by Emma Stebbins, *portrait*, Boston, 1878; etc. (5)

35. Clemens (S.L.) A Connecticut Yankee in King Arthur's Court, illustrations, New York, 1891 – Wilson (B.) The New America, *presentation copy from the author*, 1903 – Hickey (W.) Constitution of the United States of America, *half morocco*, Philadelphia, 1851; etc. (4)

36. Clemens (S.L.) The Man that Corrupted Hadleyburgh, etc. by Mark Twain, *frontispiece, presentation copy, with autograph inscription: 'To Bram Stoker, from his friend the Author, London, Aug. 24/00, '1900* – Tom Sawyer, Detective, portrait, presentation *copy 'To B.S. from M.T. with warm regards, London, December, 1896'*, 1897; and others by the same author (7)

37. Dibdin (Thos. Of Theatres Royal, Covent Garden etc.) Reminiscences 2 vol. *portrait*, 1827 – Garrick (David) Life, by Percy Fitzgerald, 2 vol. *portrait*, 1868 – Murphy (A.) Life of David Garrick, *uncut, Dublin*, 1801

38. American Statesmen, edited by John T. Morse junior, 16 vol. 1896, *etc.*

39. Shakespeare (Wm.) Works, reduced facsimile of First Folio, with Introduction by J.O. Halliwell-Phillipps, 1876 – Bormann (E.) The Shakespeare Secret, *illustrations*, roy.8vo, 1895 – Shakespeare's Garden of Girls, *frontispiece*, 1885 – Donnelly (I.) The Cipher in the Plays and on the Tombstone, 1900, *two copies*; and others relating to Shakespeare (12)

40. Brereton (Austin) Henry Irving, a Biographical Sketch, 17 portraits *imp. 8vo* New York, 1884

41. Stevenson (Robert Louis) Works, EDINBURGH EDITION, including his Letters to his Friends, Appendix, etc. 30 vol. *portrait, etc. Red cloth, uncut Edinb.* 1894– 99

42. Stevenson (R.L.) Misadventures of John Nicolson, New York, *n.d.*; The Merry Men, *ib.* 1887; A Footnote to History, *ib.* 1892; Across the Plains, FIRST EDITION, *buckram, uncut*, 1892 (4)

43. Stevenson (R.L.) Father Damien, an Open Letter to the Reverend Doctor Hyde of Honolulu, pp. 30, *original wrappers, uncut* 1890

44. Tennyson (A.) Ode on the Death of the Duke of Wellington, FIRST EDITION, 1852; another edition, 1853 – Corbet (W.J.) Battle of Fontenoy, *Dublin* 1871; etc. *some presentation copies to Bram Stoker from the authors* (20)

45. Tennyson (A.) Maud and other Poems, FIRST EDITION, *original cloth*, 1855; Gareth and Lynette, FIRST EDITION, *original cloth, initials on title*, 1872

46. Dibdin (C.) Complete History of the English Stage, vol. I–II, 2 vol. *uncut, n.d.* – Calcraft (J.W.) Defence of the Stage, *uncut, Dublin*, 1839 – Senior (Wm.) The Old Wakefield Theatre, *frontispiece*, uncut, Wakefield, 1894; and others (14)

47. Stirling (E.) Old Drury Lane, Fifty Years' Recollections 2 vol. 1881– Hazlitt (W.) Criticisms and Dramatic Essays of the English Stage, 1854; and others relating to the stage, etc. (24)

48. Cibber. Theophilus Cibber to David Garrick, Esq. With Dissertations on Theatrical Subjects, with Appendix, *frontispiece and plates, one inserted*, 1759 – Shaw (A.) Theatrical World of 1894, with Introduction by G.B. Shaw, 1895 – Brereton (A.) Dramatic Notes, *half morocco*, 1885; and others, Plays etc. *A parcel*

49. Shakespeare (W.) Maude Abams' Acting Edition of Romeo and Juliet, *illustrations*, New York 1889 – Talfourd (T.N.) Ion, a Tragedy 1836 – Beecher (H.W.) Eulogy on General Grant, *autograph signature of Ellen Terry on wrapper and title, New York* 1885 – Falconer (E.) Francesca, A Dream of Venice, 1865; etc. (14)

50. Shipman (L.E. A Group of Theatrical Characatures, 12 *plates by W. J. Gladding, New York*, 1897 – Brereton (A.) Some Famous Hamlets, with Appendix, 1884 – Fargus F.J.) Bound Together, vol. 1, presentation copy, with autograph inscription: *'To Florence Bram Stoker from Hugh Conway, Aug. 12 /84'*, 1884 (4)

51. Hilles (Malcolm W.) A Queen's Love, a Drama, FIRST EDITION, *presentation copy, with autograph inscription: 'Presented to Henry Irving, Esq. With the Author's Compts. 13 Jan. 1880', Keighley*, 1879 – Long Island Publications, No. 1, The Battle of Brooklyn, a Farce in Two Acts, *presentation copy to 'Mr. Bram Stoker', only a few copies reprinted for private distribution, New York*, 1776, *reprinted Brooklyn*, 1873

52. Fargus (F.J.) Called Back, by Hugh Conway, FIRST EDITION, *morocco, g.e. presentation copy, with autograph inscription: To Bram Stoker from Hugh Conway, F. J. Fargus, Aug. 1,* 1884' *Bristol*, 1884

53. Wilkins (Wm.) Songs of Study, FIRST EDITION, *presentation copy, with autograph inscription: 'Bram Stoker, Esq. With the Author's kind regards'* 1881

54. Field (Eugene) A Little Book of Western Verse, New York, 1893; Second Book of Verse, ib 1893 – Eugene Field, a Study in Heredity and Contradictions, by Mason Thompson, 2 vol. *portraits, views and facsimile illustrations, uncut, New York*, 1901 (4)

55. Bancroft. Mr. And Mrs. Bancroft on and off the Stage, written by themselves 2 vol. *portraits, half calf gilt, m.e. presentation copy, with autograph inscription: 'To Bram Stoker from S.B. Bancroft, Christmas 1889'* 1888

56. Watson (Wm.) Lachrymæ Musarium and other Poems, 1892; Poems 1892; The Eloping Angels, 1893; Excursions in Criticism, 1893 (4)

57. Caine (Hall) The Mahdi, or Love and Race, a Drama in Story, *no. 66 of 100 copies, privately printed for copyright, uncut, inscription on the title: 'Private Copy, Hall Caine'* 1894

58. Lloyd (John Uri) The Right Side of the Car, *illustrations on Japanese paper, buckram gilt, uncut, presentation copy, with pencil autograph inscription: 'Will Mr. Bram Stoker accept this little token of the Author's regard, with the Author's best wishes? Sincerely John Uri Lloyd, Cincinnati, March 5th, 1904'* Boston, 1897

59. Lloyd (J.U.) Red Head, *illustrations and decorations* by R.B. Birch, *white cloth gilt, uncut, t.e.g. presentation copy, with autograph inscription: 'To Mr. Bram Stoker, with kind regards and best wishes of John Uri Lloyd, Thanksgiving, 1903'* New York, 1903

60. Lloyd (J.U.) Scroggins, *illustrations and decorations* by R.B. Birch, *linen boards, uncut, t.e.g. presentation copy, with pencil autograph inscription 'To my friend Mr. Bram Stoker, with many happy recollections and pleasant hours spent together, John Uri Lloyd'* ib. 1904

61. Lloyd (J.U.) Warwicks of the Knobs, *illustrations of Knob County, presentation copy, with pencil autograph note on fly-leaf: 'My dear Stoker. Should you read this book I beg you to bear in mind that I consider it my best (excepting Red Head) study of Kentucky character, sincerely yours John Uri Lloyd. To my friend Bram Stoker'* ib. 1901

62. Jacobi (C.T.) Some Notes on Books and Printing, *uncut,* 1903 − Winter (Wm.) The Press and the Stage, *linen boards, uncut, presentation copy, with autograph inscription: To Mr. and Mrs. Bram Stoker, with the regards of their old friend, William Winter, June 24, 1889'*, New York, 1889 (2)

63. Stoker (Bram) Under the Sunset, *illustrations by W. Fitzgerald and W.V. Cockburn, vellum, g.e.* 1882

64. Walton and Cotton. The Complete Angler, edited by G.W. Bethune with Notes, Bibliographical Preface, etc. *Portraits, plates, etc. Calf gilt g.e. roy. 8vo.* New York, 1880

65. Jacobs (W.W.) A Master of Craft, 12 *illustrations,* 1900; Light Freights, 12 *illustrations,* 1902; The Lady of the Barge, *illustrations,* 1902; Captains All, *illustrations,* 1905; and other novels (12)

66. Churchill (Winston) Richard Carvel, *Illustrations, presentation copy, with autograph inscription: 'To Bram Stoker, October 31, 1899. Another Gentleman who belongs to both sides of the Atlantic, W. C.'* 1889 − Moore (F.F.) According to Plato, *presentation copy, with autograph inscription: 'To Florence A. L. Stoker with affectionate regards from F. Frankfort Moore'*, New York, 1901 (2)

67. Molloy (J. Fitzgerald) Romance of the Irish Stage, 2 vol. *2 portraits presentation copy, with autograph inscription: 'To Bram Stoker with best wishes from Fitzgerald Molly'*, 1897: Life and Adventures of Edmund Keane, Tragedian, 2 vol. *autograph inscription: 'To Bram Stoker, Esq. With Fitzgerald Molloy's kind regards'*, 1888

68. Cunningham (Peter) Story of Nell Gwyn and the Sayings of Charles the Second, with Index, *uncut, New York*, 1883 – Bowker (Alfred) King Alfred Millenary, *illustrations, presentation copy, 'Bram Stoker, Esq. From Alfred Bowker',* 1902 imp. 8vo (2)

69. Caine (Hall) The Deemster, a Romance, FIRST EDITION, 3 vol. 1887; *The Little Manx Nation*, 1891; Fate of Fenella, 3 vol. *illustrations*, 1892: etc. (9)

70. Ordnance Survey of Great Britain, with Index, 110 *folding sheets on linen*, in 19 *solander cases* 1848, *etc.*

71. Clarke (Jos. I.C.) Mâlmoida, a Metrical Romance, *vellum, uncut, t.e.g. presentation copy, with autograph inscription: 'To my good friend Bram Stoker, Esq. In souvenir of many gracious acts, with the hearty good wishes of Joseph I. C. Clarke, New York, March 19, 1894'* 1893

72. Braddon (M.E.) Rough Justice, *presentation copy, with autograph inscription: 'To Bram Stoker, with kindest regards from M. E. Braddon, Richmond, March 22nd 1898',* 1898 – Parry (Judge) England's Elizabeth, *presentation copy, 'Bram Stoker, with all good wishes from Edward A. Parry, June 1st, 1904',* 1904 (2)

73. Tayler (Jeremy) Rule and Exercises of Holy Living, *presentation copy, with inscription: 'To my kind friend Bram Stoker, a souvenir of some of my happiest hours at the dear Lyceum, M.E. Braddon, December, 1892'* Bickers, 1873

74. Hoffman (E.T.W) Weird Tales, translated by J.T. Bealby, 2 vol. *portrait*, New York, 1885 – Campbell (J.G.) Superstitions and Witchcraft and Second Sight in the Highlands and Islands of Scotland 2 vol. *Glasgow*, 1902; etc.

75. Goddard (Arthur) Players of the Period, Both Series, in 1 vol. *illustrations*, 1891 – Cook (Dutton) Night and the Play, 2 vol. 1883 – Wills (W.G.) and Hon. Mrs. Greene, Drawing Room Dramas, 1873 (4)

76. Landon (L.E.) Complete Works, 2 vol. in 1, *Boston*, 1859 – Figaro Programme and Sketch Book, no. XXVI–LXXVI, in 1 vol. *portraits*, 1875 *roy. 8vo.* (2)

77. Watson (John, Ian Maclaren) Beside the Bonnie Brier Bush, 1894; The Days of Auld Langsyne, 1895; Kate Carnegie and those Ministers, 1896; Church Folks, *presentation copy with autograph inscription, 'Bram Stoker, Esq. From the Author with kind regards, Nov. 9 1900',* 1900 (4)

78. Millet (F.D.) The Danube from the Black Forest to the Black Sea, *illustrations, presentation copy 'To Bram Stoker, Esq. With regards of F. D. Millet', New York*, 1893; Egyptian Tales, second series, edited by W.M. Flinders Petrie, *illustrations*, 1895; etc. (4)

79. Donaldson (Thos.) The House in which Thomas Jefferson wrote the Declaration of Independence, *illustrations, presentation copy with autograph note on fly-leaf, 'My dear Mr. Stoker this is father's last book and please accept it as a remembrance, Thomas Blaine Donaldson',* 1898 – Whittle (J.L.) Grover Cleveland, *two portraits*, 1896: etc. (4)

80. Ruskin (John) Sesame and Lilies, revised and enlarged edition, *calf, g.e. autograph letter of the author inserted* 1871

81. Ruskin (J.) Plates to the Stones of Venice, in 1 vol. *some coloured, New York,* 1880 – Dickens (C.) *The Battle of Life, illustrations, half calf gilt,* 1846 (2)

82. Beeton's Christmas Annual. Edward the Seventh, a Play, etc. Illustrations, *presentation copy with autograph inscription, 'To Bram Stoker from Henry Irving',* 1876 – Mayall's Celebrities of the London Stage, *photographic portraits in character* (1867–68) imp. 8vo. (2)

83. Shelley (P.B.) Queen Mab, with Notes, *calf gilt* W. Clark, 1821

84. Haggard (H. Rider) Mr. Meesom's Will, FIRST EDITION, 16 *illustrations,* 1888 – Strange (T.B.) Gunner Jingo's Jubilee, *illustrations, presentation copy from the author to Col. Reginald Hennell, with interesting autograph inscriptions,* 1893 (2)

85. Kipling (Rudyard) Traffics and Discoveries, 1904: Out of India, *New York,* 1895 – Field (R.) The Bondage of Ballinger, *portrait, presentation copy with autograph inscription of the author,* 1903; etc. (6)

86. Kipling (R.) The Jungle Book, 1896, and The Second Jungle Book, 1895, 2 vol. *illustrations* by J. Lockwood Kipling etc. *blue cloth, g.e.* 1895–96

87. Gaskell (Mrs.) Cranford, with Preface by Anne T. Ritchie, *illustrations by Hugh Thomson, presentation copy with inscription, 'To Bram Stoker Esq. as a faint acknowledgement of his kindness, Hugh Thomson'* 1891

88. Pinero (A.W.) Trelawny of the 'Wells', *illustrations, New York,* 1899; His House in Order, a Comedy, *portrait and illustrations,* 1907 – Barlow (G.) An Actor's Reminiscences, and other Poems 1883; etc. (8)

89. Becke (L.) The Ebbing of the Tide, presentation copy to *'Bram Stoker, with the author's sincere regards',* 1896 – Evans (R.D.) A Sailor's Log, *illustrations,* New York, 1901 – Matsell (G.W.) Vocabulum, or, The Rogue's Lexicon, *portrait, etc. ib.* 1859; etc. (8)

90. Jennings (L.J.) Field Paths and Green Lanes, Illustrations, 1878; Rambles among the Hills, illustrations, 1880 – Fiske (S.) Holiday Stories, *presentation copy 'To Bram Stoker, with a Happy New Year, Stephen Fiske', St. Paul,* 1891; etc.

91. Dowden (Edward) Poems, *presentation copy with autograph signature of the author,* 1876 – Armstrong (G.F.) A Garland of Greece, 1882 – Veley (M.) A Marriage of Shadows, with Preface by Leslie Stephen, 1888, and others, *all presentation copies with autograph inscriptions* (8)

92. Caine (Hall) My Story, *presentation copy with autograph inscription, 'To my dear Bram, to whom this book owes much, Hall Caine, 10 Oct. 1908',* – Baker (James) The Cardinal's Page, *presentation copy with autograph inscription, To Bram Stoker, in pleasant remembrance of many a famous First-night at the Lyceum, from James Baker',* 1899 – Moore (F.F.) A Nest of Linnets, *illustrations, presentation copy 'from F. Frankfort Moore',* 1901, and others, *all presentation copies* (10)

93. Reid (Capt. Mayne) The Wild Huntress, *illustrations, presentation copy with autograph inscription, 'Bram Stoker, Esq. with Compts. Of Mayne Reid, March 21 1879', n.d.* – Law (James D.) Dreams o' Hame, and other Scotch Poems,

portrait, To Bram Stoker, Esq. with the compliments of the author, James D. Law',
1893 – Becke (Louis) Pacific Tales, *portrait, To Bram Stoker, from Louis Becke,
with kind regards, London, May 26 1897'*, 1897: and others, *all presentation copies
to Bram Stoker* (12)

94. Harte (Bret) The Heritage of Dedlow Marsh and other Tales, *presentation copy
with autograph inscription, 'To Bram Stoker from Bret Harte, London, January 1891'*,
1890 – O'Brien (Wm.) Irish Ideas, *presentation copy, To Bram Stoker, Esq. with
all best wishes, William O' Brien, July, 1894'*, 1893 (2)

95. Gifford (Mrs. W.K.) The Last Touches and other Stories, *presentation copy
with autograph inscription 'With Mrs. W. K. Clifford's very kind regards, to
Mr. Bram Stoker, Dec. 1, 1892'*, 1892; A Wild Proxy, 1893; Mere Stories, 1896;
Plays, 1909 (4)

96. Shelley (P.B.) Poetical Works, with Memoir by Leigh Hunt, 4 vol. *n.d.* – Shelley
(Mary W.) Frankenstein, the modern Man-Demon, *n.d.* – Sheridanania, or
Anecdotes of the Life of R. B. Sheridan, etc. *portrait,* 1826; etc.

97. Bohn's Extra Volumes, 6 vol. *portraits* 1846–55

98. Harley (Geo.) The Life of a London Physician, edited by Mrs A. Tweedie,
portrait, 1899 – Wicks (F.) Golden Lives: The Story of a Woman's Courage,
illustrations, 1891: The Veiled Hand, illustrations, 1893; and others, *all presentation copies with inscriptions* (10)

99. Macaulay (T.B.) Lays of Ancient Rome, *with autograph signature and initials of
the author,* 1848 – Marston (E.) Days in Clover, *frontispiece, uncut, presentation
copy, 'To Bram Stoker with the compliments and regards of E. Marston'*, 1892 –
Matthews (B.) Vignettes of Manhattan, *illustrations, presentation copy from the
author, New York,* 1894; etc. (5)

100. Omar, Rubáiyát of Omar Kháyyám, in English Verse, translated by Edward
Fitzgerald, with notes, etc. *half vellum, uncut, New York,* 1888 – Federalist (The),
reprinted from the Original Text, edited by H.B. Dawson, *presentation copy to
Bram Stoker from Henry Ward Beecher, with autograph inscription, ib.* 1864 (2)

101. Barnes (Wm.) Poems of Rural Life in the Dorset Dialect, 1879 – Fergusson
(Jas. R.) Poems and Ballads, *presentation copy with autograph letter of author
inserted,* 1876 – Le Fanu (J. Sheridan) The Watcher and other Weird Stories,
21 *illustrations by Brinsley Sheridan le Fanu,* 1894; etc. (8)

102. Yeats (W.B.) The Countess Kathleen and various Legends and Lyrics, *frontispiece, half vellum uncut, presentation copy with autograph inscription, 'To Bram
Stoker with the compliments and best regards of W. B. Yeats, Sept. 1893'*, 1892
– Cochrane (A.) Collected Verses, *frontispiece, half morocco, uncut, t.e.g. presentation copy, 'To Bram Stoker, with the author's best regards, April, 1904'*, 1903 (2)

103. Smith (Goldwin) Lectures and Essays, *Toronto,* 1881 – Verey (Jos.) Poems,
Grave and Gay, 1880 – Bell (Mackenzie) Charles Whitehead, a Forgotten
Genius, 1894: Spring's Immortality and other Poems, 1893; and others, *all
presentation copies to Bram Stoker* (15)

104. Faustus, his Life, Death and Descent into Hell, translated from the German, *coloured frontispiece, linen boards, uncut* 1825

105. Heinemann (Wm.) The First Step, A Dramatic Moment, 1895; Summer Moths, a Play, 1898, *original boards, uncut, presentation copies to Bram Stoker, with autograph inscriptions of the author* 1895–98

106. Hatton (Jos.) By Order of the Czar, a Drama, *presentation copy, 'In Auld Lang Syne, Bram Stoker from his friend Joseph Hatton, July 1904'*, 1904 – Page (T.M.) Santa Claus' Partner, *coloured illustrations, New York*, 1899, Daskam (J.D.) Fables for the Fair, 1901; etc. (8)

107. Alden (H.M.) God in his World, *presentation copy with autograph letters of author inserted, New York*, 1894 – Miller (E.) The Yoke, a Romance, 1904 – Scott (Clement) Poppy Land, *presentation copy, 'To Bram from Clem, 17 April 1886'*, 1886; etc. (24)

108. Gabbitas (P.) Heart Melodies, for Storm and Sunshine from Cliftonia the Beautiful, *portrait*, 1885 – Wiggin (Kate D.) Diary of a Goose Girl, *illustrations, Boston*, 1902 – Caster (Eliz. B.) 'Boots and Saddles', or Life in Dakota, with General Caster, *portrait, presentation copy, New York, n.d.*; etc. (4)

109. Patterson (E.) The Mermaid and other Pieces, FIRST EDITION,★ *presentation copy with autograph inscription, To Bram Stoker, Esq. with the author's humble compliments, his sincere good wishes and his honest desire for further acquaintance, Cardiff, Sep. 22/97, E. Patterson', published by the author Cardiff* 1897
★The first book published by the author, only 300 copies of the book were printed.

110. Clapp (H.A.) Reminiscences of a Dramatic Critic, with Essay on the Art of Henry Irving, *portraits of Japanese paper, Boston*, 1902 – Mead (Thos, Comedian) Lady of the Rose and other Poems, *portrait, uncut, 'To Mr. B. Stoker, with the kind regards of T. Mead'*, 1881 (2)

111. Garrick. Catalogue of the Library, Splendid Books of Prints, Poetical and Historical Tracts of David Garrick, Esq. with prices and purchasers' names, *half russia* 1823

112. Winter (Wm.) Shadows of the Stage 3 vol. *New York*, 1892–95 – Smalley (G.W.) Studies of Men, *autograph letter of author inserted*, 1895 – Todminter (J.) True Tragedy of Rienzi and Alcestes, a Dramatic Poem, 2 vol. presentation *copies to Bram Stoker, 'with the author's kind regards*, 1879–81; etc. (8)

113. Dodgson (C.L.) Sylvie and Bruno, FIRST EDITION, *46 illustrations by H. Furniss, red cloth g.e.* 1889

114. Aldrich (T.B.) Ponkapong Papers, *presentation copy, Boston*, 1903; Judith of Bethula, a Tragedy, *portrait, presentation copy, 'To Bram Stoker with affectionate regards from Thomas Bailey Aldrich, Boston, September 1906'*, ib. 1905; Mercedes and Later Lyrics, FIRST EDITION, *presentation copy i.b.* 1884 (3)

115. Mayhew Boros. Whom to Marry and how to get Married, *illustrations by G. Cruikshank*, 1854 – Anstey (F.) Lyre and Lancet, *illustrations, presentation copy to Bram Stoker*, 1895 (2)

116. Benson (Robt.) Sketches of Corsica, *plates, one coloured*, 1825 – Baker (J.) Imperial Guide, with Picturesque Plans of the Great Post Roads, *plates, half calf*, 1802 – Collection of Proverbs, Bengali and Sanscrit, with their Translation, etc. by W. Morton, *Calcutta*, 1832 (3)

117. Le Gallienne (Richard) The Book–Bills of Narcissus, *buckram, uncut, t.e.g.* 1892 – Arnold (Sir E.) Gwen, a Drama, 1880 – Jacobi (C.T.) Gesta Typographica, *1897; another copy, one of 50 copies printed on Japanese vellum, uncut*, 1897 (4)

118. Remembrances for Order and Decency to be kept in the Upper house of Parliament by the Lords when His Majesty is not there, MANUSCRIPT, *old red morocco, g.e. autograph signature of J. Britton on fly-leaf* SÆC. XVIII

119. Toole (J.L.) Reminiscences, chronicled by Jos. Hatton, *portrait and illustrations, autograph inscription: 'With J. L. Toole's kind regards to his Friend Bram Stoker, May 13/92.'* 1892 – Jones (S.) The Actor and his Art, 1899 – Wallace (Wm.) The Devine Surrender, *uncut*, 1895 – Betty (W.H. West, *the Young Roscius*) Memoirs of his Life, *half morocco, Liverpool*, 1804; etc. (5)

120. AUTOGRAPHS. Collection of interesting Autograph Signatures, etc. including famous Actors, etc.: Charles Dickens, with original sketch, W.C. Macready, J.P. Hartley, J.A. Van Amburg with original sketch, John Braham, Anna Mordaunt, Drinkwater Meadows, G.Y. Bennett, E.W. Elton, Fra Diavolo, Mark Lemon, M.W. Balfe, A.E. Betts, E. Vestris, with pencil sketch, W.H. Oxberry, W. Farren, Charles Peake, R. Keeley, George Lefanu, C.J. Matthews, H.J. Wallack, Fanny Stirling etc. with Index, in a vol. of *half roan*

121. Fitzgerald (Wm.) Collection of Oriental Pencil Sketches, in a vol. *half roan*

122. Riley (Jas. Whitcomb, *the Hoosier Poet*★) Sketches in Prose, 1891; Rhymes of Childhood, 1891; Pipes O' Pan at Zekesbury, 1891; Old-Fashioned Roses, 1891; Flying Islands of the Night, 1892; Green Fields and Running Brooks, 1893; A Child World, 1897; Home Folks, 1900; Book of Joyous Children, 1903; His Pa's Romance, 1903; etc. together 11 vol. *portraits, etc. all presentation copies to Bram Stoker, with autograph inscriptions, some with original lines by the author, and an Autograph letter Indianapolis, etc.* 1891–1903

★ 'Irving' says Bram Stoker in his Reminiscences of the great actor, 'like all who had ever known him, loved the "Hoosier" Poet. We saw a great deal of him when he was in London, and whenever we were in Indianapolis, to meet him was one of the expected pleasures. Riley is one of the most dramatic reciters that live, and when he gives one of his own poems it is an intellectual delight.'

WALT WHITMAN

For many years Mr. Bram Stoker was an intimate friend of Walt Whitman. He first became acquainted with his works through the volume of Selections, issued in 1868 by Mr. W. M. Rossetti, which, as he observes in his 'Reminiscences', provoked his ardent admiration, in spite of the hostility and ridicule with which it was generally received.

123. Whitman (Walt) Leaves of Grass, Author's Edition, with Intercalations, *half calf gilt, g.e. presentation copy, with autograph inscription: 'Bram Stoker, from his friend the Author'* Camden, New Jersey, 1876

124. Whitman (Walt) Leaves of Grass, Author's Edition, *green cloth, presentation copy from the author with autograph inscription: 'Bram Stoker from the Author W.W.' ib.* 1882

125. Whitman (Walt) Leaves of Grass, *portrait, brown cloth* Philadelphia, 1884

126. Whitman (Walt) Leaves of Grass, including Sands at Seventy, Goodbye my Fancy, *green cloth, uncut, with autograph signature of Bram Stoker ib.* 1894

127. Whitman (Walt) Two Rivulets, including Democratic Vistas, Centennial Songs, and a Passage to India, Author's Edition, *portrait (inserted) with autograph signature, half calf gilt, presentation copy, with autograph inscription: 'Bram Stoker from his friend the Author'* Camden, New Jersey, 1876

128. Whitman (Walt) Complete Prose Works, *green cloth, uncut, t.e.g. autograph signature of Bram Stoker inside cover* Philadelphia, 1892

129. Whitman (Walt) As a Strong Bird on Pinions Free, and other Poems, *autograph signature of the author on title, presentation copy, with inscription: 'Bram Stoker Esq. with compliments of Thos. Donaldson July 31/85'* Washington, 1872

130. Whitman (Walt) November Boughs, *portrait of the author in his 70th year, red cloth, t.e.g. with autograph receipt from the author: 'Camden, New Jersey, U.S. America. Received from Bram Stoker, Twenty-five Dollars (Deepest thanks and remembrances), Walt Whitman', and Autograph Letter, 4pp. From Thomas Donaldson to Bram Stoker, having reference to Walt Whitman* 1889

131. Whitman (Walt) Specimen Days and Collect, *brown cloth* Philadelphia, 1882–83

132. Whitman (Walt) Drum-Taps, FIRST EDITION, *brown cloth, presentation copy, with note and inscription by Thomas Donaldson: Given me by Walt Whitman May 31, '85', 'Bram Stoker, with regards of Thos, Donaldson'* New York, 1865

133. Whitman (Walt) After All, Not to Create only, recited at the American Institute Sept. 7, 1871, *Boston,* 1871 – Trimble (W.H.) Walt Whitman and Leaves of Grass, *presentation copy to Bram Stoker from the Author,* 1905 (2)

134. Whitman. Donaldson (Thomas) Walt Whitman the Man, *portrait illustrations and facsimiles, buckram, uncut, Autograph Letter from the author to Bram Stoker enclosed* New York, 1896

135. Whitman (Walt) In re Walt Whitman: edited by his literary Executors, Horace L. Traubel, Richard Maurice Bucke, Thomas B. Harned, *original cloth, uncut* Philadelphia, 1893

136. WHITMAN (WALT) A COLLECTION OF FRAGMENTS OF WALT WHITMAN'S WRITINGS, all in his Autograph, consisting of Eighteen various Pieces, some written in ink and some in pencil, together with his portrait, containing his autograph signature, all mounted or inlaid in a vol. *given to Bram Stoker by Thomas Donaldson*

★ 'He sometimes wrote on scraps of paper, on the inside of envelopes addressed to him, on the backs or unwritten portions of letters received by him or on paper received around packages, in fact on anything that could carry ink. His manuscript was like Joseph's coat, of many colours. Sometimes he used half a dozen kinds of paper on which to complete one poem, – a verse or two on each, and then he would pin them together. His poems he worked over and over again. He would roll a complete poem, or a book, or an article up, wrap it about with a piece of twine, and throw it in the corner of the room. In his bedroom were packages of manuscript in baskets, in bundles, or in piles. Some of them were mixed up with lots of short-cut pine wood, which he kept to fire up his sheet iron stove. He used the crook on his cane to hook out what he wanted from the pile on the floor. Usually before sending a poem or a manuscript to a paper, or away, he had it set up in type and sent it to the publisher printed.' – *Thomas Donaldson in his 'Walt Whitman the Man', 1896, pp. 73–4.*

137. WHITMAN (WALT) Lecture by Walt Whitman on Abraham Lincoln, THE ORIGINAL PRINTED NOTES, with autograph emendations and corrections, as given to Thomas Donaldson by Walt Whitman, Aug. 11/86; a Portrait of Walt Whitman, with his autograph signature; a Portrait of Abraham Lincoln; and an exceedingly interesting Autograph Letter to Thomas Donaldson (author of 'Walt Whitman the Man'), *mounted on cardboard and enclosed in a cover, with autograph notes of Thos. Donaldson*

★ 'A Message from the Dead.' We did not reach Philadelphia till towards the end of January 1894. In the meantime Walt Whitman had died, March 26, 1892. On 4th February I spent the afternoon with Donaldson in his own home. Shortly after I came in he went away for a minute and came back with a large envelope which he handed to me. 'That is for you from Walt Whitman. I have been keeping it till I should see you.' The envelope contained in a rough card folio pasted down on thick paper the original notes from which he delivered his lecture on Abraham Lincoln at the Chestnut Street Opera House on April 15, 1886. With it was a letter to Donaldson, in which he said 'Enclosed I send a full report of my Lincoln Lecture for our friend Bram Stoker.' This was my Message from the Dead.' – *Bram Stoker in his 'Henry Irving', 1906, vol. II, p. 3*

138. WHITMAN (WALT) An exceedingly interesting Autograph Letter from Walt Whitman to Bram Stoker, with Introductory Note, 1p. 4to, 24 lines, dated from Canden, N. Jersey, U. S. America, March 6/76: 'My physique is entirely shatter'd, doubtless permanently from paralysis and other ailments. But I am up & dress'd & get out every day a little – live here quite lonesome but hearty & good spirits. Write to me again. Walt Whitman', *mounted within covers*

★ One evening in 1876 at the 'Fortnightly Club', a club of Dublin men who met occasionally for free discussions, a violent attack was made on Walt Whitman, which drew forth a most impassioned protest from Edward

Dowden. Bram Stoker followed on the same side, and together they carried the question. Stoker excited by the stress of the meeting, went home, and before he went to bed, poured out his heart in a long letter to Walt Whitman. Bye and bye came the characteristic letter from the Poet described above.

139. FIELD (EUGENE) 'Willie' an Autograph Poem from Eugene Field to Bram Stoker, written in black and red and signed by the author, Jan. 11, 1888, *inserted in a cover, with explanatory note*

★ Bram Stoker, who knew Eugene Field well, and greatly admired his delightful poems for and about children, one day expressed a wish for the poet's autograph. Shortly afterwards, to his amusement and delight, he received the accompanying dainty verses, entitled 'Willie'. As far as is known, and it is obviously unlikely, they have never been printed.

140. Riley (James Whitcomb) Armazindy, *presentation copy, with autograph inscription* 1894

★ This volume contains the poem Leonainie, with which many literary critics were successfully hoaxed in the early seventies. It was supposed to be an hitherto unknown poem by Edgar A. Poe, which had been found written on a fly leaf of a book once in the possession of Poe.

141. Whistler (J. McNeil) Exhibition of Etchings, with a note on the Etchings of Whistler by F. Wedmore, *frontispiece, uncut* 1903

142. Whistler (J. McNeil) Etchings and Dry Points. Venice, Second Series, *n.d.;* 'Notes', 'Harmonies', 'Nocturnes' Second Series 1886, *uncut* (2)

143. LINCOLN (PRESIDENT) A Death Mask and Hands, closed, of President Lincoln, in bronze, and a plaster cast of the left hand, opened (4)

★ The death mask and closed hands were cast by the celebrated sculptor Augustus St. Gaudens in 1886 from the original moulds made by Volk before Lincoln went to Washington for his first Presidency, and were found by Volk's son twenty-five years later. Twenty men joined to purchase the moulds and present them to the American nation, two of the twenty being Henry Irving and Bram Stoker, and each of the subscribers received casts in bronze of the face and hands with his name in each case cut in the bronze (*see Bram Stoker's Henry Irving', 1906, vol. II, pp. 108–9*).

144. Lincoln (President) THE ORIGINAL MANUSCRIPT of Bram Stoker's Lecture on Abraham Lincoln, First Notes and Variantes, *in a solander case*

145. Lincoln (President) Reminiscences, by distinguished Men of his Time, edited by A.T. Rice, *portraits, etc. New York*, 1866 – Stoddard (W.O.) Abraham Lincoln, the True Story of a great Life, *portrait, illustrations, etc. ib.* 1885 – Arnold (I.M.) Life of Abraham Lincoln, *half morocco, Chicago*, 1885

146. Lincoln (President) The Lincoln Memorial, Album Immortelles, etc. collected and edited by O.H. Oldroyd, *portrait and illustrations*, 1882 – Holland (J.G.) Life of Abraham Lincoln, *portrait, Springfield,* Mass. 1866 – Nicolay (J.G.) Short Life of Abraham Lincoln, *portrait, New York*, 1906 (3)

147. Lincoln (President) Barrett (J.H.) Life of Abraham Lincoln), *portrait*, 1865 – Curtis (W.E.) The True Abraham Lincoln *portrait and illustrations*, 1903 – Brooks (Noah) Abraham Lincoln, a Biography, *portrait and illustrations*, 1888; etc. (8)

148. Hope (A.) Adventure of the Lady Ursula: a Comedy, *illustrations*, New York, 1898 – Days with Sir Roger de Coverley, *illustrations*, 1866; etc. (5) QUARTO

149. Lavater (J.C.) Essays on Physiognomy, translated by Henry Hunter, 5 vol. *numerous portraits and plates, by T. Holloway, blue morocco gilt, ornamental borders on the sides, silk linings, g.e.* 1789

150. Budge (E.A. Wallis) The Book of the Dead. The Papyrus of Ani, in the British Museum, the Egyptian Text, with Translation, etc. *half morocco, uncut, t.e.g.* 1895

151. Shakespeare (Wm.) Works, 'Henry Irving Edition', edited by Henry Irving and F.A Marshall, with Notes and Introductions, EDITION DE LUXE *one of* 150 copies, 8 vol. *numerous illustrations by Gordon Browne, linen boards, uncut, t.e.g.* 1888–90

152. Quasi Cursores. Portraits of the High Officers and Professors of the University of Edinburgh, *drawn and etched by William Hole, uncut, presentation copy 'Bram Stoker, Esq. in memory of a very pleasant visit, W. B. Blaikie, Edinburgh, 2ⁿᵈ Nov 1894' Edinb.* 1884

153. History of the Two Americas, 2 vol. *portraits and illustration, half morocco, m.e.* New York, 1880 – Young (L.R.) Around the World with General Grant, 2 vol. *illustrations, half morocco, m.e. New York, n.d.* (4)

154. Irving (W.) Rip Van Winkle, illustrations by F.T. Merrill, *linen boards, g.e. Boston* 1888 – Walsh (W.S.) Faust, the Legend and the Poem, *etchings by H. Faber, Philadelphia*, 1888; etc. (4)

155. Smith (Adam) Inquiry into the Nature and Causes of the Wealth of Nations, Second Edition, 2 vol. *calf, presentation copy* 'From the Author' 1788

156. Byron (Lord) Childe Harold's Pilgrimage, Cantos I–II, FIRST EDITION, *binding broken* 1812

157. Thackeray (W.M.) Orphan of Pimlico, FIRST EDITION, *illustrations, half morocco*, 1876 – Archer and Barker: A National Theatre Scheme and Estimates, 1907; etc.

158. Leather (R.K.) and Ricd. Le Gallienne. The Student and the Body Snatcher, etc. LARGE PAPER, *one of* 50 copies, *buckram, uncut*, 1890; The Hardships of Publishing, *one of* 120 *copies, uncut, privately printed* 1873

159. Caldecott (R.) Some of Æsop's Fables with Modern Instances, *illustrations* 1883

160. Greey (E.) The Golden Lotus and other Legends of Japan, *presentation copy 'Bram Stoker San, with compliments of the author, Edward Greey'*, Boston 1883; The Royal Ronins, translated from the Japanese of Tamenaga Shunsai, by E. Greey, etc. *illustrations, presentation copy 'with the compliments of Edward Greey'*, 1884; etc. (5)

161. Kipling (R.) Verses written for Nicholson's Almanac of Sports for 1898, with the Almanac, *illustrations, presentation copy 'Mr. Bram Stoker, with compliments of Pamela Colman Smith'*, 1899 – Garcia (G.) The Actor's Art, *illustrations by A. Forestier*, 1882; etc. (4)

162. Calmour (Alfred C.) Fact and Fiction about Shakespeare, with Notes, *illustrations, presentation copy from the author to Bram Stoker, with autograph note on fly-leaf*, 1894 – Berg (A.E.) The Drama. Painting, Poetry and Song, *illustrations, NewYork*, 1884 –Yellow Book (The), vol. IV. *illustrations* 1895 (3)

163. Balfour (A.) Second, Third and Fourth Reports of the Wellcome Research Laboratories at the Gordon Memorial College, Khartoum, 3 vol. *map and illustrations, some coloured, Khartoum*, 1906–11; etc. (4)

164. Le Gallienne (Ricd.) Volume in Folio, *one of 50 copies, signed by the author, uncut* 1889

165. Green Sheaf (The) edited by Pamela Colman Smith, nos. I–VI and no. IX, *illustrations, some coloured by hand by the editor, autograph letter and receipt of the editor inserted* 1903–4

166. Hawks (F.L.) Narrative of the Expedition of an American Squadron to the China Seas and Japan under the Command of Commodore M. C. Perry, 3 vol. *maps, numerous illustrations, plates of costumes, etc.Washington*, 1856

167. Powell (J.W.) First and Second Annual Reports of the Bureau of Ethnology, 1880–1, *numerous plates,Washington*, 1881–3; Second Annual Report, another copy, 1883 (3)

168. Blake. Blair (Robert) The Grave, a Poem, portrait of W. Blake, *and 12 etchings from Blake's original designs by Schiavonetti, Bensley*, 1813

169.Wiley (W.H. and S.K.) The Yosemite, Alaska and the Yellowstone, portrait and illustrations, 1893; Collection of Newspaper Cuttings relating to the Drama, etc. in a vol. (2)

170.Whistler (J.M.) Gentle Art of Making Enemies, FIRST EDITION, *one of the 15 special large paper presentation copies, uncut, t.e.g. with autograph letter of W. Heinemann inserted* 1890

171.Whistler (J.M.) Memorial Exhibition, Catalogue of Paintings, Drawings, Etchings and Lithographs, EDITION DE LUXE, *portrait and illustrations, uncut, t.e.g.* 1905

172.Whistler (J.M.) Catalogue of Paintings, etc. 1905 – Page (The) vol. I, in 12 *parts as issued (wanting nos. VIII, IX and X) portraits, woodcuts, etc. only 140 copies printed*, 1898 (10)

173. Febure (Nic. De) Compleat Body of Chymistry, rendered into English by P. D. C. *plates, covers gone*, 1670 – Temple (Sir J.) The Irish Rebellion, FIRST EDITION, *old calf*, 1646

174. [Mathews (C.J.)] Catalogue Raisonnée of Mathews's Gallery of Theatrical Portraits, *calf, presentation copy with autograph inscription, 'John Pritt Harley Esq. from his great Admirer and Friend Anne Mathews, Saturday September 16, 1848'* 1833

175. Dryden (John) An Evening's Love or the Mock Astrologer, 1671; The Rival Ladies, a Tragi-Comedy, 1675; The Assignation or Love in a Nunnery, 1678; Secret Love, or the Maiden Queen, 1679; Marriage a-la-Mode, a Comedy, 1684; The Wild Gallant, a Comedy, 1684; The Indian Emperor, or the Conquest of Mexico, 1686; The conquest of Grenada, 1687; The Spanish Fryar, 1690; The Kind Keeper, or Mr. Limberham, A Comedy, 1690; Amphitryon, or the two Sosias, 1691; and others by the same author, some FIRST EDITIONS, in 1 vol. *old calf* 1671–91

176. Play-Bills. Collection of Play-Bills of the Theatre-Royal, Edinburgh ranging from Nov. 25, 1820, to Aug. 17, 1824, in 1 vol. 182—24

The following Six Manuscripts are mainly in the autograph of the Author, but some passages appear to be in the handwriting of an Amanuensis. They are all sold subject to the copyright being reserved.

177. Stoker (BRAM) Personal Reminiscences of Henry Irving, 'THE ORIGNAL MANUSCRIPT' 1906

178. Stoker (B.) Lady of the Shroud, 'THE ORIGINAL MANUSCRIPT' with the outline of the Story 1908

179. Stoker (B.) Snowbound, the Record of a Theatrical Touring Party (the last four chapters only), 'THE ORIGINAL MANUSCRIPT' 1908

180. Stoker (B.) Under the Sunset, 'THE ORIGINAL MANUSCRIPT' 1882

181. Stoker (B.) Lair of the White Worm (the last book written by the Author), 'THE ORIGINAL MANUSCRIPT' 1911

182. Stoker (B.) Original Notes and Data for his 'Dracula', *in a solander case* (1) FOLIO

183. Harris (John) Complete Collection of Voyages and Travels in Europe, Asia, Africa and America, 2 vol. *maps and plates,* calf 1744

184. Norden (F.L.) Travels in Egypt and Nubia, enlarged by P. Templeman, 2 vol. *plates, old calf* 1757

185. Lightning Sea-Column (The) or Sea Mirrour, discovering all the Coasts and Islands of Europa, Africa, America, and Asia, with a plain description thereof: translated from the Dutch, printed, ingraved and sold by Jacob Robyn, *numerous curious old maps and plans, old calf binding, broken, a few leaves torn, and some mended, sold not subject to return Amst.* 1689

186. Jansson (I.) Novus Atlas sive Theatrum Orbis Terrarum, in quo Magna Britannia seu Angliæ ey Scotiæ nec non Hiberniæ regna exhibentur, *numerous maps, binding broken ib.* 1659

187. Hamilton (Sir W.) Collection of Vases mostly of pure Greek Workmanship, discovered in Sepulchres in the Kingdom of the two Sicilies, 3 vol. *numerous engravings, calf, y.e.* Naples, 1791–95

188. Hay (Robt.) Illustrations of Cairo, *lithographs, half morocco imp. folio.* 1840

189. Budge (E.A. Wallis) Book of the Dead. Facsimile of the Papyrus of Ani, in the British Museum, *coloured plates, half morocco* 1894

190. Borgeois (E.) Century of Louis XIV, its Arts, its Ideas, translated by Mrs. Cashel Hoey, *numerous portraits and illustrations* 1895

191. Walter (Jas.) Shakespeare's Home and Rural Life, illustrations, presentation copy from the author, 1874 – Tennyson (A.) Vivien and Guinevere, in 1 vol. *illustrations by G. Doré, morocco, g.e.* 1867

192. Chaucer (G.) Works, with the Story of the Siege of Thebes, by J. Lidgate, and Life of Chaucer, *black letter, frontispiece, half calf, stained and wants last leaf,* 1687

193. Chaucer (G.) Works, edited by John Urry, with a Glossary, Life of Author, etc. LARGE PAPER, *portrait inserted, calf* 1721

194. Barnes (J.) History of Edward III, and the Black Prince, *portrait,* calf, Cambridge, 1688 – Denon (V.) Egypt Delineated, *portrait, plates, etc. calf, binding broken,* 1825 (2)

195. Omar, Rubaiyat of Omar Khayyam, rendered into English Verse by Edward Fitzgerald, *engravings from drawings by Elihu Vedder, brown cloth gilt, t.e.g. Boston,* 1884

196. Crane (W.) Mrs. Mundi at Home, outline engravings by Walter Crane, *oblong, n.d.* – Wood (L.) Prehistoric Proverbs, *12 coloured illustrations, n.d.* (2)

197. Statutes made and established from the time of Kyng Henry the thirde, unto the fyrste yere of the reigne of Henry the VIII, *black letter, old calf, r.e.* 1543

198. Rastall (Wm) Collection of Statutes now in force from Magna Charta, until the reigne of Queene Elizabeth, *black letter, old calf, 2 leaves of old vellum MS. as fly-leaves C. Barke*r, 1599

199. Sadeler (M.) Vestigi delle Antichita de Roma, *engraved title and 50 engravings, vellum oblong. Roma, n.d.*

200. Brereton (Austin) Henry Irving, a Biographical Sketch, LARGE PAPER, *one of* 100 *copies,* 17 *portraits on india paper, vellum, uncut, t.e.g.* 1884

201. Brereton (A.) Henry Irving, another copy, *vellum, uncut, t.e.g. ex-libris of Richard D'Oyly Carte* 1884

202. Report from Select Committee on Dramatic Literature, with minutes of Evidence, *Mr. Bram Stoker's copy, with MS. notes, etc. in his handwriting* 1832

203. Theatre (The) A Weekly Critical Review, vol. 1, 1877 – Players (The), vol. I–III in 1 vol. *portraits, wanting no.* 1, 1860 – Newspaper cuttings in 1 vol. (3)

204. Stirling (W.) Some Apostles of Physiology, Account of their lives and Labours, *numerous portraits, etc. vellum Privately printed,* 1902

205. Fourcand (L. de) Maîtres Modernes, Bastien-Lepage, sa Vie et ses Œuvres, *fine engravings, india proofs, etc. Paris,* 1884

206. Harvey (F.) List of Portraits, Views, Autograph letters and Documents contained in an Illustrated Copy of the Princess Marie Liechtenstein's History of Holland House, *only* 25 *copies printed, coloured frontispiece, etc. blue morocco n.d.*

207. Newspaper Cuttings, relating to America, the Drama, Eminent Persons, etc. in 5 vol. 1885–87, etc. (6)

208. Play-Bills. Miscellaneous, in 3 vol. and case (4)

209. Play-Bills. Three of Drury Lane Theatre, 1804, *in gilt glazed frames*, and seven of the Theatre Birmingham, including Mrs. Jordan's Last Night, and Mrs. Siddons' Benefit, 1805–6

210. Ballads, Songs, etc. Collection of, *in portfolio* – Stevenson (R.L.) The Body Snatcher, as it appeared in the Pall Mall Gazette, Jan. 31, 1895 (2)

211. Boston Theatre. Plains for the Boston Theatre, by Edward C. Cabot, *drawn on linen, in roll* (1)

Abbreviations
g.e. gilt edges
m.e. marbled edges
n.d. no dates
t.e.g. top edges gilt
y.e. yellow edges

Author's Note

Bram Stoker's books and manuscripts realised a total of £400 12s. The highest prices were paid for the set of R.L. Stephenson's 'works' – £61 (Bain). A set of presentation copies of the works of James Whitcomb Riley, the 'Hoosier' poet of America, in 11 volumes, each with autograph inscription – £46 (Quartrich). The collection of fragments of Walt Whitman's writings, all in his handwriting – £16 10s (Crawley) and the original MS. of the dramatised version of Wilkie Collins's *Woman in White* – £20 (Sessler). The highest price realised for a Bram Stoker manuscript in this sale was £4 15s paid by Mr Holland for the *Personal Reminiscences of Henry Irving* while a certain Mr Drake was fortunate enough to secure Bram's original notes and data for *Dracula* for £2 2s.

The 529-page typescript bearing the original handwritten title of *The Undead* that had remained lost for almost a century, failed to reach at its minimum reserve price at Christie's in 2002. A spokesman for the auction house said they were 'disappointed' as it had been expected to fetch more than £1 million.

SELECT BIBLIOGRAPHY

Allen, Vivien, *Hall Caine: Portrait of Victorian Romancer* (Sheffield: Sheffield Academic Press, 1997).

Anon, *Parnellism and Crime* (London: C. Terry & Co., *c*. 1887).

Anon [Varney], *The Vampire: or, The Feast of Blood* (London: E. Lloyd, 1845–47).

Archer, William, *The Theatrical World of 1893–1897*, 5 vols (London: Walter Scott, 1894–98).

Arnold, Walter, *The Life and Death of the Sublime Society of Beef Steaks* (London: Bradbury, Evans & Co., 1871).

Atwater, Edward C., 'The Medical Profession in a New Society, Rochester, New York (1811–60)', *Bulletin of the History of Medicine*, vol. 37 (1973), pp. 228–35.

Auberon, Reginald [Horace Wyndham], *The Nineteen Hundreds* (London: Allen & Unwin, 1922).

Baedeker, Karl, *Southern Germany and Austria, including Hungary and Transylvania, Handbook for Travellers* (Leipzig: Karl Baedeker, 1887).

Baird, Nancy D., 'The Yellow Fever Plot', *Civil War Times Illustrated*, vol. 13, no. 7 (November), pp. 16–23.

Barber, Paul, *Vampires, Burial and Death, Folklore and Reality* (New Haven, CT: Yale University Press, 1988).

Baring-Gould, Rev. Sabine, *The Book of Were-Wolves* (London: Smith, Elder & Co., 1865).

Barker, Felix and Silvester-Carr, Denise, *The Black Plaque Guide to London* (London: Constable & Co., 1987).

Begg, Paul and Skinner, Keith, *The Scotland Yard Files: 150 Years of the CID* (London: Headline, 1992).

Belford, Barbara, *Bram Stoker: A Biography of the Author of Dracula* (London: Orion, 1996).

Bingham, Madeline, *Henry Irving and the Victorian Theatre* (London: Allen & Unwin, 1978).

Boner, Charles, *Transylvania: Its Products and its People* (London: Longmans, Green, Reader & Dyer, 1865).

Borowitz, Albert, *The Woman Who Murdered Black Satin: The Bermondsey Horror* (Ohio: Ohio State University Press, 1981).

Breathnach, Eileen, 'Women and Higher Education in Ireland (1879–1914)', in *The Crane Bag* Vol. 4, No. 1: *Images of the Irish Woman* (1980), pp. 47–54.

Brereton, Austin, *The Lyceum and Henry Irving* (London: Lawrence & Bullen, 1903).

Browne, Douglas G., *The Rise of Scotland Yard: A History of the Metropolitan Police* (London: George G. Harrap & Co., 1956).

Buckle, George Earle (ed.), *The Letters of Queen Victoria*, third series, vol. 1 (New York: Longmans, Green & Co., 1930).

Caine, Hall, *Capt'n Davy's Honeymoon* (London: Heinemann, 1893).

Caine, Hall, *The Manxman* (London: Heinemann, 1894).

Caine, Hall, *My Story* (New York: Appleton & Company, 1909).

Caine, Hall, *The Shadow of a Crime* (London: Chatto & Windus, 1885).

Caine, Hall, *Recollections of Dante Gabriel Rossetti* (London: Roberts Brothers, 1883).

Campbell, John Gregorson, *Witchcraft and Second Sight in the Highlands and Islands of Scotland* (Glasgow: J. MacLehose & Sons, 1902).

Catalogue of Valuable Printed Books, Autograph Letters and Illuminated and Other Manuscripts including the Library of the late Bram Stoker Esq. (London: Sotheby, Wilkinson & Hodge, 1913).

Cook, Matt, *London and the Culture of Homosexuality 1885–1914* (Cambridge: Cambridge University Press, 2008).

Craig, Edward Gordon, *Henry Irving* (London: Dent, 1930).

Cumming, Carman, *Devil's Game: The Civil War Intrigues of Charles A. Dunham* (Urbana and Chicago: University of Illinois Press, 2004).

Curran, Bob, *Celtic Vampire Legends* (New York: Fall River Press, 2002).

Dalby, Richard, *To My Dear Friend Hommy Beg: The Great Friendship of Bram Stoker and Hall Caine* (Dublin: Swan River Press, 2011).

Davison, Carol Margaret, *Bram Stoker's Dracula: Sucking Through the Century 1897–1997* (Toronto: Dundurn Press, 1997).

Dijkstra, Bram, *Idols of Perversity: Fantasies of Feminine Evil in Fin-de-Siècle Culture* (USA: Oxford Univerity Press, 1988).

Donaldson, Thomas, *Walt Whitman the Man* (London: Gay & Bird, 1897).

Dowden, Edward, *Fragments from Old Letters E.D. to E.D.W. 1869–1892* (London: J.M. Dent & Sons, 1914).

Du Maurier, George, *Trilby: A Novel* (London: Osgood, McIlvaine, 1895).

Eighteen-Bisang, Robert and Miller, Elizabeth (transcribed and annotated) *Bram Stoker's Notes for Dracula: A Facsimile Edition* (North Carolina and London: McFarland & Company, 2008).

Evans, Stewart P. and Gainey, Paul, *Jack the Ripper: First American Serial Killer* (London: Arrow, 1996).

Evans, Stewart P. and Rumbelow, Donald, *Jack the Ripper: Scotland Yard Investigates* (Stroud: The History Press, 2006).

Evans, Stewart P. and Skinner, Keith, *Jack the Ripper: Letters from Hell* (Stroud, Sutton Publishing, 2001).

Evans, Stewart P. and Skinner, Keith, *The Ultimate Jack the Ripper Sourcebook* (London: Constable and Robinson, 2000).

Farson, Dan, *The Man Who Wrote Dracula* (London: Michael Joseph, 1975).

Fido, Martin, *The Crimes, Detection and Death of Jack the Ripper* (London: Weidenfeld & Nicolson, 1987).

Fishman, William J., *East End 1888: Life in a London Borough among the Laboring Poor* (Philadelphia: Temple University Press, 1988).

Fitzgerald, Percy, *Henry Irving: A Record of Twenty Years at the Lyceum* (London: Chapman & Hall, 1893).

Fitzpatrick, Samuel Ossory, *Dublin: A Historical and Topographical Account of the City* (London: Methuen, 1907).

Frayling, Christopher, *Nightmare: The Birth of Horror* (London: BBC, 1996).

Frayling, Christopher, *Vampyres: Lord Byron to Count Dracula* (London: Faber & Faber, 1991).

Gasson, Andrew, *Wilkie Collins: An Illustrated Guide* (Oxford: Oxford University Press, 1998).

Gerard, Emily, 'Transylvanian Superstitions', *Nineteenth Century* (London, 1885), pp. 128–44.

Gerard, Frances, *Picturesque Dublin, Old and New* (London: Hutchinson & Co., 1898).

Haining, Peter (ed.), *The Dracula Scrapbook* (Holborn, London: New English Library, 1926).

Haining, Peter and Tremayne, Peter, *The Un-Dead* (London: Constable, 1997).

Hanchett, William, *The Lincoln Murder Conspiracies* (Urbana and Chicago: University of Illinois Press, 1989).

Hatton, Joseph, *The Lyceum 'Faust'* (London: Virtue & Co., 1886).

Hinkson, Henry Albert, *Student Life in Trinity College, Dublin* (Dublin: J. Charles & Son, 1892).

Holroyd, Michael, *The Dramatic Lives of Ellen Terry, Henry Irving and their Remarkable Families* (London: Vintage, 2009).

Honeycombe, Gordon, *The Murders of the Black Museum* (London: Hutchinson, 1982).

Horne's Guide to Whitby (Whitby, Yorkshire: Horne & Son, 1891).

Ildrewe, Miss, *The Language of Flowers* (London: Lea & Blanchard, 1839).

Irving, Laurence, *Henry Irving, The Actor and His World* (London: Faber & Faber, 1951).

Jones, Gareth Stedman, *Outcast London* (London: Penguin Books Ltd (Peregrine Books), 1976).

Jones-Evans, Eric (ed.), *Henry Irving and the Bells: Irving's Personal Script of the Play* (Manchester: Manchester University Press, 1980).

Joyce, P.W., *The Origin and History of Irish Names of Places* (Dublin: McGlashan & Gill, 1875).

Kohn, George C., *Encyclopaedia of Plague & Pestilence* (Ware, Hertfordshire: Wordsworth Editions Ltd, 1995).

Leatherdale, Clive, *Dracula: The Novel and the Legend* (Wellingborough, Northamptonshire: Aquarian Press, 1985).

Leatherdale, Clive (ed.), *Dracula Unearthed*, 2nd edn (Essex: Desert Island Books, 2006).

Leatherdale, Clive, *The Origins of Dracula* (London: William Kimber, 1987).

Le Fanu, J. Sheridan, *In a Glass Darkly* (London: R. Bentley & Son, 1872).

Le Fanu, J. Sheridan, *The Watcher and other Weird Stories* (London: Downey & Co., 1894).

Lock, Joan, *Marlborough Street: The Story of a London Court* (London: Robert Hale, 1980).

Ludlam, Harry, *A Biography of Dracula: The Life Story of Bram Stoker* (London: The Fireside Press, 1962).

Macilwee, Michael, *The Liverpool Underworld* (Liverpool: Liverpool University Press, 2011).

Macnaghten, Sir Melville, *Days of My Years* (London: Edward Arnold, 1914).

Macqueen-Pope, W., 'Note on the History of the Lyceum Theatre', in *Souvenir of Hamlet: Farewell to the Lyceum Theatre* (London: Lyceum Theatre, 1939), pp. xi–xvii.

Masters, Anthony, *The Natural History of the Vampire* (New York: Berkeley Publishing Corp., 1972).

Maturin, Charles Robert, *Melmoth the Wanderer* (Edinburgh: Archibald Constable & Co., 1820).

Mayo, Herbert, *On the Truths Contained in Popular Superstitions with an Account of Mesmerism* (Edinburgh and London: William Blackwood & Sons, 1851).

McDowell, R.B. and Webb, D.A., *Trinity College Dublin 1592–1952, An Academic History* (Cambridge: Cambridge University Press, 1982).

McEwan, Graham J., *Mystery Animals of Britain and Ireland* (London: Robert Hale, 1986).

McNally, Raymond T. and Florescu, Radu, *In Search of Dracula* (London: Robson Books, 1995).

Miller, Elizabeth, *Dracula: Sense and Nonsense*, 2nd edn (Essex: Desert Island Books, 2006).

Muir, Ramsey, Geddes, Andrew and Rankin, John, *A History of Liverpool*, 2nd edn (Liverpool: University Press of Liverpool, 1907).

Murray, Paul, *From the Shadow of Dracula* (London: Jonathan Cape, 2004).

Oddie, S. Ingleby, *Inquest* (London: Hutchinson & Co., 1941).

Parkinson, Rev. Thomas, *Yorkshire Legends and Tradition* (London: Elliot Stock, 1889).

Polidori, John, *The Vampyre: A Tale* (London: Sherwood, Neely & Jones. 1819).

Ramsey, Winston G., *The East End Then and Now* (London: After the Battle, 1997).

Reeve, Ada, *Take It For a Fact* (London: William Heinmann, 1954).

Riordan, Timothy B., *Prince of Quacks* (North Carolina: Macfarland Jefferson, 2009).

Rolleston T.W., *Myths and Legends of the Celtic Race*, 2nd rev. edn (London: George G. Harrap & Co. Ltd., 1911).

Roscoe, Theodore, *The Web of Conspiracy* (New Jersey: Prentice Hall, 1960).

Rule, Fiona, *The Worst Street in London* (London: Ian Allen, 2008).

Sanderson, James M., *The Langham Guide to London* (London: The Langham hotel, 1867).

Scott, Clement, *The Drama of Yesterday and Today* (London: Macmillan & Co., 1899).

Sears, Stephen W., *George B. McClellan* (New York: Da Capo Press, 1999).

Seymour, St John D. and Neligan, Harry L., *True Irish Ghost Stores* (Dublin: Figgis, 1926).

Shew, E. Spencer, *A Companion to Murder* (London: Cassell, 1960).

Shew, E. Spencer, *A Second Companion to Murder* (London: Cassell, 1961).

Short, K.R.M., *The Dynamite War: Irish American Bombers in Victorian Britain* (Dublin: Gill & Macmillan, 1979).

Slemen, Tom, *Wicked Liverpool* (Liverpool: Bluecoat Press, 2001).

Smith, Major Henry, *From Constable to Commissioner* (London: Chatto & Windus, 1910).

Stamp, Cordelia, *Dracula Discovered* (Whitby, Yorkshire: Caedmon, 2001).

Steel, Tom, *The Langham: A History* (London: The Langham Hilton, 1990).

Stephen, Sir Leslie (ed.), *Dictionary of National Biography* (Oxford: Oxford University Press, 1921–22).

Stoker, Bram, 'Buried Treasures: A Serial in Four Chapters', *The Shamrock*, Dublin, Ireland (13 March and 20 March 1875), pp. 376–9, 403–6.

Stoker, Bram, *The Chain of Destiny, The Shamrock*, Dublin, Ireland (1 May–22 May 1875), pp. 498–9, 514–16, 530–3, 546–8.

Stoker, Bram, *Dracula*, Nina Auerbach and David J. Skal (eds) (New York and London: W.W. Norton, 1997).

Stoker, Bram, *Dracula's Guest and Other Weird Stories* (London: George Routledge and Sons Ltd., 1914).

Stoker, Bram, *The Lady of the Shroud* (London: William Heinemann, 1909).

Stoker, Bram, *The Lair of the White Worm* (London: William Rider & Son Ltd, 1911).

Stoker, Bram, *The Man* (London: William Heinemann, 1905).

Stoker, Bram, *The Mystery of the Sea* (London: William Heinemann, 1902).

Stoker, Bram, *The Primrose Path: His First Novel* (Essex: Desert Island Books, 1999).

Stoker, Bram, *Personal Reminiscences of Henry Irving*, original holograph manuscript, Folger Shakespeare Library, Washington DC.

Stoker, Bram, *Under the Sunset* (London: Sampson, Low, Marston, Searle & Rivington, 1881).

Stoker, Charlotte, *On the Necessity of a State Provision for the Education of the Deaf and Dumb in Ireland* (Dublin: Alexander Thom, 1864).

Storey, Neil R., *East London Murders* (Stroud: The History Press, 2008).

Storey, Neil R., *A Grim Almanac of Jack the Ripper's London* (Stroud: Sutton Publishing, 2004).

Storey, Neil R., *London Crime, Death and Debauchery* (Stroud: The History Press, 2007).

Sugden, Philip, *The Complete History of Jack the Ripper* (London: Robinson Publishing, 1995).

Súilleabháin, Seán, *A Handbook of Irish Folklore* (Dublin: Educational Company of Ireland for the Folklore of Ireland Society, 1942).

Summers, Montague, *The Vampire: His Kith and Kin* (London: Routledge & Kegan Paul, 1928).

Summers, Montague, *The Vampire in Europe* (Wellingborough, Northamptonshire: Aquarian Press Ltd, 1980). Original edn, 1929.

Terry, Ellen, *The Story of My Life* (London: Hutchinson, 1908).

Terry, Ellen, *Ellen Terry's Memoirs*, with preface, notes and additional biographical chapters by Edith Craig and Christopher St. John (London: Victor Gollancz, 1933).

Thom's Irish Almanac and Official Directory (Dublin, various years).

Tumblety, Francis, *A Few Passages in the Life of Dr. Francis Tumblety* (Cincinnati: self-published, 1866).

Tumblety, Francis, *Narrative of Dr. Tumblety* (New York: self-published, 1872).

Tumblety, Francis, *A Sketch of the Life of Francis Tumblety* (New York: self-published, 1893).

Tyrrell, Robert Yelverton and Sullivan, Sir Edward, Bart. (eds), *Echoes from Kottabos* (London: E.G. Richards, 1906).

Ward, Genevieve, *Both Sides of the Curtain* (London: Cassell & Co., 1918).

Welland, Dennis, *Mark Twain in England* (London: Chatto & Windus, 1978).

Whitman, Walt, *Walt Whitman: The Correspondence, Volume 3: 1876–1885*, ed. E.H. Miller (New York: New York University Press, 1964).

Wilkins, Robert, *The Fireside Book of Death* (London: Robert Hale, 1990).

Wilkinson, Colin, *The Streets of Liverpool* (Liverpool: Bluecoat Press, 2011).

Wilkinson, William, *An Account of the Principalities of Wallachia and Moldavia: With Various Political Observations Relating to Them* (London: Longman, Hurst, Rees, Orme & Brown, 1820).

Wills, Freeman, *W.G. Wills Dramatist and Painter* (London: Longman, 1898).

Wilson, A.E., *The Lyceum* (London: Dennis Yates, 1952).

Winter, William, *Shadows of the Stage* (London: Macmillan, 1895).

Yeats, W.B., *Autobiographies* (London: Macmillan, 1955).

Yeats, W.B., 'Swedenborg, Mediums and the Desolate Places', in *Explorations* (London: Macmillan, 1962).

Yeats, W.B., *Writings on Irish Folklore, Legend and Myth* (London: Penguin, 1993).

Newspapers and Periodicals

Canada
Hamilton Evening Times
The Headquarters
London Free Press
Montreal Pilot
Montreal Witness
Morning Freeman
St Thomas Weekly Dispatch

Ireland
Evening Mail
Freeman's Journal and Daily Commercial Advertiser
Irish Times
Saunders Newsletter
The Shamrock

United Kingdom
Caledonian Mercury
Cassell's Saturday Journal
Daily Chronicle
Daily Mirror
East London Advertiser
East London Observer
Eastern Argus & Borough of Hackney Times
Eastern Post & City Chronicle
Echo
English Illustrated Magazine
The Era

Evening Standard
Famous Crimes
The Globe
The Graphic
Illustrated London News
The Illustrated Police News
Illustrated Sporting and Dramatic News
The Lancet
Liverpool Lantern
Liverpool Mercury
The Mirror of Literature, Amusement and Instruction
Morning Post
Nineteenth Century
Pall Mall Gazette
Penny Illustrated Paper
Police Gazette
Punch
The Stage
The Star
The Strand Magazine
The Sun
The Times
Windsor Magazine
York Herald

United States of America
Brooklyn Daily Eagle
Civil War Times Illustrated
Daily Inter Ocean
Daily News
Frank Leslie's Illustrated Newspaper
Harper's Weekly
New York Times
New York Tribune
New York World
Puck
Rochester Daily Union and Advertiser
Rochester Democrat and Republican

Manuscript Sources

Ann Stoker Collection, Trinity College Dublin
Bram Stoker Collection, Shakespeare Centre Library, Stratford-upon-Avon
Papers of Sir Thomas Henry Hall Caine (1853–1931) Manx National Heritage
Stewart P. Evans Archive

NOTES

1 Robert Eighteen-Bisang, 'Dracula, Jack the Ripper and A Thirst for Blood', *Ripperologist* 60 (July 2005).

2 Neil R. Storey, *A Grim Almanac of Jack the Ripper's London* (Stroud: Sutton Publishing, 2004), pp. 84–5.

3 Quoted in Harry Ludlam, *A Biography of Dracula: The Life Story of Bram Stoker* (London: The Fireside Press, 1962), p. 12.

4 Ann Stoker Archive, Trinity College Dublin.

5 Ludlam, *A Biography of Dracula*, p. 14.

6 Bram Stoker, *Personal Reminiscences of Henry Irving*, original holograph manuscript, Folger Shakespeare Library.

7 Bram Stoker, *Personal Reminiscences of Henry Irving* (London, 1907), vol. 1, p. 31.

8 Ludlam, *A Biography*, pp. 26–7.

9 Ludlam, *A Biography*, p. 27.

10 Ludlam, *A Biography*, p. 28.

11 Ludlam, *A Biography*, p. 29.

12 See St John D. Seymour and Harry L. Neligan, *True Irish Ghost Stories* (Dublin: Figgis, 1926), pp. 206–8.

13 See Seán Ó Súilleabháin, *A Handbook of Irish Folklore* (Dublin: Educational Company of Ireland for the Folklore of Ireland Society, 1942), pp. 442–50.

14 Bob Curran, *Celtic Vampire Legends* (Fall River Press, 2002), p. 6.

15 P.W. Joyce, *The Origin and History of Irish Names of Places* (Dublin: McGlashan & Gill, 1875), p. 331.

16 Bob Curran, *Vampires: A Field Guide to the Creatures That Stalk the Night* (Career Press, 2005), p. 65.

17 Montague Summers, *The Vampire in Europe* (1929), p. 117.

18 See Peter Haining and Peter Tremayne, *The Un-Dead* (London: Constable, 1997), p. 71.

19 See Eileen Breathnach, 'Women and Higher Education in Ireland (1879–1914)', in *The Crane Bag*, Vol. 4, No. 1: *Images of the Irish Woman* (1980), pp. 47–54.

20 Charlotte Stoker, *On the Necessity of a State Provision for the Education of the Deaf and Dumb in Ireland* (Dublin: Alexander Thom, 1864).

21 *Caledonian Mercury* (Edinburgh, Scotland), Saturday 22 November 1862.

22 *York Herald* (York, England), Saturday 20 December 1862.

23 *Freeman's Journal and Daily Commercial Advertiser* (Dublin, Ireland), Thursday 21 January 1864.

24 Stoker, *Personal Reminiscences*, vol. 2, p. 209.

25 Samuel Ossory Fitzpatrick, Dublin: *A Historical and Topographical Account of the City* (London: Methuen, 1907), pp. 123–4.

26 Bram Stoker, *The Mystery of the Sea* (London: Heinemann, 1902), p. 8.

27 Henry Albert Hinkson, *Student Life in Trinity College, Dublin* (Dublin: J. Charles & Son, 1892), p. 33.

28 Hinkson, *Student Life*, p. 11.

29 Hinkson, *Student Life*, p. 4.

30 *Freeman's Journal and Daily Commercial Advertiser* (Dublin, Ireland), Wednesday 10 February 1875.

31 Paul Murray, *From the Shadow of Dracula* (London: Jonathan Cape, 2004), p. 38.

32 *Irish Times*, 14 November 1872.

33 Stoker, *Personal Reminiscences*, vol. 2, p. 31.

34 *Penny Illustrated Paper* (London, England), 12 August 1871.

35 The speech reproduced is an edited version published in *Freeman's Journal and Daily Commercial Advertiser* (Dublin, Ireland), Thursday 14 November 1872.

36 *Saunders Newsletter* (Dublin, Ireland), Thursday 14 November 1872.

37 Stoker, *Personal Reminiscences*, vol. 1, p. 32.

38 R.B. McDowell and D.A. Webb, *Trinity College Dublin 1592–1952, An Academic History* (Cambridge: Cambridge University Press, 1982), p. 298.

39 Murray, *From the Shadow of Dracula*, p. 33.

40 *Saunders Newsletter* (Dublin, Ireland), Thursday 14 November 1872.

41 Stoker, *Personal Reminiscences*, vol. 1, pp. 7–8.

42 Hinkson, *Student Life*, p. 42.

43 Stoker, *Personal Reminiscences*, vol. 2, pp. 93–5.

44 The Walt Whitman Archive, edited by Ed Folsom and Kenneth M. Price.

45 Stoker, *Personal Reminiscences*, vol. 2, pp. 95–6.

46 The Walt Whitman Archive, edited by Ed Folsom and Kenneth M. Price.

47 The Walt Whitman Archive, edited by Ed Folsom and Kenneth M. Price.

48 Bram Stoker, *The Man* (London: William Heinemann, 1905), pp. 77–9.

49 Stoker, *Personal Reminiscences*, vol. 1, p. 20.

50 Stoker, *Personal Reminiscences*, vol. 1, pp. 1–2.

51 Stoker, *Personal Reminiscences*, vol. 1, pp. 3–4.

52 Stoker, *Personal Reminiscences*, vol. 1, p. 8.

53 Ludlam, *A Biography*, pp. 34–5.

54 Stoker, *Personal Reminiscences*, vol. 2, pp. 167–8.

55 Stoker, *Personal Reminiscences*, vol. 2, p. 169.

56 Stoker, *Personal Reminiscences*, vol. 1, pp. 305–6.

57 Murray, *From the Shadow of Dracula*, p. 60.

58 Bram Stoker, *The Primrose Path: His First Novel* (Essex: Desert Island Books, 1999).

59 Bram Stoker, 'Buried Treasures: A Serial in Four Chapters', *The Shamrock* (13 March and 20 March 1875), pp. 376–9, 403–6.

60 Bram Stoker, *The Chain of Destiny*, *The Shamrock* (1 May to 22 May 1875), pp. 498–9, 514–16, 530–3, 546–8.

61 Stoker, *The Chain of Destiny*, in Stoker, *Dracula's Guest and Other Stories* (Ware, Hertfordshire: Wordsworth Editions, 2006), pp. 171–2.

62 Stoker, *Dracula* (New York: Grosset & Dunlap, copyright 1987), p. 2, read online: www.archive.org/details/draculaoostokvoft

63 See Stoker, *The Chain of Destiny*, in Stoker, *Dracula's Guest and Other Stories*, pp. 171–2.

64 Stoker, *Dracula*, p. 35.

65 Stoker, *Dracula*, p. 37.

66 Reflecting his legal background and knowledge, instead of another theatre critic Stoker quotes Oliver Wendell Holmes. Holmes was editor of the *American Law Review*, one of the early founders of law and economics jurisprudence and the man who went on to publish the respected legal tome *The Common Law* in 1881.

67 *Evening Mail* (Dublin, Ireland), 1 December 1876.

68 Stoker, *Personal Reminiscences*, vol. 1, p. 25.

69 Stoker, *Personal Reminiscences*, vol. 1, pp. 25–6.

70 Stoker, *Personal Reminiscences*, vol. 1, p. 28.

71 Stoker, *Personal Reminiscences*, vol. 1, p. 29.

72 Stoker, *Personal Reminiscences*, vol. 1, p. 30–1.

73 Stoker, *Personal Reminiscences*, vol. 1, p. 31.

74 Stoker, *Personal Reminiscences*, vol. 1, p. 33.

75 Laurence Irving, *Henry Irving, The Actor and His World* (London: Faber & Faber, 1951), p. 31.

76 Eric Jones-Evans (ed.), *Henry Irving and the Bells: Irving's Personal Script of the Play* (Manchester: Manchester University Press, 1980), p. 6.

77 Dan Farson, *The Sexual Impulse in The Man Who Wrote Dracula* (London: Michael Joseph, 1975), pp. 203–24; also see Talia Schaffer, 'A Wilde Desire Took Me: The Homoerotic History of Dracula', *ELH* 61 (1994), pp. 381–425.

78 Sir Leslie Stephen (ed.), *Dictionary of National Biography* (Oxford: Oxford University Press, 1921–22), p. 795.

79 Irving, *Henry Irving*, p. 152.

80 Madeline Bingham, *Henry Irving and the Victorian Theatre* (Allen & Unwin, 1978), p. 70.

81 Irving, *Henry Irving*, p. 152.

82 Irving, *Henry Irving*, p. 152.

83 Irving, *Henry Irving*, p. 152.

84 *Pall Mall Gazette* (London, England), Monday 25 January 1869.

85 *Morning Post* (London, England), Monday 25 January 1869.

86 *The Era* (London, England), Sunday 7 February 1869.

87 *The Era* (London, England), Sunday 7 February 1869.

88 See Miss Ildrewe, *The Language of Flowers* (London: Lea & Blanchard, 1839).

89 Murray, *From the Shadow of Dracula*, p. 65.

90 Barbara Belford, *Bram Stoker: A Biography of the Author of Dracula* (London: Orion, 1996), p. 68.

91 Stoker, *Personal Reminiscences*, vol. 1, p. 54.

92 Stoker, *Personal Reminiscences*, vol. 1, pp. 55–6.

93 Stoker, *Personal Reminiscences*, vol. 1, p. 56.

94 Stoker, *Dracula*, p. 36.

95 Stoker, *Personal Reminiscences*, vol. 1, pp. 60–1.

96 Stoker, *Personal Reminiscences*, vol. 1, p. 32.

97 Stoker, *Personal Reminiscences*, p. 61.

98 Austin Brereton, *The Lyceum and Henry Irving* (London: Lawrence & Bullen, 1903), p. 54.

99 *The Mirror of Literature, Amusement and Instruction* (London, England), 2 August 1834.

100 *The Mirror of Literature, Amusement and Instruction* (London, England), 2 August 1834.

101 Stoker, *Personal Reminiscences*, vol. 1, pp. 61–2.

102 Stoker, *Personal Reminiscences*, vol. 1, p. 62.

103 Stoker, *Personal Reminiscences*, vol. 1, pp. 62–3.

104 MS. Letter from H.J. Loveday to Hall Caine (Papers of Sir Thomas Henry Hall Caine (1853–1931) Manx National Heritage (MNH) MS 09542). (Hereafter T.H.H.C. Papers).

105 Vivien Allen, *Hall Caine: Portrait of a Victorian Romancer* (Sheffield: Sheffield Academic Press, 1997), p. 34.

106 Stoker, *Personal Reminiscences*, vol. 1, p. 20.

107 Stoker, *Personal Reminiscences*, vol. 2, pp. 116–17.

108 *Windsor Magazine* (London, England), p. 564.

109 Hall Caine, *My Story* (New York: Appleton & Company, 1909), pp. 10–11.

110 *Windsor Magazine* (London, England, 1895), vol. 2, p. 565.

111 *Manx Quarterly* (Isle of Man), October 1921.

112 Allen, *Hall Caine: Portrait*, p. 24.

113 Caine, *My Story*, p. 36.

114 Caine, *My Story*, p. 33.

115 Caine, *My Story*, p. 34.

116 Caine, *My Story*, p. 38.

117 Caine, *My Story*, pp. 40–1.

118 Caine, *My Story*, p. 40.

119 Ramsey Muir, Andrew Geddes and John Rankin, *A History of Liverpool*, 2nd edn (Liverpool: University Press of Liverpool, 1907), pp. 307–8.

120 Caine, *My Story*, p. 48.

121 Caine, *My Story*, p. 50.

122 See 'Soiree of the Learned Societies of Liverpool', *Liverpool Mercury* (Liverpool, England), Saturday 1 February 1879.

123 Caine, *My Story*, p. 50.

124 *Liverpool Mercury* (Liverpool, England), Saturday 22 February 1879.

125 The full poem 'Dr. Tumblety' was published in *A Few Passages in the Life of Dr. Francis Tumblety* (Cincinnati: self-published, 1866), pp. 10–12, attributed to the Saint John Albion, Tumblety actually penned the verse himself.

126 See 'Tumblety's Protege Talks: Interview with Martin H. McGarry', *New York World* (New York, USA), 5 December 1888.

127 *New York World* (New York, USA), 5 December 1888.

128 *Rochester Democrat and Republican* (New York, USA), 3 December 1888.

129 See Timothy B. Riordan, *Prince of Quacks* (North Carolina: Macfarland Jefferson, 2009), pp. 15–17.

130 See Edward C. Atwater, 'The Medical Profession in a New Society, Rochester, New York (1811–60)', *Bulletin of the History of Medicine*, vol. 37 (1973), pp. 228–35.

131 *London Free Press* (Ontario, Canada), 6 May 1856.

132 *Brooklyn Daily Eagle* (New York, USA), 10 May 1865.

133 See Riordan, *Prince of Quacks*, pp. 29–30.

134 *Montreal Pilot* (Montreal, Canada), 16 September 1857.

135 *Montreal Witness* (Montreal, Canada), 26 September 1857; *Montreal Pilot* (Montreal, Canada), 2 October 1857; *La Minerve* (Montreal, Canada), 29 September 1857.

136 *Montreal Pilot* (Montreal, Canada), 2 October 1857 and *La Minerve* (Montreal, Canada), 29 September 1857.

137 *Montreal Pilot* (Ontario, Canada), 23 September 1857.

138 *Montreal Pilot* (Ontario, Canada), 25 September 1857.

139 *Montreal Pilot* (Ontario, Canada), 25 September 1857.

140 *Montreal Pilot* (Ontario, Canada), 26 September 1857.

141 *Montreal Pilot* (Ontario, Canada), 26 September 1857.

142 *Montreal Pilot* (Montreal, Canada), 30 October 1857.

143 'Call Without Delay, and See The Indian Herb Doctor', advertising booklet (1857) in the Stewart P. Evans Archive.

144 'News To The Afflicted!!! Certificates from the Citizens of Montreal to Dr. Tumblety,' in broadside Bibliothèque et Archives Nationales du Québec.

145 *Morning Freeman* (St John, New Brunswick), 3 July 1860.

146 Private letter from William Smith, Deputy Minister of Marine, Ottawa, to James Barber Esq. of St. John, recalling his memories of Tumblety, 1 December 1888 (courtesy of Stewart P. Evans).

147 *Morning Freeman* (New Brunswick, Canada), 11 August 1860.

148 *Daily News* (Newport, Rhode Island, USA), Thursday 23 August 1860.

149 *Morning Freeman* (New Brunswick, Canada), 13 September 1860.

150 *Morning Freeman* (New Brunswick, Canada), 29 September 1860.

151 *Morning Freeman* (New Brunswick, Canada), 29 September 1860.

152 See MS. Testimony of James Hamilton recorded at the inquest of James Potmore, Friday 28 September 1860 (Legislative Library of New Brunswick).

153 Tumblety, *A Few Passages*, p. 15.

154 Tumblety, *A Few Passages*, p. 16.

155 Tumblety, *A Few Passages*, p. 20.

156 See Stephen W. Sears, *George B. McClellan* (New York: Da Capo Press, 1999), pp. 36–7.

157 *Rochester Daily Union and Advertiser* (Rochester, New York), 5 April 1881.

158 *Democrat and Republican* (Rochester, New York), 3 December 1888.

159 *The Headquarters* (New Brunswick, Canada), 12 February 1862.

160 *St. Thomas Weekly Dispatch* (Ontario, Canada), 20 March 1862.

161 See Riordan, *Prince of Quacks*, pp. 96–7.

162 *Brooklyn Daily Eagle* (New York, USA), 4 May 1865.

163 *Brooklyn Daily Eagle* (New York, USA), 10 May 1864.

164 Tumblety, *A Few Passages*, pp. 21–2.

165 Tumblety, *A Few Passages*, p. 16.

166 Tumblety, *A Few Passages*, p. 20.

167 Francis Tumblety, *Narrative of Dr. Tumblety* (New York: self-published, 1872), p. 17.

168 *Brooklyn Daily Eagle* (New York, USA), 4 May 1865.

169 *Brooklyn Daily Eagle* (New York, USA), 4 May 1865.

170 *New York Times* (New York, USA), Friday 5 May 1865.

171 MS on file. United States National Archives, War Department Records, Judge Advocate General Office, File 'B' Doc 261, cited in Stewart Evans and Paul Gainey, *Jack the Ripper: First American Serial Killer* (London: Arrow, 1996).

172 See Nancy D. Baird, 'The Yellow Fever Plot', *Civil War Times Illustrated*, vol. 13, no. 7 (November 1974), pp. 16–23.

173 *New York Tribune* (New York, USA), Friday 12 May 1865.

174 *Hamilton Evening Times* (Hamilton, Ontario, Canada), 29 May 1865.

175 Tumblety, *Narrative of Dr. Tumblety*, p. 44.

176 Queenstown was renamed Cobh after the foundation of the Irish Free State in 1922.

177 Riordan, *Prince of Quacks*, pp. 131–2.

178 Tumblety, *Narrative*, p. 60.

179 See Tom Steel, *The Langham: A History* (The Langham Hilton, 1990), p. 17.

180 Steel, *The Langham*, p. 25.

181 See James M. Sanderson, *The Langham Guide to London* (London: The Langham hotel, 1867), p. 4.

182 Tumblety, *Narrative*, p. 62.

183 Tumblety, *Narrative*, p. 61.

184 Tumblety, *Narrative*, pp. 59–61.

185 See Riordan, *Prince of Quacks*, pp. 134–5.

186 See Michael Macilwee, *The Liverpool Underworld* (Liverpool: Liverpool University Press, 2011), pp. 1–10.

187 See *The Times* (London), 1 December 1873.

188 *Daily Inter Ocean* (Chicago, USA), 20 November 1888.

189 *Liverpool Mercury* (Liverpool, England), Wednesday 2 September 1874.

190 Allen, *Hall Caine: Portrait*, pp. 35–6.

191 *New York World* (New York, USA), 2 December 1888.

192 *Liverpool Mercury* (Liverpool, England), Monday 2 November 1874.

193 *Liverpool Mercury* (Liverpool, England), Wednesday 27 January 1875.

194 MS. Letter from Armstrong (undated) and letter from Tumblety to Caine mentioning Armstrong 'showed the white feather', 8 February 1875, T.H.H.C. Papers (1853–1931) MNH MS 09542.

195 *Liverpool Mercury* (Liverpool, England), Tuesday 19 January 1875.

196 (Liverpool, England), Tuesday 19 January 1875.

197 See the *Sheffield & Rotherham Independent* (Sheffield, England), Thursday 29 January 1875 and the *York Herald* (York, England), Saturday 30 January 1875.

198 *Liverpool Mercury* (Liverpool, England), Wednesday 24 February 1875.

199 Murphy was Tumblety's solicitor in Liverpool.

200 MS. Letter from Tumblety to Hall Caine, 28 January 1875, T.H.H.C. Papers (1853–1931) MNH MS 09542.

201 MS. Letter from Tumblety to Hall Caine, 8 February 1875, T.H.H.C. Papers (1853–1931) MNH MS 09542.

202 Matt Cook, *London and the Culture of Homosexuality 1885–1914* (Cambridge: Cambridge University Press, 2008).

203 MS. Letter from Tumblety to Hall Caine, 16 February 1875, T.H.H.C. Papers (1853–1931) MNH MS 09542.

204 MS. Letter from Tumblety to Hall Caine, 23 February 1875, T.H.H.C. Papers (1853–1931) MNH MS 09542.

205 MS. Letter from Tumblety to Hall Caine, 24 February 1875, T.H.H.C. Papers (1853–1931) MNH MS 09542.

206 MS. Letter from Tumblety to Hall Caine, 16 March 1875, T.H.H.C. Papers (1853–1931) MNH MS 09542.

207 MS. Letter from Tumblety to Hall Caine, 24 March 1875, T.H.H.C. Papers (1853–1931) MNH MS 09542.

208 MS. Letter from Tumblety to Hall Caine, 27 March 1875 (HCA.)

209 MS. Letter from Tumblety to Hall Caine, 29 March 1875, T.H.H.C. Papers (1853–1931) MNH MS 09542.

210 MS. Letter from Tumblety to Hall Caine, 31 March 1875, T.H.H.C. Papers (1853–1931) MNH MS 09542.

211 Telegram sent by Tumblety from Ludgate Circus to Hall Caine, 9 April 1875, T.H.H.C. Papers (1853–1931) MNH MS 09542.

212 MS. Letter Tumblety to Hall Caine, undated but fits sequence for April 1875, T.H.H.C. Papers (1853–1931) MNH MS 09542.

213 See *Liverpool Mercury* (Liverpool, England), Saturday 3 April 1875.

214 *The Standard* (London, England), Saturday 3 April 1875.

215 *Bradford Observer* (Bradford, England), Saturday 3 April 1875.

216 *Liverpool Mercury* (Liverpool, England), Tuesday 20 April 1875.

217 MS. Letter Tumblety to Hall Caine, 4 May 1875, T.H.H.C. Papers (1853–1931) MNH MS 09542.

218 Tumblety to Hall Caine, undated letter, envelope postmarked 21 June 1875, T.H.H.C. Papers (1853–1931) MNH MS 09542.

219 MS. Letter from Tumblety to Hall Caine, 13 July 1875, T.H.H.C. Papers (1853–1931) MNH MS 09542.

220 *Liverpool Mercury* (Liverpool, England), Thursday 15 July 1875.

221 MS. Letter from Tumblety to Hall Caine, 4 August 1875, T.H.H.C. Papers (1853–1931) MNH MS 09542.

222 MS. Letter from Tumblety to Hall Caine, 6 August 1875, T.H.H.C. Papers (1853–1931) MNH MS 09542.

223 MS. Letter from Tumblety to Hall Caine, 10 August 1875, T.H.H.C. Papers (1853–1931) MNH MS 09542.

224 MS. Letter from Tumblety to Hall Caine, 14 August 1875, T.H.H.C. Papers (1853–1931) MNH MS 09542.

225 MS. Letter from Tumblety to Hall Caine, 31 August 1875, T.H.H.C. Papers (1853–1931) MNH MS 09542.

226 MS. Letter from Tumblety to Hall Caine, 24 September 1875, T.H.H.C. Papers (1853–1931) MNH MS 09542.

227 MS. Letter from Tumblety to Hall Caine, 29 September 1875, T.H.H.C. Papers (1853–1931) MNH MS 09542.

228 MS. Letter from Tumblety to Hall Caine, 30 December 1875, T.H.H.C. Papers (1853–1931) MNH MS 09542.

229 MS. Letter from Tumblety to Hall Caine, 31 March 1876, T.H.H.C. Papers (1853–1931) MNH MS 09542.

230 Edward Gordon Craig, *Henry Irving* (London: Dent, 1930), p. 160.

231 A.E. Wilson, *The Lyceum* (London: Dennis Yates, 1952), p. 16.

232 Reginald Auberon [Horace Wyndham], *The Nineteen Hundreds* (London: Allen & Unwin,), pp. 129–30.

233 Stoker, *Personal Reminiscences*, vol. 2, p. 190.

234 Stoker, *Personal Reminiscences*, portrait facing p. 206.

235 Murray, *From the Shadow of Dracula*, p. 110.

236 *Lloyd's Weekly Newspaper* (London, England), Sunday 24 September 1882.

237 *Lloyd's Weekly Newspaper* (London, England), Sunday 24 September 1882.

238 Ellen Terry, *The Story of My Life* (London: Hutchinson, 1908), p. 140.

239 Irving, *Henry Irving*, p. 209.

240 Irving, *Henry Irving*, pp. 209–10.

241 Stoker, *Dracula*, p. 60.

242 W. Macqueen-Pope, 'Note on the History of the Lyceum Theatre', in *Souvenir of Hamlet: Farewell to the Lyceum Theatre* (London: Lyceum Theatre, 1939), p. xvi.

243 Freeman Wills, *W.G. Wills Dramatist and Painter* (London: Longman, 1898), p. 202.

244 Wills, *W.G. Wills*, pp. 209–11.

245 Craig, *Henry Irving*, pp. 163–4.

246 See Walter Arnold, *The Life and Death of the Sublime Society of Beef Steaks* (London: Bradbury, Evans & Co., 1871), pp. 26–8.

247 Irving, *Henry Irving*, pp. 336–7.

248 *Pall Mall Gazette* (London, England), Wednesday 3 September 1890. The Sublime Society of Beef Steaks was revived in 1966 and continue to meet, usually at the Boisdale Club but once a year at White's Club where the president's chair and the society's nineteenth-century dining table reside.

249 Stoker, *Personal Reminiscences*, vol. 2, p. 53.

250 Terry, *The Story of My Life*, p. 166.

251 *Sunday Referee* (London, England), 7 October 1888.

252 See K.R.M. Short, *The Dynamite War: Irish American Bombers in Victorian Britain* (Gill & Macmillan, 1979), pp. 75–6.

253 Born Charles Allen Lechmere, his mother remarried to policeman Thomas Cross in 1858 and Charles took his surname.

254 *Daily Telegraph* (London, England), Monday 3 September 1888.

255 *The Star* (London, England), Saturday 8 September 1888.

256 *Daily Telegraph* (London, England), Tuesday 11 September 1888.

257 See *The Star* (London, England), Saturday 8 September 1888.

258 *The Times* (London, England), Friday 14 September 1888.

259 *Daily Telegraph* (London, England), Friday 14 September 1888.

260 *Daily Telegraph* (London, England), Thursday 27 September 1888.

261 Belford, *Bram Stoker*, p. 149.

262 See Stoker, *Dracula*, p. 71.

263 *Echo* (London, England), 10 September 1888.

264 *Daily News* (London, England), 10 September 1888.

265 *Pall Mall Gazette* (London, England), 3 October 1888.

266 *East London Advertiser* (London, England), 6 October 1888.

267 Ada Reeve, *Take It For a Fact* (London: William Heinmann, 1954).

268 Terry, *My Life*, p. 174.

269 Stoker, *Personal Reminiscenes*, vol. 1, p. 107.

270 See Stoker, *Personal Reminiscences*, vol. 1, p. 23.

271 See Stoker, MS. *Personal Reminiscences*, Original Holograph Manuscript, Folger Shakespeare Library.

272 Caine, *My Story*, p. 198.

273 Robert Eighteen-Bisang and Elizabeth Miller (transcribed and annotated), *Bram Stoker's Notes for Dracula: A Facsimile Edition* (North Carolina and London: McFarland & Company, 2008), pp. 16, 28.

274 British Government documents released in 2005 revealed Vámbéry had been employed by the British Foreign Office as a spy to observe and help combat Russian attempts to gain ground in Central Asia, which were threatening the British position on the Indian subcontinent.

275 Stoker, *Personal Reminiscences*, vol. 1, p. 372.

276 See Farson, *The Man Who Wrote Dracula*, p. 126.

277 Eighteen-Bisang and Miller, *Bram Stoker's Notes for Dracula*, pp. 143–9.

278 Bram Stoker interview with 'Lorna' (Jane Stoddard), *British Weekly*, 1 July 1897, p. 185.

279 Cordelia Stamp, *Dracula Discovered* (Whitby: Caedmon, 2001), p. 14.

280 Stoker, *Dracula*, p. 59.

281 Eighteen-Bisang and Miller, *Bram Stoker's Notes for Dracula*, p. 384.

282 Eighteen-Bisang and Miller, *Bram Stoker's Notes for Dracula*, pp. 252–71.

283 Eighteen-Bisang and Miller, *Bram Stoker's Notes for Dracula*, p. 168.

284 Stoker, *Dracula*, p. 211.

285 William Wilkinson, *An Account of the Principalities of Wallachia and Moldavia: With Various Political Observations Relating to Them* (London: Longman, Hurst, Rees, Orme & Brown, 1820), p. 17.

286 Wilkinson, *An Account of the Principalities*, p. 19.

287 Wilkinson, *An Account of the Principalities*, p. 19.

288 Elizabeth Miller, *Dracula: Sense and Nonsense*, 2nd edn (Essex: Desert Island Books, 2006), pp. 40–1.

289 See *The Morning Times* (Washington, DC, USA), 18 December 1895.

290 In the Bram Stoker Collection at the Shakespeare Library in Stratford-upon-Avon many of the cuttings are still affixed to the supply company slips, most are from Romeike & Curtice's Press Cutting Agency, 359 Strand, London, and carry dates of cutting supplied throughout the 1890s.

291 Stoker, *Personal Reminiscences*, vol. 1, p. 56.

292 Stoker, *Personal Reminiscences*, vol. 1, p. 352.

293 Stoker, *Personal Reminiscences*, vol. 1, p. 359.

294 *Dundee Courier & Argus* (Dundee, Scotland), Monday 9 November 1891.

295 Eighteen-Bisang and Miller, *Bram Stoker's Notes for Dracula*, p. 281.

296 Stoker, *Personal Reminiscences,* vol. 2, p. 175.

297 Stoker, *Personal Reminiscences*, vol. 2, p. 171.

298 'London Theatre Gossip', reprinted in *Hampshire Telegraph and Sussex Chronicle* (Portsmouth, England), Wednesday 2 November 1881.

299 *Dracula: Author's Preface* translated from the Icelandic by Sylvia Sigurdson for Transylvania Press, Inc. Reproduced by kind permission of Robert Eighteen-Bisang.

300 This train of thought stems from Farson, *The Man Who Wrote Dracula*, pp. 213–16.

301 See Penelope Shuttle and Peter Redgrove, *The Wise Wound: Menstruation and Everywoman* (London: Paladin, 1986), p. 252.

302 MS. Stoker, *Personal Reminiscences*, Folger Shakespeare Library.

303 The sheet still exists and is reproduced in Richard Dalby, *To My Dear Friend Hommy Beg: The Great Friendship of Bram Stoker and Hall Caine* (Swan River Press, 2011), p. 20.

304 Hall Caine, *The Last Confession*, pp. 143–4.

305 Caine, *The Last Confession*, pp. 153–4.

306 Caine, *The Last Confession*, p. 221.

307 See *Brooklyn Daily Eagle* (New York, USA), 10 May 1865.

308 See *Hamilton Evening Times* (Ontario, Canada), 29 May 1865.

309 *Rochester Democrat and Republican* (New York, USA), 3 December 1888.

310 *Rochester Democrat and Republican* (New York, USA), 3 December 1888.

311   *New York World* (New York, USA), 2 December 1888.

312   Hall Caine, *Capt'n Davy's Honeymoon, The Last Confession and The Blind Mother* (London: Heinemann, 1893), pp. v–vi.

313   See MS. Letters and telegrams from Piccadilly Circus and Glasshouse Street, T.H.H.C. Papers (1853–1931) MNH MS 09542.

314   See Cook, *London and the Culture of Homosexuality*.

315   Stoker, *Dracula*, p. 247.

316   Stoker, *Dracula*, p. 247.

317   Stoker, *Dracula*, p. 243.

318   *Morning Advertiser* (London, England), 19 October 1888.

319   See Neil R. Storey, *Victorian Prisons and Prisoners* (Stroud, The History Press, 2010).

320   Stoker, *Dracula*, p. 165.

321   *Hampshire Telegraph and Sussex Chronicle* (Portsmouth, England), Saturday 8 December 1894.

322   *Leeds Mercury* (Leeds, England), Tuesday 4 December 1894.

323   *The Graphic* (London, England), Saturday 8 December 1894.

324   *Birmingham Daily Post* (Birmingham, England), Tuesday 4 December 1894.

325   *Liverpool Mercury* (Liverpool, England), Tuesday 27 November 1894.

326   Saunderson was admitted to Broadmoor Criminal Lunatic Asylum on 5 February 1895, and he remained there until his death nearly fifty years later in 1943.

327   Stoker, *Dracula*, p. 243.

328   *Evening Star* (New York, USA), Monday 3 December 1888.

329   Carman Cumming, *Devil's Game: The Civil War Intrigues of Charles A. Dunham* (Urbana and Chicago: University of Illinois Press, 2004), p. xi.

330   Cumming, *Devil's Game*, p. xii.

331   See Michael Hawley, 'Charles A. Dunham: For the Better Good', *The New Independent Review*, 2 January 2012, p. 10.

332   See Stewart P. Evans and Keith Skinner, *Jack the Ripper: Letters from Hell* (Stroud: Sutton Publishing, 2001), pp. 275–6.

333   For a few examples of many references to an 'assassin' throughout the period of the Whitechapel murders see reports in: *Daily Telegraph* (London, England), 6 September 1888; *Pall Mall Gazette* (London, England), 10 September 1888; *London Evening News* (London, England), 1 October 1888; *The Star* (London, England), 15 November 1888.

334   *Daily Telegraph* (London, England), Friday 14 September 1888.

335   Stewart P. Evans and Keith Skinner, *The Ultimate Jack the Ripper Sourcebook* (London: Constable & Robinson, 2000), pp. 313–14.

336   *New York World* (New York, USA), 29 January 1889.

337   See Riordan, *Prince of Quacks*, pp. 189–91.

338   *Washington Post* (Washington DC, USA), 18 November 1890.

339   *New York Herald* (New York, USA), 5 September 1891.

340   See Francis Tumblety, *A Sketch of the Life of Francis Tumblety*, 2nd edn (New York: self-published, 1893), pp. 150–6.

341 'Hommy Beg' is Manx for 'Little Tommy', see p. 12.

342 MS. Letter from Bram Stoker to Hall Caine, 3 June 1896, T.H.H.C. Papers (1853–1931) MNH MS 09542.

343 Poster: Dracula or, The Undead, Tuesday 18 May 1897 (Bram Stoker Collection, Shakespeare Centre and Library, Stratford-upon-Avon).

344 Ludlam, A Biography, pp. 113–14.

345 Glasgow Herald (Glasgow, Scotland), 10 June 1897.

346 Daily Telegraph (London, England), 3 June 1897.

347 Pall Mall Gazette (London, England), 1 June 1897.

348 Stoker, Personal Reminiscences, vol. 2, p. 297.

349 Stoker, Personal Reminiscences, vol. 2, p. 353.

350 Stoker, Personal Reminiscences, vol. 2, p. 354.

351 Henry Irving was the first British actor to receive a knighthood, conferred upon him by HM Queen Victoria in 1895.

352 Peel City Guardian (Peel, Isle of Man), 7 September 1907.

353 See Haining and Tremayne, The Un-Dead, pp. 152–9.

354 See Vivienne Forrest, 'Castle Dracula', The Leopard Magazine (September 1991).

355 This matter has been debated at length over the years. In From the Shadow of Dracula, pp. 268–70, Murray consulted three modern consultants who concurred with the diagnosis 'Locomotor Ataxia' as a result of syphilis. I have also discussed the matter with a prominent medical historian who agrees with this conclusion.

356 Daily Telegraph (London, England), Wednesday 24 April 1912.

357 The Times (London, England), Thursday 25 April 1912.

358 See Allen, Hall Caine: Portrait, p. 292.

359 See Allen, Hall Caine: Portrait, p. 423.

INDEX